DRAGON QUEST ™

VIII

Journey of the Cursed King

OFFICIAL STRATEGY GUIDE

Written By Dan Birlew

TABLE OF CONTENTS

ATLAS

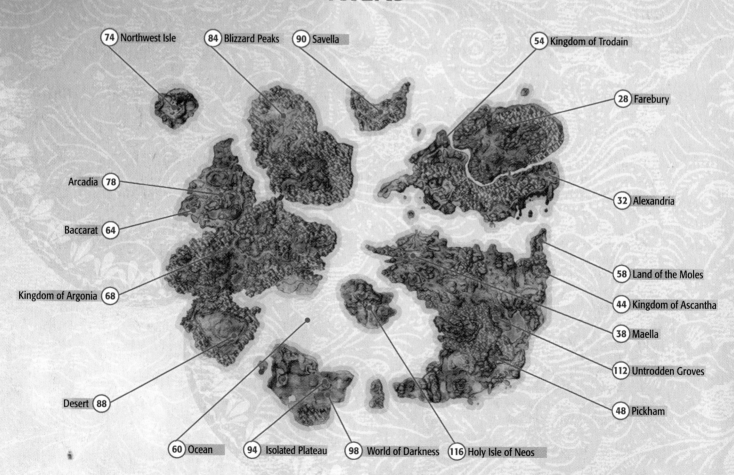

ABOUT THIS GUIDE

Everyone at BradyGames is excited and proud to bring you the *Dragon Quest VIII: Journey of the Cursed King* official strategy guide. This book is different from our other publications. Working closely with the developers of *Dragon Quest* and the staff at Square-Enix, we have created a reference manual for the game designed in part by the game makers themselves. Together, we wanted to guarantee that players could fully enjoy the intense experience of a *Dragon Quest* game, without losing any of the suspense or surprises. Our intent is for the atlas to suggest the path of exploration, revealing a plethora of possibilities among the hills and valleys of this awe-inspiring world. What happens thereafter remains in your capable hands.

An atlas is a bound collection of maps with supplementary illustrations and analyses. Therefore, the brief area descriptions in the "Atlas" chapter are designed to lead you right up to the point where the story begins, allowing you to take it from there. With our help, and by paying close attention to the words of the characters you meet in the game, there should be no point at which you start to feel lost. The walkthrough isn't written in the typical handholding manner you may have come to expect. Don't worry, plenty of information is provided in the correct order to help players find items and figure out whom to speak with to get the proverbial ball rolling in each new location.

The side chapters are full of information regarding items and monsters, but don't overlook the "Game Basics" chapter. It should be noted, though, that some of the reference material (such as certain monsters and items) have not been included to avoid spoiling one of the game's biggest surprises.

Furthermore, in our quest to avoid spoilers, we have left out some information concerning the secrets revealed near the end of the game. Suffice it to say, once you think you've finished *Dragon Quest VIII*, save your game and keep on playing!

HERO

The Hero is a versatile character who can be developed in many ways. Although he is a strong fighter, he may be used primarily as a healer early on in the game. Angelo will take over this role later, but you should continue to develop the Hero's healing abilities. Since the Hero is your second-most resilient character, he'll often survive attacks that kill Angelo, and may be the only character capable of saving a weakened party. To give him more healing options, spend some skill points on Courage.

In addition to his defensive spells and offensive might, the Hero has a special friend that goes by the name of Munchie. As you find and make various cheeses, put them in the Hero's inventory and feed them to Munchie in combat to unleash powerful spell effects. These effects are primarily useful against groups of enemies.

STARTING STATS

LV	1	STRENGTH	8
HP	22	AGILITY	6
MP	0	RESILIENCE	6
		WISDOM	5

COURAGE AND SWORD SKILLS

100 POINTS: God of the sword + Truly valiant
ABILITY = GIGAGASH: The ultimate sword technique. Utterly destroys a group of enemies.

SWORD SKILLS

Swords are the most common weapons the Hero will encounter on his travels, so it makes sense to focus on their use. Sword skills are cheap to use (many cost 0 MP) and they are usually quite powerful. However, every sword skill except Gigaslash targets only a single enemy. That's no problem when fighting powerful monsters and bosses, but you'll need to rely on spells (or Munchie) and boomerang skills when tackling large groups of enemies on the battlefield.

4 POINTS: Basic sword fighting techniques
TRAIT: +5 attack power when equipped with a sword.

9 POINTS: Proficient swordsman
ABILITY = DRAGON SLASH: An attack that causes heavy damage to dragons.

15 POINTS: Renowned swordsman
ABILITY = FLAME SLASH: Channels the power of a raging fire into the blade of your sword.

22 POINTS: Expert swordsman
TRAIT: +10 attack power when equipped with a sword.

30 POINTS: Supreme swordsman
ABILITY = METAL SLASH: An attack that can damage enemies with metal bodies.

40 POINTS: Ace of the sword
TRAIT: Increased chance of critical hit with swords.

52 POINTS: Master of the sword
ABILITY = FALCON SLASH: A double slicing attack, faster than a falcon on the wing.

66 POINTS: Star of the sword
TRAIT: +25 attack power when equipped with a sword.

82 POINTS: Sword of legend
ABILITY = MIRACLE SLASH: A secret sword technique that heals your own wounds each time you strike a foe.

100 POINTS: God of the sword
ABILITY = GIGASLASH: A legendary sword technique for cutting down a group of enemies.

SPEAR SKILLS

Spears are very powerful weapons, and their skill set offers a lot of versatility. Multithrust and Clean Sweep are great options when battling large groups of foes, and the spear's basic attack power should be sufficient when battling bosses. Unfortunately, spears are quite rare, so you won't have many opportunities to upgrade. For that reason, you may want to split your skill points between spears and another skill set like swords, courage, or fisticuffs.

3 POINTS: Basic spear fighting techniques
TRAIT: +5 attack power when equipped with a spear.

7 POINTS: Proficient spearman
ABILITY = MERCURIAL THRUST: A lightning-fast thrust.

12 POINTS: Expert spearman
ABILITY = THUNDER THRUST: Difficult to perform, but has a high chance of doing critical damage.

18 POINTS: Master spearman
TRAIT: +10 attack power when equipped with a spear.

25 POINTS: Famed lancer
ABILITY = MULTITHRUST: A flurry of thrusts that can pierce multiple enemies.

34 POINTS: Legendary lancer
TRAIT: Increased chance of critical hit with spears.

45 POINTS: Star lancer
ABILITY = CLEAN SWEEP: Drives back a group of enemies with a sweep of the spear.

59 POINTS: Grand lancer
ABILITY = LIGHTNING THRUST: Lands a critical hit when it connects.

77 POINTS: Heavenly lancer
TRAIT: +25 attack power when equipped with a spear.

100 POINTS: Almighty Lancer
ABILITY = LIGHTNING STORM: Strikes down all enemies with mighty thunderbolts.

Spells

LEVEL 3	**HEAL**: Restores at least 30 HP to a single ally.
LEVEL 4	**SQUELCH**: Cures a single ally of the effects of poison.
LEVEL 6	**EVAC**: Allows you to exit instantly from dungeons, caves, and towers.
LEVEL 11	**SIZZ**: Singes a group of enemies with a blazing fire.
LEVEL 18	**MIDHEAL**: Restores at least 75 HP to a single ally.
LEVEL 20	**SIZZLE**: Burns a group of enemies with a blazing wall of fire.
LEVEL 27	**FULLHEAL**: Restores all HP to a single ally.
LEVEL 29	**ZING**: Resurrects a fallen ally with a 50% success rate.
LEVEL 32	**KASIZZLE**: Scorches a group of enemies with the blazing flames of the underworld.
LEVEL 65	**DRAGON SOUL**: Unknown…

Starting Equipment

SOLDIER'S SWORD
PLAIN CLOTHES
BANDANA

Boomerang Skills

The boomerang is the only weapon in the game that can hit every enemy on the field. It inflicts the most damage to the first monster it hits and less to each subsequent target. Boomerangs are invaluable against large groups of enemies, but they're practically useless against bosses. Since boomerang skills offer little in the way of variety, you may want to keep an alternative weapon in reserve at all times.

6 POINTS: Basic boomerang combat techniques
ABILITY = CROSSCUTTER THROW: Traces an X in the air as it ploughs into the enemy.

12 POINTS: Baby boomer
TRAIT: +5 attack power when equipped with a boomerang.

18 POINTS: Big boomer
ABILITY = POWER THROW: A full-force throw that damages all enemies equally.

25 POINTS: Iron boomer
TRAIT: +10 attack power when equipped with a boomerang.

32 POINTS: Great boomer
ABILITY = FIREBIRD THROW: Transforms your boomerang into a firebird that incinerates your enemies.

40 POINTS: Boomer knight
TRAIT: +15 attack power when equipped with a boomerang.

52 POINTS: Boomer lord
ABILITY = SUPER THROW: A fearsome attack that uses all your strength to cause extreme damage to all foes.

66 POINTS: Boomer star
TRAIT: +20 attack power when equipped with a boomerang.

82 POINTS: Boomeranger
ABILITY = STARBURST THROW: Bathes all enemies in a shower of burning light.

100 POINTS: King boomeranger
ABILITY = GIGATHROW: Pulverises a single enemy with the force of a thunderbolt.

Fisticuffs Skills

With so many tasty weapons available, it's difficult to justify spending skill points on hand-to-hand combat! Nevertheless, the Hero can be quite good at fisticuffs, learning Stones' Throw and Knuckle Sandwich early and eventually working his way up to Boulder Toss and a meaty +50 attack bonus!

4 POINTS: Basic unarmed combat techniques
TRAIT: +5 attack power when unarmed.

11 POINTS: Brawler
ABILITY = DEFENDING CHAMPION: A defensive ability that greatly reduces the damage inflicted by physical attacks.

17 POINTS: Brawny brawler
ABILITY = STONES' THROW: Hurls rocks at a single group of enemies.

24 POINTS: Black belt brawler
ABILITY = KNUCKLE SANDWICH: A powerfully focused and damaging bare-fisted strike.

33 POINTS: Famous fistfighter
TRAIT: +20 attack power when unarmed.

42 POINTS: Fighting mentor
ABILITY = THIN AIR: Generates a powerful vacuum-vortex that slices all enemies to ribbons.

52 POINTS: Fighting instructor
TRAIT: Increased chance of critical hit when unarmed.

70 POINTS: Fighting master
ABILITY = MULTIFISTS: A vicious four-hit strike on a random enemy.

82 POINTS: Fabled fighter
ABILITY = BOULDER TOSS: Showers all enemies with enormous boulders.

100 POINTS: Fist of legend
TRAIT: +50 attack power when unarmed.

Courage

The courage skill set contains a wide variety of spells and traits that can unlock the Hero's potential as a spell caster. If you invest in this skill set, you'll be rewarded during the last portion of the game with potent offensive and defensive magic, in the form of the Zap spells and Omniheal. Courage is the swordsman's greatest asset. Mastery of both courage and the sword unlocks Gigagash, the Hero's most powerful attack skill!

8 POINTS: Gains courage to set forth on his journey
SPELL = ZOOM: Allows you to return instantly to certain places you have visited before.

16 POINTS: Brave
SPELL = TINGLE: Cures all party members of the effects of sleep and paralysis.

28 POINTS: Intrepid
SPELL = HOLY PROTECTION: Generates a holy aura that causes weaker monsters to avoid your party.

40 POINTS: Courageous
SPELL = FIZZLE: Prevents a group of enemies from using magic.

48 POINTS: Dauntless
SPELL = ZAP: Calls down lightning on all enemies.

56 POINTS: Fearless
TRAIT: Cast spells with 3/4 of the MP usually required.

70 POINTS: Bravehearted
SPELL = KAMIKAZEE: Sacrifices your own life to destroy all enemies.

82 POINTS: Lionhearted
SPELL = OMNIHEAL: Restores all HP to all party members.

90 POINTS: Dragonhearted
TRAIT: Cast spells with 1/2 of the MP usually required.

100 POINTS: Truly valiant
SPELL = KAZAP: Calls down powerful thunderbolts on a group of enemies.
ABILITY = GIGASLASH: A legendary sword technique for cutting down a group of enemies.

YANGUS

Yangus's greatest strength is his incredible fortitude. He has the highest HP, the most resilience, and access to some of the best armour. This makes Yangus an ideal choice for your party's top spot, where he can soak up the most enemy attacks. Devastating spells may often leave only Yangus standing, so make sure he's carrying a variety of recovery items that can help your party recover.

Although Yangus has many strengths, wisdom and agility are not among them. When choosing a skill set, factor in the MP costs of the various skills since Yangus has half the MP of Angelo and the Hero. To compensate for this shortcoming, give Yangus lots of seeds of magic. You may want to avoid giving him seeds of agility, though. Unless you focus on fisticuffs, Yangus will always go last in combat.

STARTING STATS

LV	1	STRENGTH	11
HP	30	AGILITY	5
MP	0	RESILIENCE	7
		WISDOM	2

AXE SKILLS

Helm Splitter is one of the best skills in the game, and it costs a mere six skill points! Even if you opt not to pursue the axe skill set, learn Helm Splitter and switch to an axe for the first few rounds of boss fights. Axe skills are powerful, but they don't offer much versatility until you learn the group-affecting Axes of Evil attack.

6 POINTS: Basic axe-fighting techniques
ABILITY = HELM SPLITTER: A skull-splitting smash that lowers an opponent's defence as it inflicts damage.

12 POINTS: Junior cleaver
TRAIT: +5 attack power when equipped with an axe.

19 POINTS: Iron woodsman
ABILITY = HATCHET MAN: An unpredictable attack that can slay an enemy with a single blow… if it connects.

26 POINTS: Axe-fighter
TRAIT: Increased chance of critical hit with axes.

34 POINTS: Axemaster
TRAIT: +10 attack power when equipped with an axe.

42 POINTS: Ace axer
ABILITY = PARALLAX: A focused strike capable of occasionally paralysing an enemy.

54 POINTS: Axelord
ABILITY = AXES OF EVIL: Generates a vortex from your axe blade that chews into a group of enemies.

66 POINTS: Great axeman
ABILITY = EXECUTIONER: A powerful roundhouse strike that fells an opponent in one blow if it hits.

82 POINTS: Axe royale
TRAIT: +20 attack power when equipped with an axe.

100 POINTS: Almighty axeman
ABILITY = TYPHOEUS' MAUL: An ancient axe technique that works wonders on monsters of the beast family.

CLUB SKILLS

While the best axe skills are free, all club skills cost a few MP to use. Heart Breaker and Mind Breaker are solid attacks, but you won't earn many gold coins from Penny Pincher or Gold Rush.

9 POINTS: Basic club fighting techniques
TRAIT: +5 attack power when equipped with a club or hammer.

19 POINTS: Li'l slugger
ABILITY = HEART BREAKER: An attack that occasionally causes the target to miss a turn.

25 POINTS: Heavy hitter
ABILITY = PENNY PINCHER: A special technique that steals gold coins from an enemy.

32 POINTS: Hammer artist
ABILITY = MONSTER MASHER: A powerful smash that works wonders on monsters of the material family.

48 POINTS: Skullsplitter
TRAIT: +10 attack power when equipped with a club or hammer.

59 POINTS: Big bludgeoner
TRAIT: Increased chance of critical hit with club or hammer.

71 POINTS: Armour-cracker
ABILITY = MIND BREAKER: A superior club attack that dominates foes and renders them unable to attack.

82 POINTS: Big-league brainer
TRAIT: +25 attack power when equipped with a club or hammer.

93 POINTS: Consummate clubber
ABILITY = GOLD RUSH: A powerful strike that steals an opponent's gold coins as it inflicts damage.

100 POINTS: Lord of destruction
ABILITY = DEVIL CRUSHER: An esoteric club technique effective on demon and material family monsters.

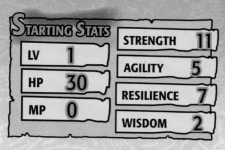

SCYTHE SKILLS

While the prospect of stealing rare items from foes may excite some, the odds of success with the Steal Sickle abilities are somewhat low. Fortunately, there are other effective scythe skills available. Abilities like Grimmer Reaper and Big Banga, acquired late in the game, are among Yangus's best.

12 POINTS: Basic scythe fighting techniques
TRAIT: +5 attack power when equipped with a scythe.

22 POINTS: Competent chopper
ABILITY = STEAL SICKLE: Occasionally allows you to steal items from those you slash.

32 POINTS: Superb sickler
ABILITY = WIND SICKLES: Sends a whirlwind of sickles pirouetting into the enemy.

42 POINTS: Sickle sweetie
TRAIT: +10 attack power when equipped with a scythe.

50 POINTS: Junior reaper
ABILITY = GRIM REAPER: A swing of Death's scythe that can instantly kill one or more foes in a group.

60 POINTS: Sickle-sonic
TRAIT: Increased chance of critical hit with scythes.

70 POINTS: Renowned reaper
ABILITY = STAINLESS STEAL SICKLE: An improved version of the Steal Sickle attack technique.

80 POINTS: Demon sickler
TRAIT: +25 attack power when equipped with a scythe.

90 POINTS: Reaper lord
ABILITY = GRIMMER REAPER: The aura of Death incarnate annihilates the living and obliterates the undead.

100 POINTS: Death's apprentice
ABILITY = BIG BANGA: An enormous explosion that consumes everything in its path.

STARTING EQUIPMENT

OAKEN CLUB
BANDIT'S GRASS SKIRT
LEATHER HAT

FISTICUFFS SKILLS

Every character has the option of pursuing fisticuffs skills, but they compliment Yangus the best. If you focus on unarmed attacks, Yangus will end up causing less damage than he will with weapons, but will compensate for it with improved agility. Thin Air is one of only a few abilities that hit all enemies for large amounts of damage, and you can get it early in the game. Be forewarned, however, that fisticuffs skills aren't free, and Yangus's lack of MP may become an issue.

3 POINTS: Basic unarmed combat techniques
TRAIT: +5 attack power when unarmed.

7 POINTS: Streetfighter
TRAIT: +10 agility when unarmed

12 POINTS: Village champ
ABILITY = KNUCKLE SANDWICH: A powerfully focused and damaging bare-fisted strike.

18 POINTS: Local champ
TRAIT: Increased chance of critical hit when unarmed.

25 POINTS: Regional champ
TRAIT: +20 attack power when unarmed.

33 POINTS: National contender
SPELL = PADFOOT: A secret technique for disguising your presence so as to avoid monsters.

42 POINTS: National champ
ABILITY = THIN AIR: Generates a powerful vacuum-vortex that slices all enemies to ribbons.

60 POINTS: Continental champ
ABILITY = MULTIFISTS: A vicious four-hit strike on a random enemy.

77 POINTS: World champion
TRAIT: +45 attack power when unarmed.

100 POINTS: Super grandmaster
ABILITY = BOULDER TOSS: Showers all enemies with enormous boulders.

HUMANITY

Among the highlights of the humanity skill set are Nose for Treasure, ideal for those who insist on finding everything, and Kerplunk, which can completely turn things around when all hope seems lost. Underpants Dance and Golden Oldies aren't particularly useful, but they're worth learning just for the comic relief.

4 POINTS: Soft-hearted
SPELL = WHISTLE: Summons monsters with a whistle.

10 POINTS: Kind-hearted
SPELL = HEAL: Restores at least 30 HP to a single ally.

16 POINTS: Busybody
SPELL = NOSE FOR TREASURE: Instantly reports the number of nearby treasures.

22 POINTS: Sentimental
ABILITY = WARCRY: A hideous battle cry that paralyses a group of enemies with fear.

32 POINTS: Considerate
SPELL = SHARE MAGIC: Shares some of your MP with an ally.

42 POINTS: Confidant
SPELL = KABUFF: Raises the defence of all party members.

55 POINTS: Big brother
ABILITY = UNDERPANTS DANCE: Paralyses all enemies with embarrassment.

68 POINTS: Gangleader
SPELL = MIDHEAL: Restores at least 75 HP to a single ally.

82 POINTS: Big boss
SPELL = KERPLUNK: Sacrifice your own life to resurrect all other party members.

100 POINTS: Beloved boss
ABILITY = GOLDEN OLDIES: A multi-hit battle royale from King Trode and friends.

JESSICA

Jessica is perhaps your party's most powerful character and the focal point of your offensive line. Not only are her spells devastating, but her melee attacks pack quite a surprising punch as well.

Jessica has access to some excellent abilities, but a lot of her most potent attacking options can be found in her standard spell list. Highlights include the field-clearing Bang series of spells, and Oomph, which can turn anyone into a monster-smashing machine. For all her might, keeping Jessica alive is a full-time job due to her low HP. Whenever you acquire new armour, accessories, or seeds of defence, consider giving them to Jessica.

KNIFE SKILLS

When you put 30 skill points into the knives skill set, Jessica gains the ability to equip swords. While they lack versatility, swords are her most powerful weapon choice.

4 POINTS: Basic knife fighting techniques
TRAIT: +5 attack power when equipped with a knife.

9 POINTS: Knife fighter
ABILITY = TOXIC DAGGER: A knife-fighting technique that envenomates a single enemy.

15 POINTS: Master blader
TRAIT: +10 attack power when equipped with a knife.

22 POINTS: Serious slicer
ABILITY = ASSASSIN'S STAB: A fearsome technique that fells an opponent instantly by attacking their vital parts.

30 POINTS: Edgemaster
TRAIT: Can now use swords as well as knives.

40 POINTS: Swordfighter
TRAIT: Increased chance of critical hit with knife or sword.

52 POINTS: Famous fencer
TRAIT: +20 attack power when equipped with a knife or sword.

66 POINTS: Blade ballerina
ABILITY = TOXIC SWORD: A sword-fighting technique which envenomates an enemy with each strike.

82 POINTS: Sword princess
TRAIT: +30 attack power when equipped with a knife or sword.

100 POINTS: Sword Valkyrie
ABILITY = SUDDEN DEATH: A fatal flash that strikes down an enemy like a bolt out of the blue.

WHIP SKILLS

Whips hit every enemy in a group and cause a decent amount of damage, making them useful against large groups of foes. The whip is also very effective against bosses. The key is the Twin Dragon Lash, which causes more damage for its cost (a mere 3 MP) than any straight attack spell can inflict.

5 POINTS: Basic whip fighting techniques
TRAIT: +5 attack power when equipped with a whip.

10 POINTS: Whippersnapper
ABILITY = WHIPLASH: A paralysing crack of the whip.

16 POINTS: Ready whipper
TRAIT: +10 attack power when equipped with a whip.

23 POINTS: Whipping artist
ABILITY = TWIN DRAGON LASH: A double-strike that lashes a random group of enemies.

32 POINTS: Whipper ripper
ABILITY = LADY'S THONG: A secret whip technique that steals HP as it damages an enemy.

43 POINTS: Lusty lasher
TRAIT: +15 attack power when equipped with a whip.

55 POINTS: Whip fairy
ABILITY = LASHINGS OF LOVE: Harness your inner passion to paralyse enemies.

68 POINTS: Superstar scourger
TRAIT: +25 attack power when equipped with a whip.

82 POINTS: Whipping angel
ABILITY = QUEEN'S THONG: A fearsome attack that steals the HP of a group of enemies.

100 POINTS: Lady of the lash
ABILITY = SERPENT'S BITE: A technique that transforms your whip into a snake that attacks a group of enemies.

Starting Stats

LV	9	STRENGTH	11
HP	41	AGILITY	26
MP	22	RESILIENCE	9
		WISDOM	25

Spells

START	**FRIZZ:**	Singes a single enemy with a small fireball.
START	**SAP:**	Reduces the defence of a single enemy.
LEVEL 10	**CRACK:**	Pierces a single enemy with razor-sharp icicles.
LEVEL 11	**SIZZ:**	Singes a group of enemies with a blazing fire.
LEVEL 11	**EVAC:**	Allows you to exit instantly from dungeons, caves, and towers.
LEVEL 12	**SNOOZE:**	Puts a group of enemies to sleep.
LEVEL 14	**BANG:**	Damages all enemies with a small explosion.
LEVEL 16	**CRACKLE:**	Rips into a group of enemies with sharp icicles.
LEVEL 19	**OOMPH:**	Increases the attack of a single party member.
LEVEL 20	**SIZZLE:**	Burns a group of enemies with a blazing wall of fire.
LEVEL 21	**FRIZZLE:**	Burns a single enemy with a large fireball.
LEVEL 23	**BOOM:**	Engulfs all enemies in a large explosion.
LEVEL 25	**INSULATE:**	Forms a barrier that protects all party members from fire- or ice-based attacks.
LEVEL 33	**KABOOM:**	Blasts all enemies with an incredibly violent explosion.
LEVEL 35	**KAFRIZZLE:**	Incinerates a single enemy with an enormous fireball.

Starting Equipment

LEATHER WHIP
WAYFARER'S CLOTHES
HAIRBAND

Sex Appeal

From a purely practical standpoint, the sex appeal abilities don't do much for Jessica since she already has powerful spells and plenty of MP to use them. However, you can spend 18 skill points to learn the monster-charming trait. This causes lustful enemies to randomly skip their turns in battle without any further effort on your part!

8 POINTS: Jessica realises just how sexy she can be
ABILITY = BLOW KISS: A special kiss that can temporarily prevent enemies from attacking.

18 POINTS: Others realise just how sexy Jessica can be
TRAIT: Has a 1/16 chance to charm monsters.

26 POINTS: Head-turner
SPELL = FUDDLE: Sends a group of enemies into confusion.

38 POINTS: Charming lady
ABILITY = PUFF-PUFF: Charms and excites an enemy into paralysed submission.

48 POINTS: Pretty lady
ABILITY = HIP DROP: Pelvic punishment! Curvaceous hips equal big damage.

54 POINTS: Lovely lady
ABILITY = SEXY BEAM: Focus the power of passion into a beam that sows destruction and confusion.

68 POINTS: Sexy lady
SPELL = KASNOOZE: Puts a group of enemies into a deep sleep.

78 POINTS: Gorgeous lady
TRAIT: Chances of charming monsters increases to 1/8.

88 POINTS: Sultry lady
ABILITY = PINK TYPHOON: A sudden typhoon that rips a group of enemies into ribbons.

100 POINTS: Sexy dynamite
ABILITY = HUSTLE DANCE: Restores at least 70 HP to all party members

Staff Skills

Use the staff skill set to teach Jessica spells like Kasap, Magic Barrier and Kazing. Your investment will be rewarded with traits that ensure she has the MP to use them. Once Jessica becomes a junior sorceress, you can literally cast spells on almost every turn without running out of MP!

3 POINTS: Basic magical staff techniques
SPELL = ACCELERATLE: Raises the agility of all party members.

7 POINTS: Junior staffer
SPELL = KASAP: Reduces the defence of a group of enemies.

13 POINTS: Staff analyst
TRAIT: +20 max MP when equipped with a staff.

21 POINTS: Magic staffer
SPELL = BOUNCE: Forms a protective barrier that reflects the enemy's and party's spells alike.

31 POINTS: Chief of staff
SPELL = MAGIC BARRIER: Forms a protective barrier that reduces the effectiveness of foes' offensive spells.

44 POINTS: Junior magician
TRAIT: +50 max MP when equipped with a staff.

57 POINTS: Staff magician
ABILITY = CADUCEUS: A blessing from the heavens that restores a single party member's HP.

70 POINTS: Junior sorceress
TRAIT: Recovers MP every turn when equipped with a staff.

84 POINTS: Staff sorceress
TRAIT: +100 max MP when equipped with a staff.

100 POINTS: Queen sorceress
SPELL = KAZING: Resurrects a fallen ally.

Fisticuffs Skills

Fisticuffs offers another option for players who choose to focus on Jessica's spells. Invest a mere 52 skill points in Fisticuffs and Jessica can obtain an invaluable defensive boost.

5 POINTS: Basic unarmed combat techniques
TRAIT: +5 attack power when unarmed.

13 POINTS: Femme fighter
TRAIT: +10 agility when unarmed

19 POINTS: Gladiatrix
ABILITY = STONES' THROW: Hurls rocks at a single group of enemies.

28 POINTS: Semifinalist
TRAIT: Increased chance of critical hit while unarmed.

35 POINTS: Finalist
TRAIT: +20 attack power when unarmed.

45 POINTS: Colosseum champ
ABILITY = HARVEST MOON: Pummel all enemies with a chain of cartwheels and backflips.

52 POINTS: Fightin' fairy
TRAIT: Increased chance of dodging enemy attacks.

68 POINTS: Punching princess
ABILITY = THIN AIR: Generates a powerful vacuum-vortex that slices all enemies to ribbons.

85 POINTS: Battle Queen
TRAIT: +35 attack power when unarmed.

100 POINTS: Queen of the Grapplers
SPELL = MAGIC BURST: Unleashes all remaining magic power in a fearsome explosion.

Jessica's tension increases by 100!!!

ANGELO

Early in the game, Angelo is a jack-of-all-trades with decent combat abilities and a wide variety of useful spells (Kabuff and Thwack are among the highlights). Later in the game, a natural talent for healing will become Angelo's defining trait, as he can learn spells like Multiheal and Kazing.

What Angelo does when he isn't healing is up to you. You can pursue staves to focus on spell casting, swords to become a force in melee combat, or bows for versatility. Whichever you choose, commit to it early as Angelo receives skill points at a much slower rate than any other character!

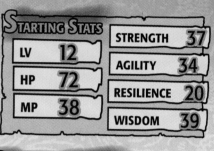

STARTING STATS

LV	12	STRENGTH	37
HP	72	AGILITY	34
MP	38	RESILIENCE	20
		WISDOM	39

SWORD SKILLS

Although Angelo can't learn quite as many sword abilities as the Hero, he acquires most of them approximately 10 to 20 skill points sooner. Miracle Slash can be very useful, and Falcon Slash is a steal at 40 skill points. Instead of maxing out at Gigaslash, Angelo learns Lightning Storm when he masters the art of swordsmanship.

4 POINTS: Basic sword fighting techniques
TRAIT: +5 attack power when equipped with a sword.

9 POINTS: Renowned knight
ABILITY = FLAME SLASH: Channels the power of a raging fire into the blade of your sword.

15 POINTS: Gentle knight
TRAIT: +10 attack power when equipped with a sword.

22 POINTS: Knight of the lilies
ABILITY = METAL SLASH: An attack that can damage enemies with metal bodies.

30 POINTS: Knight of the roses
TRAIT: +20 attack power when equipped with a sword.

40 POINTS: Knight of the crest
ABILITY = FALCON SLASH: A double slicing attack, faster than a falcon on the wing.

52 POINTS: Knight of the sun
TRAIT: Increased chance of critical hit with swords.

66 POINTS: Miraculous knight
ABILITY = MIRACLE SLASH: A secret sword technique that heals your own wounds each time you strike a foe.

82 POINTS: Holy knight
TRAIT: +25 attack power when equipped with a sword.

100 POINTS: Royal knight
ABILITY = LIGHTNING STORM: Strikes down all enemies with mighty thunderbolts.

BOW SKILLS

The highlights of the bow skill set are Cherub's Arrow and Seraph's Arrow, abilities that restore some of Angelo's MP. Since his healing duties require a lot of MP, repeated use of these abilities will ensure that Angelo retains a healthy stash for when the going gets tough.

6 POINTS: Basic archery techniques
ABILITY = SANDMAN'S ARROW: A magical arrow capable of putting a single enemy to sleep.

18 POINTS: Archer
ABILITY = CHERUB'S ARROW: A secret bow technique that regenerates your own MP.

25 POINTS: Arrow sniper
ABILITY = NEEDLE SHOT: Capable of felling an enemy instantaneously if a vital area is hit.

32 POINTS: Arrow soldier
TRAIT: +10 attack power when equipped with a bow.

44 POINTS: Arrow knight
ABILITY = MULTISHOT: A hail of blows directed randomly against one or more enemies.

59 POINTS: Arrow artist
TRAIT: Increased chance of critical hit with bows.

66 POINTS: Wonder archer
ABILITY = SERAPH'S ARROW: A secret technique that recovers even more MP than Cherub's Arrow.

76 POINTS: Miracle archer
TRAIT: +25 attack power when equipped with a bow.

88 POINTS: Saint archer
ABILITY = SHINING SHOT: An arrow attack that bathes all enemies in a destructive magical light.

100 POINTS: Arrow emperor
ABILITY = NEEDLE RAIN: A rain of arrows that can occasionally obliterate all enemies in a single salvo.

Spells

START	**HEAL**: Restores at least 30 HP to a single ally.
START	**BUFF**: Raises the defence of a single party member.
START	**WOOSH**: Slices through a group of enemies with a small whirlwind.
START	**ZOOM**: Allows you to return instantly to certain places you have visited before.
LEVEL 13	**TINGLE**: Cures all party members of the effects of sleep and paralysis.
LEVEL 14	**KABUFF**: Raises the defence of all party members.
LEVEL 15	**MIDHEAL**: Restores at least 75 HP to a single ally.
LEVEL 17	**WHACK**: A cursed incantation that sends an enemy to the hereafter.
LEVEL 18	**SWOOSH**: Slices through a group of enemies with a powerful whirlwind.
LEVEL 19	**ZING**: Resurrects a fallen ally with a 50% success rate.
LEVEL 22	**THWACK**: A cursed incantation that sends a group of enemies to the hereafter.
LEVEL 24	**FULLHEAL**: Restores all HP to a single ally.
LEVEL 30	**MULTIHEAL**: Restores at least 100 HP to all party members.
LEVEL 32	**KASWOOSH**: Slices through a group of enemies with a ferociously destructive whirlwind.
LEVEL 34	**KAZING**: Resurrects a fallen ally.

Starting Equipment

RAPIER
TEMPLAR'S UNIFORM
TEMPLAR'S RING

Charisma

Most of the early abilities in the charisma skill set are narrow in application, but Fuddle and Divine Intervention certainly have their uses. The final two abilities are powerful attacks that are as good as anything from Angelo's weapon skill sets; Charming Look scorches all foes while Pearly Gates deals massive damage to a group.

Staff Skills

The investment in staff skills will pay off when you learn Kathwack and Oomph, which are both fantastic spells. If you stick with it until the end, Angelo will have an abundance of MP for every fight.

3 POINTS: Basic magical staff techniques
SPELL = **DAZZLE**: Envelops a group of enemies in illusions

6 POINTS: Warlock
SPELL = **FIZZLE**: Prevents a group of enemies from using magic.

9 POINTS: High warlock
SPELL = **BOUNCE**: Forms a protective barrier that reflects the enemy's and party's spells alike.

12 POINTS: Conjurer
SPELL = **DRAIN MAGIC**: Steals MP from a single enemy.

28 POINTS: High conjurer
TRAIT: +20 max MP when equipped with a staff.

48 POINTS: Wizard
ABILITY = **CADUCEUS**: A blessing from the heavens that restores a single party member's HP.

56 POINTS: High wizard
SPELL = **KATHWACK**: A cursed incantation that sends all enemies to the hereafter.

65 POINTS: Arch wizard
SPELL = **OOMPH**: Increases the attack of a single party member.

80 POINTS: Holy wizard
TRAIT: +50 max MP when equipped with a staff.

100 POINTS: Majestic wizard
TRAIT: Recovers MP every turn when equipped with a staff.

Fisticuffs Skills

You must spend 35 skill points before Angelo learns his first fisticuffs ability. However, the traits he'll learn in the meantime make up for it, especially the agility boost and the increased chance of dodging enemy attacks. If you can master fisticuffs, you'll be rewarded with the Angelo-exclusive Miracle Moon ability, a powerful attack that restores Angelo's HP.

7 POINTS: Basic unarmed combat techniques
TRAIT: +7 attack power when unarmed.

14 POINTS: Monk
TRAIT: +10 agility when unarmed.

21 POINTS: Warrior monk
TRAIT: Increased chance of dodging enemy attacks.

28 POINTS: Master monk
TRAIT: +15 attack power when unarmed.

35 POINTS: Paladin
ABILITY = **KNUCKLE SANDWICH**: A powerfully focused and damaging bare-fisted strike.

42 POINTS: Great paladin
ABILITY = **HARVEST MOON**: Pummel all enemies with a chain of cartwheels and backflips.

54 POINTS: Saintly paladin
TRAIT: Increased chance of critical hit when unarmed.

68 POINTS: Guardian
ABILITY = **DEFENDING CHAMPION**: A defensive ability that greatly reduces the damage inflicted by physical attacks.

82 POINTS: Holy guardian
TRAIT: +40 attack power when unarmed.

100 POINTS: Royal guardian
ABILITY = **MIRACLE MOON**: A miraculous technique that pummels all enemies while regenerating your own HP.

3 POINTS: Ladykiller
SPELL = **SQUELCH**: Cures a single ally of the effects of poison.

7 POINTS: Dreamboat
SPELL = **FUDDLE**: Sends a group of enemies into confusion.

13 POINTS: Playboy knight
ABILITY = **SARCASTIC SNIGGER**: Reduces a single enemy's tension by one level.

19 POINTS: Hot knight
ABILITY = **ANGEL EYES**: A powerful glance capable of paralysing a single enemy.

27 POINTS: Idol knight
SPELL = **DIVINE INTERVENTION**: Reduces a group of enemies' resistance to magical attacks.

39 POINTS: Charismatic knight
SPELL = **BAN DANCE**: Stops one group of enemies from dancing for several turns.

52 POINTS: Romantic knight
ABILITY = **CHILLING CHUCKLE**: Reduces the tension of an entire group of enemies by a degree.

66 POINTS: Crystal knight
SPELL = **KAFUDDLE**: Confuses all enemies.

81 POINTS: Knight of knights
ABILITY = **CHARMING LOOK**: A glance so powerfully captivating that it burns all enemies in its path.

100 POINTS: Knight of legend
SPELL = **PEARLY GATES**: Opens heaven's door to baptise a group of foes with sacred light.

GAME BASICS

Dragon Quest VIII: Journey of the Cursed King is a role-playing game (RPG) that takes place in a world dominated by monsters and magic. The objective is to lead a group of characters, known as "the party," on a quest to overcome the great evil that threatens the land. Achieve this objective by exploring the world, including all of the towns, castles, dungeons, and wilderness areas. Speak to the townspeople, merchants, clergymen, politicians, and kings who populate the cities and villages to learn about the world, and to garner clues as to where the party needs to travel next and what challenges lie ahead.

All that stands between the party and their peaceful goal is an infinite number of monsters and beasts. In order to survive encounters with these ravening hordes, the party must be equipped with the best weapons, armour, and accessories available. You can acquire useful items and armour by searching every location thoroughly, defeating terrible foes, or purchasing the goods from a merchant.

Each victory makes the characters stronger, and soon they will learn powerful new skills. If the party can survive encounter after encounter and explore their surroundings, they just might save the world from domination by the forces of evil. Against such overwhelming odds, that would be quite an accomplishment!

STARTING A GAME

After inserting the *Dragon Quest VIII* disc into the PlayStation 2 console, wait for the opening demo to finish and then choose one of the starting options. If you've never played before, select "Create a new adventure log." Make sure that a memory card is plugged into one of the two slots on the PlayStation 2 console before starting.

Enter a name for the adventure log file to be created. This name will also be the name of the main character, referred to as the Hero throughout this guide. You can choose any name you like, as long as it's not the sort that will interfere with the gameplay.

When you've entered a name for the Hero, choose "End." Select a memory card slot in which to save your game file. You can put up to 30 saves on a memory card. Choose an empty file and press the ⊗ button to complete the adventure log creation sequence.

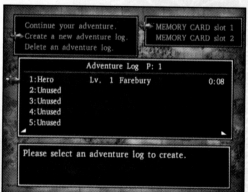

Once you've created an adventure log, you can continue where you left off by choosing the "Continue your adventure" option from the start menu. Select a memory card inserted into MEMORY CARD slot 1 or slot 2, then choose the file that contains the game you would like to load up. Usually, the cursor automatically points to the most recent saved game.

SAVING A GAME

Any time you want to stop playing, return to the nearest church and speak to the priest or nun standing at the altar. Priests offer many services, some of which require monetary donations. To record your progress to a memory card inserted into the PlayStation 2 console, choose the "Confession (Save)" option. Then select a memory card slot and a file location in which to save. If you choose a file location that already contains save data, the priest or nun then asks if you want to overwrite the data. Select "Yes" or "No" to indicate your preference, or select a blank file to create a new adventure log.

CREATE A LOG LIBRARY

If you create new adventure logs every time you save, you can go back to previous saves and replay events. This is useful if you find out that you missed a valuable item or failed to explore an area as well as you should have. However, creating new adventure logs requires additional space on the memory card, and you might need more than one memory card to create enough adventure logs.

CONFERRING WITH PARTY MEMBERS

The other party members provide hints and clues on where to go and what to do next. If you can't figure out the game's next objective, or just need a reminder of your progress after a long respite, just press the Start button for a subtle clue.

CONTROLS

CHARACTER CONTROLS

Directional buttons	Walk
Left Analog Stick	Move (Speed depends on distance stick is moved), next message
Right Analog Stick	Camera Angle
R1	Rotate camera and character right
L1	Rotate camera and character left
R2	Switch to character's point of view (First Person View)
L2	Set camera angle behind character's back
L3 (Press Left Stick)	Search, open door or chest, speak with person (same function as ✕)
R3 (Press Right Stick)	Switch to character's point of view (First Person View)
✕	Search, open door or chest, speak with person, next message, climb, pick up and throw pots and barrels
⊙	Open Main Menu, open door or chest depending on where character is standing, investigate well, read signs, climb
△	Skip messages, cancel out of options screen, disembark ship, dismount sabrecat, land godbird
▢	View Map
▶	Speak to party members
SELECT	Open Battle Records Menu

MENU CONTROLS

Directional buttons	Move cursor
Left Analog Stick	Move cursor
R1	Next page
L1	Previous page
L2	Cancel, return to previous menu
L3 (Press Left Stick)	Select menu option
✕	Select menu option
⊙	Select menu option
△	Cancel, return to previous menu
▢	Exit Menu, Exit from Battle Records to Main Menu if applicable
SELECT	Cancel, return to previous menu

BATTLE CONTROLS

Directional buttons	Move cursor
Left Analog Stick	Move cursor
L1	Select menu option
L2	Cancel, return to previous menu
L3 (Press Left Stick)	Select menu option
✕	Select menu option
⊙	Select menu option
△	Cancel, return to previous menu
▢	Exit Menu, Exit from Battle Records to Main Menu if applicable
SELECT	Cancel, return to previous menu

FIRST-PERSON VIEW CONTROLS

Left Analog Stick	Move camera
Right Analog Stick	Move camera
R2	Return to normal third-person view
R3 (Press Right Stick)	Return to normal third-person view
✕	Return to normal third-person view
⊙	Return to normal third-person view
▢	Return to normal third-person view
△	Return to normal third-person view

MAP SCREEN CONTROLS

L1	World Map: Toggles between Zoom Out, Zoom In, Hide Cursor. Town Map: Toggles icons on and off.
L3 (Press Left Analog Stick)	World Map: Toggles between Zoom Out, Zoom In, Hide Cursor. Town Map: Toggles icons on and off.
✕	World Map: Toggles between Zoom Out, Zoom In, Hide Cursor. Town Map: Toggles icons on and off.
⊙	World Map: Toggles between Zoom Out, Zoom In, Hide Cursor. Town Map: Toggles icons on and off.
L2	Close Map
△	Close Map
▢	Open Map/Close Map
SELECT	Close Map

PLAY WITH ONE HAND!

Notice that the controller is mapped in such a way that the player can interact with the game solely using his or her left hand on the controller! Use the Left Analog Stick to move, and press it (L3) to interact with the environment, open doors, open chests, and so on. Press L1 to rotate and press L2 to center the camera behind the character. This allows you to play the game with one hand, and hold this strategy guide with the other!

MAIN MENU

After the opening scenes, press the ⊙ button to open the main menu. The main menu is divided into four pages indicated by the four menu tabs on the top (Items, Magic, Attributes, and Misc.), and you switch pages by pressing the R1 or L1 buttons or left or right on the directional button. Enter the chosen page by pressing the ⊙ or ✕ button. Open the main menu whenever you want to perform one of the following actions:

- View each character's inventory and items in the Bag.
- Change the characters' equipment.
- Use healing items or cast healing spells between battles.
- Use important items that summon sabrecats or transform the party into the flying Godbird (when available).
- Read important notes and recipes.
- View the status and attributes, including magic, spells and abilities, of each party member.
- Change a character's battle tactics.
- Change the party lineup.
- Change screen, sound, and camera settings.
- Open the Battle Records menu.
- Open the alchemy pot menu (when available).
- Open the Monster Team menu (when available).

ITEMS PAGE

The first page of the main menu is the Items page, displaying all of the items held by each character and extra items contained in the Bag. The party's total amount of gold coins is shown in the lower-right corner of this screen.

Press the ⊙ or ✕ button while viewing the Items page to move the cursor to the first character in the party's lineup. Then move the cursor to the character whose items you want to view, or to the Bag.

CHARACTER ITEMS

To interact with the items in a character's possession, move the cursor and select that character. Then move the cursor to the desired item and press the ✖ button to bring up the popup item option. The help window at the bottom of the item screen displays the description of selected items. Each character can carry up to 12 items. *The items in a character's inventory are the only items that can be accessed in battle.*

BAG OPTIONS

View Bag's Contents: Enter the Bag and interact with the items inside. While viewing items in the Bag, press R1 to scroll to the next page of items in the Bag, and press L1 to view the previous page of items.

Organise Items: Allows you to instantly dump all unequipped items that one or all characters are carrying. For instance, if the Hero's item slots are full but he's only equipped with five items, use this option to move the unequipped extras to the Bag without having to transfer them one by one. Items that can be used for combat (such as cheeses and certain weapons that can be used as items) will not be moved to the Bag.

Sort Bag's Contents: Rearranges the items in the Bag based on type or alphabetical order. When you sort by type, items are arranged in the following order: Items, Important Items, Weapons, Armour, Shields, Helms, and Accessories.

POPUP ITEM OPTIONS

Move the cursor to any item in a character's inventory, or in the Bag, and press ◉ or ✖ to bring up the popup item options.

Use: The highlighted character uses the item, either on himself or another party member, if applicable. If the item is a restorative herb or medicine, the character's status ailment is cured or they regain HP/MP. If the selected item is a tool, its function is enabled.

Transfer: The item becomes attached to the cursor, and you can then transfer it to the inventory of another character or to the Bag. To transfer an item to another character, he or she must have an open slot in their inventory.

Equip/Remove: If the item is a piece of equipment such as a weapon, garment or accessory, use this option to equip or remove the item and receive any status benefits/impediments the item provides. The attribute affected by a piece of equipment is displayed below the character's item slots. A decrease in the attribute is displayed in red numbers, and an increase is marked in green.

Discard: The selected item is removed from the character's inventory or from the Bag. Discarded items are lost permanently.

Nothing: Cancels action and closes the popup item option.

MAGIC PAGE

Certain spells can be used in battle, but some can only be used outside of battle in the field. The second page of the menu screen allows you to cast spells that can be used in the field. These include healing or status ailment-curing spells, protective spells, and teleport spells that allow the party to escape from a dungeon or return to a previously visited town. Open this menu screen and use the characters' spells to prepare for upcoming battles.

ATTRIBUTES PAGE

The Attributes page of the menu screen allows you to view all of the statistics regarding a character's combat skills and abilities. Highlight a character with the cursor, and press ◉ or ✖ to access their attribute pages on the right of the screen. Move the directional button or the left analog stick to the right or left to scroll through the pages. The pages are displayed in the following order: Equipment and Attributes, Field Magic, Battle Spells, Battle Abilities, and Traits.

When the Field Magic, Battle Spells, and Battle Abilities pages are displayed, press ◉ or ✖ to make the cursor appear. Use the cursor to highlight spells and skills, and read their descriptions at the bottom of the screen. It's a good idea to know the function of a spell or ability *before* attempting to use it in battle!

MISCELLANEOUS PAGE

The fourth page of the main menu allows you to perform a variety of actions.

Heal All: Restores the HP of each party member as efficiently as possible. If the characters know healing spells and have sufficient MP, the lowest possible amount of MP will be used to fully heal the party. If no spells have been learned, healing items are used from the characters' inventories (OR party's inventory).

Tactics: Allows you to determine whether characters are controlled manually or automatically during combat. If you choose a tactic other than "Follow Orders," the character acts automatically in battle according to the guidelines of the chosen tactic. Tactics can be switched during combat as well. More details on tactics are given in the "Combat" section of this chapter.

Line-up: Use this option to change the order of the party. The character at the top of the party line-up is the character displayed onscreen when you're navigating through fields, towns, and dungeons. Characters placed toward the top of the line-up are more likely to be on the receiving end of enemy attacks. Characters further down in the line-up are more likely to evade attacks, and won't be targeted as often. We'd like to suggest that you keep Jessica at the bottom of the party line-up at all times, due to her typically lower defence and HP attributes.

Equipment: Provides an alternate method of changing the character's equipment. Items in the selected character's inventory are displayed according to type, rather than all together.

Settings: Here, you can change the aspect ratio of the display to better suit widescreen monitors, adjust the volume of music, sound effects, and character voices, and change camera control options.

Help: At key points during the beginning of your adventure, you will be shown some helpful hints and explanations about the game. Refer to this section for reminders.

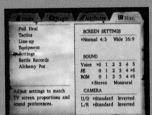

Battle Records: Another method of opening the Battle Records menu, detailed in the next section.

Alchemy Pot: Opens the Alchemy Pot menu, when available.

Monster Team: Opens the Monster Team menu and allows you to select available monsters to fight in Morrie's Monster Arena. More details on the arena are provided in the "Side Quests" chapter.

Battle Records Menu

While King Trode accompanies the heroes on their journey, he keeps a log of everything they experience. Trode records data on enemies defeated, items handled, and alchemy pot recipes collected. View this information in the Battle Records menu.

The main page of the Battle Record displays the log overview, including statistics such as the distance travelled, the battles fought and won, and other facts regarding your adventure. Choose one of the three options to view one of Trode's collected volumes.

Defeated Monster List

All of the creatures that the party defeats in battle are added to the Defeated Monster List. Various statistics are listed for each monster, such as Experience Points (EXP) and gold coins (Gold) acquired when the monster is defeated, the number defeated thus far, and any items it's dropped. Items must be dropped by the creature at the end of the battle in order to be added to the Defeated Monster List. The monster's main habitats are also listed.

Collected Item List

Every item obtained by the party, irrespective of whether it's still in your possession, is added to King Trode's Collected Item List. Items and their descriptions may be viewed all at once, in order by type, or by individual type. This menu is handy if you're shopping and want to purchase something you used to own, but cannot quite remember its function.

Alchemy Recipe Book

As the heroes continue on their journey, King Trode eventually decides to reestablish the ancient practice of combining items to form new ones in a device called an alchemy pot. The combination of two or more items is called a *recipe*. All of the alchemy recipes that the heroes successfully combine, read about in books, or hear rumors of are collected and catalogued in King Trode's Alchemy Recipe Book. This book is viewable both from the Battle Records menu and the Alchemy Pot menu.

Recipes can be viewed all at once, or according to the type of resultant item. It's also possible to view only those recipes that have been heard of or hinted at, but haven't been used to create an item.

If the resulting item or the ingredient is a known item, the name will appear in a black font. If the item produced from the recipe is unknown, three red question marks are shown. If the party has only a vague idea of what the item or the ingredient might be, a clue appears in green letters.

MOVEMENT

Move the character around towns, castles, dungeons, and the field with the left analog stick. The character moves in the same direction onscreen as the left analog stick. Therefore, if you move the left analog stick left, the character runs toward the left side of the screen. Move the left analog stick to the right, and the character goes right. Move the left analog stick up, and the character moves toward the horizon. Move the left analog stick down, and the character moves toward the screen. The character can also move in any diagonal direction relative to the movement of the left analog stick.

The character's speed of movement is determined by how far you move the left analog stick. Move the left analog stick as far as it will go to run at full speed, or only a little way to walk. The directional button can be used to make the character walk as well.

Walking is sometimes better than running, especially if the ground is icy or slippery. Running over an icy bridge can be dangerous, because the party might fall over the edge!

MUNCHIE

Munchie is the small mouse-like pet of the Hero. However, he serves a greater purpose than just being cute and fun to play with. Munchie is tiny enough to crawl into small holes in walls, especially if the party is having trouble getting inside a locked room. Once Munchie is on his own, you can guide his movement the same as any of the other characters. Use the left analog stick to maneuver, and press the ◉ button to perform a forward roll for fun. Since Munchie is so tiny in stature, he can't jump up and unlock doors for the Hero to walk through. But perhaps there's something in the room that's light enough for Munchie to carry back to his master…

ACQUIRING ITEMS

Aside from winning battles, the second best way to improve the fighting abilities of the characters is to collect the best possible items and equipment. There are several ways to collect items. To get the most out of the game, be sure to practice all of the following item acquisition techniques, all of the time.

HERO finds a set of wayfarer's clothes and puts it in the bag.

TYPES OF ITEMS

Finding items is important, but knowing what to do with those items is essential. Keep in mind the types of items on hand, and use them as soon as needed to keep the characters healthy, strong, well protected, and fighting at full potential in every battle.

MEDICINES

Medicines take the form of herbs, roots, mixtures, elixirs, and potions. You can use medicines only once, and they disappear from the inventory when used. They can be used in the field or during combat, if contained in a character's personal inventory.

SEEDS

A character can eat a seed to improve an attribute. This allows you to develop characters more effectively than by simple leveling up, by strengthening the defence of a character who seems to take too much damage from physical attacks (Jessica), for example, or by boosting the agility of a slower character who's always getting left behind (Yangus).

MISCELLANEOUS USE ITEMS

Miscellaneous items include field-affecting items and attack items usable in combat. For instance, phials of holy water stop random battles with weaker monsters from occurring as long as their effects are active or the character remains in the area of effect. Chimaera wings can be used to warp the party instantly to any previously visited town or city, when they need rest or additional supplies. A rockbomb shard is an attack item that can be used in combat to cause damage to all enemies. This category also contains unique items such as Baumren's bell, which summons a sabrecat for riding swiftly across long distances.

CHEESE

The Hero can feed cheese to Munchie during combat, provided that a piece is handy in the Hero's personal inventory. What happens when Munchie eats certain types of cheese in battle, no one knows. We leave it to you to experiment during battle and find out the surprising results on your own. A variety of cheeses with various effects can be created in the alchemy pot.

ALCHEMY ITEMS

Some items are used exclusively in the alchemy pot. When combined with one or two other items, they mix together to form a new item. For instance, fresh milk and rennet powder have no use individually. But when combined in the alchemy pot and allowed to simmer, the two mix together to form plain cheese. And we all know what happens to Munchie when he eats cheese during battle. Or do we?

RARE COINS

By opening certain chests or defeating special monsters, the party can acquire rare coins that can be sold or traded at a high profit. Although coins can be sold to any merchant, mini medals are another story. Someone in the world is rumored to be searching for them…

IMPORTANT ITEMS

Important items often serve a function in the game when the party merely possesses them. For instance, owning the world map allows you to view the entire world at a glance when travelling in the field. The thief's key allows the party to unlock treasure chests that may have extra security. Some important items are found or received, and some are created in the alchemy pot. Sympathetic people

along the journey will hand many important items to the party. Most important items have a story-driven purpose and may be required by other non-player characters in the course of events. If you acquire an important item and have no idea what to do with it, speak with all of the people you've met. With the item in your possession, they may have something of relevance to say.

WEAPONS

Of the five types of equippable items in the game, weapons are perhaps the most interesting! A weapon improves the attack power of the character who wields it. The type of weapon also determines whether the character can attack one enemy or several enemies per turn. Without weapons, the character must rely on leveling and bare mitts to get the job done. Then again, maybe there's something to be said for barehanded brawling…

ARMAMENTS

Armaments are divided into four types of protective items that a character can wear to improve his or her durability in combat. Armaments include suits of armour, shields, helmets, and certain accessories. Stronger armour reduces the amount of damage taken during battle. Sometimes armaments may have additional benefits, such as reflecting spells or regenerating the wearer's HP every round. Check item descriptions in the menu for details.

ACCESSORIES

Small accoutrements, such as rings and bracelets, that improve one of a character's attributes are known as accessories. Equipping such items may raise a character's attack, defence, wisdom, or agility, improving damage, protection, magical power, or combat speed, respectively. Accessories may also have a secondary ability, such as making a wearer resistant to certain status ailments.

TYPICAL ITEM LOCATIONS

When you're searching towns, go into homes and places of business to find useful items and equipment. In dungeons or caves, items are often located in side rooms off the main corridors. Items are rarely out in the open, but are usually inside containers of various types. If you learn to identify the types of containers that may hold items, finding plenty of useful things to wear or sell should be no problem.

BARRELS AND POTS

Wooden barrels and clay pots can be picked up by the character, carried around, and then shattered on the floor. If an item is inside the barrel or pot, the character obtains it immediately.

To pick up a barrel or pot, stand facing the object and press the ✗, ●, or the L3 button. You can throw the container immediately, or carry it to a clearer spot. Press any of these three buttons a second time to toss the breakable object to the ground, smashing it.

CABINETS

You can open cabinets with doors while searching towns and castles for items. Stand facing the cabinet doors, and press the ✗, ●, or the L3 button to open them and search the inside. If an item is available, the party collects it immediately.

ITEM BAGS

Bags hung from pegs on walls may also contain items. To search a hanging bag, face it and press one of the search buttons. The character sticks his arm in and feels around.

BOOKSHELVES

Sometimes important books can be found on bookshelves. By reading these sagely volumes, you might be able to learn clues regarding upcoming challenges. Some books contain interesting information regarding the history of the world in which the characters live. However, some bookshelves contain absolutely nothing of interest. Whenever you decide to stop and glance across the titles on the book spines, you risk wasting your time, but the rewards can be great. Some books may allude to recipes for the alchemy pot. This is, in fact, the number one method of learning alchemy recipes in the game.

CHESTS

Treasure chests must be opened from the front, so examine the chest in first-person view if needed to determine which side to stand near. Press the search button to open the chest and collect the item inside. Be cautious, however, because horrible monsters called mimics like to pretend to be treasure chests sometimes. If a party opens a chest that turns out to be a mimic or a cannibox, a fierce battle ensues.

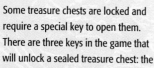

Some treasure chests are locked and require a special key to open them. There are three keys in the game that will unlock a sealed treasure chest: the **thief's key**, the **magic key**, and the **ultimate key**. Each key is greater than the last and opens more types of treasure chests. Once you find the ultimate key, all the previous keys can be discarded or used in the alchemy pot, if possible.

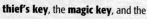
The treasure chest is locked!

DEFEATED ENEMIES

Sometimes when the party wins a battle against a monster party, one or more of the monsters may drop an item. This is another way to acquire items. If you need an item for the alchemy pot, and you know that a particular monster in a certain region sometimes drops that item, do some additional hunting there for a while.

ALCHEMY POT

Certain items can only be acquired by combining them with other items in the alchemy pot. Therefore, it can be hard to discard or sell any item because it may be a key ingredient in a rare mixture. We leave it up to you to determine which items must be obtained via alchemy. This research shouldn't be hard, especially if you use the recipes found in the "Alchemy Pot Recipes" chapter.

King Trode
Now, form an image in your mind of what you'd like to make, and choose the ingredients carefully.

NON-PLAYER CHARACTERS

Anybody you meet during the course of the adventure who's not in your party is considered a non-player character, or *NPC*. These NPCs are the number one source of clues and information in the game, and speaking with them is the best way to learn where to travel next and what dangers may lie in wait there. Speak to any NPC by approaching within a few steps of them, facing them, and pressing the ✖, ⬤, or the L3 button.

NPCs move around and live their lives just like ordinary people. For this reason, they're usually not found in the exact same location after the sun goes down. Many times, the things an NPC says at night differ from what they say during the daytime. Therefore, it's important to speak to everyone in the light of day, and again after dark.

*: Well, let me tell you, it made me so angry that I threw a great clod of horse muck up at it!

*: Ah-phew, ah-phew...

MAPS

While visiting a populated town, city, or castle, press the ⬤ button to view a colorful hand-drawn map of the area. Maps show the streets and buildings, which can aid navigation. Icons placed over important locations in town show you where to stop for a night's stay, a quick confession, or a stout drink.

MAP ICONS

(INN) Inn	📜 Item Shop	🍺 Pub
✝ Armour Shop	♛ Church	🪣 Well
⚔ Weapon Shop	Ⓖ Gold Bank	

Towns and Castles

When travelling through populated areas, the party normally doesn't encounter monsters unless they invade a town in the course of the story. Therefore, it's alright to relax and take things easier when you're hanging out with the locals. Towns also have several beneficial services that the party can take advantage of, usually for a price.

Inns

The party can rest at a local inn, either overnight or until evening, usually for a fee. Whether you decide to stay until evening or overnight, resting at an inn fully restores the HP and MP of all party members. The rate differs from town to town and depends on how many people you have in your party. Usually, the towns you visit later in the game will charge higher rates per person. Please note that staying at an inn will not bring back a fallen party member.

By staying overnight, the party can set out at first light when the monsters are weaker. By resting until evening, the party can visit areas at night when the circumstances are different, or cross the fields when the monsters are more challenging.

Shops

Merchants set up permanent stores in towns. Typically, these peddlers stock an assortment of items and equipment that protect travellers from the monsters in the region. For example, the peddlers in Farebury sell weaker equipment for a lower price, whereas the merchants in Ascantha sell more expensive gear. The monsters in the Kingdom of Ascantha are much more powerful and dangerous than the ones near Farebury, so it all makes sense.

When you want to see what a merchant has for sale, observe proper etiquette by speaking to the clerk from across the counter. If you go behind the counter and speak to a merchant, typically they won't sell you items. However, they may still have something interesting to say…

Pubs

Pubs are where the common folk gather, along with the runts and rogues. The town pub is the place to go if you're looking to meet someone important, or if you want to hear the local gossip and rumors.

Churches

A priest or a nun inside a church, usually standing behind an altar, will hear the party's confession for free. Confession is a fancy way of saving your progress in the game. Anytime you want to stop playing, warp back to the nearest town and make a confession before quitting the game.

Churches offer many other helpful services, as listed on the church menu. Many of them require a donation, which sometimes costs more than you want, or can afford, to pay.

DIVINATION

The priest or nun looks deep into the soul of each character and determines how many more experience points he or she needs to accumulate before reaching the next level. Divination is free, and it's extremely useful when you're planning whether to push onward or spend some time hunting monsters in the field.

RESURRECTION

Death is a reality of battle, and when allies fall in combat, the entire party is weaker as a result. Retreat to the nearest church and seek the aid of a priest or nun in resurrecting dead characters. The church requires a fee to bring each deceased character back to life. The clergy quotes the amount of gold coins required to perform this action. The higher the level of the deceased person, the more gold coins the church requires.

If the entire party falls in battle, the bodies are collected and taken to the church in the nearest town you've visited. All characters are revived automatically, at a cost of half the party's gold coins.

PURIFICATION

Poison is a status ailment that continues afflicting characters even after battle. If an antidote or the proper spell isn't available, return to the nearest church and seek the aid of a priest or nun. Purification is an extremely cheap service. The further from civilisation you go, the more it will cost you.

BENEDICTION

Curse is another status ailment that affects characters in the field. Although some enemies can curse characters during battle, the effect is usually temporary. However, some weapons and equipment are cursed permanently. When they're equipped, the character becomes cursed immediately and cannot take action in battle. The only way to remove the cursed equipment is to return to a local church and seek benediction services. Benedictions aren't nearly as cheap as purifications, and the amount of gold coins required is determined by the affected character's level.

GOLD BANKS

A few major cities and even a few offbeat locations provide financial storage solutions. The point of giving money to Gold Banks for safekeeping is to avoid losing half your earnings if the party is wiped out in battle. The church cannot touch money stored in a Gold Bank, so it's safe. Gold Banks become available as the party explores new areas, so be sure to store most of your wealth there, and carry only what little gold coins you need to get by.

HOUSES

Many people live in towns, and they generally dwell in houses. Speak to the people inside these homes, and search their cabinets, barrels, pots, bags, and chests for useful items. Some people obviously have no idea what kinds of cool stuff they have tucked away in their cupboards, because they don't seem to mind parting with it!

CASINOS

Gambling halls in the towns of Pickham and Baccarat provide a fun diversion from the trials of saving the world from evil. To play the slots, bingo, and roulette, you need tokens. There's usually a counter inside the casino where you can buy them, at a rate of 20 gold coins per token. Try to keep the price of a token in mind when you're placing bets of five or more on a single spin of the wheel. Tokens can be exchanged for the weapons, equipment, and items offered at the exchange counter, also located inside the casino. As long as you have at least a single token, you can view all the wares that are available at the exchange counter to determine how many tokens you will need for the item you want.

WELLS

Towns need a source of water, and many have old-fashioned wells. The characters can climb down into a well and find hidden chambers underneath the towns. The discarded items you find inside a well may turn out to be of great benefit to the party!

DAY AND NIGHT EFFECTS

The daytime is when towns usually have the most activity. At night, many of the townspeople traipse home for some well earned rest. As nighttime settles in, NPCs change locations and shops close. The only places that stay open 24 hours are the churches, inns, and casinos. Sometimes people lock their front doors against intruders, so it may be harder to search for items at night. But some citizens only come out after dark, so perhaps the nighttime is just as good a time as any to visit a town!

FIELD

Whenever the party leaves the comforts of a town, city, or castle, they enter a giant wilderness known as the field map. While moving in the field, the heroes encounter randomly generated parties of monsters roughly every 10-25 steps, depending on the terrain and the time of day. Without the safety of nearby inns and churches, search and survival skills in the field are extremely important.

COMPASS

While you're navigating in the field, a directional compass appears in the lower-left corner of the screen. Use the compass to move north, south, east, and west. Sometimes certain NPCs will tell the party to head south to find a certain location. Without a world map handy, the compass is the best tool to help you get there.

TERRAIN

The type of terrain the character walks upon determines several factors, including the frequency of monster encounters and the types of monsters. Areas with plenty of trees are referred to as forests, sandy areas are beaches or deserts, and everywhere else is fields. Even walking on a dirt road is safer than walking in the green grass. Pay careful attention to the type of terrain surrounding the character.

The party takes constant damage when walking over certain types of terrain, such as poisonous swamps. The types of monsters in swamps are more likely to inflict status ailments on characters as well.

FIELD TREASURE CHESTS

Look for lone treasure chests while navigating across the field map. Most of them aren't located right by the beaten path, but rather behind cliffs or at the edges of lakes. Field treasure chests contain items just like the ones located in towns and dungeons. Many field treasure chests are locked and cannot be opened until you find the proper key.

HERO finds a farmer's scythe and puts it in the bag.

INFAMOUS MONSTERS

In certain areas in the field, monsters are visible on the map. As the character approaches, the monster may run away or may rush forward and attack. If it attacks, a battle begins. Monsters that are visible in the field are unique creatures that aren't encountered anywhere else in the game. Some infamous monsters only appear at night while others only appear during the

day. Certain ones also appear in as many as four different locations! If you defeat them, infamous monsters often drop rare coins that can be sold for high amounts of gold coins. And you may find out that the infamous monsters serve another purpose in the game, if you talk to the right people…

DAY AND NIGHT IN THE FIELD

The more time you spend exploring the field map, the darker the day becomes. As dusk fades and the stars come out, the situation changes in the field. Not only is the environment harder to see, but the monsters you encounter at night are much tougher than the ones you fight during the day. When inexperienced characters are caught in the field at night, it may be a wise idea to warp back to the nearest town and sleep in a safe inn bed. Better that than recklessly plunging forward and losing allies in unnecessary battles, especially when you consider how much it will cost to resurrect them. Then again, if the encounters in your current region have started to lose their flavour, perhaps travelling at night is just the challenge the party needs to keep leveling up at a good pace.

TRANSPORTATION

Because travelling the field requires the party to go long distances, it's impossible to reach all parts of the world on foot. Once you've explored the farthest reaches of the eastern hemisphere, the party must seek out some means of sea travel. Then you can chart the vast oceans and find out what else this fantastic world has to offer. The party continues to have random battles against monsters that board the ship at sea.

Dock the ship by moving toward any piece of land until the option to disembark appears onscreen. The party docks the ship and goes ashore to explore on foot. To board the ship again, move along the ship's portable pier until the characters take to the seas once more. Using chimaera wings or a Zoom spell is no problem, because the ship changes location to be conveniently accessible to the party no matter where they go.

Great sabrecats are another way of travelling long distances quickly. To acquire a sabrecat for riding, the party should speak to someone who trains them for a living. You can dismount from a sabrecat at any time by pressing the ● button. The party continues having random battles while riding sabrecats, although at a greatly reduced rate per distance. Perhaps another means of easy travel is available… something in the sky?

Dungeons

The term *dungeon* refers to any unpopulated indoor location with a heavy concentration of monsters, possibly a few tricks and traps, and maybe one or two environmental puzzles to unravel. You'll also run into the leaders of the monsters, also known as the *bosses*.

Mobile Statues

Sometimes you can move objects such as statues across flat areas. To move an object, face the side of it and press the ✕, ◉, or the L3 button to grab hold. Then use the directional button or the left analog stick to make the character push the object forward, left, or right, or to pull it backward. Statues can be moved in one of four directions, depending on where the character is facing. To move the statue at a slightly better angle, change to another side of the statue and try moving it from there.

Levers and Switches

Machinery in dungeons presents a conundrum. Pulling a lever or switch may help the party down the road, or it may release a trap that instantly springs into action! Levers sometimes reveal hidden corridors or raise collapsed mechanical staircases so that the party can access new areas.

Traps

You'll find various types of traps in dungeons. What looks like a perfectly normal door could be a spring-loaded trap that pushes the party through a hole in the floor to the level below, so they have to fight their way back up. Another setback is when you navigate through a room improperly and are locked in a corridor leading back to the starting point, rather than heading for the exit. Whenever you begin to sense a trap, it's better to stand still and think about how to proceed, rather than plunging blindly ahead.

What appears to be a door is actually just a painting on the wall.

Dangerous Ground

As in the field, walking on certain types of terrain may cause damage to the party, such as purple or green acid pools and spiked floors. When the character starts flashing red and you hear a striking sound effect, it means that everyone in the party is suffering small amounts of damage with each step.

Combat

Your party lines up directly across from the monster party, in the order determined by the Line-up function in the main menu. Characters at the head of the line-up are more likely to be targeted, and more likely to take damage from enemy attacks. During combat, you issue menu commands to the characters. The characters then carry out their orders when it's their *turn*. The monsters respond with attacks or actions of their own. When all monsters and all characters have had a turn, one *round* of combat has passed.

Yangus attacks!

Read the following sections to better understand the combat system, and to learn how to resolve conflicts swiftly and efficiently with the least amount of damage to the party.

Cockateer G uses Wind Sickles!

Random Encounters

Every step the onscreen character takes into a monster-filled region or dungeon is counted, and this count determines when the next battle occurs. In the field, the characters can walk roughly 20-25 steps before triggering an enemy encounter. In rougher terrain, such as the forest, beach, snow, or desert, battles occur every 15-20 steps or so. In dungeons, battles occur every 10-20 steps, depending on the difficulty level of the lair. Sudden battles triggered by character movement are known as *random encounters*. Speaking to or touching unique monsters or NPCs may also trigger battles.

ROUND COMMANDS

At the start of each round, the Round Command menu appears. Before doing anything else, you can flee from battle, intimidate and try to scare the enemies off, or change each character's battle tactics.

Fight: Issuing this command opens the Character Turn Command menu, where you input commands for characters who are set to Follow Orders. Characters set to automatic tactics behave accordingly.

Flee: This command makes the party flee from battle. Whether or not the party gets away depends on whether escape is allowed. During many event battles, fleeing isn't permitted. However, during most random encounters, the party has a chance to escape.

The chance of fleeing is determined by a number of factors. Although it is mainly based on luck, there are other things to consider. For example, the more turns that take place in battle, the higher the chance there is to flee. Also, if the party's level is much higher than the monsters' level, the chance to flee is 100%. If one or more characters are killed during battle, try to flee in the next round to avoid complete annihilation. Fleeing prevents characters from receiving experience points or gold coins, even if monsters have been eliminated.

After fleeing, use chimaera wings or a Zoom spell to return to the nearest town with a church if you're low on HP.

Intimidate: This command makes the characters attempt to frighten off enemies, reducing the size of the monster party and making it easier to win the battle. The character who's first in the lineup gets the first chance to try. Making an ugly face and screaming, he or she tries to drive off the monsters.

Intimidating monsters may scare them away from the battle, or it may have the opposite effect. Higher-level monsters may become enraged and get an extra attack. Therefore, it's not wise to go around intimidating monsters haphazardly, especially when your party is at very low levels or are just entering a new region. Each time you give the Intimidate command, the next character in the lineup tries to intimidate the enemies. Intimidation never works on boss monsters, but it may drive off any underlings serving them.

TACTICS

This command allows you to change how characters are controlled during the course of the battle. Characters set to the Follow Orders tactic are controlled manually using the Character Turn Command menu. Characters who have been assigned any other tactic fight automatically, casting spells and using abilities according to the tactic selected. Tactics can also be changed between battles using the main menu. The Hero cannot be assigned a tactic; you have to input his commands every round.

Show No Mercy: Characters unleash their most powerful attacks against foes, regardless of MP cost or item consumption.

Fight Wisely: Characters use spells and abilities with minimal MP cost, unless they or an ally are close to death.

Focus on Healing: Characters use healing spells and abilities on any ally in the party who's below their maximum HP.

Don't Use Magic: Characters use only physical attacks to strike foes. Be sure to switch to this tactic when characters are running low on MP.

Get Psyched Up: The character psyches up to increase tension every turn until strong enough to cause high damage. The character won't attack or use spells or abilities until the appropriate amount of tension is reached.

Follow Orders: The default setting for all new party members. You manually input a command for each character every round. This is the surest way to make sure each character is behaving appropriately during combat.

CHARACTER TURN COMMANDS

When you select the Fight command from the initial command menu, the Character Turn Command screen appears. You can choose battle commands for the Hero and any other characters who are set to the Follow Orders tactic.

ATTACK

The character physically assaults the targeted enemy or enemies. Equipped weapons determine whether characters can strike single or multiple targets, and strengthen their attack. Physical attacks are the best way to defeat most monsters.

SPELLS

As characters reach higher levels, they will automatically learn some magic spells for use in combat and in the field. Some spells can be learned only by speaking to a certain NPC. Choosing the Spell command opens the selected character's Spell menu. Move the cursor to highlight spells, and choose an appropriate one based on the situation and the spell's description. Most spells

require MP consumption and cannot be cast if the character has 0 MP. Replenish MP by consuming items such as magic water and elfin elixir, or by resting at an inn.

ABILITIES

After gaining a few levels, characters start to receive skill points upon leveling up. While the victory display is still active, you can distribute skill points to any of the characters' weapon or personality skills. When enough skill points are attributed to a skill, the character learns a new ability.

Abilities associated with weapons might only become available in combat when a character equips a certain type of weapon. Many abilities consume MP and cannot be used if the character has insufficient MP remaining. Abilities tend to allow characters to damage enemies while inflicting status ailments upon them.

DEFEND

When you issue the Defend command, characters raise their guard (and/or a shield, if equipped) in preparation for attack. The character can do nothing else for the remainder of the round. Note that if the enemy's attack valve is low and the party's defence value is high, there is a higher chance that the enemy's attack will miss. Issue

the Defend command if it looks like the enemy is about to perform a particularly powerful attack that could greatly reduce the characters' HP or even kill them.

ITEMS

Choose this command during combat to view the personal inventory of the selected party member. Characters cannot use items stored in the Bag during combat, so it's important for each hero to tote around a few healing items and perhaps some powerful attack items, such as a piece of cheese or a rockbomb shard. Some weapons

and armour pieces can be used during combat to cast spells, so try filling your characters' inventories with a variety of items and using them in combat.

PSYCHE UP

This command causes the character to focus their energies, raising their tension level. No other action can be performed during the turn. Each time a character's tension level rises, all of his attributes increase. This means that characters can cause more damage with their attacks or spells, are slightly less likely to be hit, sustain less damage from enemy attacks, and administer greater healing when items or spells are used.

The first time a character psyches up, his or her tension increases by 5. The second time, it increases by 20. So it's important to psyche up at least twice just to be serious about it.

On the third attempt, there's a chance of failure to psyche up. The character doesn't lose any tension, but doesn't gain any either. If the third attempt is successful, the character's tension increases by 50. At this point the character reaches a state of *high tension*.

As characters increase in experience level, past level 20, they can reach an even higher tension level. Reach a tension increase of 50, then try to psyche up again to a tension increase of 100. In this extremely intense state, you can even kill powerful foes with one strike.

When there are many enemies in the monster party, it's difficult to psyche up because the characters leave themselves vulnerable to attack. It may be wiser to have one character psyche up and attack while the rest of the party performs regular attacks and healing procedures every round. During boss fights, when the party usually faces only one foe, it's easier to spend the first few turns raising tension.

When the Hero reaches super high tension, he transforms!

However, observe boss monster attack patterns and use tension appropriately. Many boss monsters can drop the tension level of one or more characters back to normal, negating all the effort it took to psyche up. If a boss is capable of this, avoid spending too many turns trying to psyche up to higher levels.

Certain monsters can use tension to make themselves stronger and harder to defeat.

After choosing an attack, spell, or ability from the Character Turn Command menu, you need to choose an appropriate target for the attack. Move the cursor across the row of enemies, and select the foe that's most likely to cause the most damage or inflict status ailments that could impair the party or prevent them from attacking.

EARLY STRATEGIES

Targeting is extremely important during the early portion of the game, especially when only Yangus and the Hero are playable. *In every battle, the first order of business is to reduce the number of enemies in the monster party.* This way, the enemies get fewer turns to act. When your party enjoys more turns per round than the enemies, healing and raising tension becomes much easier.

As should be evident in even the very first battle in the woods west of Farebury, Yangus is a bit stronger than the Hero and inflicts more damage. This means Yangus can defeat an enemy in a single turn, whereas the Hero may need to attack a foe two or more times to defeat it. When you're targeting enemies, make sure that the Hero targets one foe while Yangus targets another. Yangus should have no problem wiping out his enemy, while the Hero's foe is wounded but still active. On the next turn, have Hero finish off the enemy he attacked in the previous round, while Yangus targets the third foe.

Yangus attacks!

If you use targeting properly, this strategy enables you to eliminate three foes in two rounds. If the Hero and Yangus both target the same foe every turn, you'll find that Yangus is always cleaning up after the Hero. The longer a battle goes on, the more opportunities your foes will have to attack, and the more restorative items your party will therefore need to consume.

THE PARTY EXPANDS

Even after more members join the party, targeting remains important. Jessica uses multiple-target spells and weapons such as whips. With her abilities, she can target and strike groups of same-species monsters that are in line. For example, if a monster party consists of a slime, three candy cats, and another slime, Jessica can attack the three candy cats simultaneously with a whip or a multi-target spell. Since the candy cats separate the two slimes in the lineup, Jessica cannot strike both slimes at once.

Therefore, command Hero to target the first slime, command Yangus to target the last slime, and command Jessica to target the three candy cats in the middle. At the end of the first round, one slime should be dead, along with one or more of the candy cats in the middle. The other slime and the remaining candy cats should be wounded and easy to take out in the next round. With this strategy, you can take out a large number of foes in as few rounds as possible.

Jessica attacks!

FOUR FOR ONE AND ONE FOR ALL

When Angelo finally joins the party in the fourth spot, targeting becomes less of a concern. Use the first round to increase the attack power or defence of the characters with Angelo's spells, or heal up in preparation for impending damage. Continue forming strategies that remove as many enemies from the battlefield as possible, as quickly as possible, reducing the number of enemy turns and enabling the party to retain the upper hand.

Sometimes one or more highly powerful foes appear in a party, as well as several weaker enemies. If it's evident that a character can't take out one of the bigger foes in a single turn, it may be more efficient to spend the first round taking out all of the smaller foes. For instance, if a monster party consists of three she-slimes and three hammerhoods, take out all of the she-slimes immediately. Although the hammerhoods cause more damage than the she-slimes, the monster party has fewer turns available per round because the smaller foes are all eliminated. Now it should be easy to double-team the hammerhoods for the next few rounds until they're defeated.

Angelo casts Kabuff!

Defeat any monsters with character-debilitating abilities before the ones that only perform normal attacks. For instance, if one of the monsters can inflict Curse, rendering one of your characters immobile for the next several turns, that monster must die as soon as possible!

Yangus takes 1 point of damage!

Enemies that can summon additional enemies to join the battle are your highest priority. Dingalings are some of the first enemies that can call allies to their aid. When they ring, they call forth an endless number of powerful jargon monsters. The party's survival depends on eliminating the dingalings immediately, no matter how many jargons appear in the meantime.

Yangus attacks!

INITIATIVE

After you've issued commands to all characters with Follow Orders as their tactic, the battle ensues. How quickly a character can execute his or her action is based on their agility attribute, in comparison to the agility of allies and the monster party. For instance, of all the party members, Jessica's agility is usually the highest, so she will most

likely act first. Yangus's agility is a lot lower, and therefore he probably won't get to attack until after all of the others. In fact, depending on the enemies, Yangus might have to wait until after all of the enemies have had their turns too!

Pay attention to how initiative is working out in battles. If a character like Yangus isn't effective during a fight, equip him with agility-boosting rings or accessories. After all, Yangus is the heavy hitter. The sooner he attacks, the less damage the party sustains from enemy hits.

SURPRISE ATTACKS

Occasionally, the party may get the jump on a monster party when a battle begins. This is indicated by a battle message at the bottom of the screen that the monsters are "too stunned to move." This means that none of the enemies have any turns for the first round, allowing you to act first. Use this opportunity to attack the enemies and reduce their numbers, to heal, or to psyche up and build tension.

Sometimes monsters ambush the party and get to perform attacks or actions without allowing the heroes to counterattack. It may be important to spend the first round healing characters who have sustained multiple hits before you return fire.

HEALING

Damage from enemy attacks reduces the party members' hit points (HP). When a character's HP drops to zero, he or she dies. Dead characters can't act in battle and don't receive experience points from defeated foes. To prevent beleaguered characters from dying, use items and magic to replenish their HP.

In the field, the best method of healing is with magic spells. The Hero and Angelo both learn healing magic fairly early on, so it falls to them to keep the rest of the party in shape. Make sure the Hero and Angelo get to wear the best protective equipment possible, so that they die less often and can heal or revive the others. Yangus might also learn a few minor healing spells, depending on how his skill points are assigned. However, magical healing is only possible as long as the spell caster has magic points (MP) remaining.

In the early stages of the game, before the Hero learns to heal magically, you must use items to regain HP. Purchase plenty of medicinal herbs at shops, and be sure to transfer them to the personal inventory slots of Yangus and the Hero. Even after the characters start to learn healing spells, make sure each character carries a few herbs just in case MP runs low. This is a good strategy to consider until Angelo joins the party

The best method of restoring HP and MP is at an inn. For a reasonable price, the party can sleep in a comfy room and wake up some hours later with full HP and MP. Don't get too comfy, though. If the party never ventures farther than the first inn, how can you ever finish the quest?

MP can only be recovered during battle by consuming magic water or elfin elixir, or by using certain abilities. These items aren't sold at most shops and are rarely found in towns, dungeons, or the field. When the party starts running low on MP, the best idea is to return to the nearest town and get some rest.

RESURRECTION

As mentioned previously in this chapter, you can resurrect fallen comrades by visiting a church and making a sizable donation to the clergy. As characters like Angelo and Jessica increase in experience, they begin learning spells that resurrect fallen allies during a battle or in the field. Lower-level resurrection spells have a chance of failure, however,

so it could take several turns and MP to get a dead man back on his feet. However, using Zing or Kazing spells to revive allies is better than going to a church. As the game wears on, the fees get higher, and higher, and higher…

STATUS AILMENTS

Enemies can inflict a variety of conditions that inhibit your party's abilities in combat. Learn to identify status ailments quickly, and try to keep the proper mixtures of items or spells on hand to remedy the situation. Prevent status conditions by equipping the proper armour and accessories, depending on the enemies in the area. You can lose a battle quickly if everyone isn't fighting at their full potential. You can use status ailments against enemies as well, giving the party a further advantage in combat. Any status ailment that expires after a few combat turns will also be lifted when the battle ends.

Death: A character dies if their HP falls to zero. Revive dead characters by visiting a church or casting Zing or Kazing spells.

Poison: Poisoned characters continually lose HP until the condition is cured. Poisoning continues to affect characters after the battle is over, draining HP each time they take a step. Use antidote items or the Squelch spell to cure poisoning.

Sleep: Dozing characters cannot perform in battle and lose turns as a result. Physical attacks can sometimes wake a character up, depending on how deeply asleep they are. Spells cannot waken a sleeping party member, even if they're taking damage. Cure sleepiness with the Tingle spell. Otherwise, sleep typically wears off after a few rounds.

Jessica is asleep!

Confusion: When stars swirl around an ally's head, he cannot tell friend from foe. Confused characters may attack themselves or others. Confusion wears off after a few rounds, and sometimes abates when an enemy attacks.

Enthrall

Some monsters are capable of seducing or charming allies into not fighting. Enthralled characters usually have hearts swirling around their heads, and will not attack until the effect wears off.

Yangus is absolutely enthralled!

Paralysis: Paralysis prevents the character from moving for several combat rounds, rendering him or her useless and vulnerable. Cure paralysis with the Tingle spell. It also wears off on its own, though you may be in for a long wait…

Yangus is paralyzed and cannot move!

Laughing/Dancing/Stun: Many monsters do funny things to catch the party off-guard. A character who is laughing or dancing loses a turn. The effect doesn't last longer than one round.

HERO begins dancing uncontrollably!

Knocked Down: Some monsters strike so hard that they can knock an ally right on their backside. Allies who have the wind knocked out of them lose two to three turns before they can get back up.

HERO still cannot stand up!

Curse: A Curse is an evil spell, often cast by the undead or the servants of darkness. It prevents characters from acting in battle for several turns.

Yangus is cursed and cannot move!

Illusion/Blind: Characters blinded by light or enveloped in illusions cannot see as well as normal. Although these characters can act in battle, their ability to successfully attack and cast spells is greatly reduced, often resulting in a miss. Illusions and blindness wear off after several rounds, or at the end of battle.

Yangus's eyes are blinded by the sand!

Critical: When a character's HP drops low enough, they double over in pain between turns and their name changes from the normal white font to yellow. If their HP drops still lower, they crumple over even more and their name turns orange. When a character's HP falls to critical status, heal them as quickly as possible.

Yangus uses the medicinal herb!

Attribute Up/Down: Certain spells, cast by enemies and allies alike, can raise or lower attributes such as attack, defence, and agility, improving or decreasing the combat abilities of the characters.

VICTORY

When the final monster falls, the party achieves victory. Experience points are awarded to all surviving party members, and all of the monsters drop a predetermined amount of gold coins. Some monsters will also randomly drop items. If a character has enough experience to increase in level, a special message is displayed along with a sound effect.

Each party member receives 1193 experience points!

LEARNING SPELLS AND SKILLS

Characters who level up at the end of a battle may learn new magic spells. They may also receive skill points, which you can assign to the character's weapon or personality skills. After adding skill points to any of the character's attributes, their skill level may increase. Sometimes a skill level increase allows the character to cause more damage with the specified weapon. Skill level increases also allow characters to learn new abilities.

Although we prefer to leave the allocation of skill points to your discretion, we suggest that you don't spread them out. If a character is equipped with a certain type of weapon, it may be best to increase the skill level of that type in order to achieve benefits in the short term. Therefore, the character becomes more powerful with the weapon in hand, rather than with a weapon type you don't yet own.

FAREBURY REGION

WORLD MAPS

MAP KEY

- Treasure Chest
- Treasure Chest, requires thief's key
- Item Bag

ITEMS FOUND

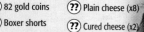

- 82 gold coins
- Boxer shorts
- Seed of life
- Mini medal
- Tool bag*
- Holy water
- Seed of agility

- (??) Plain cheese (x8)
- (??) Cured cheese (x2)
- (??) Angel cheese (x2)
- (??) Mild cheese (x4)
- (??) Highly-strung cheese

*Appears upon fulfilling special circumstances

INFAMOUS MONSTERS

- Axoraptor
- Shortshooter
- One Knight Stand
- Pain in the Neck
- Automaton Aviator

Farebury

Waterfall Cave

WATERFALL HUT

Explore the area to the south of the Waterfall Cave to find a path leading to an isolated residence on the hilltop overlooking the falls.

The eastern view from this area should prove interesting…

THE LONE RED TREE

An isolated tree bearing red leaves grows on the rise near the eastern path. A perfect place for taking a nap…if you had the time.

An important item may appear at the base of this tree after you speak to a certain woodsman.

MONSTER APPEARANCES

FIELD—ANY TIME

NO.	NAME	HP	MP	EXP	GOLD
2	Candy cat	10	0	2	2
3	Lips	11	0	2	3

FOREST—ANY TIME

NO.	NAME	HP	MP	EXP	GOLD
1	Slime	7	0	1	1
2	Candy cat	10	0	2	2
6	Capsichum	15	4	3	3
7	Bunicorn	16	0	5	5
9	Firespirit	14	3	5	4

*Appear only in southeastern portion of region.

FIELD—DAY

NO.	NAME	HP	MP	EXP	GOLD
1	Slime	7	0	1	1
5	Satyr	13	0	3	4
7	Bunicorn	16	0	5	5
*11	Mecha-mynah	9	4	5	8

FIELD—NIGHT

NO.	NAME	HP	MP	EXP	GOLD
4	Dracky	10	0	2	3
9	Firespirit	14	3	5	4
12	Bubble slime	20	0	5	7
13	Dancing devil	20	0	7	10
*17	Beetleboy	16	0	12	10

FAREBURY

Recommended Level: 1

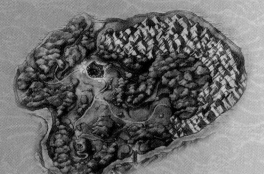

MAP KEY

- (INN) Inn
- Armour Shop
- Weapon Shop
- Item Shop
- Church
- Pub
- Well

ITEMS FOUND

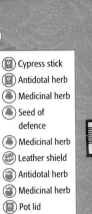

2 gold coins	Cypress stick
3 gold coins	Antidotal herb
4 gold coins	Medicinal herb
4 gold coins	Seed of defence
5 gold coins	Medicinal herb
7 gold coins	Leather shield
8 gold coins	Antidotal herb
10 gold coins	Medicinal herb
20 gold coins	Pot lid
Medicinal herb	Medicinal herb
Antidotal herb	Cypress stick
Holy water	Dagger
Plain clothes	Mini medal
Plain clothes	Thief's key recipe
Chimaera wing	

WEAPON SHOP LIST

WEAPON	COST (G)	EQUIP ON
Cypress stick	10G	Hero
Oaken club	110G	Yangus
Giant mallet	240G	Yangus
Copper sword	270G	Hero, *Jessica (knife skill)
Boomerang	420G	Hero

ARMOUR SHOP LIST

ARMOUR	COST (G)	EQUIP ON
Bandit's grass skirt	35G	Yangus
Wayfarer's clothes	70G	Hero, Yangus, Jessica, Angelo
Leather armour	180G	Hero, Angelo
Leather shield	70G	Hero, Yangus, Angelo
Leather hat	65G	Hero, Yangus, Jessica, Angelo

ITEM SHOP LIST

ITEM	COST (G)	EQUIP ON
Medicinal herb	8G	N/A
Antidotal herb	10G	N/A
Chimaera wing	25G	N/A
Plain clothes	30G	Hero, Yangus, Jessica, Angelo

NOTEWORTHY LOCALS

Kalderasha
Once a great fortune teller, people used to come from far and wide to obtain the legendary foresight and advice offered by "The Great Kalderasha."

However, his clairvoyant abilities have become less reliable over time. Is it simply that Kalderasha is losing his uncanny ability, or is there something else behind the sudden decline in the accuracy of his fortune telling?

Valentina
The sweet, caring daughter of Kalderasha lives with her father in the house near the town's well. Valentina is greatly concerned by the recent decline in her father's fortune telling abilities. Although Kalderasha seems willing to pretend that his senses are as keen as ever, Valentina knows why her father's renowned abilities have waned.

SEARCHING FOR MASTER RYLUS

Speak to every character in Farebury. Any one of them could be Master Rylus, or may know where he is.

Seeking to treat King Trode's malady by finding the culprit who is responsible, the journeying heroes make their first stop in the small, fortified town of Farebury. There, they hope to track down the legendary Master Rylus and gain his support in determining where the evil Dhoulmagus has fled. By speaking to the townsfolk of Farebury, the adventuring party can learn about Master Rylus and perhaps a few other interesting things, too.

SHOPPING IN FAREBURY

The merchants in Farebury offer plenty of items and equipment to help get this journey started. The only problem is finding the gold coins to pay for it!

Farebury has many shops featuring various types of useful items and equipment. Unfortunately, the party only have a small amount of gold coins in their possession. Use some of those gold coins to purchase some **medicinal herbs**, available at the item shop just inside the main gate. Until the heroes acquire more gold coins, most of the equipment in Farebury will remain beyond your reach.

BUYING FROM A MERCHANT

When attempting to purchase goods from a merchant, address him or her from the proper side of the counter. By approaching a shop clerk from behind the counter, he or she will only respond with friendly conversation.

UNDER-THE-COUNTER ITEMS

In one case, it is advisable that the party go behind the counter to speak to the clerk. Speak with the armour shop clerk from inside his marketplace stand. He offers an invaluable item for 500 gold. When the party acquires enough gold, return to Farebury and speak with him again. Pursuing this merchant's under-the-counter item may prove beneficial, so do whatever he says and follow any clues that he provides.

The armour shop clerk offers an especially rare item for a staggering price, but the reward for pursuing this item is definitely worth the cost!

FINDING ITEMS

Note the inclusion of several **medicinal herbs** in the Items Found list at the start of this section, in addition to other valuable traveller commodities. To find items in Farebury, pick up and throw barrels and clay pots to reveal hidden goods. Enter the buildings and dwellings and open cabinets and treasure chests to find items as well. Lastly, don't forget to search inside bags hanging from the walls! Have fun searching and try to find all the items and gold coins listed in the Items Found list!

A young woman on the upper floor of the inn describes in detail how to search for items and gold.

Search inside bags hanging on the wall to find items and gold.

Farebury's pub has two entrances, as do many other shops in town. The back door of the establishment leads to the bartender's area, behind the counter. Make a point to search around the bartender's area to perhaps find some additional items.

Certain locked treasure chests in town require a special key to open them. Speak to everyone in town to learn clues about

SAVING YOUR PROGRESS

Speak to the priest behind the altar during the day, or the nun standing off to the side at night, to access the Church menu.

Stop by the church and speak with the priest to open the Church menu. Use the "Confession (Save)" option to save your game to a memory card. Perilous times and dangerous creatures lie ahead, so saving the game is the best protection against having to replay large portions of the adventure again.

Several other options on the Church menu enable the player to seek the Goddess's aid in curing various status ailments inflicted during battle. The "Divination" option requests that the priest determine the number of Experience Points each character requires to reach the next level.

Don't forget to search all of the back rooms inside the church to find useful items and meet interesting people. It's also possible to ascend to the bell tower that overlooks all of Farebury!

The bell tower is empty for now, but an important clue will appear here after speaking to a certain someone in town…

THE FORTUNE TELLER

After exploring every nook and cranny in Farebury, enter the pub and approach the counter. The rotund man to the right has some important information for visitors. The other man seated at the bar is Kalderasha, and whether the party knows it or not, they have business with him.

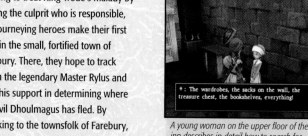

Approach Kalderasha to trigger a string of storyline events in Farebury.

WATERFALL CAVE

Recommended Level: 6

ITEMS FOUND

- Waterfall Cave map
- Chimaera wing
- Medicinal herb
- Leather hat
- Copper sword
- **??** Crystal ball

- Treasure Chest

MONSTER APPEARANCES

NO.	NAME	HP	MP	EXP	GOLD
1	Slime	7	0	1	1
4	Dracky	10	0	2	3
9	Firespirit	14	3	5	4
10	Mischievous mole	15	0	4	5
11	Mecha-mynah	9	4	5	8
12	Bubble slime	20	0	5	7
13	Dancing devil	20	0	7	10
15	Skipper	21	5	12	10
22	Hammerhood	33	0	21	9

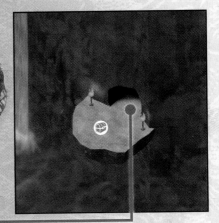

ATLAS

FAREBURY REGION

Level 1

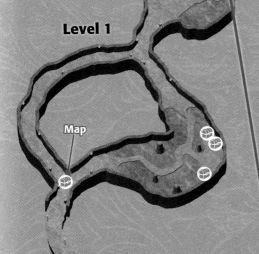

Map

START

Level 2

Level 3

HAMMERHOOD GUARD

A hammerhood blocks the doorway on the second dungeon level. Speak to this monster to find out what it wants. With a little bravery, it's possible to get this monster to move from the path.

The hammerhood is slightly more powerful than other monsters inside the Waterfall Cave. This is the only appearance of a hammerhood in this area.

ALEXANDRIA REGION

WORLD MAPS

INFAMOUS MONSTERS

Buffalo Bill   Family Doctor   Quick Silver

MAP KEY

◉ Treasure Chest

ITEMS FOUND

| ⊚ Slime earrings | ⊚ Seed of strength |
| ⊚ 100 gold coins | ⊚ Seed of life |

Alexandria

Tower of Alexandra

Port Prospect

MONSTER APPEARANCES

FIELD—ANY TIME

NO.	NAME	HP	MP	EXP	GOLD
14	Bodkin archer	21	2	10	8
15	Skipper	21	5	12	10
16	Drackmage	19	6	9	7
19	Funghoul	22	0	13	12
23	Jailcat	29	6	19	8
27	Spiked hare	42	0	30	13

FIELD—DAY

NO.	NAME	HP	MP	EXP	GOLD
11	Mecha-mynah	9	4	5	8
20	Fencing fox	25	8	20	16
22	Hammerhood	33	0	21	9

FIELD—NIGHT

NO.	NAME	HP	MP	EXP	GOLD
17	Beetleboy	16	0	12	10

FOREST—ANY TIME

NO.	NAME	HP	MP	EXP	GOLD
16	Drackmage	19	6	9	7
17	Beetleboy	16	0	12	10
19	Funghoul	22	0	13	12
22	Hammerhood	33	0	21	9
27	Spiked hare	42	0	30	13

BEACH—ANY TIME

NO.	NAME	HP	MP	EXP	GOLD
16	Drackmage	19	6	9	7
24	Frogface	36	6	20	13
237	See urchin	16	4	24	20
238	Man o' war	35	0	23	12
239	Yabby	41	2	31	18

ALEXANDRIA

Recommended Level: 8

MAP KEY

(INN) Inn	🏛 Church
⚒ Armour Shop	🪣 Well
🗡 Weapon Shop	

ITEMS FOUND

🪙 5 gold coins	👕 Wayfarer's clothes
🪙 11 gold coins	🌱 Seed of magic
🪙 18 gold coins	🌿 Moonwort bulb
🌿 Medicinal herb	👗 Jessica's outfit
💧 Holy water	?? Jessica's letter
🪶 Chimaera wing	
🧀 Plain cheese	

WEAPON SHOP LIST

WEAPON	COST (G)	EQUIP ON
Oaken club	110G	Yangus
Giant mallet	240G	Yangus
Copper sword	270G	Hero, *Jessica (knife skill)
Boomerang	420G	Hero
Stone axe	550G	Yangus

ARMOUR SHOP LIST

ARMOUR	COST (G)	EQUIP ON
Leather kilt	220G	Yangus
Scale armour	350G	Hero, Angelo
Scale shield	180G	Hero, Yangus, Jessica, Angelo
Medicinal herb	8G	N/A
Holy water	20G	N/A
Chimaera wing	25G	N/A

33

NOTEWORTHY LOCALS

Bangerz
Bangerz is a rascally youth who seems to have designated himself as the official town guard. Although he displays a natural animosity toward outsiders, he greatly favors Jessica Albert and anyone associated with her.

Rosalind
Rosalind is the mother of Jessica Albert. Her family is currently in mourning following a tragic loss. For this reason, she does not want Jessica to leave the family estate in Alexandria.

Mash
Mash is basically Bangerz's accomplice, which makes him second in command behind Alexandria's self-appointed guard. He follows Bangerz just about anywhere, except out of town.

RECENT TRAGEDY IN ALEXANDRIA

Although the official "welcome" here may come as quite a surprise, speak to all of the citizens and merchants of Alexandria to learn about the recent events that have unfolded regarding the town's most prominent family, the Alberts. After doing so, walk up the nearby hill and enter the mansion.

Most of the citizens are very knowledgeable regarding recent events in the area, plus they all seem to know about the long history of the Albert family.

Find out more facts by speaking to the staff of the mansion, and Rosalind and Lorenzo on the second floor. Bangerz and Mash guard the door to Jessica's quarters and refuse to allow anyone inside. This means that there must be another method of entry. Head through the northwest door of the mansion and ascend to the attic. Speak to the maid there to view a telling clue.

Search the attic walls for a way to continue exploring the mansion in Alexandria.

TOWER OF ALEXANDRA

Recommended Level: 9

AREA MAPS
MAP KEY

ITEMS FOUND

- 7 gold coins
- 11 gold coins
- 22 gold coins
- Tower of Alexandra map
- Medicinal herb
- Medicinal herb
- Moonwort bulb
- Seed of agility
- Seed of strength
- Scale shield
- Antidotal herb
- (??) (item not found until later)

MONSTER APPEARANCES

NO.	NAME	HP	MP	EXP	GOLD
12	Bubble slime	20	0	5	7
16	Drackmage	19	6	9	7
17	Beetleboy	16	0	12	10
18	Imp	28	0	15	11
19	Funghoul	22	0	13	12
21	Healslime	24	12	18	13
24	Frogface	36	6	20	13

- Treasure Chest
- Breakable Pot
- Breakable Barrel

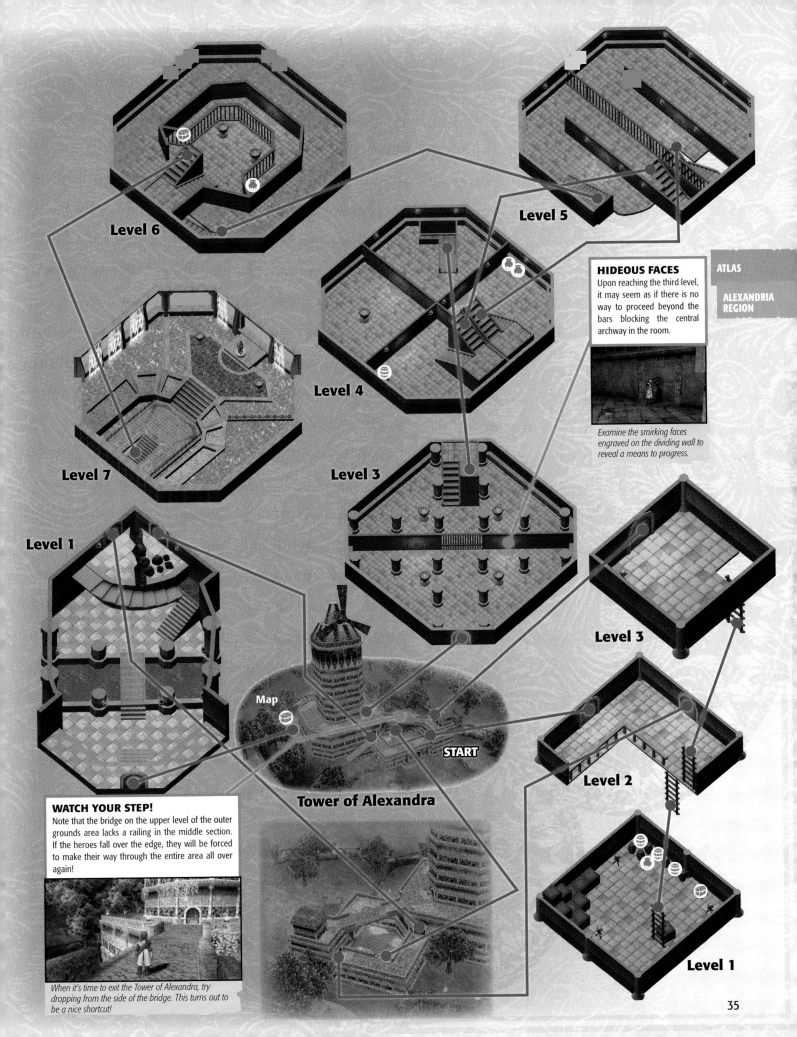

Level 6

Level 5

Level 4

Level 7

Level 3

Level 1

HIDEOUS FACES
Upon reaching the third level, it may seem as if there is no way to proceed beyond the bars blocking the central archway in the room.

Examine the smirking faces engraved on the dividing wall to reveal a means to progress.

Level 3

Map

START

Level 2

Tower of Alexandra

WATCH YOUR STEP!
Note that the bridge on the upper level of the outer grounds area lacks a railing in the middle section. If the heroes fall over the edge, they will be forced to make their way through the entire area all over again!

When it's time to exit the Tower of Alexandra, try dropping from the side of the bridge. This turns out to be a nice shortcut!

Level 1

35

PORT PROSPECT

Recommended Level: 11

MAP KEY

- Inn
- Armour Shop
- Weapon Shop
- Item Shop
- Church
- Pub
- Well

ITEMS FOUND

- Chimaera wing
- Medicinal herb
- Seed of wisdom
- 17 gold coins
- Holy water

ITEM SHOP LIST

ITEM	COST (G)
Medicinal herb	8G
Antidotal herb	10G
Holy water	20G
Chimaera wing	25G

ARMOUR/WEAPON SHOP LIST

ARMOUR	COST (G)	EQUIP ON
Stone axe	550G	Yangus
Iron lance	750G	Hero
Farmer's scythe	910G	Yangus
Leather kilt	220G	Yangus
Scale armour	350G	Hero, Angelo
Scale shield	180G	Hero, Yangus, Jessica, Angelo

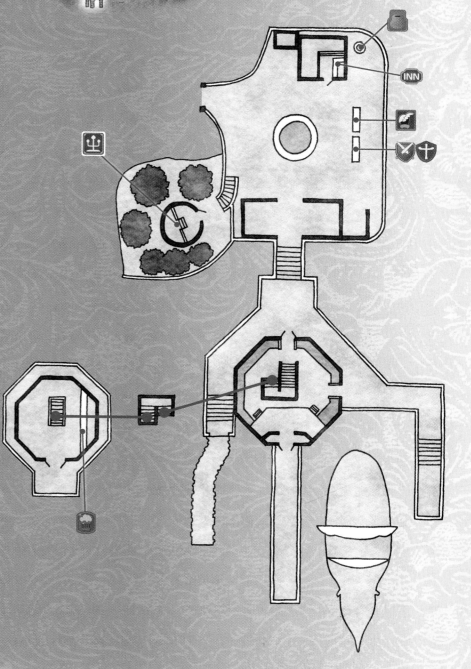

WISE WOMEN OF SKILLS

Speak to the two women standing underneath the awning near the armour/weapon shop (during the day or night) to learn a few tips regarding weapons, each character's different skills, and allocation of skill points when characters level up.

Speak to either woman underneath the awning for tips on how to improve character attacks and abilities.

MONSTER MESSAGE

Find and speak to a friendly monster located somewhere in Port Prospect. What this monster has to say could prepare the heroes for the rough waters ahead…

PORT PROSPECT'S HERB MERCHANT

During the daytime, a young lady stands on the path between the market portion of town and the lighthouse where the pub is located. Speak to her to learn that she sells an unknown type of herb for 10G. Choosing to buy one from her turns out to be either a great deal, or a waste of money. She may sell a medicinal herb (which is usually cheaper at any item shop), or she may hand over more valuable herbs. If the heroes have any spare gold, purchase some herbs from this woman to see if any bargains are available.

Find the young woman standing in front of the lighthouse during the daytime and try your luck at buying herbs.

ATLAS

ALEXANDRIA REGION

FERRY
Recommended Level: 12

AREA MAPS

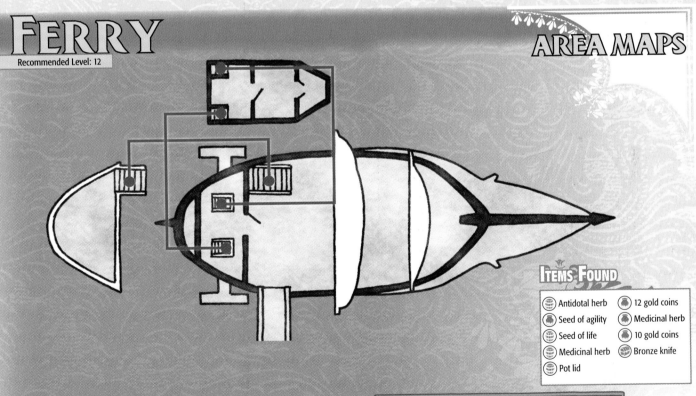

ITEMS FOUND

Antidotal herb	12 gold coins
Seed of agility	Medicinal herb
Seed of life	10 gold coins
Medicinal herb	Bronze knife
Pot lid	

CROSSING THE WATER

If the trip from Port Prospect to Peregrin Quay seems to be taking a long time, seek out and speak to King Trode. He has a wonderful new device to reveal!

MAELLA REGION

WORLD MAPS

MAP KEY

- 🔵 Treasure Chest
- 🔵 Treasure Chest, requires thief's key
- 🔵 Treasure Chest, requires magic key

ITEMS FOUND

- 🟢 Magic water
- 🟢 Stone axe
- 🟢 Feathered cap
- 🟢 Seed of magic
- 🟢 Seed of strength
- 🟢 Seed of wisdom
- 🟢 Bunny tail
- 🟢 Mini medal

INFAMOUS MONSTERS

 Mullet Mallet

 Bricklayer

 Hollow Knight

 Root of Evil

Peregrin Quay

Maella Abbey

Simpleton

MONSTER APPEARANCES

FIELD—ANY TIME

NO.	NAME	HP	MP	EXP	GOLD
8	She-slime	18	0	8	6
26	Winky	40	0	32	12
28	Chainine	38	0	36	11

FOREST—ANY TIME

NO.	NAME	HP	MP	EXP	GOLD
28	Chainine	38	0	36	11
29	Giant moth	36	6	37	12
30	Dingaling	28	4	31	16
31	Jargon	73	0	64	32
33	Bullfinch	40	0	30	14
38	Morphean mushroom	45	0	40	11

FIELD—DAY

NO.	NAME	HP	MP	EXP	GOLD
30	Dingaling	28	4	31	16
31	Jargon	73	0	64	32
33	Bullfinch	40	0	30	14

NORTHEASTERN AREA—ANY TIME

NO.	NAME	HP	MP	EXP	GOLD
37	Scorpion	40	4	42	8
38	Morphean mushroom	45	0	40	11
39	Brownie	53	0	43	12
45	Hell hornet	37	0	51	12
49	Treeface	64	0	67	23

FIELD—NIGHT

NO.	NAME	HP	MP	EXP	GOLD
25	Lump mage	38	12	31	18
29	Giant moth	36	6	37	12

PEREGRIN QUAY

Recommended Level: 12

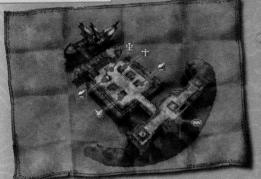

MAP KEY

Inn	Item Shop
Armour Shop	Church
Weapon Shop	Pub

ITEMS FOUND

- 8 gold coins
- Chimaera wing
- Antidotal herb
- Seed of defence
- Medicinal herb
- Iron nail
- 200 gold coins
- Boomerang
- Mini medal
- Seed of magic
- Leather kilt
- Medicinal herb
- Oaken club

ITEM SHOP LIST

ITEM	COST (G)
Medicinal herb	8G
Antidotal herb	10G
Holy water	20G
Chimaera wing	25G

ITEM SHOP LIST*

ITEM	COST (G)	EQUIP ON
Cypress stick	10G	Hero
Pot lid	40G	Yangus, Jessica
Bandana	45G	Hero
Hairband	150G	Jessica
Slime earrings	400G	Hero, Yangus, Jessica, Angelo

WEAPON SHOP LIST

WEAPON	COST (G)	EQUIP ON
Bronze knife	150G	Jessica
Thorn whip	350G	Jessica
Iron lance	750G	Hero
Farmer's scythe	910G	Yangus

ARMOUR SHOP LIST

ARMOUR	COST (G)	EQUIP ON
Scale armour	350G	Hero, Angelo
Silk robe	420G	Jessica, Angelo
Chain mail	500G	Yangus
Scale shield	180G	Hero, Yangus, Jessica, Angelo
Pointy hat	70G	Yangus

THE THIEF'S KEY

Enter the inn and speak to the traveller seated at the table. The man gives an **iron nail** to the party. Combine this item with a bronze knife in the alchemy pot and let the ingredients bubble for a while. Spend the interim speaking with other townsfolk, or proceed through the inn into the wilds of the Maella region to battle new enemies. If you choose the latter course of action, we strongly recommend setting out at dawn rather than at night, because the enemies are much tougher on the new continent!

*: But if you're clever an' you mix it wiv somefin' else, maybe you'll be able to get it to work for ya. You'll 'ave to figure that out for yerself though.

Speak to the traveller from Port Prospect, now seated inside the inn, to obtain a vital alchemy pot item.

While continuing to play, listen for the chime of the alchemy pot. When the chime sounds, open the pot, wherein the party will have concocted the **thief's key**. This special key opens many of the locked chests encountered throughout the game, especially on the field map. Remember that there were some locked chests as far back as Farebury…

You made a thief's key!

The thief's key opens many, but not all, of the locked treasure chests in the world.

After making the thief's key, do not let the alchemy pot sit idle just because you do not know any recipes. A wide variety of weapon and armour upgrades can be created to make the characters a little bit stronger, while saving a nice chunk of gold in the meantime.

Kick things off with new hats for everyone. By combining a leather hat with a chimaera wing you can make a **feathered cap** (Defence 9). Combine two bandanas to make a **turban** (Defence 8). Stick a bunny tail (dropped randomly by local enemies) onto a hairband to make Jessica some **bunny ears** (Defence 14).

Boost your defence even more by giving the Hero or Yangus a sturdy new shield. Throw a leather shield and a bronze knife into the alchemy pot, and out comes a **bronze shield** (Defence 10).

Whip together a few new weapons, too. Upgrade Jessica's leather whip to a **snakeskin whip** (Attack 23) by combining it with a scale shield, resulting in a significant power upgrade and creating a rare item not sold in any shops. Combine two farmer's scythes to make a powerful and pricey **iron axe** (Attack 38).

You can sell any one of these items for much more than the cost of its ingredients. So there's no reason not to keep cranking out these items for profit! When no other ingredients are on hand, just toss a pair of medicinal herbs into the pot to produce more powerful doses of **strong medicine**.

RECIPE SUMMARIES

Turban = bandana + bandana

Bunny ears = hairband + bunny tail

Feathered cap = leather hat + chimaera's wing

Bronze shield = leather shield + bronze knife

Snakeskin whip = leather whip + scale shield

Iron axe = farmer's scythe + farmer's scythe

Strong medicine = medicinal herb + medicinal herb

THE CLOSED ITEM SHOP

After creating the thief's key, help the man in the market area who was having trouble opening treasure chests. The equipment he sells may not seem very advantageous at this point in the game, however, such things may prove very useful now that the alchemy pot is at your disposal…

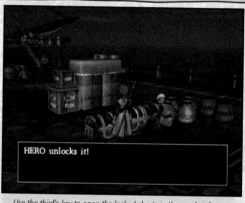

HERO unlocks it!

Use the thief's key to open the locked chests in the marketplace area. The merchant then opens a shop selling items useful in the alchemy pot.

MAELLA ABBEY

Recommended Level: 12

AREA MAPS MAP KEY

🏛 Church

ITEMS FOUND

26 gold coins	Mini medal
Holy water	Mini medal
Mini medal	(??) World map

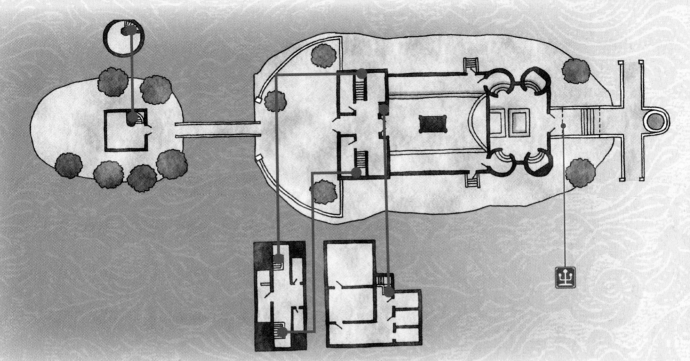

NOTEWORTHY LOCALS

Marcello

The Captain of the holy order of the Templars commands his men with a mixture of fear and respect. All save Angelo, a Templar who often disregards Marcello's orders and threats, even to the point of outright lying to Marcello's face. The Templar Captain has a peculiar air about him. Although he appears to be benevolent and—at times—even helpful to the party, he may be someone to keep an eye on.

Abbot Francisco

The Abbot of Maella would appear to be somewhat reclusive, living in a little mansion on a small island surrounded by a moat behind Maella Abbey. But this is not the summary of his character; he is in fact quite fond of secondhand jokes and bad puns. The books in the private library within his dwelling contain jokes and witticisms reflecting the lowbrow nature of his humor. Yet Abbot Francisco remains a good natured and benevolent holy man, having taken in and raised orphans such as Angelo and Marcello, as well as most of the Templars. If the heroes can find a means to appease the Abbot's scores of fervent bodyguards, perhaps he can shed some light on Dhoulmagus's plans.

LIFE AMONG THE TEMPLARS

Proceed through the abbey to an enclosed courtyard. Approach the double doors at the end of the outdoor area where two guards stand. The guards become threatening and even violent in their efforts to prevent the party from entering the Templar's area and visiting the Abbot. It looks like the heroes may need assistance from someone inside the Templar group. Perhaps such a person could be found in one of the nearby towns?

The guards refuse to allow the party access to the Templar's dorms and Abbot Francisco's residence.

SIMPLETON

Recommended Level: 13

MAP KEY

(INN) Inn	Item Shop
Armour Shop	Church
Weapon Shop	Pub

ITEMS FOUND

- 6 gold coins
- Mini medal
- (??) Templar's ring

WEAPON SHOP LIST

WEAPON	COST (G)	EQUIP ON
Rapier	300G	Angelo
Thorn whip	350G	Jessica
Wizard's staff	1300G	Jessica, Angelo
Long spear	1700G	Hero
Sledgehammer	1700G	Yangus

ITEM SHOP LIST

ITEM	COST (G)	EQUIP ON
Medicinal herb	8G	N/A
Antidotal herb	10G	N/A
Holy water	20G	N/A
Chimaera wing	25G	N/A
Chain mail	500G	Yangus
Turban	410G	Hero, Yangus

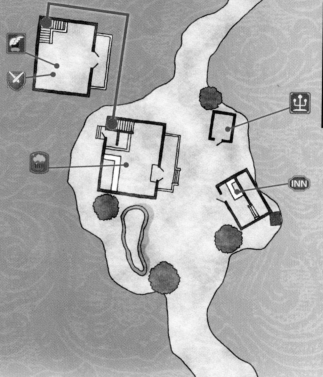

WHERE THE SIMPLE FOLK LIVE

The weapon and item shops are located on the upper level of the pub. Speak to the two men seated at the table near the bunny girl waitress (she's close to the dumb waiter) to learn about the Simpleton economy and to view their list of available items.

*: People think just because I'm from Simpleton, I can't run a successful business. But I'm a decent trader, you know. Wanna buy something?

The merchants on the upper level of the pub have items for sale.

WANT TO BE STARTING SOMETHING?

Trouble seems to be brewing in the pub. Speak to the men gathered around the table in the corner of the downstairs level to initiate a chain of events that eventually forces the heroes outside. After receiving a special item, the party will be able to explore sections of the Templar's dormitory in Maella Abbey that were previously inaccessible.

Speak to the man seated across the table from the thugs depicted in this screenshot to get the ball rolling in Simpleton.

RUINED ABBEY

Recommended Level: 14

MONSTER APPEARANCES

NO.	NAME	HP	MP	EXP	GOLD
32	Drackyma	33	6	28	9
33	Bullfinch	40	0	30	14
34	Bag o' laughs	34	10	35	25
35	Skeleton	46	3	41	15
36	Metal slime	4	Infinite	1350	5
40	Flyguy	39	8	44	16
44	Mummy boy	73	0	55	9
52	Walking corpse	94	0	59	11
62	Cannibox	61	12	76	110

ITEMS FOUND

- Waterweed mould
- Mini medal
- Iron nail
- Bandit's grass skirt
- Mini medal
- 50 gold coins
- Ruined Abbey map
- Bronze shield
- Cannibox

MAP KEY

- Treasure Chest
- Treasure Chest, requires thief's key
- Breakable Pot
- Breakable Barrel
- Cabinet

A ONE-WAY DOOR

You can only open the tightly shut door that separates the two sections of Level 3 from the north side. If your party is on the south side of the door, you can return to Level 2 and use the ladder to explore the north side of Level 3.

The door that separates the two sections of level B3F can only be opened from the north side.

RIVER OF SLUDGE

Each step taken through the purplish sludge that divides the large chamber on Level 4 causes damage to all party members. However, it's possible to use the debris strewn about the room to safely navigate from one side of the chamber to the other. Don't slip!

Use the directional button to walk slowly over the wreckage. Avoid falling into the muck or the entire party suffers damage.

Level 1

START

Level 2

Map

Level 3

Level 3

Level 4

METAL SLIMES

Occasionally, a metal slime may appear with groups of enemies within the Ruined Abbey. Causing damage to them is extremely difficult, but try anyhow. If you can manage to defeat a metal slime before it runs away, each party member receives a huge amount of experience!

Avoid defeating other monsters before fighting the metal slimes. If left alone, metal slimes will flee.

ALCHEMY POT TIPS: INGREDIENTS IN THE RUINED ABBEY

There are two key alchemy pot ingredients located inside the Ruined Abbey. One is the iron nail and the other is the gold rosary, which you obtain upon defeating the boss inside the dungeon. Use them to produce some significant weapon upgrades for the Hero.

If you spent the Hero's skill points on boomerang skills, then combine the iron nail with a boomerang to produce a **reinforced boomerang** (Attack 32). If you allocated skill points to the Hero's Spear ability instead, then mixing the gold rosary with a long spear will produce an equally exciting weapon, the **holy lance** (Attack 39).

RECIPE SUMMARIES

Reinforced boomerang = boomerang + iron nail

Holy lance = long spear + gold rosary

KINGDOM OF ASCANTHA

WORLD MAPS

MAP KEY

 Treasure Chest

Treasure Chest, requires thief's key

Treasure Chest, requires magic key

ITEMS FOUND

- 154 gold coins
- Chain mail
- Seed of life
- 230 gold coins
- Seed of defence
- Seed of agility
- Fresh milk (x5)

- Mini medal
- Steel broadsword
- Agility ring
- Seed of magic
- Mini medal
- Silk robe

INFAMOUS MONSTERS

Sharpshooter   Little Nipper   Fantom of Chopera

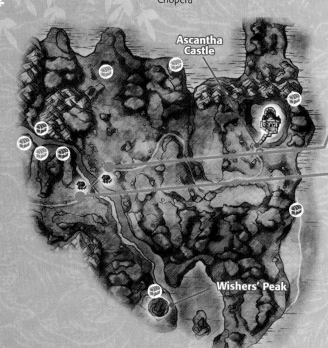

Ascantha Castle

Wishers' Peak

RIVERSIDE CHAPEL

This church on the eastern side of the bridge is also the site of the cheapest resting spot in the country.

RIVERSIDE COTTAGE

The small cottage on the western bank of the river that divides the Kingdom of Ascantha is the homestead of an elderly lady whose beloved granddaughter serves the King of Ascantha. This is important information to remember later on.

Interact with the citizens on the outskirts of the Kingdom of Ascantha.

MONSTER APPEARANCES

WEST OF RIVER—FIELD, DAY

NO.	NAME	HP	MP	EXP	GOLD
8	She-slime	18	0	8	6
21	Healslime	24	12	18	13
31	Jargon	73	0	64	32
34	Bag o' laughs	34	10	35	25
39	Brownie	53	0	43	12
41	Puppeteer	75	12	45	21
46	Pan piper	48	0	54	18

EMBANKMENT—ANY TIME

NO.	NAME	HP	MP	EXP	GOLD
36	Metal slime	4	Infinite	1350	5
50	Kisser	49	0	53	15
236	Khalamari kid	44	0	37	9
237	See urchin	16	4	24	20
240	King kelp	86	8	56	16

EAST OF RIVER—FOREST, ANY TIME

NO.	NAME	HP	MP	EXP	GOLD
37	Scorpion	40	4	42	8
39	Brownie	53	0	43	12
45	Hell hornet	37	0	51	12
49	Treeface	64	0	67	23
51	Diemon	64	10	58	19

WEST OF RIVER—FIELD, NIGHT

NO.	NAME	HP	MP	EXP	GOLD
21	Healslime	24	12	18	13
29	Giant moth	36	6	37	12
38	Morphean mushroom	45	0	40	11
40	Flyguy	39	8	44	16
43	Night sneaker	52	12	52	20
44	Mummy boy	73	0	55	9
47	Slime knight	52	4	55	22

EAST OF RIVER—FIELD, ANY TIME

NO.	NAME	HP	MP	EXP	GOLD
21	Healslime	24	12	18	13
47	Slime knight	52	4	55	22

EAST OF RIVER—FIELD, NIGHT

NO.	NAME	HP	MP	EXP	GOLD
43	Night sneaker	52	12	52	20
44	Mummy boy	73	0	55	9
50	Kisser	49	0	53	15

NORTH OF RIVER—FIELD, ANY TIME

NO.	NAME	HP	MP	EXP	GOLD
48	Clockwork cuckoo	32	0	56	31
51	Diemon	64	10	58	19
53	Fat bat	52	5	61	9
56	Chimaera	54	6	64	12
79	Boh	80	Infinite	65	16

WEST OF RIVER—FOREST, ANY TIME

NO.	NAME	HP	MP	EXP	GOLD
27	Spiked hare	42	0	30	13
32	Drackyma	33	6	28	9
38	Morphean mushroom	45	0	40	11
39	Brownie	53	0	43	12
45	Hell hornet	37	0	51	12
47	Slime knight	52	4	55	22
78	Mum	65	20	68	25

EAST OF RIVER—FIELD, DAY

NO.	NAME	HP	MP	EXP	GOLD
26	Winky	40	0	32	12
39	Brownie	53	0	43	12
41	Puppeteer	75	12	45	21
78	Mum	65	20	68	25
80	Jum	75	10	60	4
81	Boe	68	10	59	4

NORTH OF RIVER—FOREST, ANY TIME

NO.	NAME	HP	MP	EXP	GOLD
48	Clockwork cuckoo	32	0	56	31
49	Treeface	64	0	67	23
51	Diemon	64	10	58	19
53	Fat bat	52	5	61	9
56	Chimaera	54	6	64	12

EAST SHORE AREA—ANY TIME

NO.	NAME	HP	MP	EXP	GOLD
16	Drackmage	19	6	9	7
50	Kisser	49	0	53	15
236	Khalamari kid	44	0	37	9
239	Yabby	41	2	31	18
240	King kelp	86	8	56	16

SOUTH OF ASCANTHA CASTLE—FIELD, DAY

NO.	NAME	HP	MP	EXP	GOLD
21	Healslime	24	12	18	13
41	Puppeteer	75	12	45	21
42	Bodkin bowyer	48	Infinite	43	17
46	Pan piper	48	0	54	18
47	Slime knight	52	4	55	22
79	Boh	80	Infinite	65	16

SOUTH OF ASCANTHA CASTLE—FIELD, NIGHT

NO.	NAME	HP	MP	EXP	GOLD
21	Healslime	24	12	18	13
34	Bag o' laughs	34	10	35	25
35	Skeleton	46	3	41	15
43	Night sneaker	52	12	52	20
44	Mummy boy	73	0	55	9
50	Kisser	49	0	53	15

SOUTH OF ASCANTHA CASTLE—FOREST, ANY TIME

NO.	NAME	HP	MP	EXP	GOLD
8	She-slime	18	0	8	6
45	Hell hornet	37	0	51	12
49	Treeface	64	0	67	23
50	Kisser	49	0	53	15
51	Diemon	64	10	58	19

COW MILKING

Examine the cows grazing in the Kingdom of Ascantha and around the world to obtain **fresh milk**, a healthy source of calcium and also a useful item in the creation of various cheeses!

Cows aren't just for tipping anymore!

ASCANTHA CASTLE

Recommended Level: 15

AREA MAPS

MAP KEY

- Inn
- Armour Shop
- Weapon Shop
- Item Shop
- Church
- Pub
- Well

ITEMS FOUND

- Rennet powder
- 42 gold coins
- Plain clothes
- Mini medal
- Mini medal
- Mini medal
- Medicinal herb
- Red mould
- Lady's ring

ITEM SHOP LIST

ITEM	COST (G)
Medicinal herb	8G
Antidotal herb	10G
Rennet powder	10G
Holy water	20G
Chimaera wing	25G
Moonwort bulb	30G

WEAPON SHOP LIST

WEAPON	COST (G)	EQUIP ON
Dagger	350G	Jessica
Short bow	750G	Angelo
Wizard's staff	1300G	Jessica, Angelo
Edged boomerang	1360G	Hero
Steel broadsword	2000G	Hero, *Jessica (knife skill)

ARMOUR SHOP LIST

ARMOUR	COST (G)	EQUIP ON
Leather dress	380G	Jessica
Bronze armour	840G	Hero
Iron cuirass	1000G	Yangus
Bronze shield	370G	Hero, Yangus
Turban	410G	Hero, Yangus
Slime earrings	400G	Hero, Yangus, Jessica, Angelo

Level 2

Level 3 Level 4 Level 5

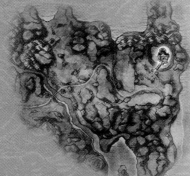

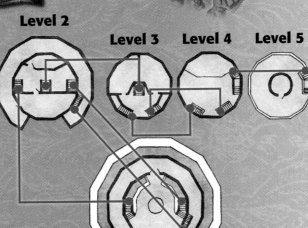

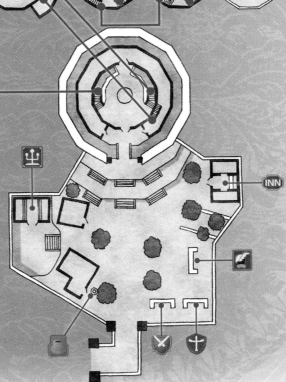

45

Emma

The King's maid is a hard worker who attempts to keep her spirits up in spite of the current situation in the castle city of Ascantha. Find her in Ascantha and speak to her when she is not busy carrying out her chores or praying in the local church. She may provide clues that could allow your party to intervene on behalf of Ascantha's troubled citizens.

King Pavan

Formerly a generous and benevolent ruler, something is deeply troubling the King of Ascantha, causing him to neglect his once-thriving kingdom. The party must try to determine the cause of the King's malady to restore balance in Ascantha.

CITY OF SADNESS

Speak to the citizens of Ascantha to determine why everyone is wearing black. Your investigation of such matters will eventually take your party inside the castle. The events transpiring in Ascantha depend upon the time of day in which you enter the town. If you enter Ascantha at night, then the party can find Emma, the King's maid, praying for guidance in the local church. She will not provide any information while praying, so spend the night at the local inn or wait until morning for things to change.

If you enter Ascantha at nighttime, look for Emma who is praying in the local church.

During the daytime, Emma is located at the top of Ascantha castle's tower, attempting to coax the King from his chambers. After witnessing this event, follow Emma back down to the throne room and speak to her to find out what is going on with the King.

Locate Emma outside the King's chambers at the top of Ascantha castle. Follow her back to the throne room to determine what can be done to help the citizens of Ascantha.

THE THRONE ROOM AT NIGHT

To act upon the information provided by Emma, the party may need to stay at the local inn, just until nightfall. Nighttime is the only time of day that the King emerges from his chambers. His Majesty is located in the throne room. By attempting to speak with the King, the party can learn something that may help them unravel the mystery of the King's condition and herald a new beginning for Ascantha.

After the scenes involving Emma, return to the throne room at night to find King Pavan.

RIVERSIDE COTTAGE (EMMA'S GRANDMOTHER'S HOUSE)

Return to the small house across the bridge from Riverside Chapel. Speak with Emma's grandmother and listen to the stories of Wishers' Peak and how to get there.

Be sure to speak to Emma's grandmother.

WISHERS' PEAK

Recommended Level: 16

ITEMS FOUND

- Wizard's staff
- Wishers' Peak map
- Templar's shield

MONSTER APPEARANCES

NO.	NAME	HP	MP	EXP	GOLD
21	Healslime	24	12	18	13
42	Bodkin bowyer	48	Infinite	43	17
44	Mummy boy	73	0	55	9
45	Hell hornet	37	0	51	12
47	Slime knight	52	4	55	22
49	Treeface	64	0	67	23
51	Diemon	64	10	58	19
52	Walking corpse	94	0	59	11
53	Fat bat	52	5	61	9

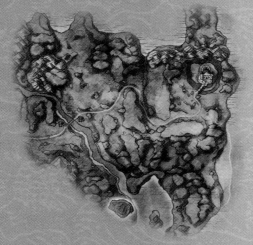

MAP KEY

Treasure Chest

ATLAS

KINGDOM OF ASCANTHA

Side A

Side B

START

Entrance

Map

Inside well

TOP OF WISHERS' PEAK

After receiving clues from certain individuals at Ascantha castle and the dwellings near the river bridge, the party's next logical move would be to attempt to unravel the mystery of Wishers' Peak. Yet the uppermost level of Wishers' Peak is devoid of all objects. Not even monsters dwell here. What can the heroes hope to find in the ruins? Perhaps only time and quite a bit of patience will tell.

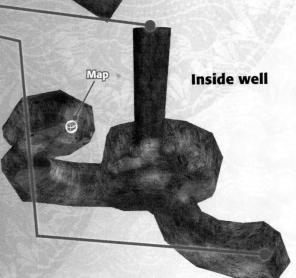

Wait atop Wishers' Peak long enough, and some present concerns may be answered.

PICKHAM REGION

WORLD MAPS

MAP KEY

- 🔵 Treasure Chest
- 🔵 Treasure Chest, requires thief's key
- 🔵 Treasure Chest, requires magic key
- 🔵 Treasure Chest, requires ultimate key

ITEMS FOUND

🔵 Iron shield	🔵 Garter
🔵 Leather whip	?? Flail of fury
🔵 450 gold coins	🔵 Mini medal
🔵 Farmer's scythe	🔵 Hairband
🔵 Fresh milk (x3)	🔵 Mini medal
🔵 Seed of defence	🔵 Seed of agility
🔵 Mini medal	🔵 Mini medal
🔵 Seed of skill	🔵 Spiked steel
🔵 Gold ring	whip

INFAMOUS MONSTERS

 Pelvic Thruster

 Squiggly Squiggler

 Old-School Drooler

 Sand Slayer

 Femme Fatale

Swordsman's Labyrinth

Pickham

LAKESIDE CABIN

Use the world map to help locate a small cabin located just off the embankment of a small lake between Ascantha and Pickham. Not only is the nightly rate competitive with other inns in the region, but there just happens to be a wandering priest staying at this cabin who will be happy to hear confessions and provide other holy services.

The lakeside cabin, located on the strip of land between Ascantha and Pickham, is an ideal stopover location.

MONSTER ARENA

The infamous Monster Arena stands in the forest area just southeast of Pickham, but the doors are locked. There must be some key or some requirement to meet to open the doors for the party.

See if you can get a better view of the area for someone who might have a clue.

RED'S DEN

Several leagues southwest of Pickham, a small homestead has been encircled by tall trees and a man-made moat. This is the lair of Red, a notorious thief and someone from Yangus's past. Speak with Red to learn of recent dealings in the underworld.

If the feisty Red has something the players want, she will want something in return. For instance, she has had her eye on a certain jewel sealed in a tomb north of her homestead…

MONSTER APPEARANCES

PICKHAM AREA—FIELD, ANY TIME

NO.	NAME	HP	MP	EXP	GOLD
57	Hood	60	0	66	14

PICKHAM AREA—FIELD, DAY

NO.	NAME	HP	MP	EXP	GOLD
48	Clockwork cuckoo	32	0	56	31
59	Minidemon	58	5	59	11
60	Gorerilla	65	0	65	10

PICKHAM AREA—FIELD, NIGHT

NO.	NAME	HP	MP	EXP	GOLD
52	Walking corpse	94	0	59	11
54	Night fox	56	6	56	16
58	Headhunter	54	0	62	18

WEST AREA—FIELD, DAY

NO.	NAME	HP	MP	EXP	GOLD
59	Minidemon	58	5	59	11
60	Gorerilla	65	0	65	10

PICKHAM AREA—FOREST, ANY TIME

NO.	NAME	HP	MP	EXP	GOLD
49	Treeface	64	0	67	23
55	Paprikan	54	6	47	10
56	Chimaera	54	6	64	12
58	Headhunter	54	0	62	18
60	Gorerilla	65	0	65	10

WEST AREA—FIELD, ANY TIME

NO.	NAME	HP	MP	EXP	GOLD
57	Hood	60	0	66	14
64	Witch	68	12	66	22
70	Hipster	70	8	69	16

WEST AREA—FIELD, NIGHT

NO.	NAME	HP	MP	EXP	GOLD
54	Night fox	56	6	56	16
58	Headhunter	54	0	62	18

WEST AREA—FOREST, NIGHT

NO.	NAME	HP	MP	EXP	GOLD
55	Paprikan	54	6	47	10
58	Headhunter	54	0	62	18
60	Gorerilla	65	0	65	10
64	Witch	68	12	66	22
70	Hipster	70	8	69	16

BEACH—ANY TIME

NO.	NAME	HP	MP	EXP	GOLD
16	Drackmage	19	6	9	7
50	Kisser	49	0	53	15
236	Khalamari kid	44	0	37	9
239	Yabby	41	2	31	18
240	King kelp	86	8	56	16
247	Merman	101	12	106	19

PICKHAM

Recommended Level: 17

MAP KEY

-  Inn
- Armour Shop
- Weapon Shop
- Item Shop
- Church
- Pub
- Well

ATLAS

PICKHAM REGION

ITEMS FOUND

- 12 gold coins
- Rennet powder
- Cowpat
- Mini medal
- Mini medal
- Amor seco essence
- 30 gold coins
- Seed of wisdom
- 35 gold coins
- Bunny tail
- Chain mail
- Holy water
- Magic water
- Mini medal
- Mini medal
- Seed of strength
- Boxer shorts
- Seed of life
- Mini medal
- 26 gold coins
- Waterweed mould
- Fresh milk
- Red mould
- 1000 gold coins
- Power shield
- Mini medal
- (Mimic)
- Rune staff

ITEM SHOP LIST

ITEM	COST (G)
Medicinal herb	8G
Antidotal herb	10G
Holy water	20G
Chimaera wing	25G
Amor seco essence	120G

WEAPON SHOP LIST

WEAPON	COST (G)	EQUIP ON
Poison moth knife	950G	Jessica
Hunter's bow	1700G	Angelo
Steel broadsword	2000G	Hero, *Jessica (knife skill)
Iron axe	2600G	Yangus
Holy lance	2700G	Hero

ARMOUR SHOP LIST

ARMOUR	COST (G)	EQUIP ON
Bronze armour	840G	Hero
Leather cape	1100G	Angelo
Dancer's costume	1300G	Jessica
Iron shield	720G	Hero, Yangus
Iron helmet	1100G	Hero, Angelo

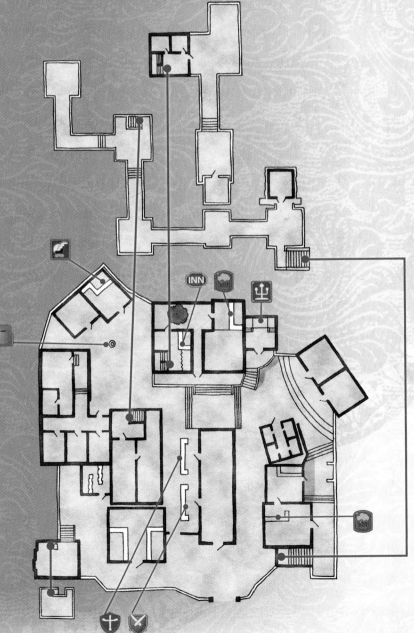

NOTEWORTHY LOCALS

Mitts

A petty thief, Mitts gets the courage to steal people's treasured possessions out of a bottle. Yet when it comes to confrontations, even liquid courage won't stop the cowardly crook from curling up like a paranoid porcupine. Mitts may have some information that the party desperately needs when a crisis arises. His storehouse, which is filled with purloined items, is located in the southwest part of Pickham.

Brains

This scholar is a well-known and widely respected source of information. A walking encyclopedia of knowledge and a brilliant user of deductive reasoning, Brains is the first person Yangus thinks of when the party runs out of clues to Dhoulmagus's whereabouts. No one can understand why an intelligent and civil man like Brains wants to live in a run-down thief's den like Pickham. Yet this is where the party must search if they want to locate Brains.

Dodgy Dave

Whispered of in rumors all over Pickham, there is a merchant known as Dodgy Dave who works from a hidden location in town and trades for rare goods. He recognizes the usefulness of the party's alchemy pot, and will offer better than fair prices for rare items produced in it. Finding Dodgy Dave can be rather tricky, and may only be possible after the party has had to endure some rather trying times.

DEN OF THIEVES

Trode finally finds a place where it is all right for him to mingle with the population without drawing unwanted attention. Unfortunately, Pickham is a hive of scum and villainy. While it is acceptable to speak to the residents to gather information, avoid giving anyone in town any money, with the exception of the legitimate shop merchants.

Avoid giving money to drunks outside the tavern in the southeast alley of town.

SEARCH THE TOWN AND SEARCH WELL

Search the town to find items and speak to the citizens to gather clues regarding the Pickham region. Because Pickham is a town full of pickpockets, there are numerous stolen items located in every nook and cranny, so be sure to search high and low.

HERO finds a pair of boxer shorts and puts it in the bag.

Items are located in all sorts of places in Pickham. Leave no bag unsearched!

DO NOT PAY TO PASS

A rogue blocking the archway connecting the town entrance to the marketplace demands a bribe of 10 gold coins each time the party attempts to pass. This is a rip-off, since the party can simply navigate through the nearby blacksmith's or down the other alley to reach the

*: This is my patch. You wanna come through 'ere, ya pay me some dosh. 10 gold coins.

northern portion of town. At night, the man is fast asleep and does not present an obstacle.

PICKHAM CASINO

Just west of Pickham's entrance is a casino where travellers can try their luck at games of chance. Speak to the bunny girl behind the counter on the left to purchase game tokens at a rate of one token per 20 gold coins. Tokens are required to play the games and are redeemable for prizes such as rare items and equipment at the other counter across the way.

*: Welcome, welcome, welcome! To the shrine of recreation... The social stampin'-ground o' the gentry... PICKHAM CASINO!

Speak to the patrons and staff inside the casino to learn how to play the games.

*: Lend me some cash, mate! I ain't got a penny. Not even enough for a drink tonight. Come on! 5 gold coins, that's all I'm askin'. Please.

BINGO

In Bingo, put down your tokens and keep your fingers crossed. Coming close to a Bingo is a thrilling experience!

Play Bingo by examining the central machine in the casino. The man wearing red standing near the machine can explain the rules. The minimum bet is five tokens, with bets made in multiples of five. Once a Bingo game starts, the creature inside the machine begins choosing numbered balls at random. The numbers are marked on the Bingo card as chosen. The center square is already marked. After several numbers are drawn, a multiplier appears in the upper-left corner of the screen. Each time a ball is chosen thereafter that does not score a Bingo, the multiplier decreases. If all 10 balls are drawn and no bingo is scored, the player loses and the game ends. But if the player scores a Bingo, then the player wins the initial bet back times whatever multiplier remains. Therefore, the sooner a Bingo is scored, the higher the winnings. However, Bingo is a passive game where the player has little control over when—or if—a Bingo is scored.

SLOT MACHINES

Examine any of the slot machines along the walls to try your luck and place a bet from one to five tokens. The number of tokens put down determines how many lines are valid. Therefore, by betting more tokens, the player can score three across in more ways, including horizontally and diagonally. The payouts for winning combinations are listed on the marquee at the top of the screen.

Slot machines provide an easy way to make lots of tokens in one shot, especially if you bet five tokens each time!

ATLAS

PICKHAM REGION

ALCHEMY POT TIPS: PICKHAM CASINO ITEMS

Try to earn enough tokens to purchase two silver platters and toss them into the alchemy pot with an iron cuirass to make a sturdy **silver cuirass** (Defence 44) for Yangus.

Agility rings are great, but wouldn't it be nicer to achieve the agility boost without wasting a character's accessory slot? Mix an agility ring with a standard bandana to generate a **Mercury's bandana** (Defence 23) for the Hero. This headgear actually raises agility as well as defence!

Staves are often more useful for their inherent abilities than their attack bonuses. Instead of using the expensive rune staff in combat, consider combining it with a standard wizard's staff to make the more powerful **staff of antimagic** (Attack 41).

RECIPE SUMMARIES

Silver cuirass = iron cuirass + silver platter + silver platter

Mercury's bandana = bandana + agility ring

Staff of antimagic = wizard's staff + rune staff

BRAINS'S PLACE

Brains's residence is only accessible by navigating across the upper level of Pickham. Ascend the stairs near the second pub in the southeast corner of the town, then cross the upper level. Descend the stairs in the northwest corner to find the information dealer's home.

PICKHAM CASINO EXCHANGE		
PRIZE	TOKEN COST	EQUIP ON
Magic water	100 tokens	N/A
Silver platter	500 tokens	Jessica
Agility ring	1000 tokens	Hero, Yangus, Jessica, Angelo
Titan belt	1500 tokens	Hero, Yangus, Jessica, Angelo
Rune staff	3000 tokens	Jessica, Angelo
Platinum headgear	5000 tokens	Hero, Angelo

SWORDSMAN'S LABYRINTH

Recommended Level: 18

- 🛢 Treasure Chest
- 🛢 Treasure Chest, requires thief's key
- 🏺 Breakable Pot

ITEMS FOUND

🏺 11 gold coins	🏺 Antidotal herb
🏺 62 gold coins	🛢 Swordsman's Labyrinth map
🏺 Cowpat	🛢 Cannibox
🏺 Mini medal	🛢 Mini medal
🏺 Mini medal	🛢 Kitty shield
🏺 Red mould	🛢 Venus' tear
🏺 Seed of magic	

MONSTER APPEARANCES

NO.	NAME	HP	MP	EXP	GOLD
*21	Healslime	24	12	18	13
44	Mummy boy	73	0	55	9
62	Cannibox	61	12	76	110
63	Goodybag	55	8	32	106
65	Mummy	66	0	67	10
67	Restless armour	61	0	74	13
68	Lost soul	52	0	62	9
69	Phantom fencer	65	0	68	12

*Appears only when called as backup.

LOWERING THE DRAWBRIDGE

On the fourth level, the party encounters an impassable river of filth, over which hangs a raised drawbridge. Another moveable statue is located nearby. Perhaps by moving the stone monument somewhere within the small area where it rests, the drawbridge might be lowered?

Moving the statue to a specific location should enable the party to lower the drawbridge, if only the proper placement of the statue can be determined…

STATUE BLOCKING THE DOORWAY

A stone statue blocks a doorway on the third level. However, this is a temporary setback. Approach the statue from the front or side and press the ✖ button to grab or release the object. Then move the left analog stick to drag the statue out of the way.

Push the statue aside to clear the doorway.

Level 4

Map

Level 3

REACHING THE CENTER?

As Yangus points out, the Venus' tear, housed in a large chest sitting at the center of the very first room, tempts unwary adventurers to enter the dungeon with the prospect of a quick profit. However, the treasure cannot simply be taken. The party must first navigate the lower levels of the dungeon and search for some means to reach the center…

Yangus relates a chilling story regarding his first attempt to nab the priceless gem for Red.

x6

Level 2

Level 1

START

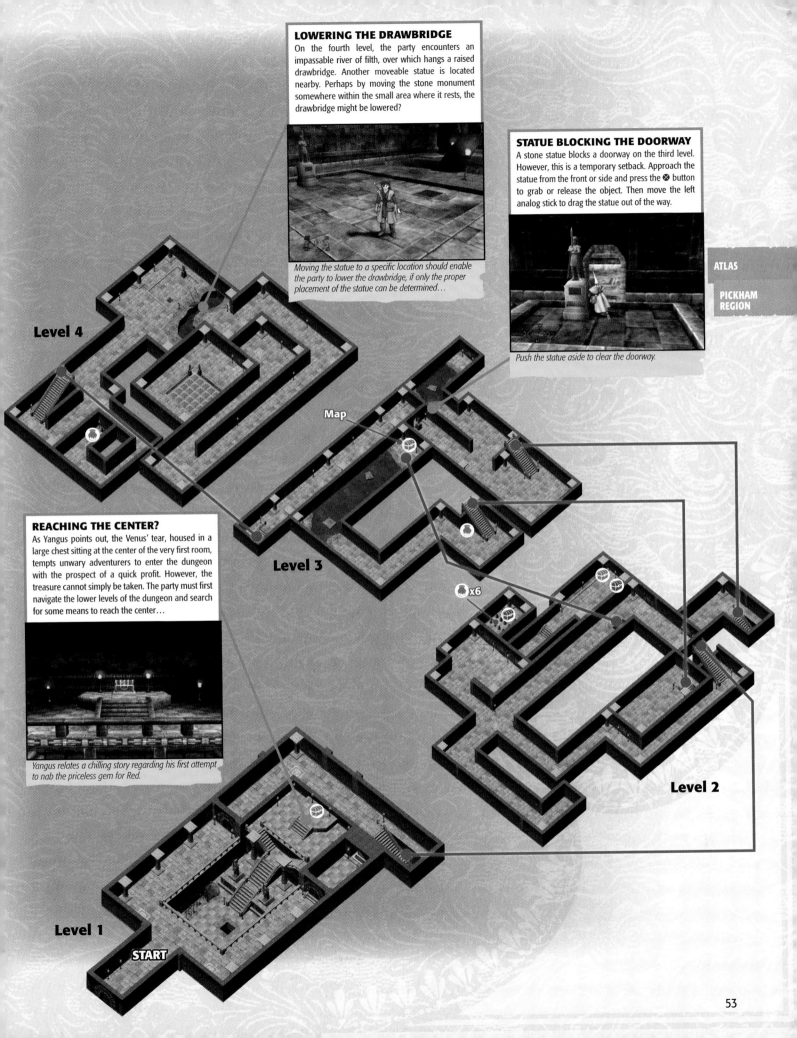

KINGDOM OF TRODAIN

WORLD MAPS

MAP KEY

- Treasure Chest
- Treasure Chest, requires thief's key
- Treasure Chest, requires magic key

ITEMS FOUND

- Cannibox
- Sledgehammer
- Seed of magic
- 630 gold coins
- Mini medal
- Fresh milk x3
- Slime crown
- Seed of defence
- Lesser panacea

INFAMOUS MONSTERS

 Potty Dragon
 Man-eater Chest
 Slimy Smiley
Punchin' Judy

ITEM SHOP LIST (WEST TRODAIN CHURCH)

ITEM	COST (G)	EQUIP ON
Medicinal herb	8G	N/A
Antidotal herb	10G	N/A
Holy water	20G	N/A
Chimaera wing	25G	N/A
Leather cape	1100G	Angelo
Fur hood	1400G	Hero, Yangus

HILLTOP HUT

Travellers heading west from Port Prospect into the Kingdom of Trodain should stop by this conveniently located hut, high atop a hill just a few dozen feet past the border. The inn's rate is exceptionally cheap, and an elderly nun can take your confession.

A well outside the Hilltop Hut just begs to be explored. Perhaps something of tremendous value can be found there, or perhaps not…

Trodain

WEST TRODAIN CHURCH

After passing through a large tunnel dug underneath the mountains, turn west and head toward the cliffs overlooking the sea to locate the West Trodain Church. Not only can visitors find an economically priced resting spot and a priest, but there is also a travelling item merchant inside. Speak to the man seated at the table to purchase any consumables that you need, as well as protective clothing.

The West Trodain Church is located near the northern sea cliffs, directly to the west of the mountain tunnel that separates north and south Trodain.

MONSTER APPEARANCES

SOUTHEAST AREA—FIELD—ANY TIME

NO.	NAME	HP	MP	EXP	GOLD
14	Bodkin archer	21	2	10	8
61	Mud mannequin	63	0	69	15
71	Rockbomb	68	20	70	11
73	Muddy hand	49	0	45	8

SOUTHEAST AREA—FIELD—DAY

NO.	NAME	HP	MP	EXP	GOLD
16	Drackmage	19	6	9	7
83	Pink pongo	81	0	78	18

SOUTHEAST AREA—FIELD—NIGHT

NO.	NAME	HP	MP	EXP	GOLD
17	Beetleboy	16	0	12	10

SOUTHEAST AREA—FOREST—ANY TIME

NO.	NAME	HP	MP	EXP	GOLD
2	Candy cat	10	0	2	2
14	Bodkin archer	21	2	10	8
74	Terror tabby	56	10	67	12
75	Devilmoth	70	0	66	19
76	Buffalo wing	74	12	62	17
80	Jum	75	10	60	4
81	Boe	68	10	59	4
83	Pink pongo	81	0	78	18

SOUTHWEST AREA—ALL TERRAIN TYPES—ANY TIME

NO.	NAME	HP	MP	EXP	GOLD
21	Healslime	24	12	18	13
72	Dieablo	78	15	72	37
76	Buffalo wing	74	12	62	17
77	Mumboh-jumboe	345	40	309	41
78	Mum	65	20	68	25
79	Boh	80	Infinite	65	16
80	Jum	75	10	60	4
81	Boe	68	10	59	4
83	Pink pongo	81	0	78	18
87	Garuda	80	21	75	12
105	Hawk man	95	26	100	24

TRODAIN CASTLE AREA—FIELD—ANY TIME				
NO.	NAME	HP	MP	EXP	GOLD
62*	Cannibox	61	12	76	110
74	Terror tabby	56	10	67	12
77	Mumboh-jumboe	345	40	309	41
78	Mum	65	20	68	25
79	Boh	80	Infinite	65	16
80	Jum	75	10	60	4
81	Boe	68	10	59	4

*Field chest appearance only.

TRODAIN CASTLE AREA—FIELD—DAY				
NO.	NAME	HP	MP	EXP	GOLD
1	Slime	7	0	1	1
2	Candy cat	10	0	2	2
72	Dieablo	78	15	72	37
87	Garuda	80	21	75	12

TRODAIN CASTLE AREA—FIELD—NIGHT				
NO.	NAME	HP	MP	EXP	GOLD
4	Dracky	10	0	2	3
13	Dancing devil	20	0	7	10
70	Hipster	70	8	69	16
75	Devilmoth	70	0	66	19

TRODAIN CASTLE AREA—FOREST—ANY TIME				
NO.	NAME	HP	MP	EXP	GOLD
17	Beetleboy	16	0	12	10
74	Terror tabby	56	10	67	12
75	Devilmoth	70	0	66	19
76	Buffalo wing	74	12	62	17
87	Garuda	80	21	75	12

ALCHEMY POT TIPS: ENHANCED ALCHEMY POT RECIPES

After you get Brains's help in Pickham, stay at inns several times. Eventually King Trode expands the alchemy pot to allow for three-ingredient recipes! A few interesting recipes might already be within reach if you have the necessary ingredients currently on hand.

For another boomerang upgrade, mix an edged boomerang with a steel scythe and a wing of bat to produce a **razor wing boomerang** (Attack 42).

Other interesting recipes require ingredients dropped by the rockbomb enemies you fought in the canyons of the Kingdom of Trodain. If you were able to score a rockbomb shard, drop it into the pot, along with a wizard's staff, to create a **magma staff** (Attack 28) capable of casting Bang without MP consumption in battle!

If all you've taken from the rockbombs is rock salt, don't despair! Drop it into the pot with fresh milk (free from any wandering cow), along with some rennet powder, to make **soft cheese**. Forget feeding this to Munchie; the real value of this cheese is that you can sell it for 600 gold coins a pop!

RECIPE SUMMARIES

Razor wing boomerang = edged boomerang + steel scythe + wing of bat

Magma staff = wizard's staff + rockbomb shard

Soft cheese = rennet powder + fresh milk + rock salt

ATLAS

KINGDOM OF TRODAIN

TRODAIN CASTLE

Recommended Level: 19

ITEMS FOUND

- Trodain Castle map
- Magic key
- Waterweed mould
- Rock salt
- 46 gold coins
- 150 gold coins
- Mini medal
- Mini medal
- 29 gold coins
- Magic beast hide
- Mini medal
- Gold bracer
- Garter
- Mini medal
- Templar's sword
- Seed of magic
- Yggdrasil dew
- Rusty old sword
- Mini medal
- Imp knife recipe

MONSTER APPEARANCES

NO.	NAME	HP	MP	EXP	GOLD
66	Cureslime	54	20	70	11
71	Rockbomb	68	20	70	11
82	Hunter mech	71	0	76	20
84	Liquid metal slime	8	Infinite	10050	18
86	Wailin' weed	59	0	73	17
87	Garuda	80	21	75	12
88	Infernal armour	88	0	90	19
89	Dragonthorn	164	0	101	25

ENTANGLED ENTRANCE

Although thorny vines block the front entrance to the castle, do not let the plants deter you. Examine the vines to make Jessica use her magic to burn them away. This allows you to open the doors and proceed.

Vines cover the main entrance to the castle. But Jessica can easily take care of them…

AREA MAPS

MAP KEY

- Breakable Barrel
- Breakable Pot
- Item Bag
- Cabinet/Wardrobe/Cupboard
- Treasure Chest
- Treasure Chest, requires thief's key
- Treasure Chest, requires magic key

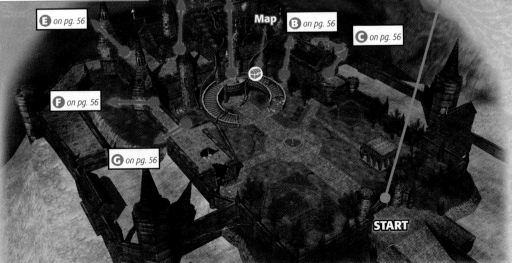

D on pg. 56   A on pg. 56

E on pg. 56

Map   B on pg. 56

C on pg. 56

F on pg. 56

G on pg. 56

START

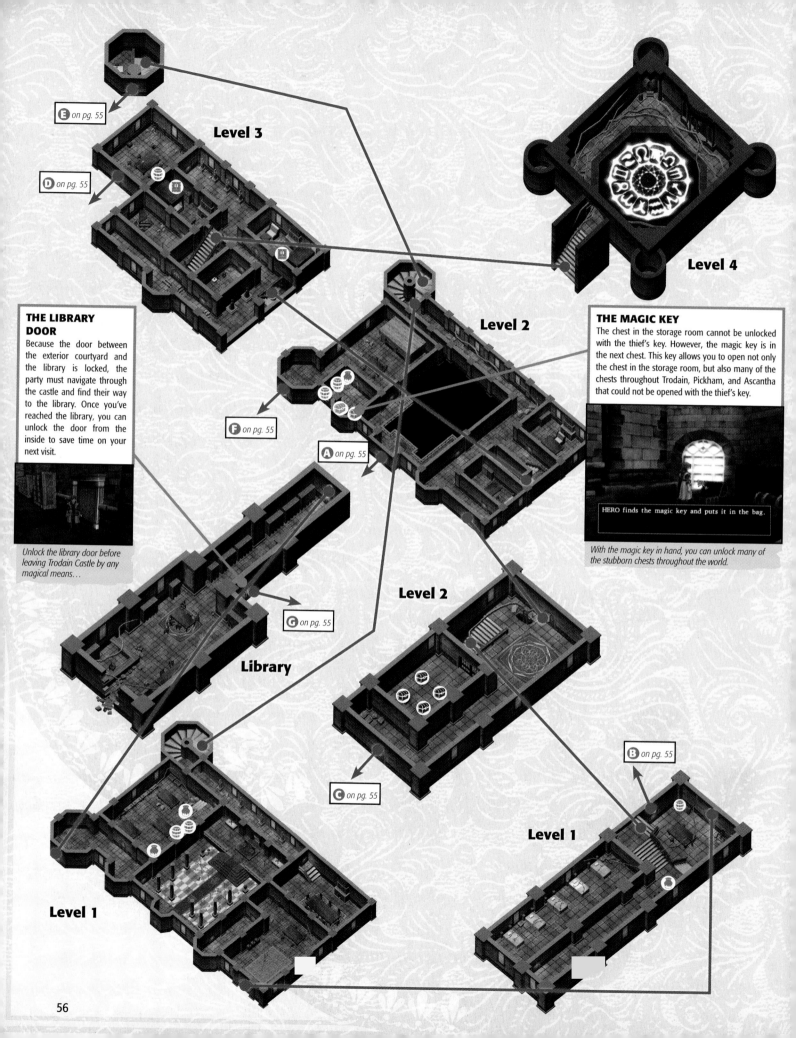

E on pg. 55

Level 3

D on pg. 55

Level 4

THE LIBRARY DOOR

Because the door between the exterior courtyard and the library is locked, the party must navigate through the castle and find their way to the library. Once you've reached the library, you can unlock the door from the inside to save time on your next visit.

Unlock the library door before leaving Trodain Castle by any magical means…

Level 2

F on pg. 55

A on pg. 55

THE MAGIC KEY

The chest in the storage room cannot be unlocked with the thief's key. However, the magic key is in the next chest. This key allows you to open not only the chest in the storage room, but also many of the chests throughout Trodain, Pickham, and Ascantha that could not be opened with the thief's key.

HERO finds the magic key and puts it in the bag.

With the magic key in hand, you can unlock many of the stubborn chests throughout the world.

G on pg. 55

Library

Level 2

C on pg. 55

B on pg. 55

Level 1

Level 1

ALCHEMY POT TIPS:
NEW INGREDIENTS IN TRODAIN CASTLE

Thorough exploration of Trodain Castle reveals several new ingredients, although their alchemy uses may not be obvious. For example, the magic beast hide seems to do nothing except transform strong armaments into mere leather. But if you have two of them, you can combine them to form a fur poncho (Defence 29) for Yangus that reduces damage from both physical and magical attacks.

The garter is a fine defensive item for Jessica, but the alchemy pot can make it into something even better. Mix the garter with a hunter's bow to form **Eros' bow** (Attack 45), an exceptional weapon for Angelo.

The gold bracer and Templar's sword found within the castle are also valuable ingredients that can be used for future recipes. *Do not sell them,* because no merchant in the game supplies replacements.

RECIPE SUMMARIES

Eros' bow = hunter's bow + garter

Fur poncho = magic beast hide + magic beast hide

ATLAS

KINGDOM OF TRODAIN

BENEATH ASCANTHA

AREA MAPS

Recommended Level: 20

MONSTER APPEARANCES

NO.	NAME	HP	MP	EXP	GOLD
10	Mischievous mole	15	0	4	5
63	Goodybag	55	8	32	106
73	Muddy hand	49	0	45	8
85	Mad mole	65	0	68	16
90	Mars rover	78	0	56	17

To Field

To Ascantha Castle

START

A TUNNEL UNDER THE KINGDOM?

Looks like someone has broken into the area beneath Ascantha Castle! Who could've done such a thing? What were they after? And how were they able to get in?

Venture through the hole in the wall and see where it leads.

LAND OF THE MOLES

WORLD MAPS

INFAMOUS MONSTER

Mole Major

MAP KEY

🗝 Treasure Chest, requires thief's key

🗝 Treasure Chest, requires magic key

ITEMS FOUND

🍼 Fresh milk

🌱 Seed of life

🏅 Mini medal

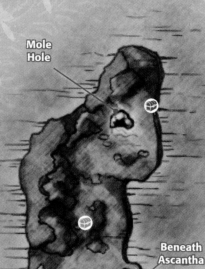

Mole Hole

Beneath Ascantha

MONSTER APPEARANCES

LAND OF THE MOLES—ANY TIME

NO.	NAME	HP	MP	EXP	GOLD
10	Mischievous mole	15	0	4	5
56	Chimaera	54	6	64	12
85	Mad mole	65	0	68	16
90	Mars rover	78	0	56	17
105	Hawk man	95	26	100	24

MOLE HOLE

Recommended Level: 20

ITEMS FOUND

- Mole Hole map
- Mini medal
- Seed of defence
- Stone hardhat
- (??) Moonshadow harp

MONSTER APPEARANCES

NO.	NAME	HP	MP	EXP	GOLD
10	Mischievous mole	15	0	4	5
71	Rockbomb	68	20	70	11
73	Muddy hand	49	0	45	8
85	Mad mole	65	0	68	16
90	Mars rover	78	0	56	17
91	Peeper	78	32	75	14

MAP KEY

- Breakable Pot
- Treasure Chest
- Treasure Chest, requires thief's key

ATLAS

LAND OF THE MOLES

START

Map

FRIENDLY MOLES

Although most moles you encounter in the Mole Hole are ready for battle, some of them have other things than battle on their minds.

Speak to moles standing throughout all levels of the Mole Hole to learn the situation here, and to receive some vital warnings.

Level 1

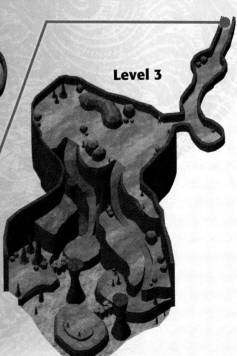

Level 3

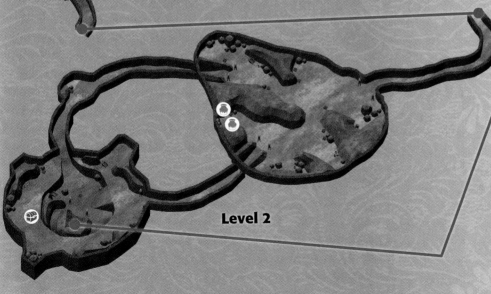

Level 2

OCEAN

WORLD MAPS

INFAMOUS MONSTERS

 Jewel Juggler

 Colossal Clione

 Nightstalker

 Death Tabby

 Terror Talons

 Muscly Mohawker

 Loopy Lupus

 Gigantes Gangster

 Metal Babble

MAP KEY

- 🜸 Treasure Chest
- 🜸 Treasure Chest, requires thief's key
- 🜸 Treasure Chest, requires magic key

ITEMS FOUND

- 🜸 Fresh milk x2
- 🜸 950 gold coins
- 🜸 Bronze knife
- 🜸 Mini medal
- 🜸 Seed of life
- 🜸 Iron armour
- 🜸 Iron mask

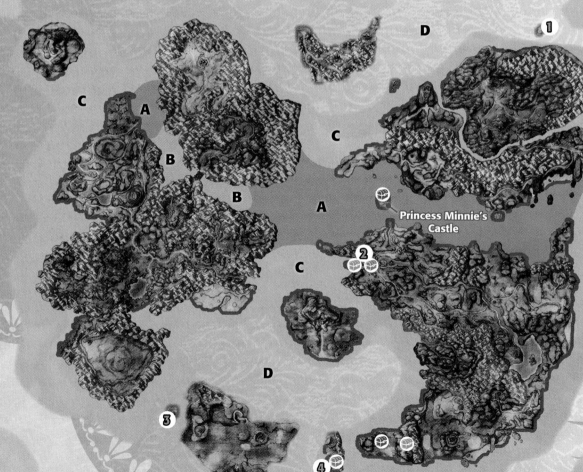

Princess Minnie's Castle

SHIP TRAVEL—AREA A—ANY TIME

NO.	NAME	HP	MP	EXP	GOLD
105	Hawk man	95	26	100	24
237	See urchin	16	4	24	20
241	Wild boarfish	62	0	60	11
246	Eveel	96	0	92	11

SHIP TRAVEL—AREA B—ANY TIME

NO.	NAME	HP	MP	EXP	GOLD
105	Hawk man	95	26	100	24
237	See urchin	16	4	24	20
241	Wild boarfish	62	0	60	11
251	Sea dragon	123	24	114	51

SHIP TRAVEL—AREA C—ANY TIME

NO.	NAME	HP	MP	EXP	GOLD
236	Khalamari kid	44	0	37	9
243	See angel	82	15	79	18
248	King squid	261	0	116	46
254	Siren	112	16	123	43

SHIP TRAVEL—AREA D—ANY TIME

NO.	NAME	HP	MP	EXP	GOLD
118	Hades condor	102	16	99	22
236	Khalamari kid	44	0	37	9
238	Man o' war	35	0	23	12
240	King kelp	86	8	56	16
248	King squid	261	0	116	46
252	Foul anchor	47	16	121	33
259	Tentacular	502	20	303	52

SHIP TRAVEL—AREA E—ANY TIME

NO.	NAME	HP	MP	EXP	GOLD
129	Shade	86	0	78	14
236	Khalamari kid	44	0	37	9
242	Anchorman	80	16	75	19
248	King squid	261	0	116	46
250	Pigmalion	100	12	109	13
253	Poison eveel	110	0	116	16
259	Tentacular	502	20	303	52
260	Abyss diver	230	21	255	38

UNNAMED ISLE 1—ANY TIME

NO.	NAME	HP	MP	EXP	GOLD
36	Metal slime	4	Infinite	1350	5
99	Orc	105	Infinite	94	31
101	Treevil	109	0	95	27
108	Redtail hipster	103	0	92	36
116	Bomboulder	115	10	111	11

UNNAMED ISLE 2—ANY TIME

NO.	NAME	HP	MP	EXP	GOLD
66	Cureslime	54	20	70	11
97	Bodkin fletcher	88	0	86	23
106	Tap devil	85	0	78	21
112	Iron scorpion	64	21	82	21
119	Frogman	116	16	88	18

UNNAMED ISLE 3—ANY TIME

NO.	NAME	HP	MP	EXP	GOLD
98	Venom wasp	92	0	89	13
102	Battle beetle	57	12	96	22
111	King slime	210	25	110	51
113	Toxic zombie	116	0	75	17
115	Volpone	107	24	102	43

UNNAMED ISLE 4—FIELD—ANY TIME

NO.	NAME	HP	MP	EXP	GOLD
95	Puppet player	100	15	90	41
104	Skeleton soldier	94	12	93	26
107	Mushroom mage	81	10	75	13
109	Jumping jackal	111	0	103	32
117	Skullrider	109	0	97	32

UNNAMED ISLE 4—FOREST—ANY TIME

NO.	NAME	HP	MP	EXP	GOLD
98	Venom wasp	92	0	89	13
102	Battle beetle	57	12	96	22
111	King slime	210	25	110	51
113	Toxic zombie	116	0	75	17
115	Volpone	107	24	102	43

CAPE WEST OF PICKHAM—ANY TIME

NO.	NAME	HP	MP	EXP	GOLD
116	Bomboulder	115	10	111	11
121	Magic dumbbell	78	14	41	9
132	Hoodlum	123	0	106	32
136	Jabberwockee	645	13	318	100
137	Jab	90	Infinite	81	25
138	Ber	75	0	71	25
139	Kee	75	10	61	25
140	Woc	75	12	61	25
142	Robo-robin	99	99	96	43
143	Puppet master	130	8	132	51

ATLAS

OCEAN

TRAVEL BY SEA

Once the party has obtained a sailing vessel from somewhere within the Kingdom of Trodain, you can voyage around the world via any ocean or any river connected to an ocean. When travelling by ship, the party will still be subject to random encounters with monsters. The sea region in which the party is sailing determines the types of monsters encountered. Use the color-coded map to determine where to battle the monsters listed in this section. However, use caution, and avoid taking on monsters that might be too tough for the party!

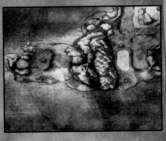

Once the party obtains a ship, they can explore many new and exciting locations inaccessible by foot. To disembark, sail up next to the land area where you want to dock and move around until the option to disembark appears onscreen. If there are no places to disembark, the option will not appear and you will be forced to find alternate ways to get to where you want to go.

If you use Zoom to zip from one continent to another, the ship relocates automatically to the nearest available shore, so you can access it from almost anywhere. The location of the party's ship is always marked on the world map.

PREVIEW FUTURE DESTINATIONS

Now you can reach many locations by docking nearby and travelling short distances on foot. The party can now visit places such as the Northwest Isle, the Holy Isle of Neos, and the small northern continent of Savella. Special events may take place while you're visiting some of these locations, and you can find some items at each stop. When you're visiting a new location (which is covered in greater detail later in the book), be sure to flip ahead to determine which items might be available.

PRINCESS MINNIE'S CASTLE

Recommended Level: 21

MAP KEY

☑ Item Shop
○ Gold Bank

ITEMS FOUND

- 🥇 Mini medal
- 📦 Double-edged sword
- 📦 Seed of strength
- 📦 Mini medal
- 📦 Seed of life

ITEM SHOP LIST

ITEM	COST (G)
Medicinal herb	8G
Antidotal herb	10G
Chimaera wing	25G
Red mould	30G
Waterweed mould	35G

NOTEWORTHY LOCALS

Princess Minnie
The princess is filling in for her ailing father, the King of Medals. When you give her the **mini medals** you've collected on your journeys, Princess Minnie bestows valuable rewards upon the party!

GLOBAL GOLD BANK

Speak to the short man behind the counter to deposit gold coins in the Gold Bank. Sometimes it's best to store excess gold coins in the bank, just in case the party is wiped out in the field and lose the gold coins in their inventory. Gold Banks are located in several places throughout the world, so depositing and withdrawing money is easy with access points in many towns.

Gold Banks help the party to preserve most of its wealth, in case of sudden hardship.

MINI MEDAL REWARDS

When the party first enters the castle, Princess Minnie is upstairs, tending to the bedridden King. She then retires to the throne room, where you can consult with her any time. Speak to Princess Minnie to remind yourself how many mini medals you've turned in, to turn in more medals, and to see how many more you need in order to claim a reward from the Princess.

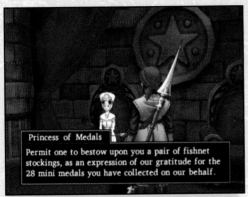

Princess of Medals
Permit one to bestow upon you a pair of fishnet stockings, as an expression of our gratitude for the 28 mini medals you have collected on our behalf.

After Princess Minnie returns to her throne, speak to her to exchange mini medals for rare equipment and items.

MINI MEDAL REWARDS

ITEM	TOTAL MINI MEDALS RETURNED
Fishnet stockings	28 medals
Posh waistcoat	36 medals
Staff of divine wrath	45 medals
Gold nugget	52 medals
Meteorite bracer	60 medals
Miracle sword	68 medals
Sacred armour	75 medals
Orichalcum	83 medals
Metal king helm	90 medals
Dangerous bustier	99 medals
Flail of destruction	110 medals

BACCARAT REGION

WORLD MAPS

MAP KEY

- Treasure Chest
- Treasure Chest, requires thief's key
- Treasure Chest, requires magic key

ITEMS FOUND

- 800 gold coins
- Seed of agility
- 1200 gold coins
- Tough guy tattoo
- Seed of defence
- Mini medal
- Fresh milk x2
- Mini medal

INFAMOUS MONSTERS

Fertiliser
Raging Rooster
Abominable Ape
Wild Spearman

Baccarat

Chateau Felix

SEAVIEW CHURCH

This church, located near the best docking point for a sea vessel in the Baccarat region, is not only a great place to save the game, but also the site of the best inn in the entire game. Thanks to the charity of the Goddess, travellers can always stay here for free!

The Seaview Church atop the northern hill in Baccarat is the best place to rest and recuperate in the world.

MONSTER APPEARANCES

NORTH BACCARAT AREA—FIELD—ANY TIME

NO.	NAME	HP	MP	EXP	GOLD
1	Slime	7	0	1	1
92	Cockateer	105	0	90	28
93	Great sabrecat	95	0	120	31
96	Spitnik	108	0	92	18
99	Orc	105	Infinite	94	31
111	King slime	210	25	110	51
116	Bomboulder	115	10	111	11

NORTH BACCARAT AREA—FOREST—ANY TIME

NO.	NAME	HP	MP	EXP	GOLD
92	Cockateer	105	0	90	28
93	Great sabrecat	95	0	120	31
98	Venom wasp	92	0	89	13
99	Orc	105	Infinite	94	31

SOUTH BACCARAT AREA—FIELD—DAY

NO.	NAME	HP	MP	EXP	GOLD
92	Cockateer	105	0	90	28
94	Metal slime knight	90	8	91	33
99	Orc	105	Infinite	94	31
109	Jumping jackal	111	0	103	32
116	Bomboulder	115	10	111	11

SOUTH BACCARAT AREA—FIELD—NIGHT

NO.	NAME	HP	MP	EXP	GOLD
49	Treeface	64	0	67	23
95	Puppet player	100	15	90	41
97	Bodkin fletcher	88	0	86	23
98	Venom wasp	92	0	89	13
100	Night emperor	100	0	93	46

EAST BACCARAT AREA—FIELD—ANY TIME

NO.	NAME	HP	MP	EXP	GOLD
49	Treeface	64	0	67	23
101	Treevil	109	0	95	27

EAST BACCARAT AREA—FIELD—DAY

NO.	NAME	HP	MP	EXP	GOLD
99	Orc	105	Infinite	94	31
109	Jumping jackal	111	0	103	32
116	Bomboulder	115	10	111	11

EAST BACCARAT AREA—FIELD—NIGHT

NO.	NAME	HP	MP	EXP	GOLD
95	Puppet player	100	15	90	41
100	Night emperor	100	0	93	46
102	Battle beetle	57	12	96	22

EAST BACCARAT AREA—FOREST—ANY TIME

NO.	NAME	HP	MP	EXP	GOLD
49	Treeface	64	0	67	23
98	Venom wasp	92	0	89	13
101	Treevil	109	0	95	27
102	Battle beetle	57	12	96	22
109	Jumping jackal	111	0	103	32

BACCARAT

Recommended Level: 24

WEAPON AND ARMOUR SHOP LIST

ITEM	COST (G)	EQUIP ON
Poison needle	1900	Jessica
Steel scythe	3700	Yangus
Dancer's costume	1300	Jessica
Iron armour	1800	Hero, Yangus
Light shield	2250	Hero, Yangus, Jessica, Angelo
Coral hairpin	950	Jessica

AREA MAPS

MAP KEY

- 🏨 Inn
- 🏦 Gold Bank
- 🍺 Pub
- ✝ Armour Shop
- 🗡 Weapon Shop
- 📦 Item Shop
- ⛪ Church
- 💧 Well

ATLAS

BACCARAT REGION

ITEMS FOUND

- 🌱 Seed of defence
- 🌱 Fresh milk
- 🌱 Seed of wisdom
- 🏅 Mini medal
- 🌱 Seed of strength
- 🏅 Bunny tail
- 🏅 Garter
- 🏅 Dancer's costume
- 🏅 Mini medal
- 🏅 Mini medal
- 🏅 Gold ring
- 🏅 Spangled dress
- 💊 Strong Medicine
- 💊 Cool cheese
- 💊 72 gold coins
- 💊 Amor seco essence
- 💊 Mini medal
- 💊 Mini medal
- 💊 Mini medal
- 💊 Rennet powder
- 💊 Magic water
- 💍 Ruby of protection
- ⁇ 600 casino tokens
- ⁇ 200 or 400 casino tokens

ITEM SHOP LIST

ITEM	COST (G)
Medicinal herb	8G
Antidotal herb	10G
Holy water	20G
Chimaera wing	25G
Moonwort bulb	30G
Amor seco essence	120G

NOTEWORTHY LOCALS

Cash
All one has to do is enter the Dragon Graveyard and obtain the mark of the family on their hands. Sounds easy, right?

Cash and Carrie

The twin children of the Baccarat casino owner, Golding, are holed up in their family mansion and have not been seen for a while. The party must determine why the twins have taken such precautions and what has become of Golding.

THE CASINO IS CLOSED

Speak to the citizens of Baccarat to determine why the casino is closed. While searching the town for items and clues about what's happening here, visit the nightclub in the basement of the hotel. Speak to the bunny-girl waitress on duty to find out where the bartender is. Then head upstairs to the top floor of the hotel to overhear an important conversation between the bartender and the casino manager. Follow the bartender back down to the nightclub to harass him for more information. This method of investigation should tally up enough clues to tell you what to do next.

Bartender
Okay, so tell me what happened the other day. The suspense is killing me!

Find the hotel nightclub's bartender in order to get the scoop on Baccarat.

CHATEAU FELIX

Recommended Level: 24

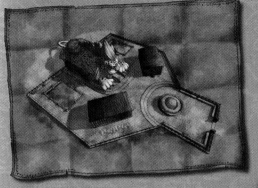

ITEMS FOUND

(??)	Sand of serenity
(??)	Baumren's bell

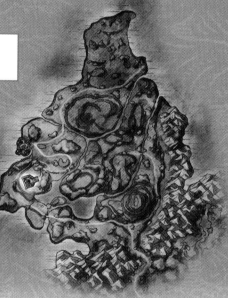

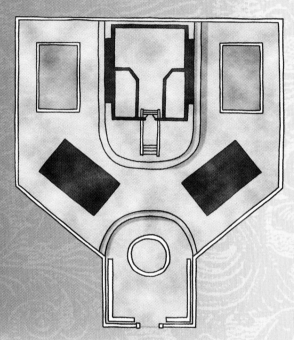

NOTEWORTHY LOCALS

Tom

Tom is the sabrecat wrangler and general all-purpose manservant of Master Felix. Although he's an extremely friendly fellow, he won't be fooled by anyone who trundles in off the well-beaten path outside the Chateau. Speak to Tom to learn more about sabrecats, Master Felix, and the function of the Chateau.

Master Felix

Master Felix is the foremost expert when it comes to sabrecats, but few know of his existence and even fewer know what he does for a living. Speak with Master Felix to learn more regarding the nature of sabrecats, and what the heroes might be able to do to help Master Felix…

KING OF THE SABRECATS

Speak with Tom at the doors of the sabrecat sanctuary. Tom is under strict orders not to let just anyone inside, so he challenges the party with a short quiz regarding their attitudes toward cats. Your answers determine whether Tom will let the party proceed to speak with Master Felix. Try different combinations of answers to his three questions, and enjoy his amusing responses. Whenever you decide to get serious and give Tom the "right" answers, he opens the doors to Chateau Felix.

Tom
I'll have to ask you some questions.
If you can prove you're a top cat, I'll let you in just now.

Tom is an interesting character with some very important questions for the party.

ATLAS

BACCARAT REGION

KINGDOM OF ARGONIA

WORLD MAPS

MAP KEY

- Treasure Chest
- Treasure Chest, requires thief's key
- Treasure Chest, requires magic key

ITEMS FOUND

- 41 gold coins
- Mini medal
- Seed of wisdom
- Yggdrasil leaf
- Lightning staff
- Prayer ring
- Prayer ring
- Light shield
- Steel shield
- Eagle dagger
- Mini medal
- Iron helmet
- Seed of strength
- 1500 gold coins
- Seed of agility
- Fresh milk x3
- Seed of skill
- Silver platter
- Mini medal
- Mini medal
- Lizard humour

INFAMOUS MONSTERS

All Day Sucker | Bundle of Joy | Hooded Hacker | Slime Creator | King of Dumbira | Al Gee | Octavius Maximus

MYSTICAL SPRING

Drinking the refreshing waters of this spring in the western mountains of the Argonian Kingdom is well worth a visit. The Mystical Spring attracts all sorts of interesting personalities. The party might encounter some extremely informative and important people here by visiting at the right time, or after certain major events.

Drink from the waters of the Mystical Spring and see what happens. Visit here often, especially after major story events and after obtaining Important Items, to learn more about the party's heroic quest.

PEDDLER'S TENT

Camped on the roadside heading west from Argonia is a band of travellers. During the daytime only, a merchant seated near the outdoor fire sells items and weapons.

The friendly campers offer help in the form of regional travel tips, alchemy pot recipes, and items for sale.

ROYAL HUNTING GROUND: HOUSE

The folks who live just outside the entrance of Argonia's Royal Hunting Ground are well-versed in the history of the area. They'll offer up their hospitality and provide helpful hints and advice concerning any upcoming tasks that the party may face.

The groundskeepers and children living by the entrance of the Royal Hunting Ground are extremely friendly and helpful people.

SEER'S RETREAT

The first time you visit the Seer's Retreat, the old hermit most likely won't be at home. The Seer can be found at the nearby spring. Join him there to learn of the Mystical Spring's qualities.

The next time you find yourself wondering how to use strange Important Items, remember how insightful the Seer is...

Argonia

ITEM SHOP LIST

ITEM	COST (G)	EQUIP ON
Medicinal herb	8G	N/A
Moonwort bulb	30G	N/A
Holy water	20G	N/A
Dream blade	4700G	Hero, *Jessica (knife skill), Angelo
Turtle shell	2300G	Yangus
Cloak of evasion	3000G	Jessica, Angelo

EASTERNMOST AREA—ANY TIME

NO.	NAME	HP	MP	EXP	GOLD
101	Treevil	109	0	95	27
112	Iron scorpion	64	21	82	21
119	Frogman	116	16	88	18
123	Magic marionette	117	0	108	27
126	Berserker	120	0	118	19

EAST CENTRAL AREA—ANY TIME

NO.	NAME	HP	MP	EXP	GOLD
101	Treevil	109	0	95	27
109	Jumping jackal	111	0	103	32
119	Frogman	116	16	88	18
123	Magic marionette	117	0	108	27
126	Berserker	120	0	118	19

SOUTHEAST AREA—ANY TIME

NO.	NAME	HP	MP	EXP	GOLD
112	Iron scorpion	64	21	82	21

SOUTHEAST AREA—DAY

NO.	NAME	HP	MP	EXP	GOLD
117	Skullrider	109	0	97	32
118	Hades condor	102	16	99	22
121	Magic dumbbell	78	14	41	9
122	Gargoyle	120	0	114	36

SOUTHEAST AREA—NIGHT

NO.	NAME	HP	MP	EXP	GOLD
113	Toxic zombie	116	0	75	17
116	Bomboulder	115	10	111	11
123	Magic marionette	117	0	108	27
125	Lump wizard	108	Infinite	112	22

CENTRAL AREA—FIELD—ANY TIME

NO.	NAME	HP	MP	EXP	GOLD
66	Cureslime	54	20	70	11
97	Bodkin fletcher	88	0	86	23
112	Iron scorpion	64	21	82	21
124	Notso macho	147	12	120	38

CENTRAL AREA—FIELD—DAY

NO.	NAME	HP	MP	EXP	GOLD
117	Skullrider	109	0	97	32

CENTRAL AREA—FIELD—NIGHT

NO.	NAME	HP	MP	EXP	GOLD
106	Tap Devil	85	0	78	21

CENTRAL AREA—FOREST—ANY TIME

NO.	NAME	HP	MP	EXP	GOLD
101	Treevil	109	0	95	27
106	Tap devil	85	0	78	21
107	Mushroom mage	81	10	75	13
119	Frogman	116	16	88	18
125	Lump wizard	108	Infinite	112	22

WEST CENTRAL AREA—FIELD—DAY

NO.	NAME	HP	MP	EXP	GOLD
121	Magic dumbbell	78	14	41	9
122	Gargoyle	120	0	114	36
124	Notso macho	147	12	120	38
127	Bulldozer	131	0	117	31
131	King cureslime	180	Infinite	136	16

WEST CENTRAL AREA—FIELD—NIGHT

NO.	NAME	HP	MP	EXP	GOLD
119	Frogman	116	16	88	18
123	Magic marionette	117	0	108	27
125	Lump wizard	108	Infinite	112	22
128	Ghoul	182	0	98	17
129	Shade	86	0	78	14

WEST CENTRAL AREA—FOREST—ANY TIME

NO.	NAME	HP	MP	EXP	GOLD
36	Metal slime	4	Infinite	1350	5
56	Chimaera	54	6	64	12
107	Mushroom mage	81	10	75	13
119	Frogman	116	16	88	18
127	Bulldozer	131	0	117	31
131	King cureslime	180	Infinite	136	16

NORTHEAST AREA—FIELD—ANY TIME

NO.	NAME	HP	MP	EXP	GOLD
130	Lethal armour	145	20	124	52

NORTHEAST AREA—FIELD—DAY

NO.	NAME	HP	MP	EXP	GOLD
66	Cureslime	54	20	70	11
122	Gargoyle	120	0	114	36
124	Notso macho	147	12	120	38
127	Bulldozer	131	0	117	31
131	King cureslime	180	Infinite	136	16
134	Demonrider	126	0	131	37

NORTHEAST AREA—FIELD—NIGHT

NO.	NAME	HP	MP	EXP	GOLD
123	Magic marionette	117	0	108	27
125	Lump wizard	108	Infinite	112	22
128	Ghoul	182	0	98	17
129	Shade	86	0	78	14
132	Hoodlum	123	0	106	32

NORTHEAST AREA—FOREST—DAY

NO.	NAME	HP	MP	EXP	GOLD
56	Chimaera	54	6	64	12
107	Mushroom mage	81	10	75	13
119	Frogman	116	16	88	18
127	Bulldozer	131	0	117	31
133	Hocus chimaera	108	8	115	35

SOUTHEAST AREA—ANY TIME

NO.	NAME	HP	MP	EXP	GOLD
106	Tap Devil	85	0	78	21
119	Frogman	116	16	88	18
123	Magic marionette	117	0	108	27

SOUTHEAST AREA—DAY

NO.	NAME	HP	MP	EXP	GOLD
95	Puppet player	100	15	90	41
117	Skullrider	109	0	97	32
122	Gargoyle	120	0	114	36

SOUTHEAST AREA—NIGHT

NO.	NAME	HP	MP	EXP	GOLD
100	Night emperor	100	0	93	46
125	Lump wizard	108	Infinite	112	22
245	Crayzee	91	16	94	25

SOUTHEAST SHORE AREA—ANY TIME

NO.	NAME	HP	MP	EXP	GOLD
122	Gargoyle	120	0	114	36
125	Lump wizard	108	Infinite	112	22
242	Anchorman	80	16	75	19
244	Squid kid	74	0	74	15
247	Merman	101	12	106	19
249	Octavian sentry	116	36	120	33
256	Seasaur	181	0	194	36

ATLAS

KINGDOM OF ARGONIA

ARGONIA

Recommended Level: 25

MAP KEY

- 🏠 Inn
- ✝ Armour Shop
- ⚔ Weapon Shop
- 🛡 Item Shop
- ⛪ Church

ITEMS FOUND

- 🪙 38 gold coins
- 🪙 50 gold coins
- 🪙 80 gold coins
- 🪙 Rennet powder
- 🪙 Rennet powder
- 🪙 Cool cheese
- 🧪 Strong medicine
- 🧪 Feathered cap
- 🧪 Strong antidote
- 🧪 Plain cheese
- 🧪 Rock salt
- 🧪 *Seed of magic (after bazaar moves inside)
- 🧪 *Mini medal (after bazaar moves inside)
- 🧪 Mini medal
- 📦 Mini medal
- 📦 Wayfarer's clothes
- 📦 Iron axe
- 📦 Hairband
- 📦 Turban
- 📦 Magic water
- 📦 Leather cape
- 📦 Seed of strength
- 📦 Elfin elixir
- 📦 30 gold coins
- 📦 Mini medal
- 📦 Mini medal
- 📦 Mini medal
- 🎒 Cloak of evasion
- 🎒 Mini medal
- 🎒 Devil's tail
- 🎒 Magical hat
- 🎒 Battle fork
- (??) Important Item
- 🎒 Mini medal
- 🎒 Skull ring
- 🎒 Moon axe

WEAPON AND ARMOUR SHOP LIST

ITEM	COST (G)	EQUIP ON
Battle-axe	4300G	Yangus
Partisan	4400G	Hero
Silver mail	4300G	Hero, Angelo
Magic vestment	4400G	Jessica, Angelo
Light shield	2250G	Hero, Yangus, Jessica, Angelo
Silver tiara	1450G	Jessica

ITEM SHOP LIST

ITEM	COST (G)
Medicinal herb	8G
Antidotal herb	10G
Holy water	20G
Chimaera wing	25G
Moonwort bulb	30G

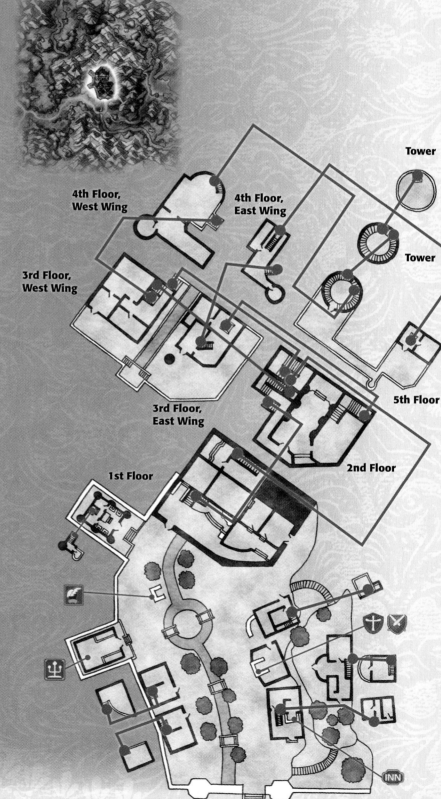

Tower

4th Floor, West Wing

4th Floor, East Wing

Tower

3rd Floor, West Wing

3rd Floor, East Wing

5th Floor

2nd Floor

1st Floor

Bazaar Weapon Shop List

WEAPON	COST (G)	EQUIP ON
Chain whip	2200G	Jessica
Razor wing boomerang	3800G	Hero
Zombiesbane	6300G	Hero, *Jessica (knife skill)
War hammer	6700G	Yangus
Falcon knife	7700G	Jessica

Bazaar Armour Shop List

ARMOUR	COST (G)	EQUIP ON
Heavy armour	5000G	Yangus
Silk bustier	5500G	Jessica
Magic armour	6100G	Hero, Angelo
Magic shield	5000G	Hero, Angelo
Magical hat	2700G	Jessica
Iron mask	3500G	Hero, Yangus

Bazaar Accessory Shop List

ACCESSORY	COST (G)	EQUIP ON
Bunny tail	50G	Hero, Yangus, Jessica, Angelo
Gold bracer	350G	Hero, Yangus, Jessica, Angelo
Gold ring	2000G	Hero, Yangus, Jessica, Angelo
Tough guy tattoo	2400G	Hero, Yangus, Jessica, Angelo
Scholar's specs	2700G	Hero, Yangus, Jessica, Angelo
Ruby of protection	3100G	Hero, Yangus, Jessica, Angelo

Bazaar Item Shop List

ITEM	COST (G)
Rennet powder	10G
Fresh milk	30G
Red mould	30G
Waterweed mould	35G

Bazaar Yggdrasil Leaf Shop List

ITEM	COST (G)
Yggdrasil leaf	1000G*

*Only for sale if you possess zero (0) Yggdrasil Leafs.

Noteworthy Locals

King Clavius
The honorable King of Argonia rules his kingdom with a fair hand. However, certain family matters are distressing him at this time. Can the heroes assist the King and his troublesome son, Prince Charmles?

Prince Charmles
The Prince is prone to hiding in the castle or running off to a neighboring town to escape his royal obligations, causing his father great concern. Charmles is worried about a forthcoming initiation ritual, in which he must go to the Royal Hunting Ground and hunt Argon lizards. What's he so afraid of?

Chancellor of Argonia
The Chancellor is truly dedicated to the causes of the King and the furtherance of the Argonian royal succession. He has a beautiful mansion located on the hill overlooking the city. Not much could cause him to abandon his post, unless there were significant troubles at home…

The Challenge of Charmles

The party is forbidden entrance to the castle without first visiting the Dark Ruins on the Northwest Isle. The party need not explore all of the Dark Ruins, but must visit there before they can enter the castle. Speak to the guards at the front doors near the church to determine the reason. The throne room of King Clavius is on the second floor. Speak to the King to learn the situation in Argonia, and how the party can help.

*: Did those travellers cause you some trouble?

King Clavius needs the assistance of a few good heroes. And it just so happens a few good ones have arrived.

ALCHEMY POT TIPS: ALCHEMY, ARGONIAN STYLE

Baccarat has a few interesting ingredients for alchemists, but most of the Important Items are waiting in Argonia. Items like the battle-axe, silver mail, and light shield should go straight from the store shelves into the alchemy pot, to be transformed into far superior items.

With the magic key available, the thief's key is now obsolete. Drop it into the alchemy pot along with the battle-axe to create the **bandit axe** (Attack 55), which sells for a nice profit. Transform the light shield into the improved **white shield** (Defence 24) using only two bottles of fresh milk. This upgrade is virtually free. And while the silver mail is a fantastic armour, you can further improve it by mixing it with Jessica's old dancer's costume to create **dancer's mail** (Defence 57).

RECIPE SUMMARIES

Bandit axe = battle-axe + thief's key

Dancer's mail = dancer's costume + silver mail

White shield = light shield + fresh milk + fresh milk

ALCHEMY POT TIPS:
NEW INGREDIENTS AT THE ARGONIA BAZAAR

The Argonia Bazaar sells a wide variety of fantastic items, many of which can be further improved with alchemy! The heavy armour, for example, has a respectable defence score of 52. Boost that by dropping it into the pot along with a bandit axe and a bandit's grass skirt, making a suit of **bandit mail** (Defence 80) for Yangus. You can also boost the magic armour by mixing it with an edged boomerang to make a suit of damage-reflecting **spiked armour** (Defence 68).

Give Jessica's wisdom a double boost by purchasing two scholar's specs, one to wear and one to mix with a magical hat (sold separately) to make a **scholar's cap** (Defence 33). Produce a second scholar's cap in the alchemy pot, and combine it with a magic vestment (sold in Argonia's regular shop) to create a **sage's robe** (Defence 55) for Angelo.

You can produce a fantastic spear by mixing a battle fork and a devil's tail (found in Argonia Castle) with a poison needle (sold in Baccarat). The resultant **demon spear** (Attack 86) can occasionally score one-hit kills!

RECIPE SUMMARIES

Bandit mail = bandit axe + bandit's grass skirt + heavy armour

Scholar's cap = magical hat + scholar's specs

Spiked armour = edged boomerang + magic armour

Sage's robe = magic vestment + scholar's cap

Demon spear = battle fork + poison needle + devil's tail

ROYAL HUNTING GROUND AREA MAPS

Recommended Level: 28

ITEMS FOUND

- Dragon scale
- Mini medal

MONSTER APPEARANCES

NO.	NAME	HP	MP	EXP	GOLD
133	Hocus chimaera	108	8	115	35
135	Killer moth	84	8	116	14
145	Jackal ripper	142	Infinite	123	32
150	Hacksaurus	171	0	216	55
153	Orc king	148	18	154	38

MAP KEY

- Treasure Chest, requires magic key
- Item Bag

STRANGE HARVEST

In the northwest section of the Royal Hunting Ground, strange fruit called salamangoes grow in a small patch. You can pick them up, carry them, and throw them just like breakable barrels or pots. Upon striking the ground, they release a small cloud of pollen that awakens and attracts Argon lizards.

Argon lizards cannot resist the smell of fresh salamango.

CAVE CRITTER

Find a way to draw the Argon lizard out of the cave.

The sleeping Argon lizard awaits.

START

EASILY SCARED

Argon lizards are highly sensitive creatures and are easily frightened off by the sight or sound of quickly approaching hunters. To sneak up on them, approach from behind by walking using the directional button.

※ : AAARG-AAARG!

Move carefully and try not to make too much noise when approaching an Argon lizard.

NORTHWEST ISLE

WORLD MAPS

MAP KEY

- Treasure Chest
- Treasure Chest, requires magic key

ITEMS FOUND

- Mini medal
- Zombie mail

INFAMOUS MONSTERS

 Old Soldier   Occult Rider   Man-at-Arms

Dark Ruins

MONSTER APPEARANCES

NORTHWEST ISLE—ANY TIME					
NO.	NAME	HP	MP	EXP	GOLD
103	Lump shaman	80	30	90	32
104	Skeleton soldier	94	12	93	26
107	Mushroom mage	81	10	75	13
113	Toxic zombie	116	0	75	17
114	Lesser demon	119	0	107	38

DARK RUINS

Recommended Level: 29

ITEMS FOUND

- Mini medal
- Dark Ruins map
- Mini medal
- Dragon scale
- (Mimic)
- Saint's ashes

MONSTER APPEARANCES

NO.	NAME	HP	MP	EXP	GOLD
44	Mummy boy	73	0	55	9
65	Mummy	66	0	67	10
120	Mimic	144	Infinite	128	72
148	Blood mummy	138	0	125	16
149	Phantom swordsman	102	0	164	34
151	Bone baron	122	0	176	56
154	Soulspawn	75	0	138	9
157	Fallen priest	138	50	183	83
164	Troll	423	0	210	46

MAP KEY

- Breakable Barrel
- Treasure Chest
- Treasure Chest, requires magic key

ATLAS

NORTHWEST ISLE

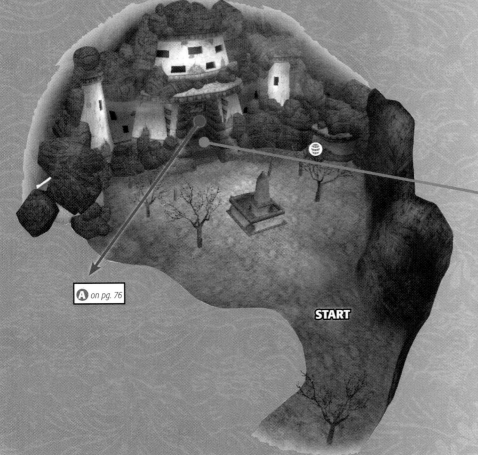

START

A on pg. 76

THE VOID

Upon entering the Dark Ruins, the party lose themselves in total darkness. Movement in any direction causes the heroes to exit the Dark Ruins. There must be some way to remove the dark veil preventing you from exploring this enigmatic location.

Examine the raised monument across from the Dark Ruins' doorway.

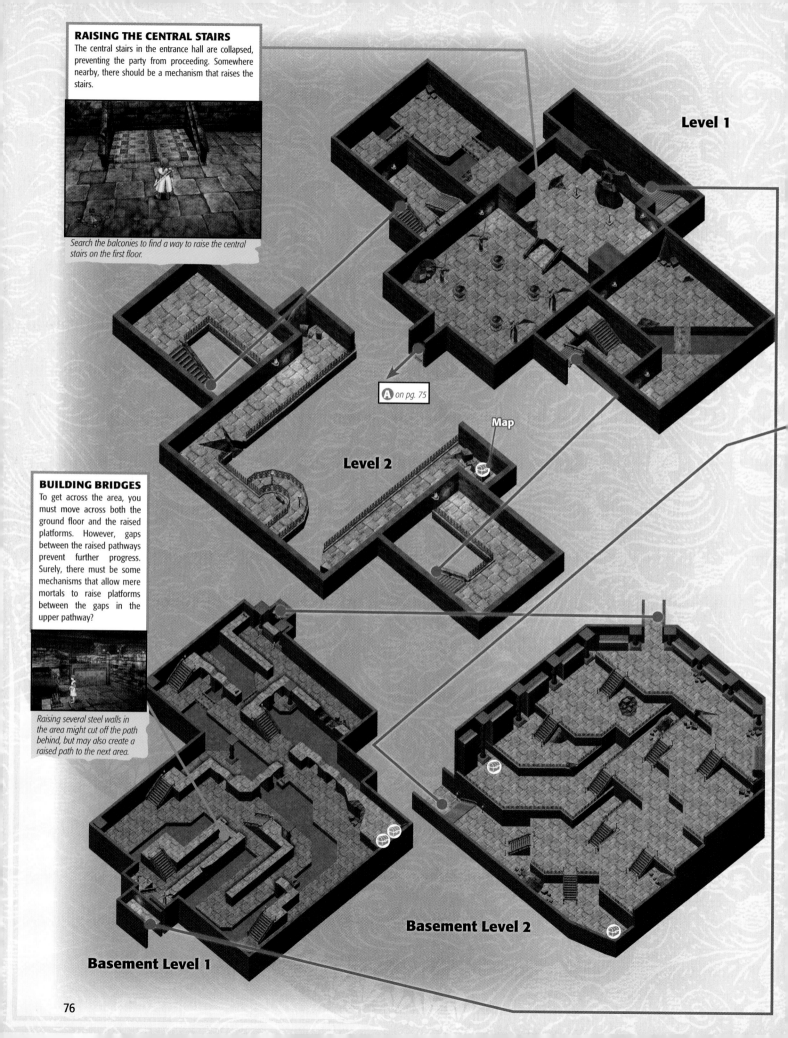

RAISING THE CENTRAL STAIRS
The central stairs in the entrance hall are collapsed, preventing the party from proceeding. Somewhere nearby, there should be a mechanism that raises the stairs.

Search the balconies to find a way to raise the central stairs on the first floor.

Level 1

A on pg. 75

Map

Level 2

BUILDING BRIDGES
To get across the area, you must move across both the ground floor and the raised platforms. However, gaps between the raised pathways prevent further progress. Surely, there must be some mechanisms that allow mere mortals to raise platforms between the gaps in the upper pathway?

Raising several steel walls in the area might cut off the path behind, but may also create a raised path to the next area.

Basement Level 1

Basement Level 2

MAP KEY

- Breakable Barrel
- Treasure Chest
- Treasure Chest, requires magic key

Basement Level 3

DEMONIC RAYS

In the room with the large mural depicting the ancient battle between good and evil, two massive statues emit scorching beams of light. If the statues could somehow be rotated, perhaps they could be made to point toward some significant portion of the giant mural…

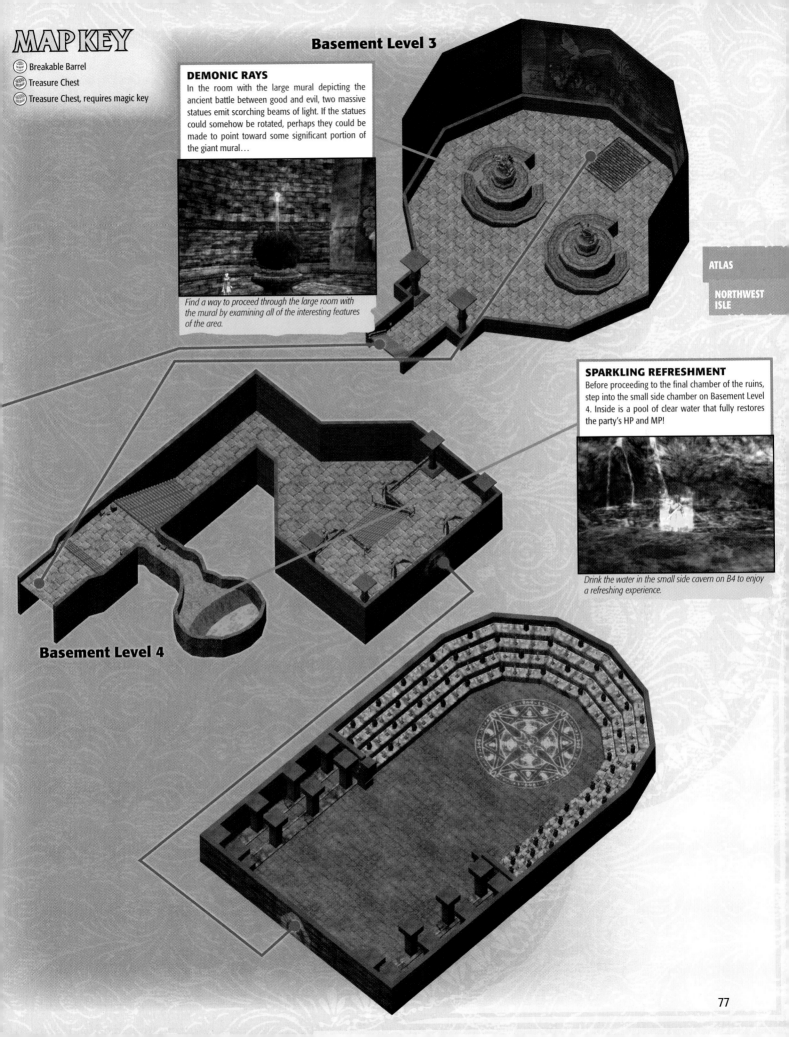

Find a way to proceed through the large room with the mural by examining all of the interesting features of the area.

SPARKLING REFRESHMENT

Before proceeding to the final chamber of the ruins, step into the small side chamber on Basement Level 4. Inside is a pool of clear water that fully restores the party's HP and MP!

Drink the water in the small side cavern on B4 to enjoy a refreshing experience.

Basement Level 4

ARCADIA REGION

WORLD MAPS

MAP KEY

- Treasure Chest, requires thief's key
- Treasure Chest, requires magic key
- Treasure Chest, requires ultimate key

ITEMS FOUND

- Fresh milk
- Elfin elixir
- Assassin's dagger
- Titan belt
- Silver tiara

INFAMOUS MONSTERS

Poisonous Sniper   Gloopy Groupie   Angel of Curing

CHAPEL OF AUTUMN

Consider a visit to the church located northwest of Rydon's Tower before and after visiting the obsessive stonemason, and before proceeding to the frozen Blizzard Peaks in the far north.

Be sure to confess and rest at this church, conveniently located on the road northwest of Rydon's Tower.

Rydon's Tower

Arcadia

MONSTER APPEARANCES

WEST AREA—FIELD—ANY TIME

NO.	NAME	HP	MP	EXP	GOLD
152	Swingin' hipster	144	0	155	45
156	Golem	225	0	237	50

WEST AREA—FOREST—ANY TIME

NO.	NAME	HP	MP	EXP	GOLD
133	Hocus chimaera	108	8	115	35
145	Jackal ripper	142	Infinite	123	32
146	Iron rhino	48	0	138	68
150	Hacksaurus	171	0	216	55
153	Orc king	148	18	154	38
164	Troll	423	0	210	46

EAST AREA—FIELD—NIGHT

NO.	NAME	HP	MP	EXP	GOLD
143	Puppet master	130	8	132	51
146	Iron rhino	48	0	138	68
151	Bone baron	122	0	176	56

WEST AREA—FIELD—DAY

NO.	NAME	HP	MP	EXP	GOLD
142	Robo-robin	99	99	96	43
153	Orc king	148	18	154	38
155	Gryphon	161	16	167	32

EAST AREA—FIELD—ANY TIME

NO.	NAME	HP	MP	EXP	GOLD
152	Swingin' hipster	144	0	155	45
156	Golem	225	0	237	50

EAST AREA—FOREST—ANY TIME

NO.	NAME	HP	MP	EXP	GOLD
133	Hocus chimaera	108	8	115	35
146	Iron rhino	48	0	138	68
153	Orc king	148	18	154	38
156	Golem	225	0	237	50
164	Troll	423	0	210	46

WEST AREA—FIELD—NIGHT

NO.	NAME	HP	MP	EXP	GOLD
32	Drackyma	33	6	28	9
143	Puppet master	130	8	132	51
146	Iron rhino	48	0	138	68

EAST AREA—FIELD—DAY

NO.	NAME	HP	MP	EXP	GOLD
142	Robo-robin	99	99	96	43
153	Orc king	148	18	154	38
155	Gryphon	161	16	167	32
164	Troll	423	0	210	46

ARCADIA

Recommended Level: 30

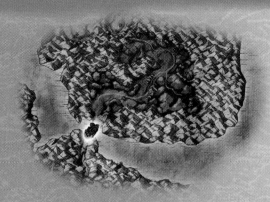

MAP KEY

(INN) Inn		Item Shop	
Armour Shop		Church	
Weapon Shop		Pub	

ATLAS

ARCADIA REGION

ITEMS FOUND

Lesser panacea	Wizard's staff	Rock salt	650 gold coins
Magic water	Seed of strength	350 gold coins	Magic vestment
Mini medal	Cloak of evasion	Magic water	Mini medal
Mini medal	Bunny tail	Amor seco essence	Mini medal
Mini medal	Poison moth knife	Fresh milk	Titan belt
Rennet powder	Leather dress	Rennet powder	Seed of magic
230 gold coins	Dragon scale	Dragon dung	Stone sword
27 gold coins	Strength ring	Cowpat	The Big Book of Barriers
Seed of life	Gold bracer	26 gold coins	
Mystifying mixture	Mini medal	Rock salt	
Mini medal	Mini medal	Giant mallet	

ITEM SHOP LIST

ITEM	COST (G)
Medicinal herb	8G
Antidotal herb	10G
Holy water	20G
Chimaera wing	25G
Moonwort bulb	30
Rockbomb shard	450G

NIGHTTIME ITEM SHOP LIST

ITEM	COST (G)
Seed of skill	2000G*

*One purchase only.

WEAPON SHOP LIST

WEAPON	COST (G)	EQUIP ON
Sword breaker	5500G	Jessica
Swallowtail	6800G	Hero
Bastard sword	8800G	Hero, *Jessica (knife skill)
Hell scythe	9500G	Yangus

ARMOUR SHOP LIST

ARMOUR	COST (G)	EQUIP ON
Cloak of evasion	3000G	Jessica, Angelo
Magic armour	6100G	Hero, Angelo
Magic bikini	13800G	Jessica
Magic shield	5000G	Hero, Angelo
Magical hat	2700G	Jessica
Iron mask	3500G	Hero, Yangus

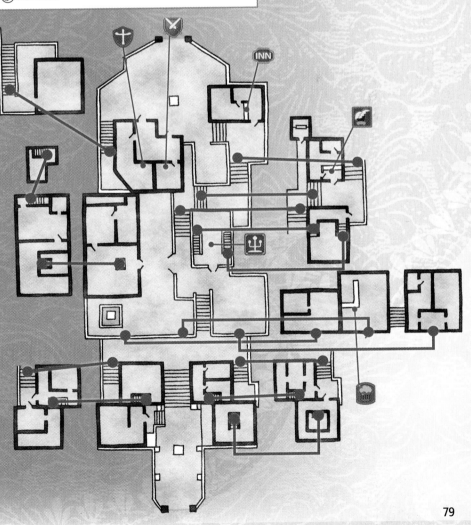

Master Dominico

Dominico is a great magician, proud descendant from a long line of wizards and mages who have presided over Arcadia. Dominico's ancient ancestors were renowned for their skill and wisdom, but Dominico and his recent forefathers have grown more complacent and conceited with each generation. Most of the townspeople bear a general disdain for Dominico, yet hide it out of respect, or perhaps in fear of his inherited magic abilities.

David

David is a young man who attempted to travel the world, in search of something he couldn't quite put his finger on. By the time he reached Arcadia, he was starving and very near death. Master Dominico took in David and gave him a place to live and work, and for that David is extremely grateful. However, David seems unable to realize that Master Dominico is always looking for any opportunity to humiliate and degrade him, and that he should have left long ago.

Sir Leopold

Master Dominico's pet is a fearsome hound, the mere sight of which chills the blood of everyone in Arcadia. Over the years, Sir Leopold has taken on many of Master Dominico's more unsavory traits, and treats the manservant David just as poorly as the master magician.

THE MOUNTAIN BRIDGE CITY

The party arrives in Arcadia in pursuit of a villain who left the Northern Checkpoint of the Argonia region in ruins. When you enter the town, all of its citizens are gathered in the streets. Beat a path to the gates of the town magistrate and tyrant, the audacious Master Dominico. Enter the house and proceed to the room upstairs to watch the events unfold, and then speak with Master Dominico to learn how to remedy the situation in Arcadia.

Citizens line the streets all the way up to the doorstep of Master Dominico's.

RYDON'S TOWER

Recommended Level: 30

ITEMS FOUND

- Rydon's Tower map
- Recovery ring
- Cheiron's bow

MONSTER APPEARANCES

NO.	NAME	HP	MP	EXP	GOLD
131	King cureslime	180	Infinite	136	16
133	Hocus chimaera	108	8	115	35
136	Jabberwockee	645	13	318	100
137	Jab	90	Infinite	81	25
138	Ber	75	0	71	25
139	Kee	75	10	61	25
140	Woc	75	12	61	25
146	Iron rhino	48	0	138	68
153	Orc king	148	18	154	38
154	Soulspawn	75	0	138	9
155	Gryphon	161	16	167	32
156	Golem	225	0	237	50
159	Living statue	266	0	306	90

MAP KEY

- Treasure chest
- Treasure chest, requires magic key

ATLAS

ARCADIA REGION

UNIQUE KEY OF ENTRY

The sign to the left of the main doors indicates that you need to insert the **stone sword** in order to enter Rydon's Tower. You can obtain the stone sword from a stonemason residing in Arcadia, but only after certain events have transpired there.

There is a hole in the door.

Use the stone sword to gain access to Rydon's Tower.

Map

A on pg. 82

START

SEESAW BRIDGES

Stepping onto the central bridge causes it to rock under the party's weight. Pause until the bridge tilts, then run across the sloping path. The bridge tilts again when the characters move just past the halfway point. Remember that your weight tilts the bridges within Rydon's Tower, and that your weight can also hold them in place…

The bridges in Rydon's Tower tilt like seesaws under the weight of the party and certain stone statues.

Level 5

Level 3

Level 2

Level 4

A on pg. 81

Level 1

STATUE-RAISING RAMPS

If you move a heavy object such as a statue onto the small square platform at the bottom of certain ramps, such as the one on Level 4, you can move the statue between levels. This way, you can use the weighted object to tilt a bridge on the level above.

When you move the statues onto the small squares at the bottom of mechanical ramps, the balancing weight is transported to the level above.

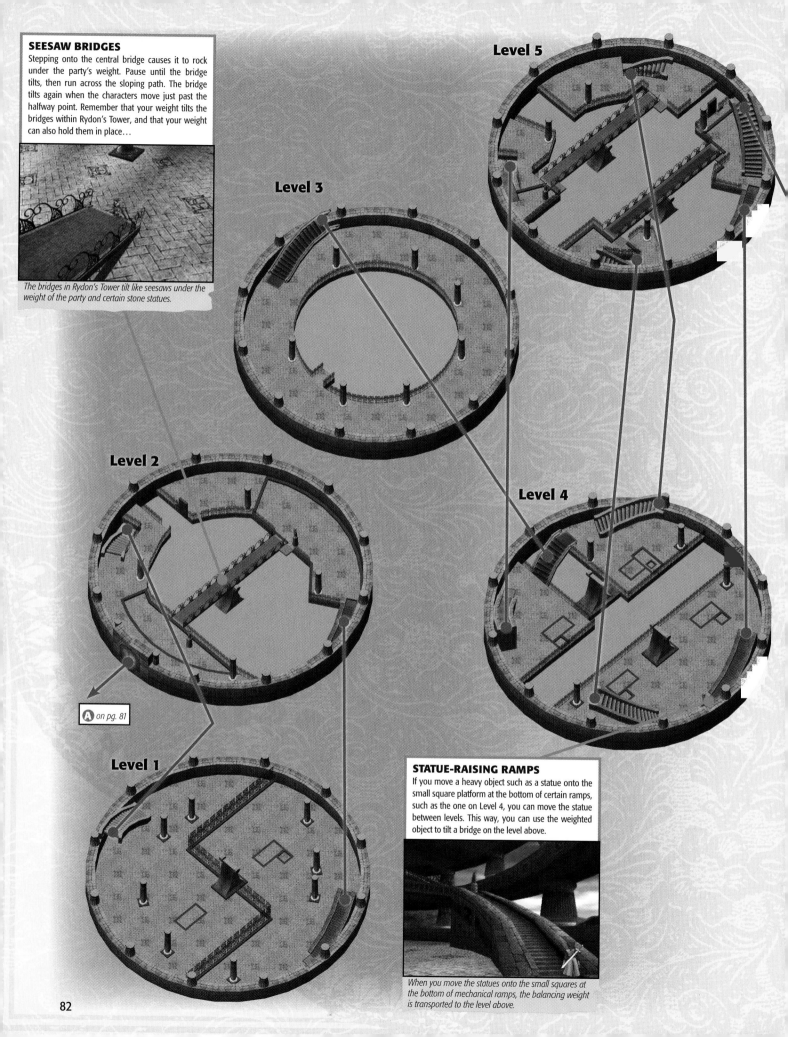

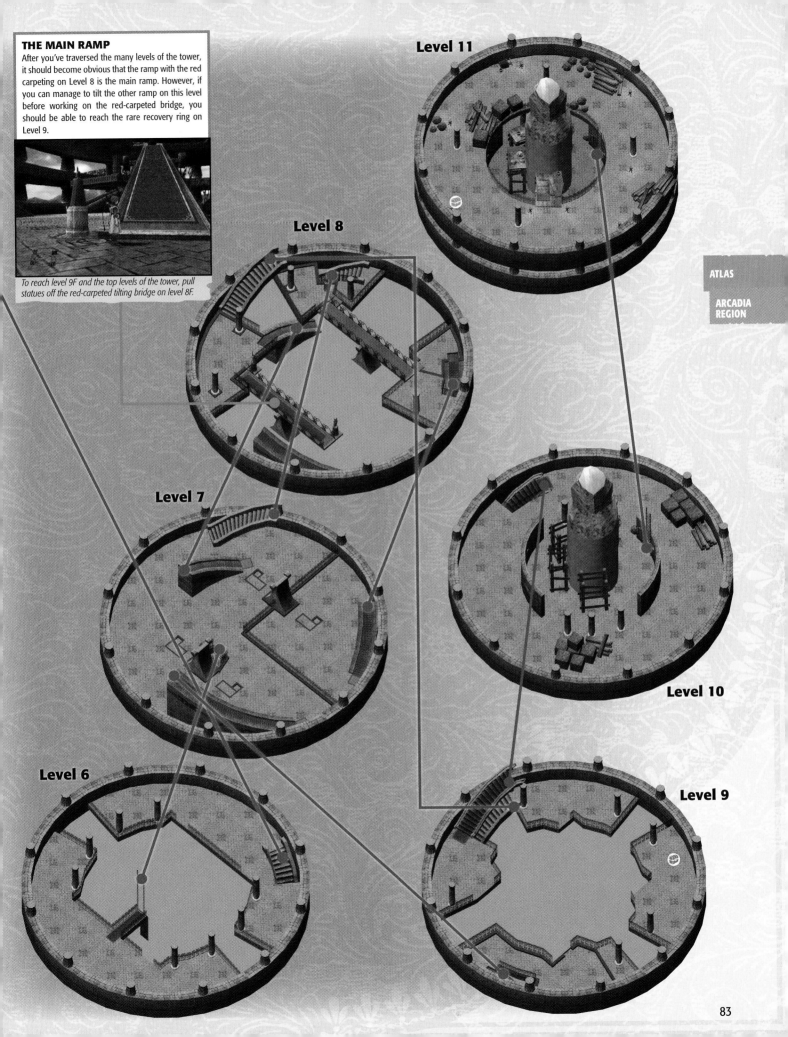

THE MAIN RAMP

After you've traversed the many levels of the tower, it should become obvious that the ramp with the red carpeting on Level 8 is the main ramp. However, if you can manage to tilt the other ramp on this level before working on the red-carpeted bridge, you should be able to reach the rare recovery ring on Level 9.

To reach level 9F and the top levels of the tower, pull statues off the red-carpeted tilting bridge on level 8F.

Level 11

Level 8

Level 7

Level 10

Level 6

Level 9

BLIZZARD PEAKS

WORLD MAPS

MAP KEY

 Treasure Chest, requires thief's key

 Treasure Chest, requires magic key

ITEMS FOUND

- Mini medal
- Special antidote
- Special medicine
- Mini medal
- Yggdrasil leaf
- Agility ring
- Holy silver rapier
- Mini medal
- (??) Important Item
- (??) Ultimate key
- (??) Nook grass x4*

Obtain from character located either at Marta's Cottage or in Orktusk town.

INFAMOUS MONSTERS

Cold Fire   Roboster Mk I   Big Blizzard   Attack Bot Mk II

MARTA'S COTTAGE

When you enter the frozen Blizzard Peaks, the party is buried under an avalanche, only to be rescued by a nice old lady named Marta and her faithful dog Boris. After awakening at Marta's Cottage, head upstairs to speak with Marta and the rest of your party seated around the table. Before leaving, check out the ancient shrine behind Marta's house.

Marta
If you go down the mountain and go to the north, you will come to a town called Orkutsk. Maybe someone will know something there.

Marta proves to be extremely knowledgeable and helpful to the party just after they enter the dangerous Blizzard Peaks.

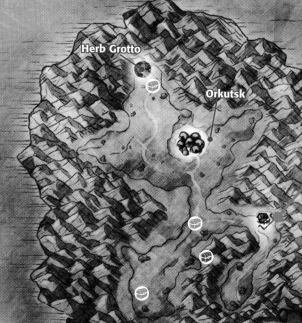

Herb Grotto

Orkutsk

MONSTER APPEARANCES

NORTH AREA—ANY TIME

NO.	NAME	HP	MP	EXP	GOLD
160	Freeze fly	126	30	160	36
165	Ice queen	221	0	186	56
166	Abominape	186	0	202	24
168	Killing machine	165	0	315	58

SOUTH AREA—ANY TIME

NO.	NAME	HP	MP	EXP	GOLD
165	Ice queen	221	0	186	56
166	Abominape	186	0	202	24
168	Killing machine	165	0	315	58
172	Frost wyvine	286	30	326	62

NORTH AREA—DAY

NO.	NAME	HP	MP	EXP	GOLD
158	Dead ringer	124	20	68	12
162	Frostburn	113	10	199	16

SOUTH AREA—DAY

NO.	NAME	HP	MP	EXP	GOLD
158	Dead ringer	124	20	68	12
162	Frostburn	113	10	199	16

NORTH AREA—NIGHT

NO.	NAME	HP	MP	EXP	GOLD
163	Hellhound	166	0	108	26

SOUTH AREA—NIGHT

NO.	NAME	HP	MP	EXP	GOLD
169	Icikiller	198	24	221	78

ORKUTSK

Recommended Level: 31

MAP KEY

🏨 Inn		🗺 Item Shop	
✝ Armour Shop		⛪ Church	
🗡 Weapon Shop		🍺 Pub	

ITEMS FOUND

🧪 Amor seco essence		🦇 Wing of bat	
🏅 Mini medal		💎 Ruby of protection	
🪨 Rockbomb shard		🪽 Chimaera wing	
🌱 Seed of defence		🧀 Chilly cheese	
🏅 Mini medal		🏅 Mini medal	
🏅 Mini medal		🪃 Edged boomerang	
💧 Magic water		⁇ Nook grass x4*	

*From character located either here or at Marta's Cottage.

ITEM SHOP LIST

ITEM	COST (G)
Medicinal herb	8G
Antidotal herb	10G
Holy water	20G
Chimaera wing	25G
Amor seco essence	120G

WEAPON SHOP LIST (NIGHT)

WEAPON	COST (G)	EQUIP ON
Swallowtail	6800G	Hero
Falcon knife	7700G	Jessica
Spiked steel whip	8300G	Jessica
Dragonsbane	11000G	Hero, *Jessica (knife skill)
King axe	17000G	Yangus

ARMOUR SHOP LIST (DAY)

ARMOUR	COST (G)	EQUIP ON
Velvet cape	9400G	Angelo
Dragon mail	12000G	Hero, Yangus
Dragon shield	6900G	Hero, Yangus
Ice shield	8500G	Hero, Angelo
Iron headgear	5500G	Hero, Yangus

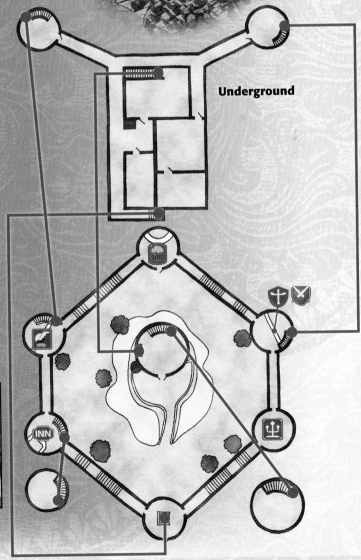

Underground

NOTEWORTHY LOCALS

Marek

Although the local herb doctor isn't a native of the Orkutsk community, the citizens deeply respect him and have come to depend on his homeopathic remedies for their wellbeing in this frigid region. When he's not busy at work in his underground apartment and lab, he often leaves on expeditions to a nearby grotto where he tends to his herb garden.

WINTRY ABODE

The town of Orkutsk is entirely enclosed, to protect its inhabitants from the harsh climate. From the pub, visitors may head through an exit to the center of the town, where the mayor's mansion is located. Within the mayor's mansion is a stairway that leads down to the warm underground level of Orkutsk, with the citizens' living quarters. Until the collapsed man can be removed from the top of the stairwell near the town's entrance, this is the only route that allows you to reach the lower levels of Orkutsk.

Speak to the mayor of Orkutsk in the central mansion to learn of Marek's whereabouts.

HERB GROTTO

Recommended Level: 32

AREA MAPS

ITEMS FOUND

- Mini medal
- Rose-wort
- Rose-root
- Mini medal
- Mini medal
- Seed of life
- Herb Grotto map
- 100 gold coins
- 2100 gold coins
- Devil's tail
- Elfin elixir
- Icicle dirk

MONSTER APPEARANCES

NO.	NAME	HP	MP	EXP	GOLD
160	Freeze fly	126	30	160	36
162	Frostburn	113	10	199	16
163	Hellhound	166	0	108	26
168	Killing machine	165	0	315	58
169	Icikiller	198	24	221	78
172	Frost wyvine	286	30	326	62

MAP KEY

- Treasure chest
- Treasure chest, requires thief's key
- Treasure chest, requires magic key
- Breakable Pot

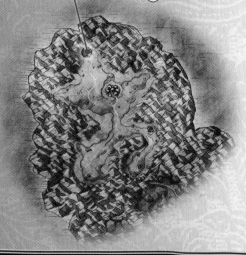

Herb Grotto

ALCHEMY POT TIPS:
THE ULTIMATE KEY AND THE ULTIMATE SWORD

With the ultimate key, you can finally unlock many doors and treasures you've passed on your travels. The alchemy pot can further enhance many of the powerful items you've found in those locations, but none as great as the rusty old sword found in Trodain Castle. That rusty old sword can transform into one of the game's most powerful swords with ingredients you might already have! Drop it into the alchemy pot along with the slime crown (from the well near the Hilltop Hut in Trodain) and a hunk of orichalcum (awarded by Princess Minnie for returning 83 mini medals) to create a **liquid metal sword** (Attack 118). This mighty blade is particularly effective against metal creatures.

Even if you don't have enough medals to obtain the orichalcum, you can still craft a number of top-class blades. Combine the double-edged sword (found in Minnie's Castle) with a pair of saint's ashes to lift the weapon's curse and create the **über double-edge** (Attack 76). Transform the dragonsbane into a **dragon slayer** (Attack 83) by combining it with a mighty armlet (a Monster Arena prize). Or craft a **blizzard blade** (Attack 90) out of the icicle dirk (found in the Herb Grotto), a bastard sword (sold in Arcadia), and a hunk of cold cheese.

RECIPE SUMMARIES

Dragon slayer = dragonsbane + mighty armlet

Über double-edge = double-edged sword + saint's ashes + saint's ashes

Blizzard blade = bastard sword + icicle dirk + cold cheese

Liquid metal sword = rusty old sword + slime crown + orichalcum

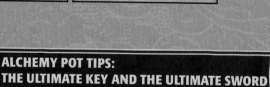

Level 1

Map

START

ATLAS

BLIZZARD PEAKS

Level 2

Level 3

Level 3

Level 4

SLIPPERY BRIDGE

Walk slowly across the ice bridge connecting the various upper portions of the initial cavern. By using the directional button, you can better control the onscreen character's movement speed and greatly reduce the likelihood of slipping off the bridge to the ground level.

Walk, don't run, across the ice bridge to avoid navigational setbacks.

ICICLE DROP

When the party passes the point where an icicle drips onto the cave floor, the frozen mass inexplicably crashes to the cave floor directly behind them. Although most of the time this serves no purpose except to startle you, it may be possible to form a makeshift ice bridge between disconnected areas in caves…

By causing icicles to fall in the caverns, you might be able to create a useful pathway.

TRAPPED BEHIND AN ICE WALL

At first it may seem as if there's no way to get around the fallen icicles that block off the eastern branch of the cave. However, examine the icicles and you may come up with a clever idea. After that, explore the area to determine if an alternate route might be created somehow…

Examine the icicles blocking the right-hand portion of the cave to determine how to resolve the situation

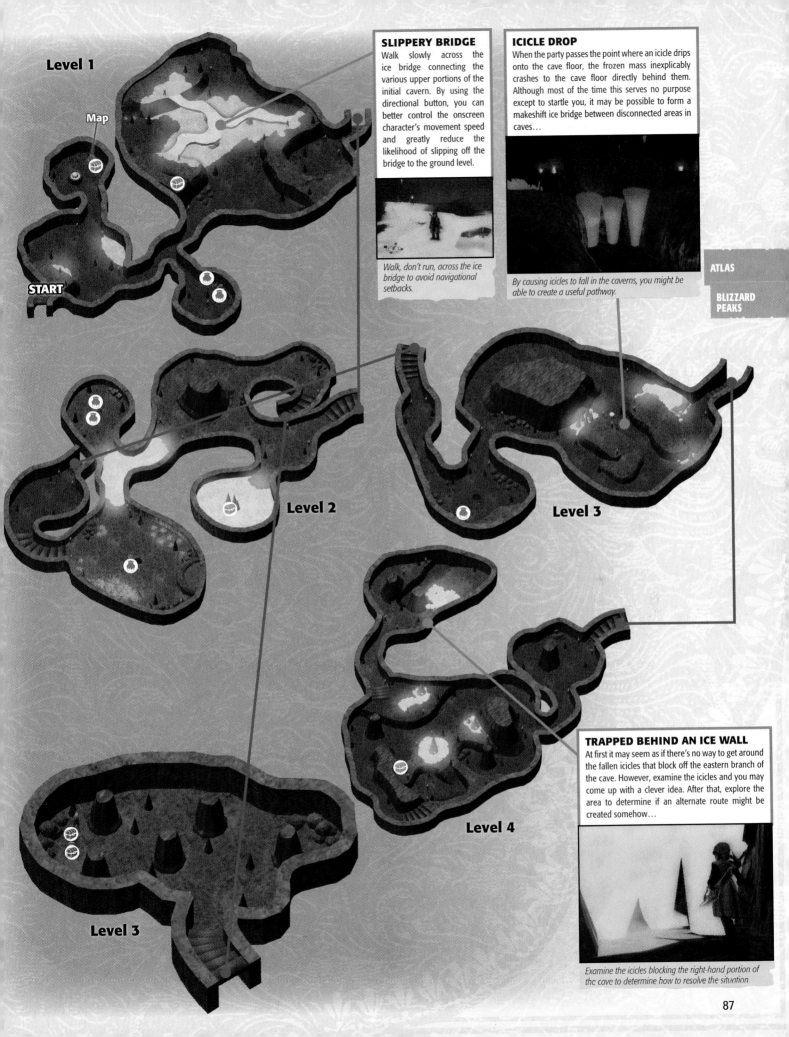

DESERT

WORLD MAPS

MAP KEY

- Treasure Chest
- Treasure Chest, requires magic key

ITEMS FOUND

- Dragon dung
- Dragon scale

INFAMOUS MONSTERS

 Living Flame   Bone Racer   Living Torch

DESERT CHAPEL

Before proceeding further into the wasteland, stop off at the Desert Chapel to confess and save your progress. A cheaply priced inn allows the party to recoup as often as needed, and a merchant behind a counter sells items. Speak to the person attending service to learn clues regarding an alchemy pot recipe.

Use the Desert Chapel to rest and save before attempting to explore the dangerous Desert.

Dragon Graveyard

DESERT WELLS

Several wells scattered all around the Desert provide more than just a cool, dark place to escape from the heat. Inside, you'll discover a faster means of travel around the desert area…

Check out the wells located around the desert. Perhaps travelling underground is a faster way to go?

ITEM SHOP LIST

ITEM	COST (G)	EQUIP ON
Medicinal herb	8G	N/A
Antidotal herb	10G	N/A
Chimaera wing	25G	N/A
Amor seco essence	120G	N/A
Dream blade	4700G	Hero, *Jessica (knife skill), Angelo

MONSTER APPEARANCES

DESERT—ANY TIME

NO.	NAME	HP	MP	EXP	GOLD
112	Iron scorpion	64	21	82	21
130	Lethal armour	145	20	124	52
144	Death scorpion	68	0	99	14
147	Dancing flame	98	0	143	14

DESERT—DAY

NO.	NAME	HP	MP	EXP	GOLD
73	Muddy hand	49	0	45	8

DESERT—NIGHT

NO.	NAME	HP	MP	EXP	GOLD
134	Demonrider	126	0	131	37

DRAGON GRAVEYARD

Recommended Level: 34

ITEMS FOUND

- Dragon Graveyard map
- Mini medal
- Dragon dung
- Dragon shield

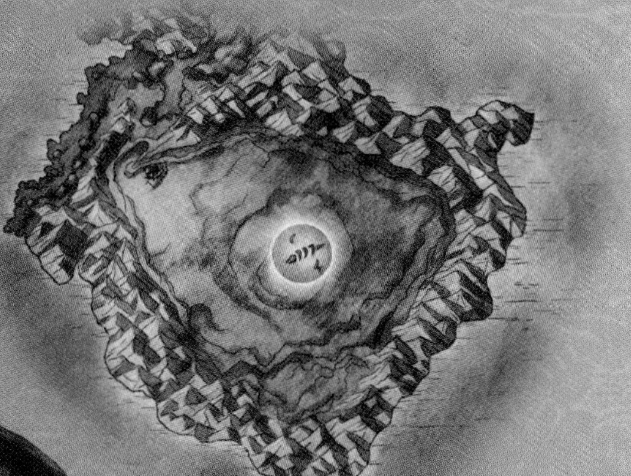

MAP KEY

- Treasure chest
- Treasure chest, requires thief's key
- Treasure chest, requires magic key
- Item Bag

MONSTER APPEARANCES

NO.	NAME	HP	MP	EXP	GOLD
167	Beelzebuzz	154	16	165	21
168	Killing machine	165	0	315	58
171	Metal king slime	20	66	30010	240
174	Dragurn	268	0	302	61
175	Smacker	131	Infinite	149	18
182	Tyrantosaurus	208	0	283	57

ATLAS

DESERT

Map

Level 1

START

Level 1

Level 1

Level 1

Level 1

Level 1

Doors of Judgement

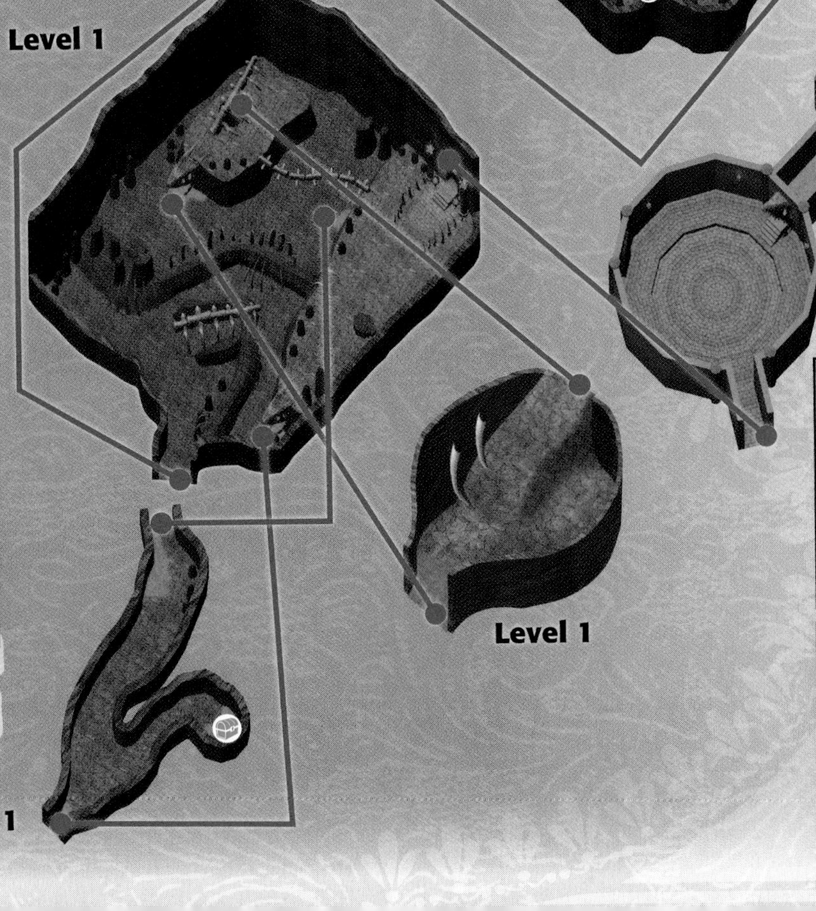

MOUTH OF THE DRAGON

It's somewhat difficult to depict on these maps, but note that the only problem with navigating through the Dragon Graveyard is that in two instances, the party must pass through the open mouth of a dragon skull to proceed.

Don't worry. This big lizard hasn't eaten any adventurers in ages!

SAVELLA AREA

WORLD MAPS

MAP KEY

- Treasure Chest
- Treasure Chest, requires magic key

ITEMS FOUND

- Magic water
- Seed of defence
- Seed of life
- Seed of magic
- Fresh milk

SWEET BIRDSONG

Cows aren't the only animals providing items on the holy island of Savella. Certain birds in the central and northwest portions of Savella also give up items when "spoken" to. The only problem is being nimble enough to catch up to these evasive little critters!

Speak with birds feeding from the grass alongside the roads in the Savella Area to obtain useful items.

Lord High Priest's Residence

Savella Cathedral

MONSTER APPEARANCES

SAVELLA AREA—DAY

NO.	NAME	HP	MP	EXP	GOLD
121	Magic dumbbell	78	14	41	9
127	Bulldozer	131	0	117	31
134	Demonrider	126	0	131	37
141	Silenus	131	0	113	38
142	Robo-robin	99	99	96	43

SAVELLA AREA—NIGHT

NO.	NAME	HP	MP	EXP	GOLD
100	Night emperor	100	0	93	46
104	Skeleton soldier	94	12	93	26
129	Shade	86	0	78	14
132	Hoodlum	123	0	106	32
135	Killer moth	84	8	116	14

SAVELLA CATHEDRAL

Recommended Level: 35

MAP KEY

- 🏠 Inn
- ✝ Armour Shop
- ⚔ Weapon Shop
- 🗡 Item Shop
- ⛪ Church

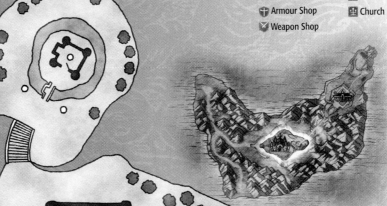

ITEMS FOUND

- 🍩 Mini medal
- 🍩 Seed of wisdom
- ❓ Dragon slayer recipe

ITEM SHOP LIST

ITEM	COST (G)	EQUIP ON
Medicinal herb	8G	N/A
Antidotal herb	10G	N/A
Holy water	20G	N/A
Chimaera wing	25G	N/A
Moonwort bulb	30G	N/A
Gold rosary	500G	Hero, Yangus, Jessica, Angelo

WEAPON SHOP LIST

WEAPON	COST (G)	EQUIP ON
Steel scythe	3700G	Yangus
Eagle dagger	3900G	Jessica
Partisan	4400G	Hero
Holy silver rapier	6600G	Angelo

ARMOUR SHOP LIST

ARMOUR	COST (G)	EQUIP ON
Full plate armour	2300G	Hero
Silver mail	4300G	Hero, Angelo
Magic vestment	4400G	Jessica, Angelo
Steel shield	2500G	Hero, Yangus
Iron mask	3500G	Hero, Yangus

RELIGIOUS HUB

Aside from the massive Goddess statue on the Holy Isle of Neos, Savella Cathedral is one of the largest and most gorgeous monuments to faith in the world. People from all walks of life come to Savella to kneel on the steps and pray to the Goddess for guidance, divination, and deliverance from evil. The people here know a great deal about the world, including hidden locations where you might not have thought to look.

*: I was sailin' down a river in the Eastern Continent when I saw this really weird cave under a bridge! What a find!

Speak to the pilgrims visiting Savella Cathedral to find out where to start the journey to find a hidden world…

PIRATE'S COVE (FAREBURY REGION)

Recommended Level: 35

ITEMS FOUND

- 790 gold coins
- Mini medal
- Magic water
- Pirate's Cove map
- Mini medal
- Mini medal
- Seed of magic
- Rock salt
- Hades helm
- Bone shield
- Mini medal
- Important Item

MAP KEY

- Treasure Chest
- Treasure Chest, requires ultimate key
- Breakable Pot
- Breakable Barrel

MONSTER APPEARANCES

NO.	NAME	HP	MP	EXP	GOLD
120	Mimic	144	Infinite	128	72
175	Smacker	131	Infinite	149	18
176	Zombie gladiator	180	16	283	71
183	Demon thunderer	179	0	250	48
238	Man o' war	35	0	23	12
240	King kelp	86	8	56	16
245	Crayzee	91	16	94	25
255	Merking	196	32	278	54
257	Octavian pirate	205	16	290	63
258	Riptide	235	13	331	113

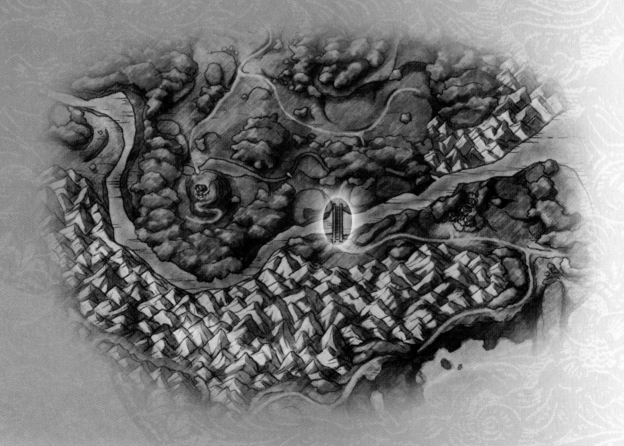

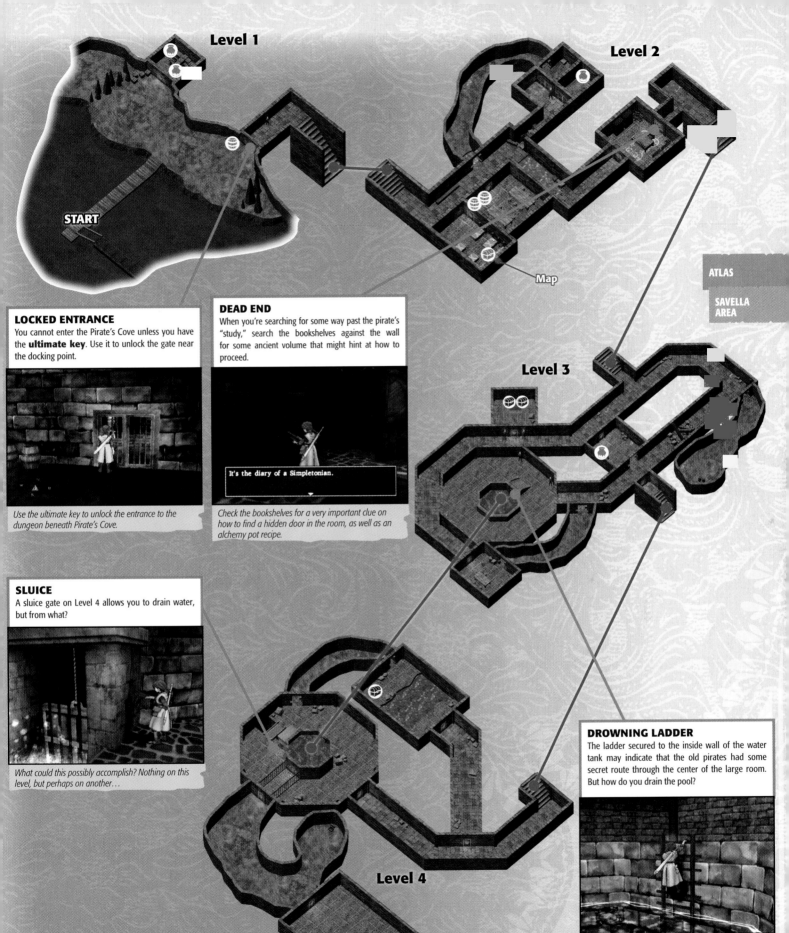

Level 1

Level 2

START

Map

ATLAS

SAVELLA
AREA

Level 3

LOCKED ENTRANCE

You cannot enter the Pirate's Cove unless you have the **ultimate key**. Use it to unlock the gate near the docking point.

Use the ultimate key to unlock the entrance to the dungeon beneath Pirate's Cove.

DEAD END

When you're searching for some way past the pirate's "study," search the bookshelves against the wall for some ancient volume that might hint at how to proceed.

It's the diary of a Simpletonian.

Check the bookshelves for a very important clue on how to find a hidden door in the room, as well as an alchemy pot recipe.

SLUICE

A sluice gate on Level 4 allows you to drain water, but from what?

What could this possibly accomplish? Nothing on this level, but perhaps on another…

Level 4

DROWNING LADDER

The ladder secured to the inside wall of the water tank may indicate that the old pirates had some secret route through the center of the large room. But how do you drain the pool?

The ladder in the water tank is a clear indication that you could climb from Level 3 to Level 4, if only the path was a bit drier.

Isolated Plateau

World Maps

Map Key

- Treasure Chest
- Treasure Chest, requires ultimate key

Items Found

- Fresh milk x6
- Mini medal
- Magical mace
- Lesser panacea
- Mighty armlet
- Elfin elixir

Infamous Monsters

Puppet Pugilist

Gigantes Guardsman

Ochre Ogre

Slime Designer

ENIGMA IN STONE

A strange monument stands on the highest hill near the center of Empycchu. Being so high and so large, perhaps it's a beacon to some force from above?

Speak to the residents of the nearby town to learn the history and function of this strange monument.

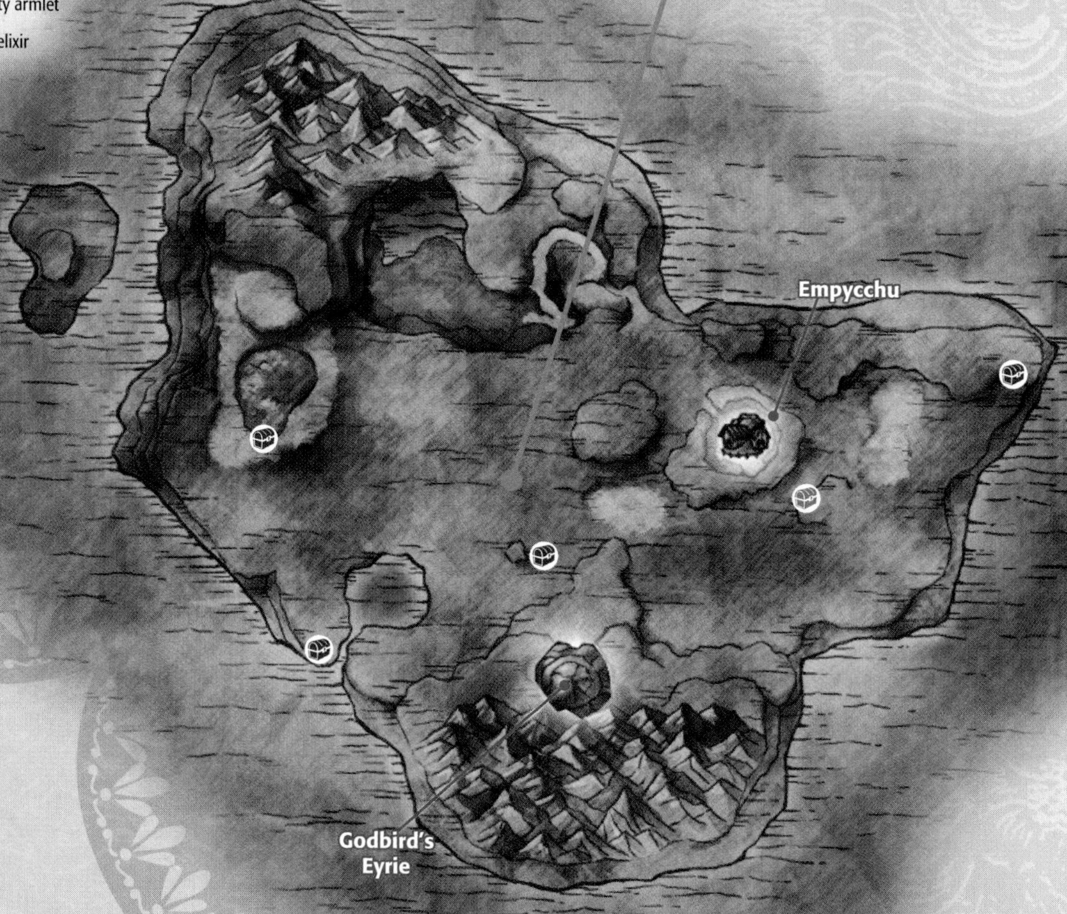

Empycchu

Godbird's Eyrie

MONSTER APPEARANCES

WEST AREA—FIELD—ANY TIME

NO.	NAME	HP	MP	EXP	GOLD
173	Elysium bird	173	32	163	43
176	Zombie gladiator	180	16	283	71

WEST AREA—FIELD—DAY

NO.	NAME	HP	MP	EXP	GOLD
1	Slime	7	0	1	1
174	Dragurn	268	0	302	61
179	Mucho macho	316	24	318	51
188	War gryphon	249	20	305	59
190	Heligator	512	0	617	138

WEST AREA—FIELD—NIGHT

NO.	NAME	HP	MP	EXP	GOLD
4	Dracky	10	0	2	3
175	Smacker	131	Infinite	149	18
183	Demon thunderer	179	0	250	48
186	Grim rider	236	9	304	72

WEST AREA—FOREST—ANY TIME

NO.	NAME	HP	MP	EXP	GOLD
164	Troll	423	0	210	46
173	Elysium bird	173	32	163	43
175	Smacker	131	Infinite	149	18
177	Stone golem	278	0	340	38
182	Tyrantosaurus	208	0	283	57
188	War gryphon	249	20	305	59

EAST AREA—FIELD—ANY TIME

NO.	NAME	HP	MP	EXP	GOLD
173	Elysium bird	173	32	163	43
176	Zombie gladiator	180	16	283	71

EAST AREA—FIELD—DAY

NO.	NAME	HP	MP	EXP	GOLD
1	Slime	7	0	1	1
179	Mucho macho	316	24	318	51
182	Tyrantosaurus	208	0	283	57
188	War gryphon	249	20	305	59
190	Heligator	512	0	617	138

EAST AREA—FIELD—NIGHT

NO.	NAME	HP	MP	EXP	GOLD
4	Dracky	10	0	2	3
175	Smacker	131	Infinite	149	18
183	Demon thunderer	179	0	250	48
186	Grim rider	236	9	304	72

EAST AREA—FOREST—ANY TIME

NO.	NAME	HP	MP	EXP	GOLD
164	Troll	423	0	210	46
175	Smacker	131	Infinite	149	18
177	Stone golem	278	0	340	38
182	Tyrantosaurus	208	0	283	57
188	War gryphon	249	20	305	59

ATLAS

ISOLATED PLATEAU

THE FLYING SHADOW

By chance, usually after visiting with the local population, the heroes might encounter a massive shadow floating across the ground near the center of Empycchu. But looking up into the sky, there does not seem to be anything that could create the shadow. Is the shadow perhaps trying to lead you somewhere?

EMPYCCHU

Recommended Level: 36

ITEMS FOUND

Seed of strength		Rock salt
Red mould		Rennet powder
Waterweed mould		Fresh milk
Mini medal		Mini medal
Mini medal		Fur poncho
Seed of skill		Special medicine
Chimaera wing		

TRADING POST SHOP LIST

ITEM	COST (G)	EQUIP ON
Holy water	20G	N/A
Magical mace	9000G	Jessica, Angelo
Mercury's rapier	10500G	Angelo
Bandit mail	13000G	Yangus
Flame shield	7100G	Yangus, Jessica
Mythril helm	13300G	Hero, Angelo

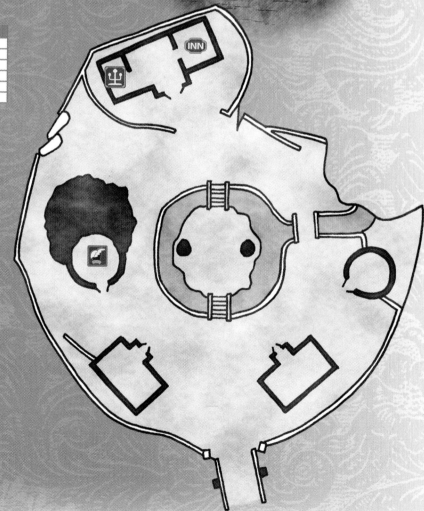

Noteworthy Locals

Chief

The village chief is the eldest and wisest member of the tribe that inhabits this region, therefore, the one person who the party can speak to about recent events in this area without hearing a bunch of superstition. The chief knows a great deal that the heroes need to learn if they have any hope of flying.

Isolated Souls

The residents of Empycchu are extremely primitive descendants of people who have been shipwrecked on this mysterious island over the centuries. Some of the denizens arrived more recently, such as a peddler who has set up shop in one of the eastern huts, and a wandering priest who wound up spreading the good word here entirely by accident.

✳: It was so rare to see her shadow, so rare for us. But recently, we see her shadow more and more often.

The people of Empycchu may be primitive, but they know a great deal about some of the more mysterious features of the island.

ALCHEMY POT TIPS: ALCHEMY IN THE LOST WORLD

Although you're far from civilisation, the ingredients you need to enhance many items sold in Empycchu are probably already available. Certainly, fresh milk is available, and there should be a cowpat to spare. These ingredients combine with a mythril helm to create a slightly stronger **raging bull helm** (Defence 42).

Good armour for Jessica is hard to come by. You can make a relatively strong **magical skirt** (Defence 55) by buying a magical mace (or finding one elsewhere on the island) and dropping it into the pot along with a magical hat and a bandit's grass skirt.

Swallowtails aren't cheap, but if you've already purchased one in Arcadia or Orkutsk, mix it with a flame shield (sold in Empycchu) to gain a 10-point boost in attack power with the **flametang boomerang** (Attack 63).

Nothing at the shop is worth much to Yangus. However, the mighty armlet found in a chest outside town is quite the gift for a hammer specialist. Mix this with a war hammer to upgrade to an **über war hammer** (Attack 69).

RECIPE SUMMARIES

Raging bull helm = mythril helm + fresh milk + cowpat

Magical skirt = magical mace + bandit's grass skirt + magical hat

Flametang boomerang = swallowtail + flame shield

Über war hammer = war hammer + mighty armlet

WORLD OF DARKNESS

WORLD MAPS

MAP KEY

- Treasure Chest
- Treasure Chest, requires ultimate key

ITEMS FOUND

- Mini medal
- Iron headgear
- Devil's tail
- Seed of agility

Dark Empycchu

Godbird's Eyrie (Dark)

MONSTER APPEARANCES

DARK EMPYCCHU—ANY TIME

NO.	NAME	HP	MP	EXP	GOLD
161	Dark slime	97	16	87	12
170	Shadow	154	0	216	14
178	Dark condor	163	36	224	26
180	Dark skeleton	240	0	304	31
181	Dark macarbour	334	0	333	56
187	Dark sea-diva	236	25	287	61
189	Dark turkey	214	12	309	73
194	Darkodile	593	0	637	138

DARK EMPYCCHU

Recommended Level: 37

MAP KEY

- 🅸🅽🅽 Inn
- 📖 Item Shop
- ⛪ Church

ITEMS FOUND

- Seed of magic
- Rock salt
- Mini medal
- 180 gold coins
- Cowpat
- Mini medal
- Cold cheese
- Premium mould
- Dragon scale
- Fresh milk
- Mini medal
- Mini medal
- Special antidote

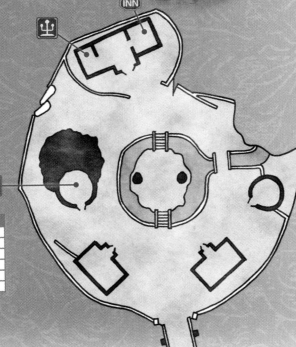

TRADING POST SHOP LIST

ITEM	COST (G)	EQUIP ON
Holy water	20G	N/A
Magical mace	9000G	Jessica, Angelo
Mercury's rapier	10500G	Angelo
Bandit mail	13000G	Yangus
Flame shield	7100G	Yangus, Jessica
Mythril helm	13300G	Hero, Angelo

The reaction of the townsfolk to the appearance of the colorful heroes in this eerily dark world is that of shock and awe. But even in the middle of the commotion, one thing that's immediately apparent is that everything in the light version of Empycchu has a mirror double here. After taking another stroll around the village to gather items and learn clues from the locals, speak to the shadowy double of the chief in the largest hut to learn about this place and its connection to the heroes' journey.

Chief
Gojoshar! Welcome to Empycchu. You've seen our village, yes? Then let me tell you something.

Speak to this dark world's version of the chief to understand what the characters can do to escape from this colorless situation.

As found in the heroes' home world, a strange stone structure stands in the center of the island. What will happen as the characters approach this mirror-image landmark?

Recommended Level: 37

ITEMS FOUND

- Godbird's Eyrie map
- Gold nugget
- Ring of truth
- Demon whip
- Saint's ashes
- (??) Important Item

MONSTER APPEARANCES

NO.	NAME	HP	MP	EXP	GOLD
161	Dark slime	97	16	87	12
170	Shadow	154	0	216	14
178	Dark condor	163	36	224	26
180	Dark skeleton	240	0	304	31
184	Dark star	236	12	301	66
185	Dark minister	193	16	316	101
187	Dark sea-diva	236	25	287	61
189	Dark turkey	214	12	309	73
191	Dark dullahan	292	0	326	138
194	Darkodile	593	0	637	138

MAP KEY

- Treasure Chest
- Treasure Chest, requires ultimate key

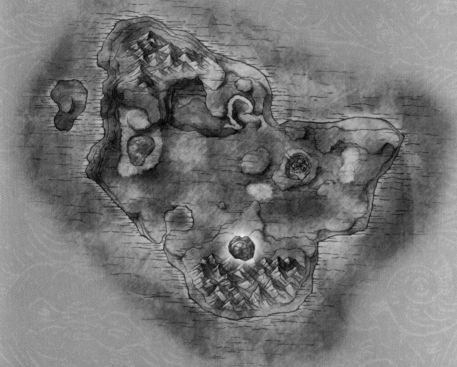

Side A

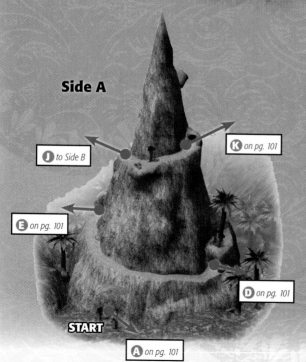

- J to Side B
- K on pg. 101
- E on pg. 101
- D on pg. 101
- START
- A on pg. 101

Side B

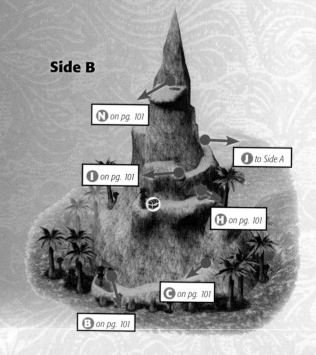

- N on pg. 101
- J to Side A
- I on pg. 101
- H on pg. 101
- C on pg. 101
- B on pg. 101

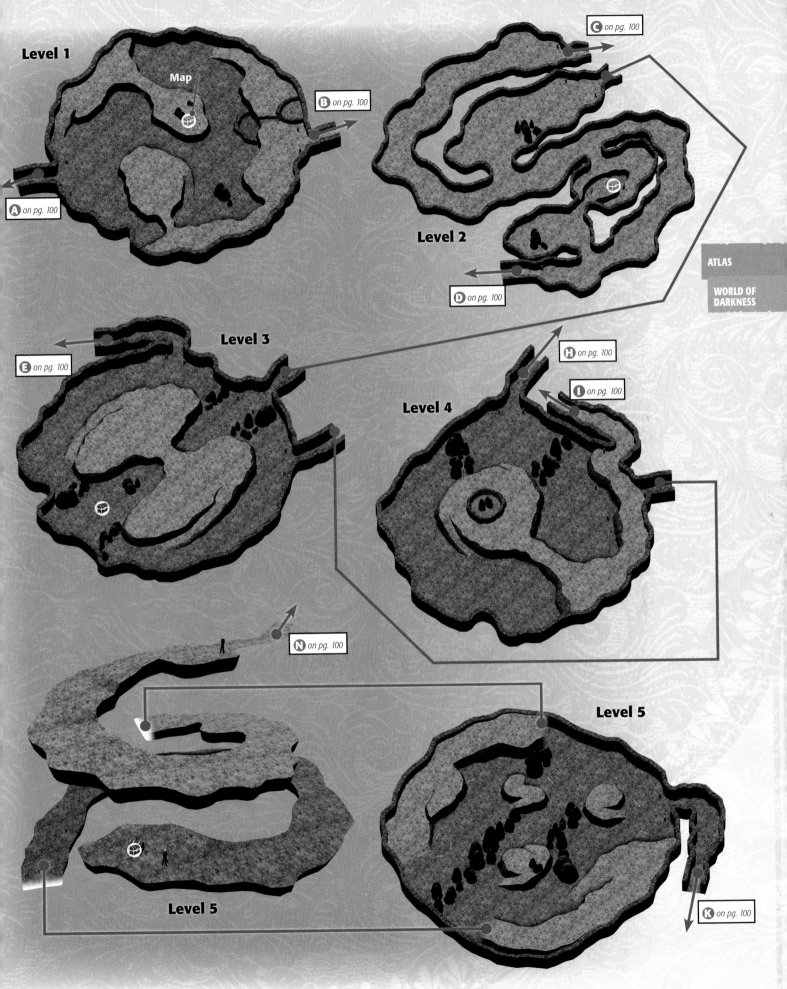

Level 1

Map

B on pg. 100

A on pg. 100

C on pg. 100

Level 2

D on pg. 100

Level 3

E on pg. 100

Level 4

H on pg. 100

I on pg. 100

N on pg. 100

Level 5

Level 5

K on pg. 100

AREAS ACCESSIBLE BY AIR

WORLD MAPS

MAP KEY

🏺 Breakable Pot

🎁 Treasure Chest

🎁 Treasure Chest, requires ultimate key

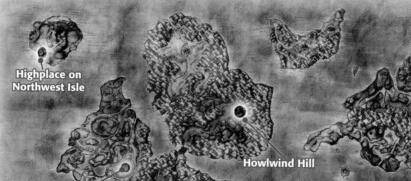

Highplace on Northwest Isle

Howlwind Hill

Egeus' Tablet

Mysterious Altar

Hill on Argonia's Western Border

Highplace near Neos

Ascantha Lake Island

Mountain Overlooking Desert

Godbird's Eyrie

Empycchu's South Rise

MONSTER APPEARANCES

AREAS ACCESSIBLE BY AIR GENERAL— ANY TIME				
NO.	NAME	HP	MP	EXP	GOLD
173	Elysium bird	173	32	163	43
196	Bloody hand	192	0	146	17

AREAS ACCESSIBLE BY AIR GENERAL—NIGHT				
NO.	NAME	HP	MP	EXP	GOLD
84	Liquid metal slime	8	Infinite	10050	18
100	Night emperor	100	0	93	46
192	Killer croaker	183	14	166	16

AREAS ACCESSIBLE BY AIR GENERAL—DAY				
NO.	NAME	HP	MP	EXP	GOLD
2	Candy cat	10	0	2	2
110	Gold golem	120	0	54	726
116	Bomboulder	115	10	111	11
188	War gryphon	249	20	305	59
193	High roller	284	28	245	87
195	Cyclops	482	0	443	69

REACHING HIGHER GROUND

By following the natural course of events and clearing dungeon after dungeon up to this point, it comes to pass that the heroes become capable of flight. This new ability allows you to land in areas that were previously inaccessible. By landing in these areas, you can gain new items and learn new clues regarding the growing threat and the history surrounding it. While soaring through the skies, look for vapory clouds hanging in the air above certain areas. Despite their uninviting appearance, you may be able to land and explore these areas.

EGEUS' TABLET

Recommended Level: 38

ITEMS FOUND

- Yggdrasil leaf
- Mini medal
- (??) Mini medal

MONSTER APPEARANCES

NO.	NAME	HP	MP	EXP	GOLD
116	Bomboulder	115	10	111	11
173	Elysium bird	173	32	163	43
188	War gryphon	249	20	305	59
190	Heligator	512	0	617	138
197	Snapdragon	436	30	356	63

Egeus' Tablet

ATLAS

AREAS
ACCESSIBLE
BY AIR

A LONELY SHRINE

The friendly monsters in the field provide valuable clues. They tell you about the engraving in the sheltered area, as well as an item hidden in the sandy area surrounding the water near the tablet.

＊: She buries everything she collects in the sand.

Speak to the friendly monsters to learn why they dwell in this mysterious location.

MYSTERIOUS ALTAR

Recommended Level: 38

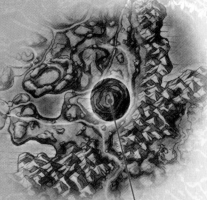

Mysterious
Altar

SHRINE TO A DRAGON GOD

This amazing structure is atop a mountain east of Chateau Felix. The origin and function of this place
is completely unknown. There's a statue of a dragon perched over the stone marker as if it were
protecting it. Who built this place and for what reason?

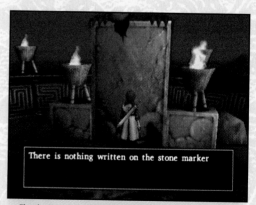

There is nothing written on the stone marker

*The character notices that the monument is not marked. Perhaps
markings might become clearer at some later time…*

HIGHPLACE ON NORTHWEST ISLE

Recommended Level: 38

INFAMOUS MONSTERS

Shadow Conductor   Troll Patroller   Stonemason

ITEMS FOUND

- Ruinous shield

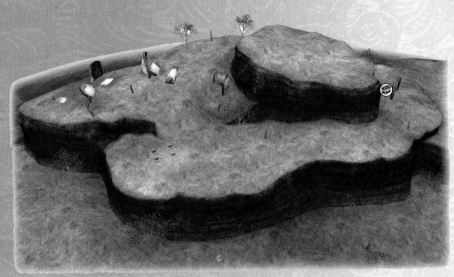

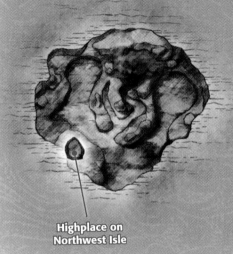

Highplace on Northwest Isle

HILL ON ARGONIA'S WESTERN BORDER

AREA MAPS

Recommended Level: 38

ITEMS FOUND

- Flametang boomerang

Hill on Argonia's Western Border

MOUNTAIN OVERLOOKING DESERT

Recommended Level: 38

INFAMOUS MONSTERS

Killer Director

ITEMS FOUND

- Mini medal
- Ogre shield

Mountain Overlooking Desert

EMPYCCHU'S SOUTH RISE

Recommended Level: 38

INFAMOUS MONSTERS

Metal Babble   Shadow Conductor

ITEMS FOUND

- Skull helm

Empycchu's South Rise

HIGHPLACE NEAR NEOS
AREA MAPS

Recommended Level: 38

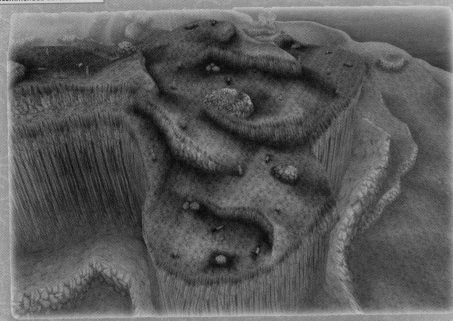

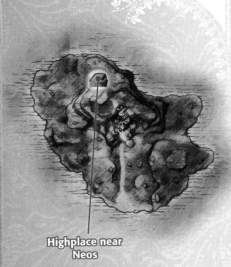

Highplace near Neos

ATLAS

AREAS
ACCESSIBLE
BY AIR

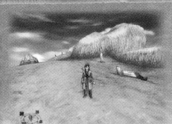

ASCANTHA LAKE ISLAND
AREA MAPS

Recommended Level: 38

INFAMOUS MONSTERS

Killer Director   Bushwhacker

ITEMS FOUND

 Yggdrasil dew

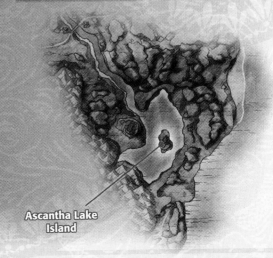

Ascantha Lake
Island

HOWLWIND HILL

Recommended Level: 38

ITEMS FOUND

 Conqueror's axe

MONSTER APPEARANCES

NO.	NAME	HP	MP	EXP	GOLD
1	Slime	7	0	1	1
8	She-slime	18	0	8	6
12	Bubble slime	20	0	5	7
21	Healslime	24	12	18	13
36	Metal slime	4	Infinite	1350	5
66	Cureslime	54	20	70	11
84	Liquid metal slime	8	Infinite	10050	18
111	King slime	210	25	110	51
131	King cureslime	180	Infinite	136	16
171	Metal king slime	20	66	30010	240

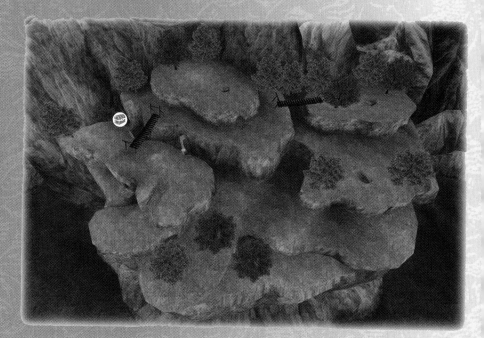

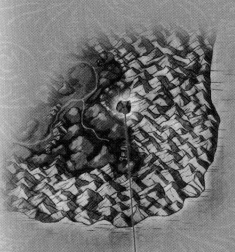

Howlwind Hill

ALCHEMY POT TIPS:
SOMETIMES A CURSE IS A BLESSING

The **Godbird's soulstone** enables the party to fly to the unreachable hills and cliffs of many familiar areas. Although the items on these high grounds may not seem fantastic at first, many are ingredients in recipes that generate some of the game's most powerful items.

The skull helm, found in the bluffs of Empycchu, is one such item. Purify it with saint's ashes to make a **sun crown** (Defence 52). But that's only the first step. Then mix the crown with a tough guy tattoo and a magic beast hide to create a **timbrel of tension**, a stunningly powerful combat item that when used in battle raises everyone's tension.

The ruinous shield found near the Dark Ruins is also cursed, and combining it with a standard dose of saint's ashes is not enough to purify it. Some orichalcum must also be thrown in, and the resulting item is the most powerful shield in the game, the **metal king shield** (Defence 65). If you don't have any orichalcum, find a piece in the Godbird's Eyrie located in the World of Light.

RECIPE SUMMARIES

Sun crown = skull helm + saint's ashes

Timbrel of tension = sun crown + tough guy tattoo + magic beast hide

Metal king shield = ruinous shield + orichalcum + saint's ashes

GODBIRD'S EYRIE

Recommended Level: 38

ITEMS FOUND

 Mini medal
 Gold nugget
 Mini medal

 Dragon dung
Orichalcum

MAP KEY

Treasure Chest
Treasure Chest, requires ultimate key

MONSTER APPEARANCES

NO.	NAME	HP	MP	EXP	GOLD
4	Dracky	10	0	2	3
84	Liquid metal slime	8	Infinite	10050	18
173	Elysium bird	173	32	163	43
174	Dragurn	268	0	302	61
175	Smacker	131	Infinite	149	18
176	Zombie gladiator	180	16	283	71
177	Stone golem	278	0	340	38
179	Mucho macho	316	24	318	51
182	Tyrantosaurus	208	0	283	57
183	Demon thunderer	179	0	250	48
186	Grim rider	236	9	304	72
192	Killer croaker	183	14	166	16
193	High roller	284	28	245	87
196	Bloody hand	192	0	146	17

ATLAS

AREAS
ACCESSIBLE
BY AIR

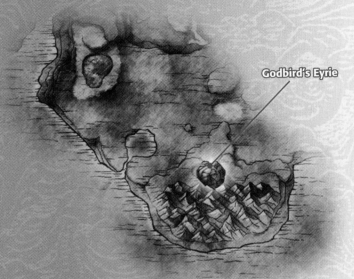

Godbird's Eyrie

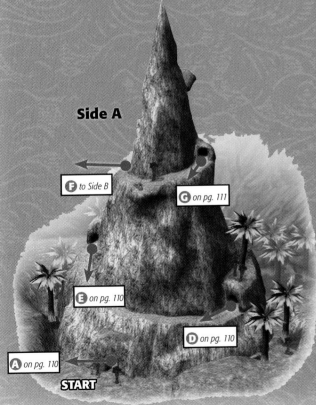

Side A

F to Side B

G on pg. 111

E on pg. 110

D on pg. 110

A on pg. 110

START

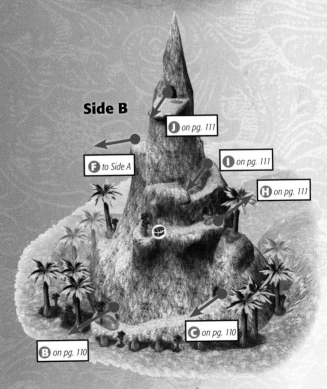

Side B

J on pg. 111

F to Side A

I on pg. 111

H on pg. 111

C on pg. 110

B on pg. 110

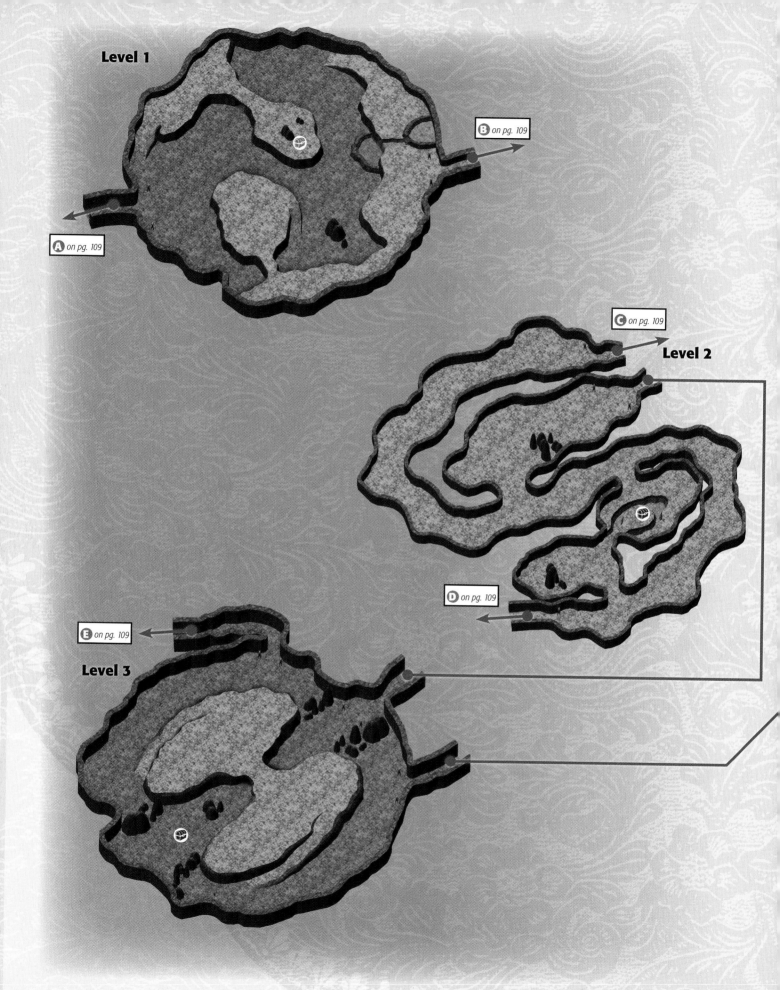

Level 1

B on pg. 109

A on pg. 109

C on pg. 109

Level 2

D on pg. 109

E on pg. 109

Level 3

110

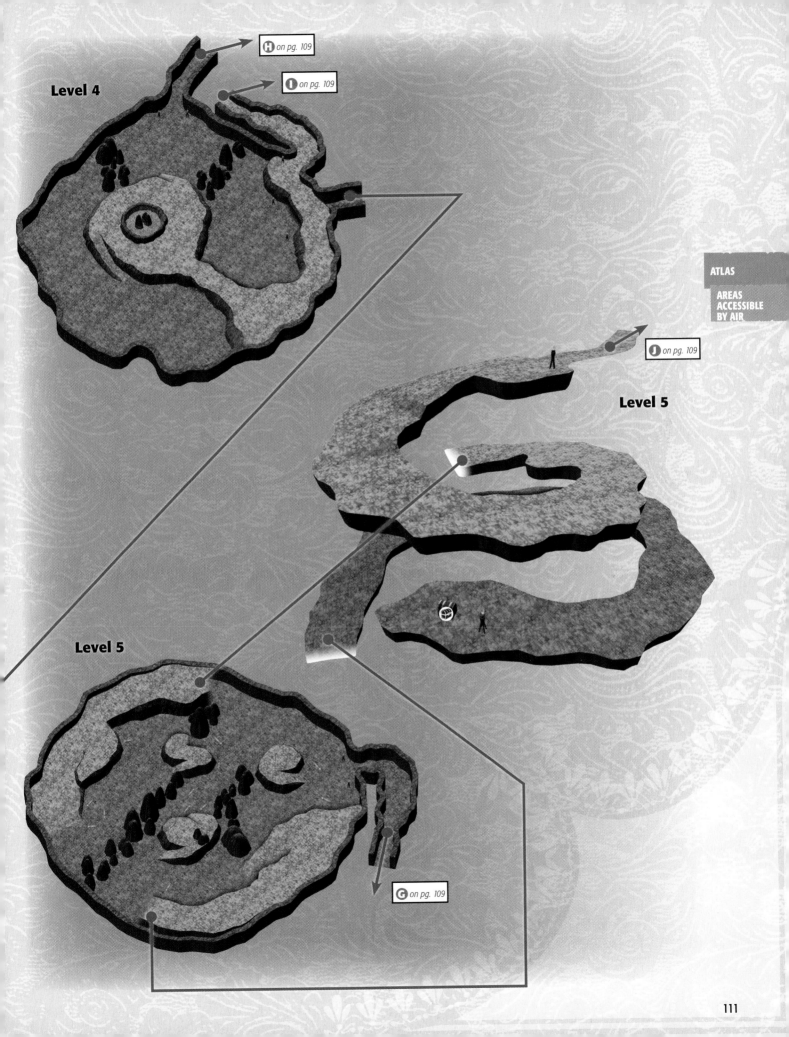

Level 4

ⓗ *on pg. 109*

ⓘ *on pg. 109*

ⓙ *on pg. 109*

Level 5

Level 5

ⓖ *on pg. 109*

UNTRODDEN GROVES

WORLD MAPS

INFAMOUS MONSTERS

 Arch-archdemon

 Big Blue Bully

MAP KEY

Treasure Chest, requires ultimate key

ITEMS FOUND

Fresh milk x2

Super spicy cheese

Mini medal

Tryan Gully

MONSTER APPEARANCES

UNTRODDEN GROVES—ANY TIME					
NO.	NAME	HP	MP	EXP	GOLD
161	Dark slime	97	16	87	12
171	Metal slime king	20	66	30010	240
184	Dark star	236	12	301	66
192	Killer croaker	183	14	166	16
193	High roller	284	28	245	87
195	Cyclops	482	0	443	69
196	Bloody hand	192	0	146	17
197	Snapdragon	436	30	356	63
198	Buffalogre	360	0	363	120
199	Mohawker	344	35	318	160
203	Claws	283	0	386	73
206	Fowlfighter	285	Infinite	376	60

TRYAN GULLY

Recommended Level: 38

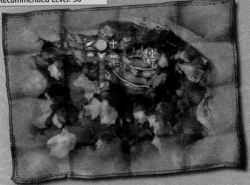

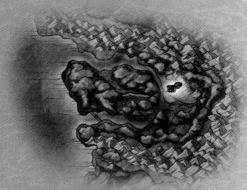

MAP KEY

(INN)	Inn	▨	Item Shop
▯	Pub	◉	Gold Bank
✚	Armour Shop	⛪	Church
◈	Weapon Shop		

ATLAS

UNTRODDEN GROVES

ITEMS FOUND

- 🏅 Mini medal
- 🏅 Elfin elixir
- 🏅 Slime crown
- 🏅 Premium mould
- 🏅 Seed of defence
- 🏅 Yggdrasil dew
- 🏅 Mini medal
- 🏅 Staff of antimagic
- 🏅 Important Item

WEAPON SHOP LIST

WEAPON	COST (G)	EQUIP ON
Dragonsbane	11000G	Hero, *Jessica (knife skill)
King axe	17000G	Yangus
Blizzard blade	21000G	Hero, *Jessica (knife skill)
Great bow	28000G	Angelo
Heavy hatchet	29000G	Yangus
Staff of resurrection	45000G	Jessica, Angelo

ARMOUR SHOP LIST

ARMOUR	COST (G)	EQUIP ON
Gigant armour	18000G	Yangus
Mirror armour	21000G	Hero, Angelo
Mirror shield	15000G	Hero, Angelo
Power shield	18000G	Hero, Yangus, Angelo
Thinking cap	13000G	Jessica, Angelo
Great helm	16000G	Hero, Yangus

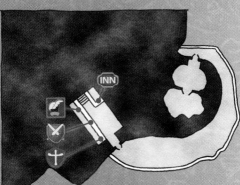

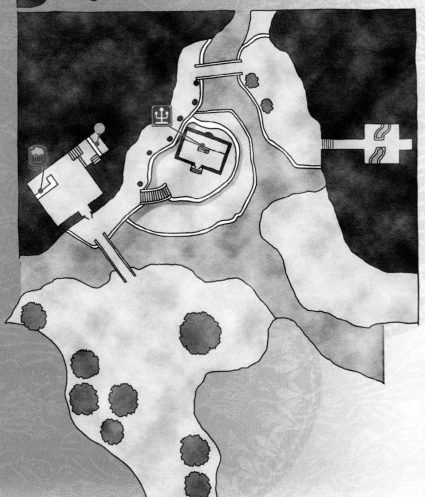

Raya

An elf maiden, Raya is one of the first creatures rescued by one of the great sages and brought to Tryan Gully to live in harmony with humans and monsters. Although she's not the leader of the community in any official way, the other residents here certainly look up to her.

TRODE'S RELIEF

Finally, a place where poor King Trode can show his hideous face without concern! Speak with the monster just outside town, as well as the bartender, to learn all there is to know about the Tryan Gully community, and why Trode should be extremely happy here. The monsters are very capable of crafting amazing weapons and equipment, so visit all the shops and purchase whatever is affordable. Then proceed across the bridge and into the small shrine to speak with Raya, Drang, and a gigantes, who are some of the co-founders of this enlightened brotherhood.

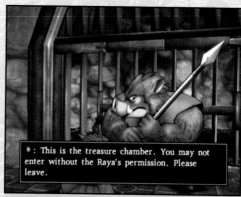

✳: This is the treasure chamber. You may not enter without the Raya's permission. Please leave.

While exploring the town, note the locked treasure room in the cave below the shops. Perhaps you should speak to someone about unlocking it…

ALCHEMY POT TIPS: A FEW FINAL CONCOCTIONS

Time to make a new bow for Angelo in the alchemy pot! Purchase the great bow from Tryan Gully's shop. In spite of its fabulousness, do not equip it. Instead, combine it in the alchemy pot with Eros' bow and Cheiron's bow to form the awesomely powerful **Odin's bow** (Attack 125).

The mirror shield sold in Tryan Gully is risky to use, since it reflects even healing and status-boosting spells. Instead of equipping the mirror shield, drop it into the pot along with a white shield and a holy water to create a **saintess shield** (Defence 46) for Jessica. Next, purchase a thinking cap and mix it with a gold nugget and a silver tiara (sold in Argonia) to make Jessica a **golden tiara** (Defence 43).

Strong shields and helmets are helpful, but nothing matches a good suit of armour. Acquiring Jessica's best costume change requires a two-stage recipe. First, mix up a **shimmering dress** (Defence 67) by combining a spangled dress (found in Baccarat) with a gold bracer and a ruby of protection. Then mix the resulting shimmering dress with the dangerous bustier that Princess Minnie awards to travellers who collect 99 mini medals. The resultant **divine bustier** (Defence 105), with its high defence, ensures that Jessica will maintain her "VA-VA-VOOM!" for the remainder of the game.

RECIPE SUMMARIES

Odin's bow = Eros' bow + Cheiron's bow + great bow

Saintess shield = white shield + mirror shield + holy water

Golden tiara = silver tiara + thinking cap + gold nugget

Shimmering dress = spangled dress + gold bracer + ruby of protection

Divine bustier = dangerous bustier + shimmering dress

Lord High Priest's Residence (Savella Area)

Recommended Level: 38

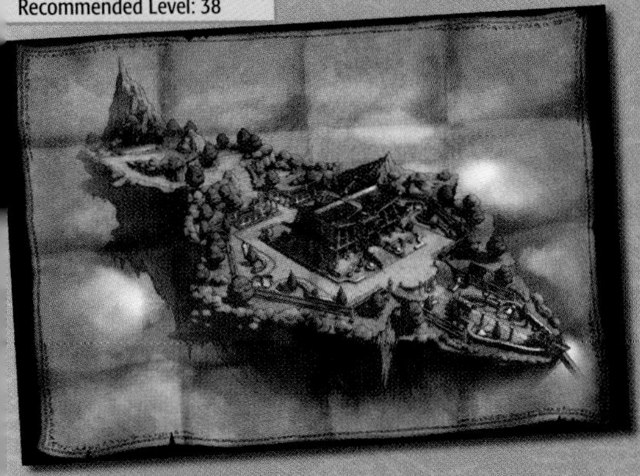

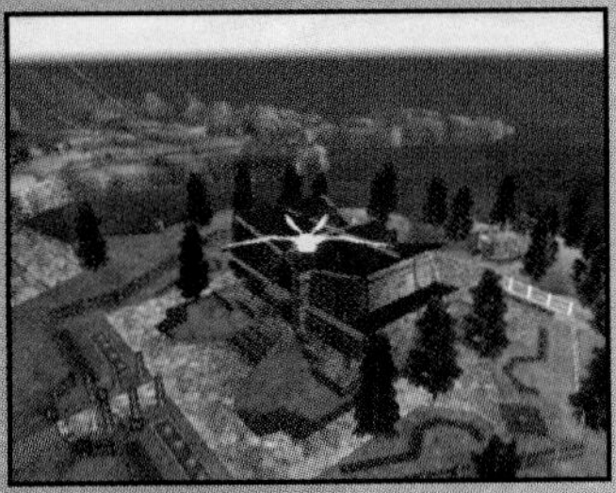

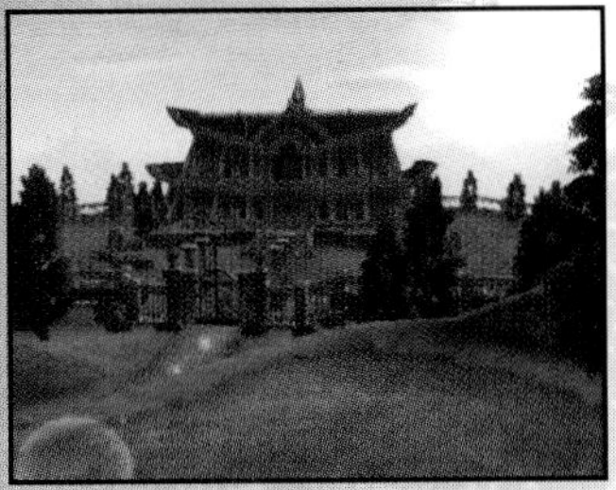

Items Found

- Mini medal
- Seed of life
- Sage's robe
- Mini medal

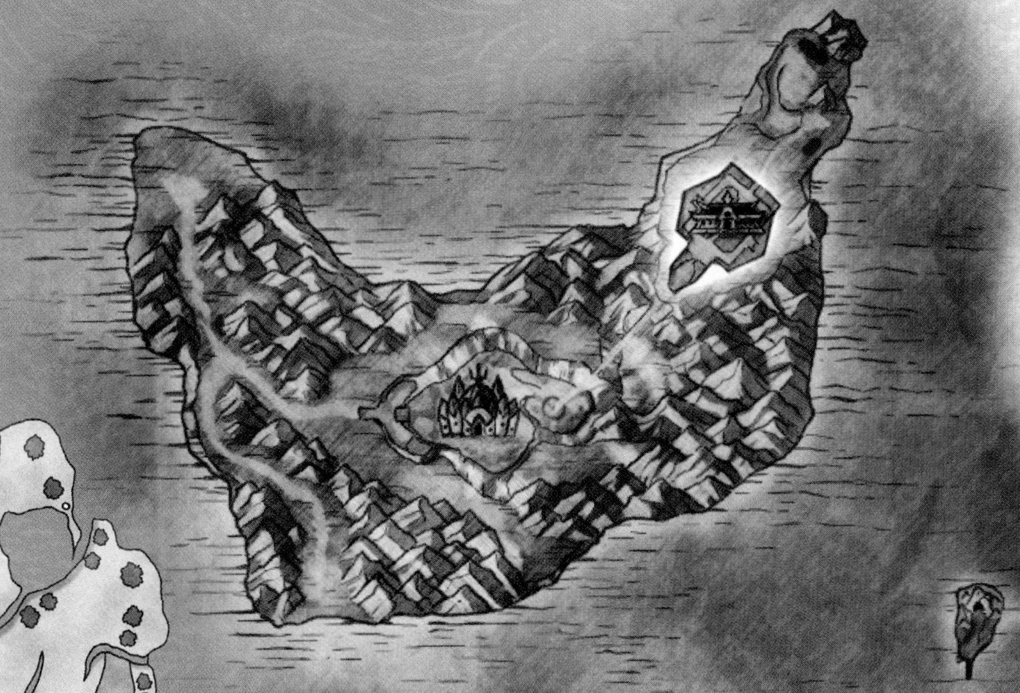

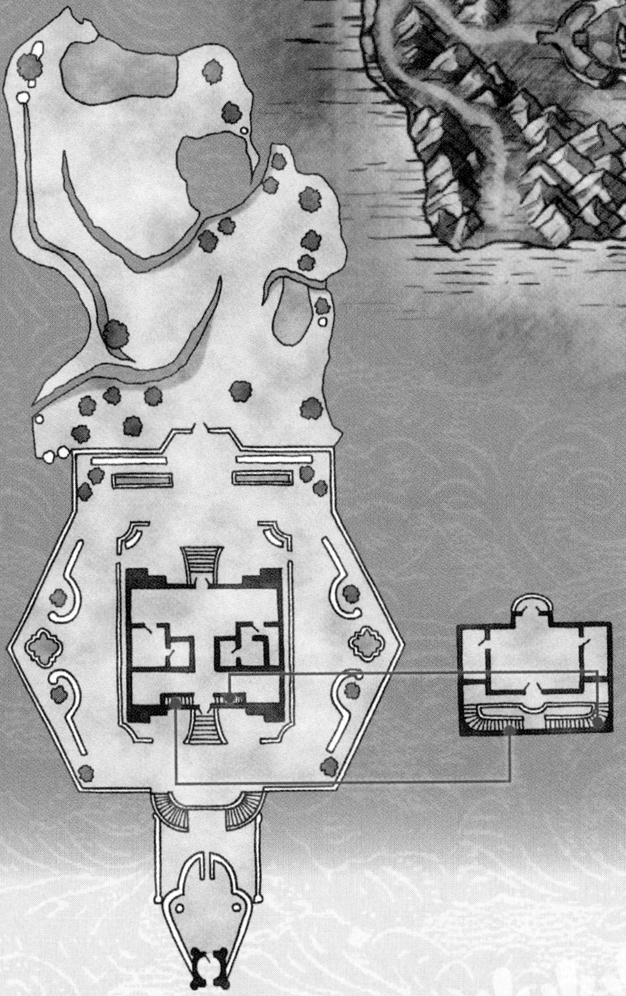

HOLY ISLE OF NEOS

WORLD MAPS

MAP KEY

 Treasure Chest

 Treasure Chest, requires magic key

ITEMS FOUND

Magic water Agility ring

INFAMOUS MONSTERS

Goldbricker

Crazed Colossus

Neos

MONSTER APPEARANCES

NEOS ISLAND—ANY TIME

NO.	NAME	HP	MP	EXP	GOLD
108	Redtail hipster	103	0	92	36

NEOS ISLAND—DAY

NO.	NAME	HP	MP	EXP	GOLD
106	Tap devil	85	0	78	21
110	Gold golem	120	0	54	726
115	Volpone	107	24	102	43
118	Hades condor	102	16	99	22

NEOS ISLAND—NIGHT

NO.	NAME	HP	MP	EXP	GOLD
100	Night emperor	100	0	93	46
104	Skeleton soldier	94	12	93	26
107	Mushroom mage	81	10	75	13
113	Toxic zombie	116	0	75	17

NEOS

Recommended Level: 39

MAP KEY

- 🏨 Inn
- 🛡 Armour Shop
- ⚔ Weapon Shop
- 📦 Item Shop

ITEMS FOUND

- Seed of magic
- Moonwort bulb
- Holy water
- 16 gold coins
- Chimaera wing
- 80 gold coins
- Scholar's specs
- Spicy cheese
- Gold rosary
- Seed of skill
- (??) Templar Captain's ring

ITEM SHOP LIST

ITEM	COST (G)	EQUIP ON
Medicinal herb	8G	N/A
Antidotal herb	10G	N/A
Holy water	20G	N/A
Chimaera wing	25G	N/A
Gold rosary	500G	Hero, Yangus, Jessica, Angelo

ARMOUR SHOP LIST

ARMOUR	COST (G)	EQUIP ON
Full plate armour	2300G	Hero
Silver cuirass	3200G	Yangus
Light shield	2250G	Hero, Yangus, Jessica, Angelo
Steel shield	2500G	Hero, Yangus
Iron mask	3500G	Hero, Yangus

*TRADING POST SHOP LIST (APPEARS AFTER CERTAIN EVENTS)

ITEM	COST (G)	EQUIP ON
Medicinal herb	8G	N/A
Moonwort bulb	30G	N/A
Holy water	20G	N/A
Dream blade	4700G	Hero, *Jessica (knife skill), Angelo
Turtle shell	2300G	Yangus
Cloak of evasion	3000G	Jessica, Angelo

WEAPON SHOP LIST

WEAPON	COST (G)	EQUIP ON
Edged boomerang	1360G	Hero
Chain whip	2200G	Jessica
Steel scythe	3700G	Yangus
Dream blade	4700G	Hero, *Jessica (knife skill), Angelo
Holy silver rapier	6600G	Angelo

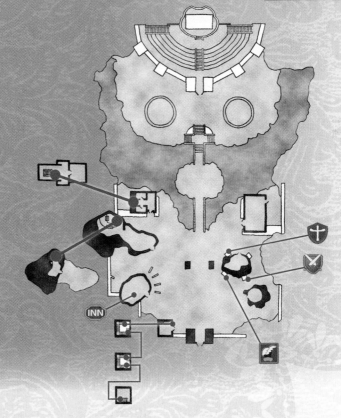

Check out the view of the Goddess statue from the top of the guard tower near the entrance of town.

THE IMMENSE GODDESS SHRINE

The pilgrims visiting the holy island and its citizens, who profit from the tourism industry, are generally friendly and informative people, but no one on the island has enough clout to get the party past the Templars guarding the entrance to the shrine at the base of the stone Goddess statue. The only way the party can enter the shrine is when the public is admitted for some sort of special occasion.

TROLLS' MAZE (???)

Recommended Level: 40

ITEMS FOUND

- Mini medal
- Hell sabre
- (??) Seed of strength x2
- (??) Seed of life x3

MONSTER APPEARANCES

NO.	NAME	HP	MP	EXP	GOLD
131	King cureslime	180	Infinite	136	16
164	Troll	423	0	210	46
195	Cyclops	482	0	443	69
197	Snapdragon	436	30	356	63
204	Boss troll	780	0	426	56
232	Great troll	1010	0	679	68

MAP KEY

- Treasure chest
- Treasure chest, requires ultimate key

THROUGH THE LOOKING GLASS

This hidden dungeon is extremely easy to navigate. Proceed across the suspended platforms that form a path to the back room, where someone of prominence in politics can be heard begging for release. Speak to the monsters in this chamber to determine what can be done to resolve the situation.

The **hell sabre** found in the Trolls' Maze is an incredibly powerful, ready-to-wield weapon for Angelo.

BLACK CITADEL (???)

Recommended Level: 41

MONSTER APPEARANCES

NO.	NAME	HP	MP	EXP	GOLD
131	King cureslime	180	Infinite	136	16
171	Metal king slime	20	66	30010	240
200	Archdemon	348	45	418	62
201	Bobonga	443	0	376	66
202	Caped caperer	216	0	199	31
203	Claws	283	0	386	73
204	Boss troll	780	0	426	56
205	Mimic king	340	Infinite	402	71
206	Fowlfighter	285	Infinite	376	60
207	Dullahan	335	24	378	48
208	Gigantes	710	0	511	36
209	Frou-frou	510	0	396	57
210	Stone guardian	450	0	422	80
211	Wight priest	258	Infinite	398	57
212	Hell gladiator	276	0	416	94

MAP KEY

- Breakable barrel
- Breakable pot
- Cabinet/Wardrobe/Cupboard
- Treasure chest
- Treasure chest, requires ultimate key

ITEMS FOUND

- Black Citadel map
- Sage's stone
- Dark robe
- Premium mould
- Rock salt
- Seed of life
- Cured cheese
- Icicle dirk
- Orichalcum
- Hard cheese
- Yggdrasil leaf
- Saint's ashes
- 500 gold coins
- 1200 gold coins
- Seed of defence
- Prayer ring
- Orichalcum
- Silver shield

COLLAPSED STAIRS

Initially, getting around in the outdoor portion of the Black Citadel is difficult because certain stairways are collapsed, such as the central one leading from the lower level up to the mezzanine. In order to reach the switch that raises these stairs, the heroes must navigate and search through this massive citadel. However, raising these connecting paths makes it easier to navigate through the Black Citadel a second time, in case you find it necessary to leave and save your game or use the alchemy pot.

Collapsed stairways force the heroes to explore every twisting nook and cranny of the outdoor area, looking for a way to reach the top of the tower.

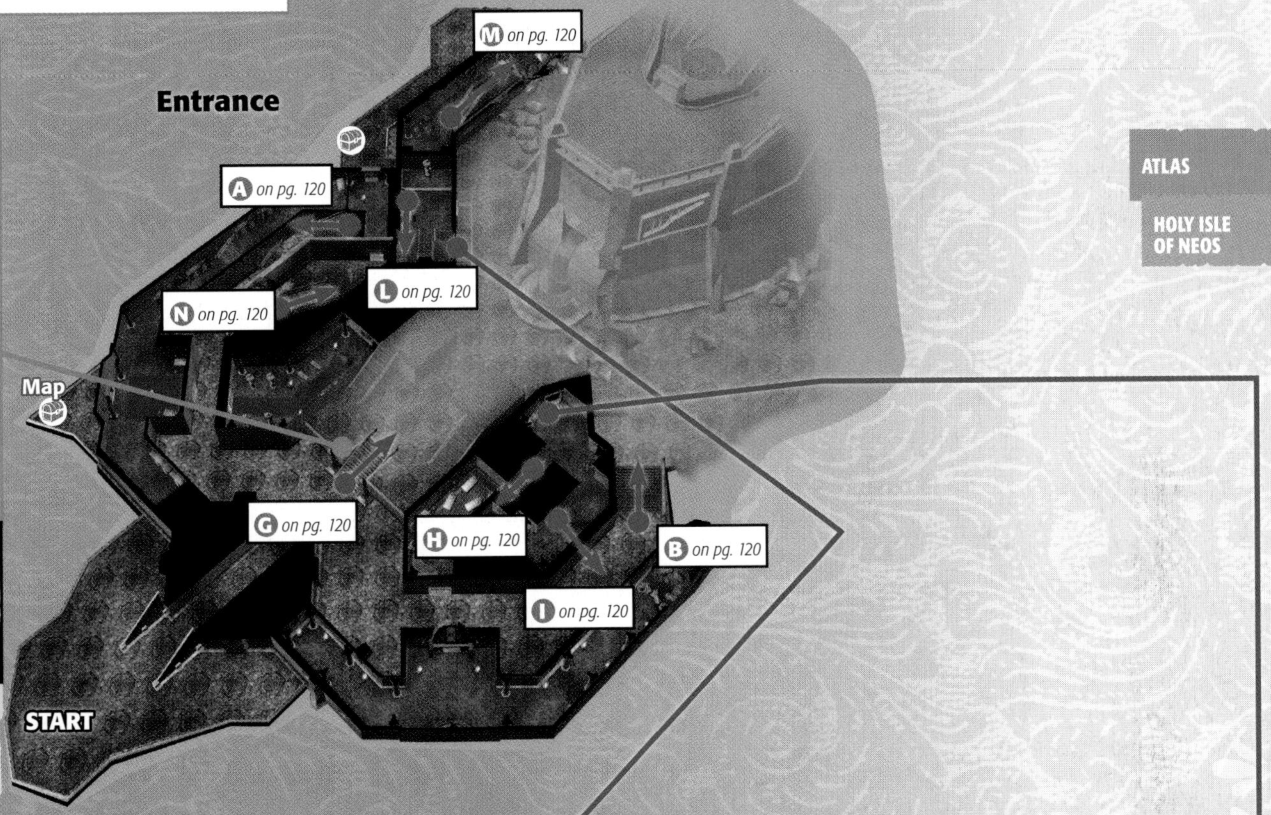

Entrance

M on pg. 120

A on pg. 120

N on pg. 120

Map

L on pg. 120

G on pg. 120

H on pg. 120

B on pg. 120

I on pg. 120

START

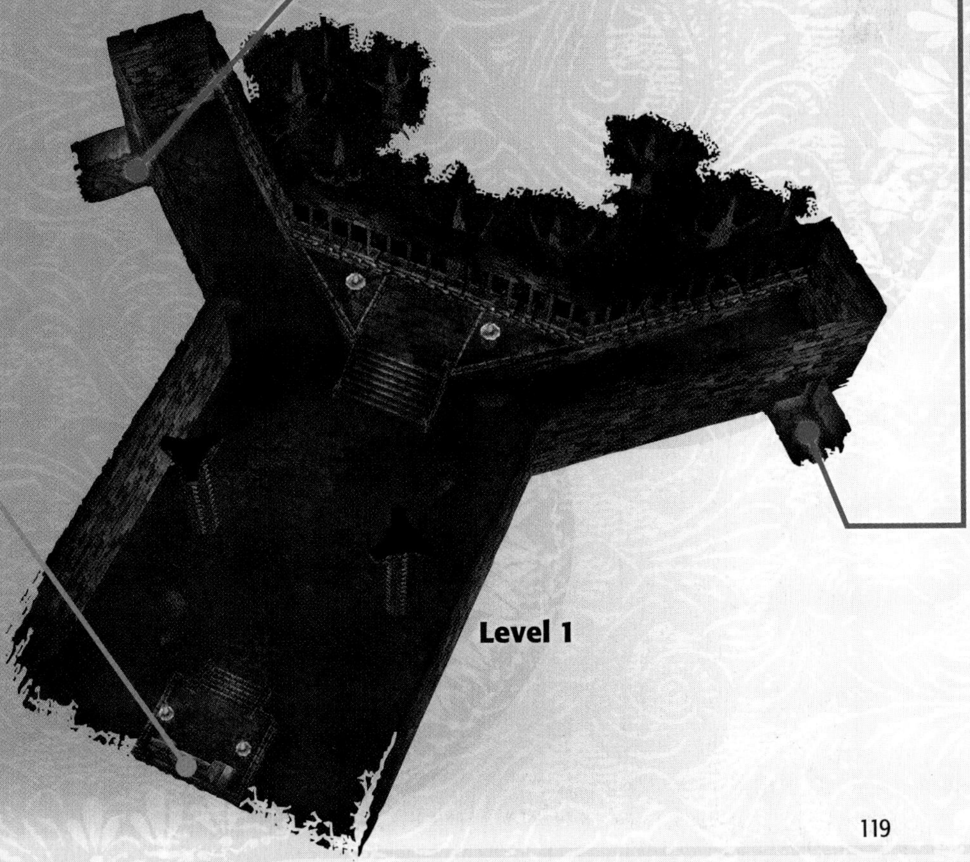

MYSTERIOUS MESSAGE

Examine the frightening plaque at the bottom of the room. Although the meaning of the inscription may seem vague, keep it in mind while navigating the confusing lower levels of the Black Citadel.

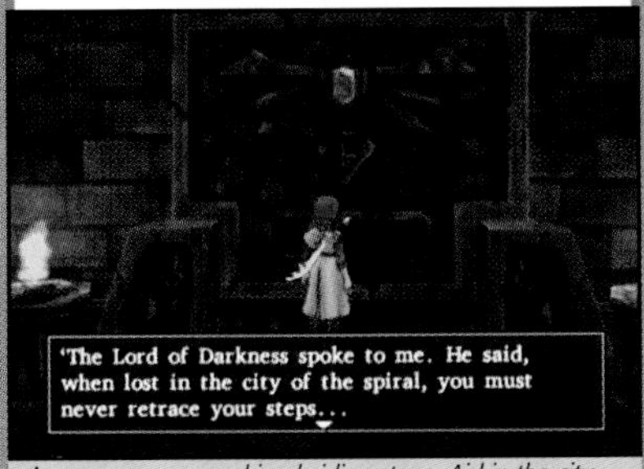

'The Lord of Darkness spoke to me. He said, when lost in the city of the spiral, you must never retrace your steps...

A message engraved in obsidian stone. Aid in the city of evil?

Level 1

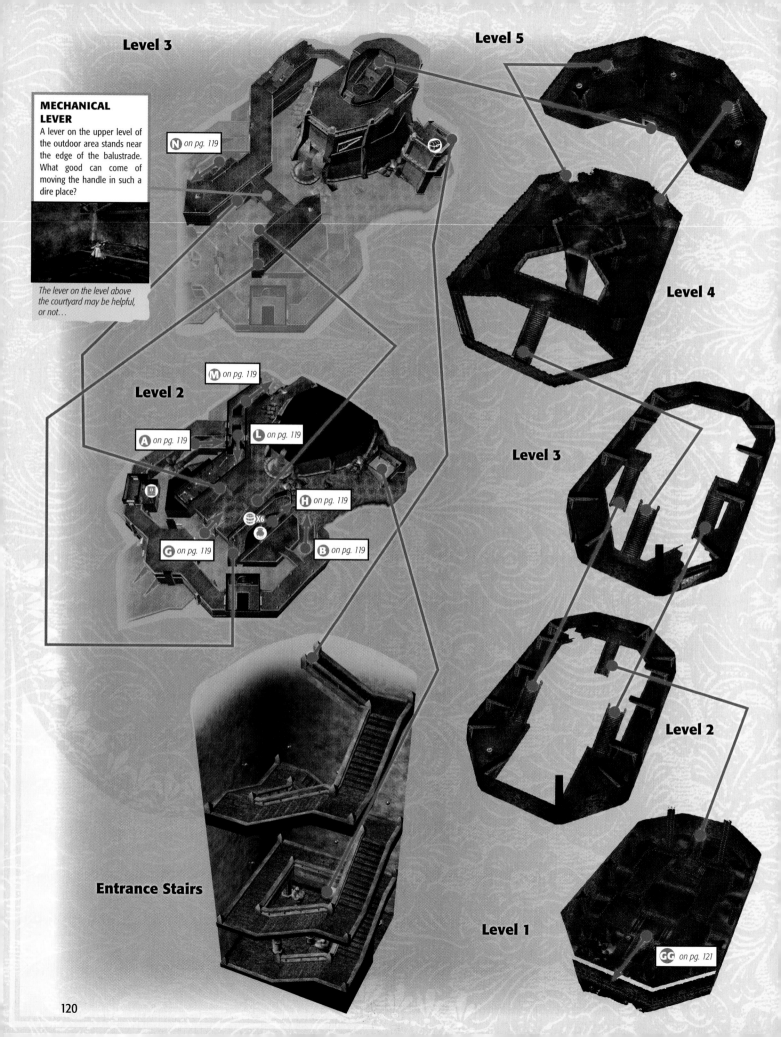

Level 3

Level 5

MECHANICAL LEVER

A lever on the upper level of the outdoor area stands near the edge of the balustrade. What good can come of moving the handle in such a dire place?

The lever on the level above the courtyard may be helpful, or not…

N *on pg. 119*

Level 4

M *on pg. 119*

Level 2

A *on pg. 119*

L *on pg. 119*

Level 3

H *on pg. 119*

X6

G *on pg. 119*

B *on pg. 119*

Level 2

Entrance Stairs

Level 1

GG *on pg. 121*

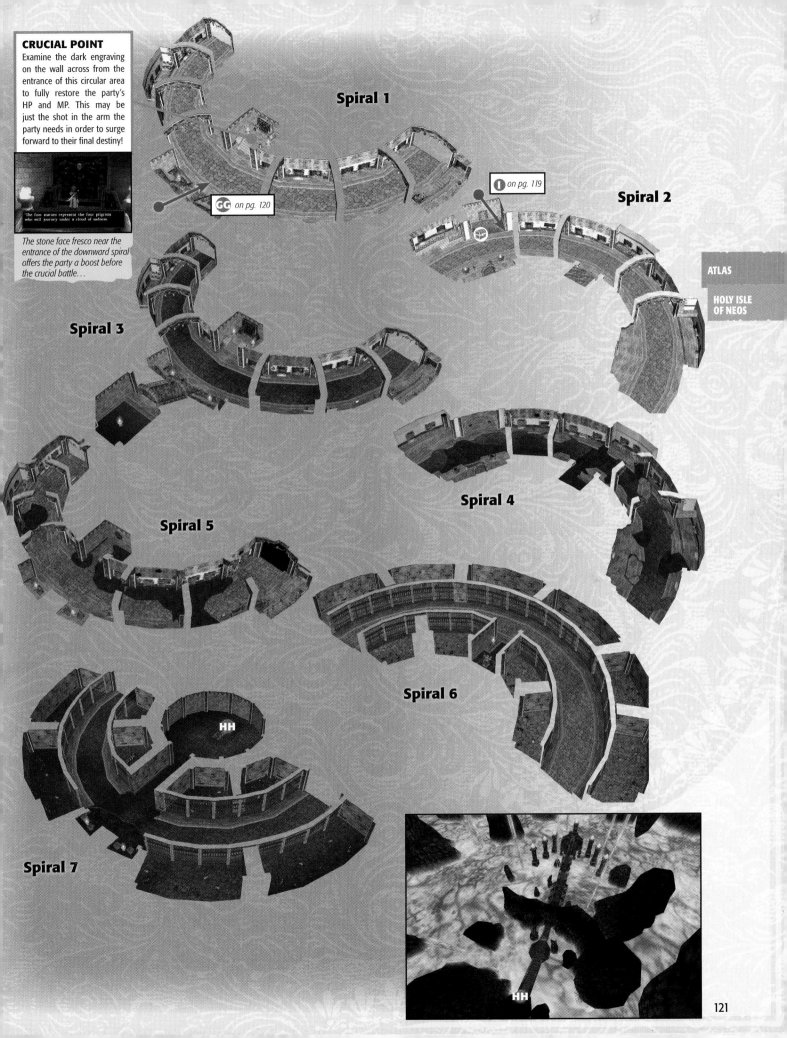

CRUCIAL POINT

Examine the dark engraving on the wall across from the entrance of this circular area to fully restore the party's HP and MP. This may be just the shot in the arm the party needs in order to surge forward to their final destiny!

'The four statues represent the four pilgrims who will journey under a cloud of sadness.'

The stone face fresco near the entrance of the downward spiral offers the party a boost before the crucial battle…

Spiral 1

GG on pg. 120

I on pg. 119

Spiral 2

ATLAS

HOLY ISLE OF NEOS

Spiral 3

Spiral 4

Spiral 5

Spiral 6

HH

Spiral 7

HH

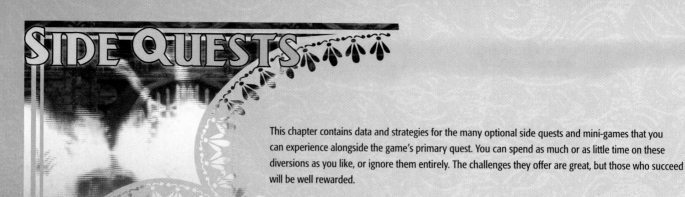

SIDE QUESTS

This chapter contains data and strategies for the many optional side quests and mini-games that you can experience alongside the game's primary quest. You can spend as much or as little time on these diversions as you like, or ignore them entirely. The challenges they offer are great, but those who succeed will be well rewarded.

MINI MEDAL COLLECTING

WHAT ARE MINI MEDALS?

There are small medals hidden throughout the game that can be found inside cabinets, treasure chests, and barrels. You can't use or sell them, but they do have a value on the tiny island kingdom that is home to Princess Minnie.

Princess of Medals
Permit one to bestow upon you a pair of fishnet stockings, as an expression of our gratitude for the 28 mini medals you have collected on our behalf.

The more medals you deliver to Princess Minnie, the more rewards you can earn. You cannot purchase or find most of her rewards anywhere else, and many of them are quite powerful. Keep your eyes peeled for medals and return to her frequently!

MINI MEDAL CHECKLIST

The following section contains a brief listing of the number of medals in their corresponding areas. Note that, in some cases, you will need to acquire an item first.

# OF MEDALS	AREA	# OF MEDALS	AREA
1	FAREBURY	1	ROYAL HUNTING GROUND
1	PEREGRIN QUAY	2	DARK RUINS
3	MAELLA ABBEY	1	DRAGON GRAVEYARD
1	SIMPLETON	8	ARCADIA
2	RUINED ABBEY	2	MARTA'S COTTAGE
3	ASCANTHA CASTLE	4	ORKUTSK
6	PICKHAM	3	HERB GROTTO
3	RED'S DEN	4	PIRATE'S COVE
3	SWORDSMAN'S LABYRINTH	3	EMPYCCHU
1	HILLTOP HUT	4	DARK EMPYCCHU
5	TRODAIN CASTLE	2	GODBIRD'S EYRIE
1	MOLE HOLE	2	TRYAN GULLY
2	PRINCESS MINNIE'S CASTLE	2	LORD HIGH PRIEST'S RESIDENCE
1	SAVELLA CATHEDRAL	8	UNKNOWN...
1	SEAVIEW CHURCH	1	TROLLS' MAZE
6	BACCARAT	15	FIELD
1	SEER'S RETREAT	1	WORLD OF DARKNESS
8	ARGONIA	1	LE CLUB PUFF-PUFF
1	ROYAL HUNTING GROUND: HOUSE		

HUNTING FOR MEDALS

The medals are hidden in towns, dungeons, the field, and even homes and inns. With one exception, they are always inside a cabinet, a pot, a barrel, a hanging bag, or a treasure chest. There are 115 medals in all, but you only need to find 110 to get the final reward. Most of them are hidden in the towns, but nearly every major area has at least one. Use Yangus's Nose for Treasure (a skill learned when you assign 16 skill points to his Humanity skill set) to make finding them a little easier.

 28 Medals
Fishnet stockings (accessory); defence: 8; equipped by Jessica

 36 Medals
Posh waistcoat (armour); defence: 48; equipped by Angelo

 45 Medals
Staff of divine wrath (staff); attack: 35, cast Swoosh when used in combat; equipped by Jessica, Angelo

 52 Medals
Gold nugget (item); used in alchemy

 60 Medals
Meteorite bracer (accessory); agility: +50; equipped by Hero, Yangus, Jessica, Angelo

 68 Medals
Miracle sword (sword); attack: 80, restores user's HP; equipped by Hero, Jessica

 75 Medals
Sacred armour (armour); defence: 84, regenerates wearer's HP; equipped by Hero, Angelo

 83 Medals
Orichalcum (item); used in alchemy

 90 Medals
Metal king helm (helmet); defence: 55, increases resistance to status effect spells; equipped by Hero, Yangus, Jessica, Angelo

 99 Medals
Dangerous bustier; (armour); defence: 1, changes Jessica's appearance; equipped by Jessica

110 Medals
Flail of destruction (weapon); attack: 125, hits all enemies; equipped by Yangus

CASINO GAMES

You can play at a casino in Pickham as soon as you reach it. Stakes are low here, so it will take perseverance to win tokens to redeem for prizes. You can earn—or lose—tokens much more quickly at the high-stakes games in Baccarat, but that casino doesn't open until much later in the game.

Instead of gold coins, you gamble with tokens that can be purchased at either casino for 20 gold coins apiece. Win enough tokens and you can redeem them for prizes, which differ in each casino. You cannot sell the tokens back for gold. Later in the game, you can also earn tokens by completing a side quest in Baccarat.

PICKHAM CASINO

You can play at this casino at any time after you reach Pickham. It offers only one-token slot machines and a bingo counter, so the stakes are quite low. You must spend a lot of time at the slots—or get lucky at bingo—to earn enough tokens to claim this casino's top prizes.

BACCARAT

This casino has higher stakes and offers better prizes. However, you must first resolve the matter of Golding's estate for it to reopen, which isn't something you can do on your first visit to Baccarat. Once it reopens, you can earn money quickly by playing roulette or the 100-token slot machine.

The prizes for redemption in Pickham are:

100 Tokens
Magic water (item); restores 30 or more MP to ally

500 Tokens
Silver platter (shield); defence: 8; equipped by Jessica

1000 Tokens
Agility ring (accessory); agility: 15; equipped by Hero, Yangus, Jessica, Angelo

1500 Tokens
Titan belt (accessory); attack: 10; equipped by Hero, Yangus, Jessica, Angelo

3000 Tokens
Rune staff (staff); defence: 30, casts Kabuff when used; equipped by Jessica, Angelo

5000 Tokens
Platinum headgear (helmet); defence: 30; equipped by Hero, Angelo

---

The prizes for redemption in Baccarat are:

1000 Tokens
Prayer ring (accessory); defence: 5, restores MP when used; equipped by Hero, Yangus, Jessica, Angelo

3000 Tokens
Spangled dress (armour); defence: 46; equipped by Jessica

5000 Tokens
Saint's ashes (item); used in alchemy

10000 Tokens
Falcon blade (sword); attack: 37; attacks twice; equipped by Hero, Jessica*, Angelo

50000 Tokens
Liquid metal armour (armour); defence: 101, reduces spell damage; equipped by Hero, Yangus, Jessica, Angelo

200000 Tokens
Gringham whip (weapon); attack: 127, hits all enemies; equipped by Jessica

SLOT MACHINES

The slots in Pickham are single token machines only, while Baccarat hosts 10-token machines and even a 100-token machine! If you have enough tokens, you can make up to five bets per pull on any machine, allowing for three-of-a-kinds

on each of the three horizontal pay lines and two diagonal ones. You can continuously play the slots, betting all five lines each time, by pressing up on the directional button or the left analog stick repeatedly. This simple control scheme allows hardcore gamblers to keep the slots rolling while they focus their attention on other things.

All slot machines are not created equal. While their reels stop at random positions, the assortment of icons on their reels can encourage occasional large payoffs or frequent small ones. You will win less often on the long-shot machines, but the payoffs for winning will make up for it.

The Best Slots in Pickham

There are eight slot machines in Pickham, although some other person will be using the third machine from the left most of the time. He's welcome to it, as it has the worst odds of the bunch! But all the machines have the odds tilted in your favor by varying degrees. The fourth machine (starting from the left) is the best performer, offering nearly a 90% profit on your investment! Machines 5 through 7 are all quite profitable as well, around the 70% range.

Keep in mind, though, that these returns are over the *long term* and factor in the odds of scoring a 777 jackpot. Machine 4 offers the best chance of scoring a 777, and even then, the odds are 1:1543. If your goal is to slowly and safely build your stake, use machine 6 (starting from the left), which will return around 30 tokens gained for every 100 spent even when the odds of the top three jackpots are stripped out of the equation.

The Best Slots in Baccarat

Among the one-token slots on the left side of the room, the third machine offers fantastic odds, but they're heavily dependent on the 1:578 chance of scoring a 500x payoff. If you don't have a lot of tokens to play the slots, you'll get more reliable odds and a nice rate of return from machine 4. The 10-token slots on the right all offer roughly the same rate of return.

The 100-token slot in Baccarat is the ultimate long-shot machine. Its reels have seven sevens instead of the usual three or four. This means your odds of scoring a 1000:1 jackpot are approximately 1:772. That's an average return of nearly 30% on your investment before you add in the payoffs from all the other rows! When totaled, they add up to an average return of over 2 tokens for every one you put in. Of course, these are long-term gains and you'll need to spend a lot of money to exploit them. If you can only afford a few pulls, you're unlikely to get the 777 you need to come out ahead.

BINGO

Bingo is the highest-stakes game in Pickham, as you can wager 100 tokens per game. (In Baccarat, the limits are raised to 300.) The point of the bingo game is to score a bingo in any direction within 10 turns (the middle square is free). The sooner you do so, the higher the payoff! You have no control of the action once you make a wager, so just sit back and see what numbers the cureslime pulls!

Bingo doesn't offer great odds, but the potential payoffs can be huge early in the game. You may want to consider playing this game at the end of every play session; save your game, go and enter the maximum bet. If you don't come out ahead, you don't need to save your progress.

BINGO PAYOFF CHART

TURN	PAYOFF	ODDS
4th	400x	.0004%
5th	200x	.02%
6th	100x	.07%
7th	50x	2%
8th	25x	4%
9th	10x	7%
10th	5x	12%

ROULETTE

The roulette table is for the real gamblers. You can lose a fortune in a flash, or earn a huge payoff. The maximum bet is 500 tokens and you can make as many bets as you want. The roulette table consists of 28 numbers. You can bet on any single number, split your bet between two or four adjacent numbers, bet on a column of three or two adjacent columns of six, or bet on a row or square of nine numbers. You can also make a bet on odd, even, red, or blue.

But it all works out to the same odds, right? Usually that's true, but the Baccarat table has several quirks that alter the usual odds. Observant players can exploit these quirks to give themselves an edge.

Zero (0) is neither even nor odd, nor blue or red. That leaves 27 numbers, 14 of which are odd, and only 13 of which are even. Fourteen of them are red and 13 are blue. So odd and red actually offer fair odds, while even and blue are sucker bets.

There are a lot of betting options but the payoffs are inconsistent. Any single number is a fair bet, with a 1:28 chance of success and a 28:1 payoff. A split bet (two adjacent

numbers with a chip between them) will double your odds and halve the payoff, which is what you'd expect. But if you bet a street (a column of three; place the token at the bottom of the column), you end up with 1:9.33 odds and only a 8:1 payoff. Those are the worst odds on the table!

While a single column offers an 8:1 payoff, a pair of adjacent columns (six numbers; place the token at the bottom between two columns) has a success rate of 1:4.67 with a 5:1 payoff,

so the payoff significantly beats the odds! A "double street" is by far the best bet on the table, and in the long run you'll earn 107 tokens for every 100 bet. Betting four double streets is a reasonably safe way to make long-term profits.

ODDS CHART

BET	PAYOFF	AVERAGE RETURN
Inside (1 number)	28:1	100%
Split (2 adjacent numbers)	14:1	100%
Street (3 numbers in column)	8:1	86%
Quad (4 numbers in square)	7:1	100%
Double Street (6 numbers in two adjacent columns)	5:1	107%
Triple Street (9 numbers in block of three columns)	3:1	96%
Row (9 numbers in horizontal line)	3:1	96%
Evens (13 numbers)	2:1	93%
Odds (14 numbers)	2:1	100%
Blue (13 numbers)	2:1	93%
Red (14 numbers)	2:1	100%

DODGY DAVE'S BLACK MARKET

After completing the chain of events that begin in Pickham and end at Red's Den, you can return to Dodgy Dave in his hidden shop behind Pickham's smaller pub. He'll ask you to make custom items for him with the alchemy pot, and he'll pay generously for them. For certain items, he'll trade some of his rare items.

Dodgy Dave doesn't reveal the recipes, just the name of the item. You must determine the recipes, or find them in a book. After giving Dodgy Dave everything he asks for, he starts over from the beginning, asking for the special medicine again. You can continue to fulfill his orders for gold, but you'll only get items in trade the first time.

DODGY DAVE'S REQUESTS

ITEM	REWARD
Special medicine	500 gold
Reinforced boomerang	1200 gold
Ring of immunity	Bandit axe
Robe of serenity	6000 gold
Sandstorm spear	Happy hat
Crimson robe	Big boss shield

Rewards from Dodgy Dave include:

Bandit axe (weapon)
Attack: 55; equipped by Yangus

Happy hat (helmet)
Defence: 31, recovers MP as you walk; equipped by Jessica, Angelo

Big boss shield (shield)
Defence: 50, casts Kasap when used; equipped by Yangus

TIPS, TRICKS, AND EASTER EGGS

The following section contains some really useful advice on strategies and some cool extras that make this game even more enjoyable. It even reveals some hidden Easter Eggs!

STEALING STUFF

Stealing items from enemies with Yangus's Steal Sickle or Stainless Steal Sickle ability requires a great deal of persistence. Fortunately, there are a few tricks to use to improve your chances of success.

Your success rate is roughly doubled when an enemy is put to sleep or paralysed. If you're determined to steal something, have Jessica cast Snooze or Kasnooze repeatedly on the target while Yangus uses Stainless Steal Sickle. (Jessica's Whiplash and Angelo's Angel Eyes are also effective.) Even if the target is already asleep or paralysed, using the spell or ability on a regular basis will lengthen the duration of the effect.

The biggest problem with Stainless Steal Sickle is that it often kills its target. To prevent this from occurring, equip the skull helm. This cursed item reduces its wearer's attack score to 0, so Yangus will do no more than 1 point of damage each time you try to steal!

Even when an enemy is sound asleep, you'll often have about a 1 in 100 chance of success. Try this to improve the odds: eliminate all the other monsters; keep your target asleep or paralysed; and have your other party members repeatedly defend. Then have Yangus (with a skull helm equipped) use the Stainless Steal Sickle repeatedly until it succeeds.

DEFEATING METAL MONSTERS

You'll encounter metallic members of the slime family throughout the game. They typically flee right away, but if you can manage to defeat one before it gets away, you will receive a ton of experience points.

When you acquire the Godbird's soulstone, fly to Howlwind Hill (just north of Rydon's Tower) to find legions of metal monsters. This is the ideal place to rack up experience once you master the small handful of skills that are effective against the creatures. Most attacks, spells and abilities cause 0 or 1 point of damage to metal monsters, regardless of the user's attack strength!

- *The best attacks are the Hero's Thunder Thrust and Lightning Thrust spear skills and Yangus's Hatchet Man and Executioner axe skills. Since critical hits deal damage regardless of the target's defence, these abilities can do several hundred points of damage, effectively killing any metal creature instantly.*

- *Another option is the Metal Slash sword skill learned by the Hero and Angelo, which can deal 1-2 points of damage. Pair this skill with a falcon blade or über falcon blade to possibly double the amount of damage.*

- *The liquid metal sword inflicts a flat 2 points of damage to any metal creature, but only on a regular attack. The damage is not doubled by the Falcon Slash skill.*

- *Characters who lack these skills should use attacks or weapons that strike twice. Since every hit has a chance of causing 1 point of damage, the more hits the better. Multishot, Multithrust and Multifists can be effective, as can Jessica's Twin Dragon Lash or Angelo's and the Hero's Falcon Slash. Also, the two-hit falcon knife, falcon blade, über falcon blade, and über double-edge are effective.*

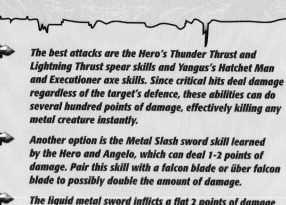

1350 Exp!

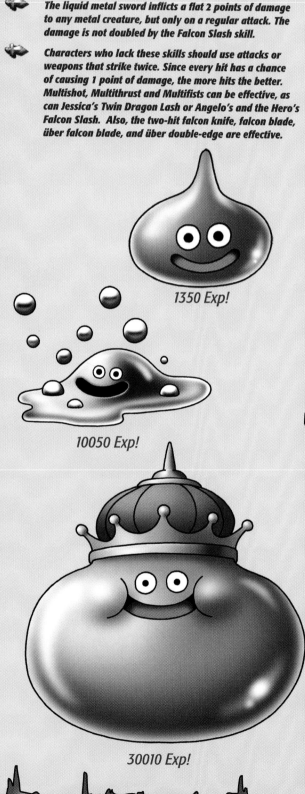

10050 Exp!

30010 Exp!

A Second Use for Baumren's Bell

After everything you went through to get Baumren's bell, it seems a pity to kill the sabrecats you encounter in combat. Fortunately, you don't have to! Whenever you encounter a sabrecat, ring Baumren's bell (keep it in a character's inventory) and they'll flee the battle.

Tricking the Yggdrasil Leaf Shop

The Yggdrasil leaf shop at the Argonia bazaar has a strict one-per-customer policy, and the shopkeeper refuses to sell leaves to anyone who has one in his or her inventory. It isn't clear how exactly she knows this fact, but her sensory powers can't seem to penetrate the metal of the alchemy pot.

To buy a second Yggdrasil leaf, drop the first one into your alchemy pot with a bottle of magic water or a set of red and waterweed moulds. Both are viable recipes, and you can buy a second leaf while the pot is working. Afterward, return to the pot and cancel the recipe to return the first leaf to your inventory.

The Secrets of Savella's Birds

You probably know that talking to a cow will get you a bottle of fresh milk, but did you know that certain birds have items as well? Two birds in the Savella Area carry items, and both are quite precious: a **seed of magic** and a **seed of life**! You'll find these tiny tweeters on the paths that lead away from the cathedral area.

COMBAT SPELLS

Characters usually learn new spells simply by gaining levels, although some are learned from spending skill points on certain skill sets (particularly Staves and each character's special skill set). A small handful of skills are learned from in-game story events.

The main stat that affects combat spells is wisdom. The higher the caster's wisdom value, the more damage the spell will cause (building tension also increases damage in most cases). With spells that apply a status effect, like sleep or paralysis, the caster's level largely determines whether the spell hits or misses. Spells that lower enemy stats or boost your characters' stats typically have fixed effects and rarely miss, although the targets may be immune to their effects.

Acceleratle

DESCRIPTION: Raises the agility of all party members.

NOTES: Raises each ally's agility by an amount equal to their base agility score. The effect lasts until the end of the battle.

TARGET: All allies

MP COST: 3

TENSION BOOST: Yes

Jessica learns at 3 Staves skill points

Yangus's agility increases by 80!

Jessica's agility increases by 110!

Bang

DESCRIPTION: Damages all enemies with a small explosion.

NOTES: Typically deals 16-24 points of damage but can cause up to 44 points of damage based on caster's wisdom.

TARGET: All enemies

MP COST: 5

TENSION BOOST: Yes

Jessica learns at level 14

Jessica casts Bang!

Inflicts an average of 40 points of damage on the enemies.

Ban Dance

DESCRIPTION: Stop one group of enemies from dancing for several turns.

NOTES: Prevents dancing attacks (like Underpants Dance) from being used for 6-9 turns. Has no effect against most foes.

TARGET: Enemy group

MP COST: 4

TENSION BOOST: No

Angelo learns at 39 Charisma skill points

Angelo casts Ban Dance!

The hipster's dance is interrupted!

Boom

DESCRIPTION: Engulfs all enemies in a large explosion.

NOTES: Typically deals 42-54 points of damage but can cause up to 102 points of damage based on caster's wisdom.

TARGET: All enemies

MP COST: 8

TENSION BOOST: Yes

Jessica learns at level 23

Jessica casts Boom!

Jessica casts Boom!

KABOOM

DESCRIPTION: Blasts all enemies with an incredibly violent explosion.

NOTES: Typically deals 104-120 points of damage but can inflict up to 200 points of damage based on caster's wisdom.

TARGET: All enemies

MP COST: 15

TENSION BOOST: Yes

 Jessica learns at level 33

Jessica casts Kaboom!

Jessica casts Kaboom!

KABUFF

DESCRIPTION: Raises the defence of all party members.

NOTES: Raises the defence of each ally by 25% of his or her base defence score each time it is cast. The effect lasts for 7-10 turns.

TARGET: All Allies

MP COST: 3

TENSION BOOST: Yes

 Yangus learns at 42 Humanity skill points

Yangus casts Kabuff!

Jessica's defence increases by 13!

Angelo learns at level 14

BOUNCE

DESCRIPTION: Forms a protective barrier that reflects the enemy's and party's spells alike.

NOTES: The barrier surrounds the caster for 6-9 turns and reflects spells cast by allies and enemies alike.

TARGET: Caster only

MP COST: 4

TENSION BOOST: No

 Jessica learns at 21 Staves skill points

Angelo casts Bounce!

 Angelo learns at 9 Staves skill points

A shining wall of light appears before Angelo!

CRACK

DESCRIPTION: Pierces a single enemy with razor-sharp icicles.

NOTES: Typically deals 20-28 points of damage but can deal up to 52 points of damage based on caster's wisdom.

TARGET: One enemy

MP COST: 3

TENSION BOOST: Yes

 Jessica learns at level 10

Jessica casts Crack!

Does 36 points of damage to orc B. Orc B is defeated.

BUFF

DESCRIPTION: Raises the defence of a single party member.

NOTES: Raises the defence of one ally by 50% of his or her base defence score. The effect lasts for 7-10 turns.

TARGET: One ally

MP COST: 2

TENSION BOOST: Yes

 Angelo knows from beginning

Angelo casts Buff!

HERO's defence increases by 118!

CRACKLE

DESCRIPTION: Rips into a group of enemies with sharp icicles.

NOTES: Typically deals 34-46 points of damage but can cause up to 86 points of damage based on caster's wisdom.

TARGET: Enemy group

MP COST: 5

TENSION BOOST: Yes

Jessica learns at level 16

Jessica casts Crackle!

Jessica casts Crackle!

WHACK

DESCRIPTION: A cursed incantation that sends an enemy to the hereafter.

NOTES: Odds of success (an instant kill) are based on caster's level and target's level of resistance.

TARGET: One Enemy

MP COST: 4

TENSION BOOST: No

Notso macho B is killed!

Notso macho B is killed!

Angelo learns at level 17

WOOSH

DESCRIPTION: Slices through a group of enemies with a small whirlwind.

NOTES: Typically deals 6-19 points of damage but can cause up to 32 points of damage based on caster's wisdom.

TARGET: Enemy group

MP COST: 2

TENSION BOOST: Yes

Angelo casts Woosh!

Inflicts an average of 22 points of damage on the orcs.

Angelo knows from beginning

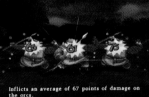

THWACK

DESCRIPTION: A cursed incantation that sends a group of enemies to the hereafter.

NOTES: Odds of success (an instant kill) are based on caster's level and targets' level of resistance.

TARGET: Enemy group

MP COST: 7

TENSION BOOST: No

Notso macho B is killed!

Notso macho B is killed!

Angelo learns at level 22

SWOOSH

DESCRIPTION: Slices through a group of enemies with a powerful whirlwind.

NOTES: Typically deals 20-44 points of damage but can inflict up to 76 points of damage based on caster's wisdom.

TARGET: Enemy group

MP COST: 4

TENSION BOOST: Yes

Angelo casts Swoosh!

Inflicts an average of 67 points of damage on the orcs. The orcs are defeated.

Angelo learns at level 18

KATHWACK

DESCRIPTION: A cursed incantation that sends all enemies to the hereafter.

NOTES: Odds of success (an instant kill) are based on caster's level and targets' level of resistance.

TARGET: All Enemies

MP COST: 15

TENSION BOOST: No

Notso macho B is killed!

Notso macho C is killed!

Angelo learns at 56 Staves skill points

KASWOOSH

DESCRIPTION: Slices through a group of enemies with a ferociously destructive whirlwind.

NOTES: Typically deals 64-144 points of damage but can cause up to 200 points of damage based on caster's wisdom.

TARGET: Enemy group

MP COST: 8

TENSION BOOST: Yes

Angelo casts Kaswoosh!

Angelo casts Kaswoosh!

Angelo learns at level 32

ZAP

DESCRIPTION: Calls down lightning on all enemies.

NOTES: Typically deals 40-56 points of damage but can cause up to 88 points of damage based on caster's wisdom.

TARGET: All enemies

MP COST: 6

TENSION BOOST: Yes

 Hero learns at 48 Courage skill points

HERO casts Zap!

HERO casts Zap!

KAZAP

DESCRIPTION: Calls down powerful thunderbolts on a group of enemies.

NOTES: Typically deals 100-140 points of damage but can inflict up to 220 points of damage based on caster's wisdom.

TARGET: Enemy group

MP COST: 15

TENSION BOOST: Yes

 Hero learns at 100 Courage skill points

HERO casts Kazap!

HERO casts Kazap!

RECOVERY SPELLS

KERPLUNK

DESCRIPTION: Sacrifice your own life to resurrect all other party members.

NOTES: Kills Yangus and reduces his MP to 0, but restores all fallen allies to life with full HP and fully heals all other allies.

TARGET: All allies

MP COST: All remaining MP (requires min 1 MP)

TENSION BOOST: No

 Yangus learns at 82 Humanity points

Yangus casts Kerplunk!

Jessica returns to life!

HEAL

DESCRIPTION: Restores at least 30 HP to a single ally.

NOTES: Restores 30-40 HP to one ally. Can be used on field or in combat.

TARGET: One ally

MP COST: 2

TENSION BOOST: Yes

Jessica recovers some HP!

Jessica recovers some HP!

 Hero learns at level 3

 Yangus learns at 10 Humanity skill points

 Angelo knows from beginning

MIDHEAL

DESCRIPTION: Restores at least 75 HP to a single ally.

NOTES: Restores 75-95 HP to one ally. Can be used on field or in combat.

TARGET: One ally

MP COST: 3

TENSION BOOST: Yes

Hero learns at level 18

Yangus learns at 68 Humanity skill points

Angelo learns at level 15

OMNIHEAL

DESCRIPTION: Restores all HP to all party members.

NOTES: Restores each ally to max HP. Can be used on field or in combat.

TARGET: All allies

MP COST: 36

TENSION BOOST: No

Hero learns at 82 Courage skill points

FULLHEAL

DESCRIPTION: Restores all HP to a single ally.

NOTES: Restores one ally to max HP. Can be used on field or in combat.

TARGET: One ally

MP COST: 6

TENSION BOOST: No

Hero learns at level 27

Angelo learns at level 24

SQUELCH

DESCRIPTION: Cures a single ally of the effects of poison.

NOTES: Can be used on field or in combat.

TARGET: One ally

MP COST: 2

TENSION BOOST: No

Hero learns at level 4

Angelo learns at 3 Charisma skill points

MULTIHEAL

DESCRIPTION: Restores at least 100 HP to all party members.

NOTES: Restores 100-120 HP to each ally. Can be used on field or in combat.

TARGET: All allies

MP COST: 10

TENSION BOOST: Yes

Angelo learns at level 30

TINGLE

DESCRIPTION: Cures all party members of the effects of sleep and paralysis.

NOTES: Can only be used in combat.

TARGET: All allies

MP COST: 2

TENSION BOOST: No

Hero learns at 16 Courage skill points

Angelo learns at level 13

ZING

DESCRIPTION: Resurrects a fallen ally with a 50% success rate.

NOTES: If successful, the fallen ally will be returned to life with half of his or her max HP. Can be used on field or in combat.

TARGET: One ally

MP COST: 8

TENSION BOOST: No

Hero learns at level 29

Angelo learns at level 19

KAZING

DESCRIPTION: Resurrects a fallen ally.

NOTES: The fallen ally returns to life with full HP. Can be used on field or in combat.

TARGET: One ally

MP COST: 15

TENSION BOOST: No

Jessica learns at 100 Staves skill points

Angelo learns at level 34

FIELD SPELLS

EVAC

DESCRIPTION: Allows you to exit instantly from dungeons, caves, and towers.

NOTES: Returns you to entrance of area. No effect if used in field or town areas.

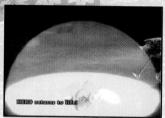

TARGET: All allies

MP COST: 2

TENSION BOOST: N/A

Hero learns at level 6

Jessica learns at level 11

HOLY PROTECTION

DESCRIPTION: Generates a holy aura that causes weaker monsters to avoid your party.

NOTES: You will not be attacked by enemies that are at a lower level than the Hero. Can be used in both field and dungeon areas.

TARGET: All allies

MP COST: 4

TENSION BOOST: N/A

Hero learns at 28 Courage skill points

NOSE FOR TREASURE

DESCRIPTION: Instantly reports the number of nearby treasures.

NOTES: N/A

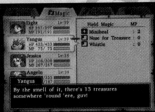

TARGET: N/A

MP COST: 0

TENSION BOOST: N/A

Yangus learns at 16 Humanity skill points

WHISTLE

DESCRIPTION: Summons monsters with a whistle.

NOTES: If used in an area with active monsters, a random encounter will begin immediately.

TARGET: N/A

MP COST: 0

TENSION BOOST: N/A

Yangus learns at 4 Humanity skill points

SPELLS

FIELD

PADFOOT

DESCRIPTION: A secret technique for disguising your presence so as to avoid monsters.

NOTES: Reduces the chance of monster encounters. Lasts longer than Holy Protection, but is less effective.

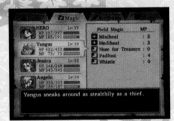

TARGET: N/A

MP COST: 4

TENSION BOOST: N/A

Yangus learns at 33 Fisticuffs skill points

ZOOM

DESCRIPTION: Allows you to return instantly to certain places you have visited before.

NOTES: Not effective if used in a roofed area (try it and see why!).

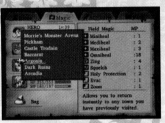

TARGET: All allies

MP COST: 1

TENSION BOOST: N/A

Hero learns at 8 Courage skill points

Angelo knows from the beginning

ABILITIES

Characters learn abilities when they assign a set number of skill points to one of their five skill sets. Each character has three weapon skills, the fisticuffs skill, and a fifth special skill available only to that character. A character can only use a weapon ability while he or she has a weapon of that type equipped. Additionally, fisticuffs abilities can only be used while the character is unarmed. Special abilities can be used regardless of a character's equipment.

Abilities increase a character's combat potential by enabling them to hit multiple times, inflict more damage, execute attacks with special effects, or hit a wider group of targets. The MP cost to use abilities is usually quite low, and some are free! But keep in mind that it is not possible to score critical hits while using most abilities; that's a special property of the standard attack option only.

AXE ABILITIES

HELM SPLITTER

DESCRIPTION
A skull-splitting smash that lowers an opponent's defence as it inflicts damage.

NOTES
Deals normal damage and reduces an enemy's defence by half of its base defence score for 7-10 turns (same as Sap spell).

Yangus uses Helm Splitter!

Does 91 points of damage to the heligator.

Axe skill: **6**
Target: **One enemy**
MP Cost: **0**
Tension Boost: **Yes**

PARALLAX

DESCRIPTION
A focused strike capable of occasionally paralysing an enemy.

NOTES
Deals 50% more damage than a standard attack and occasionally paralyses an enemy for 5-8 turns.

Yangus uses Parallax!

Yangus uses Parallax!

Axe skill: **42**
Target: **One enemy**
MP Cost: **2**
Tension Boost: **Yes**

HATCHET MAN

DESCRIPTION
An unpredictable attack that can slay an enemy with a single blow… if it connects.

NOTES
This attack misses around 50% of the time, but usually scores a critical hit when successful. Very effective against metal enemies.

Yangus hacks away like a demon!

Yangus hacks away like a demon! Critical hit!

Axe skill: **19**
Target: **One enemy**
MP Cost: **3**
Tension Boost: **Yes**

AXES OF EVIL

DESCRIPTION
Generates a vortex from your axe blade that chews into a group of enemies.

NOTES
Hits all enemies in a group from left to right. The first hit is slightly weaker than a normal attack and the damage lessens as the attack moves through the group.

Yangus uses Axes of Evil!

Yangus uses Axes of Evil!

Axe skill: **54**
Target: **Enemy group**
MP Cost: **0**
Tension Boost: **Yes**

EXECUTIONER

Yangus swings the axe with all his might!

Yangus swings the axe with all his might! Critical hit!

AXE

DESCRIPTION:
A powerful roundhouse strike that fells an opponent in one blow if it hits.

NOTES:
Replaces Hatchet Man. This attack misses around 50% of the time, but always scores a critical hit when successful. Very effective against metal enemies.

Axe skill: 66
Target: One enemy
MP Cost: 3
Tension Boost: No

POWER THROW

HERO uses Power Throw!

Inflicts an average of 155 points of damage on the enemies. The enemies are defeated.

BOOMERANG

DESCRIPTION:
A full-force throw that damages all enemies equally.

NOTES:
Does slightly less damage than a normal attack. Unlike normal boomerang attacks, the damage dealt by the boomerang does not lessen on each subsequent hit.

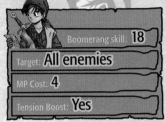

Boomerang skill: 18
Target: All enemies
MP Cost: 4
Tension Boost: Yes

TYPHOEUS' MAUL

Yangus uses Typhoeus' Maul

Yangus uses Typhoeus' Maul

AXE

DESCRIPTION:
An ancient axe technique that works wonders on monsters of the beast family.

NOTES:
Against most enemies, this causes 50% more damage than a normal attack. Against beast enemies, it does double the damage of a normal attack.

Axe skill: 100
Target: One enemy
MP Cost: 6
Tension Boost: Yes

FIREBIRD THROW

HERO uses Firebird Throw!

Inflicts an average of 40 points of damage on the demonriders.

BOOMERANG

DESCRIPTION:
Transforms your boomerang into a firebird that incinerates your enemies.

NOTES:
Deals base fire damage of 36-44 points to all enemies. The damage does not lessen on each subsequent hit.

Boomerang skill: 32
Target: All enemies
MP Cost: 6
Tension Boost: Yes

BOOMERANG ABILITIES

CROSSCUTTER THROW

HERO uses Crosscutter Throw!

Inflicts an average of 39 points of damage on the enemies. Notto macho A is defeated.

BOOMERANG

DESCRIPTION:
Traces an X in the air as it ploughs into the enemy.

NOTES:
Like a normal boomerang attack, except that the boomerang returns to hit the first enemy again. This added hit deals lower damage.

Boomerang skill: 6
Target: All enemies
MP Cost: 2
Tension Boost: Yes

SUPER THROW

HERO uses Super Throw!

Inflicts an average of 93 points of damage on the enemies. The enemies are defeated.

BOOMERANG

DESCRIPTION:
A fearsome attack that uses all your strength to cause extreme damage to all foes.

NOTES:
Replaces Power Throw. This does slightly more damage than a normal attack and the damage does not lessen on each subsequent hit.

Boomerang skill: 52
Target: All enemies
MP Cost: 4
Tension Boost: Yes

STARBURST THROW

BOOMERANG

DESCRIPTION
Bathes all enemies in a shower of burning light.

NOTES
Deals base damage of 76-84 points to all enemies.

HERO uses Starburst Throw!

Boomerang skill: **82**
Target: **All enemies**
MP Cost: **8**
Tension Boost: **Yes**

CHERUB'S ARROW

BOW

DESCRIPTION
A secret bow technique that regenerates your own MP.

NOTES
Deals the same damage as a normal attack and regenerates user's MP by 1/16 of the damage dealt.

Angelo uses Cherub's Arrow!

Does 172 points of damage to demonrider A. Demonrider A is defeated.

Bow skill: **18**
Target: **One enemy**
MP Cost: **0**
Tension Boost: **Yes**

GIGATHROW

BOOMERANG

DESCRIPTION
Pulverises a single enemy with the force of a thunderbolt.

NOTES
Deals base damage of 145-177 points to a single target, and depending on the user's level, may deal up to 233-284 points of damage.

HERO uses Gigathrow!

HERO uses Gigathrow!

Boomerang skill: **100**
Target: **One enemy**
MP Cost: **15**
Tension Boost: **Yes**

NEEDLE SHOT

BOW

DESCRIPTION
Capable of felling an enemy instantaneously if a vital area is hit.

NOTES
Has small chance of scoring a one-hit kill, but deals only 1 point of damage if that fails.

Angelo uses Needle Shot!

Angelo takes a critical hit from the Needle Shot!

Bow skill: **25**
Target: **One enemy**
MP Cost: **1**
Tension Boost: **No**

BOW ABILITIES

SANDMAN'S ARROW

BOW

DESCRIPTION
A magical arrow capable of putting a single enemy to sleep.

NOTES
Deals the same damage as a normal attack and may put an enemy to sleep for 2-5 turns. The success rate for putting enemies to sleep is the same as the Snooze spell.

Angelo uses Sandman's Arrow!

The heligator is put to sleep!

Bow skill: **6**
Target: **One enemy**
MP Cost: **2**
Tension Boost: **Yes**

MULTISHOT

BOW

DESCRIPTION
A hail of blows directed randomly against one or more enemies.

NOTES
Fires 3 to 4 arrows at randomly chosen targets. Each hit deals half the damage of a normal attack.

Angelo uses Multishot!

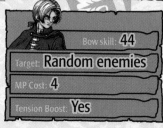

Inflicts an average of 42 points of damage on the enemies. Skullrider A is defeated.

Bow skill: **44**
Target: **Random enemies**
MP Cost: **4**
Tension Boost: **Yes**

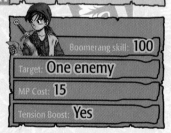
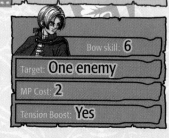

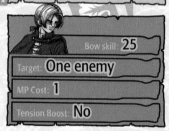

SERAPH'S ARROW

BOW

DESCRIPTION
A secret technique that recovers even more MP than Cherub's Arrow.

NOTES
Replaces Cherub's Arrow. Deals same damage as a normal attack, and regenerates user's MP by 1/8 of the damage dealt.

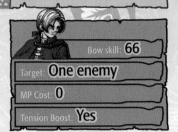

Bow skill: 66

Target: One enemy

MP Cost: 0

Tension Boost: Yes

SARCASTIC SNIGGER

CHARISMA

DESCRIPTION
Reduces a single enemy's tension by one level.

NOTES
Lowers the tension of a single enemy by 1 level.

Charisma skill: 13

Target: One enemy

MP Cost: 3

Tension Boost: No

SHINING SHOT

BOW

DESCRIPTION
An arrow attack that bathes all enemies in a destructive magical light.

NOTES
Deals base damage of 116-124 points to all enemies.

Bow skill: 88

Target: All enemies

MP Cost: 10

Tension Boost: Yes

ANGEL EYES

CHARISMA

DESCRIPTION
A powerful glance capable of paralysing a single enemy.

NOTES
Deals base damage of 15-28 points and may paralyse the target for 5-8 turns.

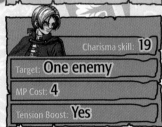

Charisma skill: 19

Target: One enemy

MP Cost: 4

Tension Boost: Yes

NEEDLE RAIN

BOW

DESCRIPTION
A rain of arrows that can occasionally obliterate all enemies in a single salvo.

NOTES
Replaces Needle Shot. Fires 3 to 4 arrows at a single target. Each arrow has a small chance of scoring a one-hit kill, but deals only 1 point of damage if that fails.

Bow skill: 100

Target: One enemy

MP Cost: 1

Tension Boost: No

CHILLING CHUCKLE

CHARISMA

DESCRIPTION
Reduces the tension of an entire group of enemies by a degree.

NOTES
Replaces Sarcastic Snigger. Lowers the tension of a group of enemies by 1 level each.

Charisma skill: 52

Target: Enemy group

MP Cost: 3

Tension Boost: No

CHARMING LOOK

Angelo peers deep into the enemies' eyes as he carries out his Charming Look!

DESCRIPTION

A glance so powerfully captivating that it burns all enemies in its path.

NOTES

Replaces Angel Eyes. Deals base damage of 65-85 points to all enemies and has a higher chance of paralysing them for 5-8 turns

CHARISMA

Charisma skill: **81**

Target: **All enemies**

MP Cost: **4**

Tension Boost: **Yes**

MONSTER MASHER

Yangus uses Monster Masher!

DESCRIPTION

A powerful smash that works wonders on monsters of the material family.

NOTES

Deals slightly more damage than a normal attack, and deals 50% more damage than a normal attack against material-type monsters.

CLUB

Club skill: **32**

Target: **One enemy**

MP Cost: **3**

Tension Boost: **Yes**

CLUB ABILITIES

HEART BREAKER

Yangus uses Heart Breaker!

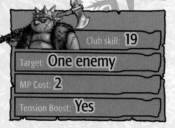

Yangus uses Heart Breaker!

DESCRIPTION

An attack that occasionally causes the target to miss a turn.

NOTES

Deals the same damage as a normal attack, but may cause the target to lose its turn.

CLUB

Club skill: **19**

Target: **One enemy**

MP Cost: **2**

Tension Boost: **Yes**

MIND BREAKER

Yangus uses Mind Breaker!

Does 108 points of damage to the tyrantosaurus.

DESCRIPTION

A superior club attack that dominates foes and renders them unable to attack.

NOTES

Replaces Heart Breaker. Deals slightly more damage than a normal attack, and has a higher chance of causing the target to lose its turn.

CLUB

Club skill: **71**

Target: **One enemy**

MP Cost: **2**

Tension Boost: **Yes**

PENNY PINCHER

Yangus uses Penny Pincher!

The party obtains 4 gold coins!

DESCRIPTION

A special technique that steals gold coins from an enemy.

NOTES

Deals the same damage as a normal attack and sometimes steals gold coins from the enemy. The amount is equal to 10% of the gold coins that monster drops. If the attack kills the monster, you cannot steal gold coins.

CLUB

Club skill: **25**

Target: **One enemy**

MP Cost: **2**

Tension Boost: **Yes**

GOLD RUSH

Yangus uses Gold Rush!

The party obtains 28 gold coins!

DESCRIPTION

A powerful strike that steals an opponent's gold coins as it inflicts damage.

NOTES

Replaces Penny Pincher. Deals slightly more damage than a normal attack, and may steal 20% of the gold coins that monster drops. If the attack kills the monster, you cannot steal gold coins.

CLUB

Club skill: **93**

Target: **One enemy**

MP Cost: **2**

Tension Boost: **Yes**

DEVIL CRUSHER

CLUB

DESCRIPTION
An esoteric club technique effective on demon and material family members.

NOTES
Replaces Monster Masher. Deals slightly more damage than a normal attack, and deals double damage to demon or material-type monsters.

Club skill: **100**
Target: **One enemy**
MP Cost: **5**
Tension Boost: **Yes**

DEFENDING CHAMPION

FISTICUFFS

DESCRIPTION
A defensive ability that greatly reduces the damage inflicted by physical attacks.

NOTES
Throughout the turn, all physical damage dealt to character is reduced by 90%.

Fisticuffs skill: **11**
Fisticuffs skill: **68**
Target: **Self only**
MP Cost: **0**
Tension Boost: **No**

FISTICUFFS ABILITIES

STONES' THROW

FISTICUFFS

DESCRIPTION
Hurls rocks at a single group of enemies.

NOTES
Deals base damage of 8-20 points to a group of enemies.

Fisticuffs skill: **17**
Fisticuffs skill: **19**
Target: **Enemy group**
MP Cost: **0**
Tension Boost: **Yes**

HARVEST MOON

FISTICUFFS

DESCRIPTION
Pummel all enemies with a chain of cartwheels and backflips

NOTES
Deals 50% more damage than a normal attack against a single foe, but the damage is distributed equally against multiple foes.

Fisticuffs skill: **45**
Fisticuffs skill: **42**
Target: **All enemies**
MP Cost: **6**
Tension Boost: **Yes**

KNUCKLE SANDWICH

FISTICUFFS

DESCRIPTION
A powerfully focused and damaging bare-fisted strike.

NOTES
Deals 50% more damage than a normal attack. This attack is not affected by tension and does not expend built-up tension.

Fisticuffs skill: **24**
Fisticuffs skill: **12**
Fisticuffs skill: **35**
Target: **One enemy**
MP Cost: **2**
Tension Boost: **No**

THIN AIR

FISTICUFFS

DESCRIPTION
Generates a powerful vacuum-vortex that slices all enemies to ribbons.

NOTES
Deals base damage of 39-48 points to all enemies, and depending on the user's level, may deal damage up to 108-132 points.

Fisticuffs skill: **42**
Fisticuffs skill: **42**
Fisticuffs skill: **68**
Target: **All enemies**
MP Cost: **2**
Tension Boost: **Yes**

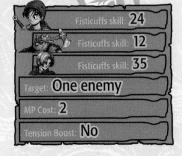

MULTIFISTS

HERO uses Multifists!

Inflicts an average of 23 points of damage on the enemies.
Skullrider B is defeated.

FISTICUFFS

DESCRIPTION
A vicious four-hit strike on a random enemy.

NOTES
Strikes against randomly chosen targets four times. Each hit deals 1/3 the damage of a normal attack

	Fisticuffs skill:	70
	Fisticuffs skill:	60
Target:	Random enemies	
MP Cost:	0	
Tension Boost:	Yes	

BOULDER TOSS

HERO tosses a boulder!

HERO tosses a boulder!

FISTICUFFS

DESCRIPTION
Showers all enemies with enormous boulders.

NOTES
Deals base damage of 72-104 to all enemies.

	Fisticuffs skill:	82
	Fisticuffs skill:	100
Target:	All enemies	
MP Cost:	4	
Tension Boost:	Yes	

MIRACLE MOON

Inflicts an average of 53 points of damage on the enemies.

Inflicts an average of 53 points of damage on the enemies.

FISTICUFFS

DESCRIPTION
A miraculous technique that pummels all enemies while regenerating your own HP.

NOTES
Replaces Harvest Moon. Deals twice the damage of a normal attack against a single foe, but the damage is distributed equally against multiple foes. Restores a portion of damage dealt as HP.

	Fisticuffs skill:	100
Target:	All enemies	
MP Cost:	6	
Tension Boost:	Yes	

144

HUMANITY ABILITIES

WARCRY

Yangus lets out an intimidating scream!

Skullrider B is shocked!

HUMANITY

DESCRIPTION
A hideous battle cry that paralyses a group of enemies with fear.

NOTES
Paralysis effect lasts only 1 turn.

	Humanity skill:	22
Target:	Enemy group	
MP Cost:	0	
Tension Boost:	No	

UNDERPANTS DANCE

Yangus does the Underpants Dance!

Yangus does the Underpants Dance!

HUMANITY

DESCRIPTION
Paralyses all enemies with embarrassment.

NOTES
Paralysis effect lasts only 1 turn, but has a higher rate of success and affects all enemies.

	Humanity skill:	55
Target:	All enemies	
MP Cost:	0	
Tension Boost:	No	

GOLDEN OLDIES

Yangus casts Golden Oldies!

A gang of old geezers gathers at King Trode's command!

HUMANITY

DESCRIPTION
A multi-hit battle royale from King Trode and friends.

NOTES
Deals base damage of 41-50 points to four random enemy targets, and depending on the user's level, may deal up to 107-131 points of damage.

	Humanity skill:	100
Target:	Random enemies	
MP Cost:	15	
Tension Boost:	No	

KNIFE ABILITIES

TOXIC DAGGER

Jessica uses Toxic Dagger!

Does a total of 31 points of damage to metal slime knight A.

DESCRIPTION
A knife-fighting technique that envenomates a single enemy.

NOTES
Deals half the damage of a normal attack, but may poison the target.

Knife skill: 9
Target: One enemy
MP Cost: 3
Tension Boost: Yes

ASSASSIN'S STAB

Jessica uses Assassin's Stab!

The jumping jackal is killed!

DESCRIPTION
A fearsome technique that fells an opponent instantly by attacking their vital parts.

NOTES
Deals the same damage as a normal attack, and has a small chance of killing the enemy instantly.

Knife skill: 22
Target: One enemy
MP Cost: 8
Tension Boost: Yes

TOXIC SWORD

Jessica uses Toxic Sword!

Noiso macho A is envenomated!

DESCRIPTION
A sword-fighting technique which envenomates an enemy with each strike.

NOTES
Replaces Toxic Dagger. Does slightly more damage than a normal attack, and has a higher chance of poisoning the target.

Knife skill: 66
Target: One enemy
MP Cost: 3
Tension Boost: Yes

SUDDEN DEATH

Jessica uses Sudden Death!

The war gryphon is killed!

DESCRIPTION
A fatal flash that strikes down an enemy like a bolt out of the blue.

NOTES
Replaces Assassin's Stab. Deals 50% more damage than a normal attack and has a higher chance of killing the enemy instantly.

Abilities

SCYTHE

Knife skill: 100
Target: One enemy
MP Cost: 8
Tension Boost: Yes

SCYTHE ABILITIES

STEAL SICKLE

Yangus uses Steal Sickle!

Yangus uses Steal Sickle!

DESCRIPTION
Occasionally enables you to steal items from those you slash.

NOTES
Deals the same damage as a normal attack, and sometimes steals an item from the enemy. The odds of success vary by enemy, but are typically very low. If the attack kills the monster, you cannot steal an item.

Scythe skill: 22
Target: One enemy
MP Cost: 0
Tension Boost: Yes

WIND SICKLES

Yangus uses Wind Sickles!

Yangus uses Wind Sickles!

DESCRIPTION
Sends a whirlwind of sickles pirouetting into the enemy.

NOTES
Deals base damage of 29-40 points to a single target, and depending on the user's level, may deal up to 122-166 points of damage.

Scythe skill: 32
Target: One enemy
MP Cost: 0
Tension Boost: Yes

GRIM REAPER

DESCRIPTION

A swing of Death's scythe that can instantly kill one or more foes in a group.

NOTES

Hits all enemies in a group from left to right. The first hit is slightly weaker than a normal attack and the damage lessens as the attack moves through the group. Occasionally kills foes instantly.

Yangus uses Grim Reaper!

SCYTHE

Scythe skill:	50
Target:	Enemy group
MP Cost:	3
Tension Boost:	Yes

BIG BANGA

DESCRIPTION

An enormous explosion that consumes everything in its path.

NOTES

Deals base damage of 175-225 points to all enemies, and depending on the user's level, may deal up to 300-400 points of damage.

Yangus unleashes Big Banga!

SCYTHE

Scythe skill:	100
Target:	All enemies
MP Cost:	30
Tension Boost:	Yes

STAINLESS STEAL SICKLE

Yangus uses Stainless Steal Sickle!

DESCRIPTION

An improved version of the Steal Sickle attack technique.

NOTES

Replaces Steal Sickle. Deals more damage than a regular attack and increases the odds of a successful theft (but the odds remain quite low). If the attack kills the monster, you cannot steal an item.

Yangus stole a hairband!

SCYTHE

Scythe skill:	70
Target:	One enemy
MP Cost:	0
Tension Boost:	Yes

SEX APPEAL ABILITIES

BLOW KISS

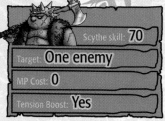

Jessica blows a kiss!

DESCRIPTION

A special kiss that can temporarily prevent enemies from attacking.

NOTES

Deals damage based on Jessica's base attack score, and may paralyse its target for a single turn.

Does 48 points of damage to cockateer C.

SEX APPEAL

Sex Appeal skill:	8
Target:	One enemy
MP Cost:	0
Tension Boost:	Yes

GRIMMER REAPER

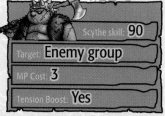

Yangus uses Grimmer Reaper !

DESCRIPTION

The aura of Death incarnate annihilates the living and obliterates the undead.

NOTES

Replaces Grim Reaper. The attack now deals normal damage to the first target, and 50% more damage to zombie monsters.

Yangus uses Grimmer Reaper !

SCYTHE

Scythe skill:	90
Target:	Enemy group
MP Cost:	3
Tension Boost:	Yes

PUFF-PUFF

Jessica performs her best puff-puff on Tyrantosaurus B!

DESCRIPTION

Charms and excites an enemy into paralysed submission.

NOTES

May paralyse a foe for a single turn. Deals no damage.

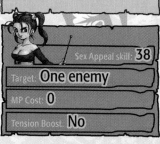

Jessica: (Puff-puff, puff-puff...)

SEX APPEAL

Sex Appeal skill:	38
Target:	One enemy
MP Cost:	0
Tension Boost:	No

HIP DROP

Jessica's Hip Drop!

Does 64 points of damage to notso macho B

Abilities

SPEAR

DESCRIPTION
Pelvic punishment! Curvaceous hips equal big damage.

NOTES
Deals 50% more damage than a normal attack.

SEX APPEAL

Sex Appeal skill: 48
Target: **One enemy**
MP Cost: 0
Tension Boost: **Yes**

HUSTLE DANCE

Angelo recovers some HP!

DESCRIPTION
Restores at least 70 HP to all party members.

NOTES
Restores 70-80 HP to each party member.

SEX APPEAL

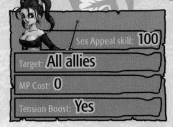

Sex Appeal skill: 100
Target: **All allies**
MP Cost: 0
Tension Boost: **Yes**

SEXY BEAM

Jessica uses Sexy Beam!

Jessica uses Sexy Beam!

DESCRIPTION
Focus the power of passion into a beam that sows destruction and confusion.

NOTES
Deals base damage of 65-75 points to a single target, and may cause confusion for 5-8 turns.

SEX APPEAL

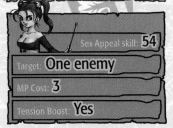

Sex Appeal skill: 54
Target: **One enemy**
MP Cost: 3
Tension Boost: **Yes**

SPEAR ABILITIES

MERCURIAL THRUST

HERO slices faster than a hurricane!

HERO slices faster than a hurricane!

DESCRIPTION
A lightning-fast thrust.

NOTES
This attack does slightly less damage than a normal attack, but strikes first in combat regardless of the user's agility.

SPEAR

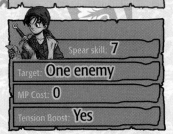

Spear skill: 7
Target: **One enemy**
MP Cost: 0
Tension Boost: **Yes**

PINK TYPHOON

Jessica uses Pink Typhoon!

Jessica uses Pink Typhoon!

DESCRIPTION
A sudden typhoon that rips a group of enemies into ribbons.

NOTES
Deals base damage of 76-84 points to a group of enemies.

SEX APPEAL

Sex Appeal skill: 88
Target: **Enemy group**
MP Cost: 5
Tension Boost: **Yes**

THUNDER THRUST

HERO's carefully aimed thrust booms like thunder!

Critical hit!

DESCRIPTION
Difficult to perform, but has a high chance of doing critical damage.

NOTES
This attack misses around 50% of the time, but usually scores a critical hit when successful. Very effective against metal enemies.

SPEAR

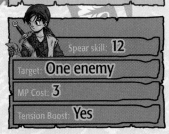

Spear skill: 12
Target: **One enemy**
MP Cost: 3
Tension Boost: **Yes**

MULTITHRUST

HERO uses Multithrust!

Inflicts an average of 39 points of damage on the magic dumbbells. The magic dumbbells are defeated.

SPEAR

DESCRIPTION
A flurry of repeated thrusts that can pierce multiple enemies.

NOTES
Strikes against randomly chosen targets three or four times. Each hit deals half the damage of a normal attack.

Spear skill:	25
Target:	Random enemies
MP Cost:	4
Tension Boost:	Yes

CLEAN SWEEP

HERO mows down the enemy!

HERO mows down the enemy!

SPEAR

DESCRIPTION
Drives back a group of enemies with a sweep of the spear.

NOTES
Hits all enemies in a group from left to right. The first hit is slightly weaker than a normal attack and the damage lessens as the attack moves through the group.

Spear skill:	45
Target:	Enemy group
MP Cost:	0
Tension Boost:	Yes

LIGHTNING THRUST

HERO's carefully aimed thrust flashes like lightning!

Critical hit!

SPEAR

DESCRIPTION
Lands a critical hit when it connects.

NOTES
Replaces Thunder Thrust. This attack misses around 50% of the time, but always scores a critical hit when successful. Very effective against metal enemies.

Spear skill:	59
Target:	One enemy
MP Cost:	3
Tension Boost:	No

148

LIGHTNING STORM

HERO calls forth bolts from the blue!

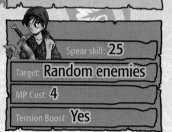

Inflicts an average of 201 points of damage on the enemies. The slimes are defeated.

SPEAR

DESCRIPTION
Strikes down all enemies with mighty thunderbolts.

NOTES
Deals base damage of 190-220 points to all enemies.

Spear skill:	100
Target:	All enemies
MP Cost:	25
Tension Boost:	Yes

STAFF ABILITIES

CADUCEUS

Angelo wields a Caduceus!

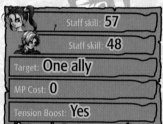

Angelo recovers some HP!

STAFF

DESCRIPTION
A blessing from the heavens that restores a single party member's HP.

NOTES
Restores 75-95 HP to one ally.

Staff skill:	57
Staff skill:	48
Target:	One ally
MP Cost:	0
Tension Boost:	Yes

SWORD ABILITIES

DRAGON SLASH

HERO uses Dragon Slash!

HERO uses Dragon Slash!

SWORD

DESCRIPTION
An attack that causes heavy damage to dragons.

NOTES
Deals damage equal to a normal attack, and an additional 50% damage to monsters from the dragon family.

Sword skill:	9
Target:	One enemy
MP Cost:	0
Tension Boost:	Yes

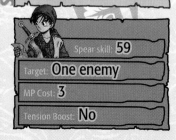

FLAME SLASH

DESCRIPTION
Channels the power of a raging fire into the blade of your sword.

NOTES
Deals fire-based damage that is 50% stronger than a normal attack.

Sword skill:	15
Sword skill:	9
Target:	One enemy
MP Cost:	0
Tension Boost:	Yes

MIRACLE SLASH

DESCRIPTION
A secret sword technique that heals your own wounds each time you strike a foe.

NOTES
Slightly more powerful than a regular attack, and restores HP to user equal to half the damage dealt.

Sword skill:	82
Sword skill:	66
Target:	One enemy
MP Cost:	4
Tension Boost:	Yes

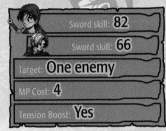

METAL SLASH

DESCRIPTION
An attack that can damage enemies with metal bodies.

NOTES
Deals normal damage to most enemies, but always deals one or two points of damage to metal enemies. (Normal attacks deal 0 or one point.)

Sword skill:	30
Sword skill:	22
Target:	One enemy
MP Cost:	0
Tension Boost:	Yes

LIGHTNING STORM

DESCRIPTION
Strikes down all enemies with mighty thunderbolts.

NOTES
Deals base damage of 190-220 points to all enemies.

Sword skill:	100
Target:	All enemies
MP Cost:	25
Tension Boost:	Yes

FALCON SLASH

DESCRIPTION
A double slicing attack, faster than a falcon on the wing.

NOTES
Attacks a single enemy twice. Each hit deals slightly less damage than a normal attack.

Sword skill:	52
Sword skill:	40
Target:	One enemy
MP Cost:	0
Tension Boost:	Yes

GIGASLASH

DESCRIPTION
A legendary sword technique for cutting down a group of enemies.

NOTES
Deals base damage of 158-190 points to a group of enemies, and depending on the user's level, may deal up to 207-239 points of damage. Can be learned from mastering either Sword or Courage skill sets.

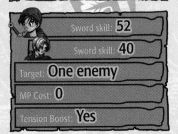

Sword or Courage skill:	100
Target:	Enemy group
MP Cost:	20
Tension Boost:	Yes

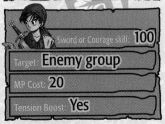

WHIP ABILITIES

WHIPLASH

Jessica uses Whiplash!

DESCRIPTION
A paralysing crack of the whip.

NOTES
Deals normal damage and occasionally paralyses targets for 5 to 8 turns.

Whip skill: 10
Target: Enemy group
MP Cost: 4
Tension Boost: Yes

LASHINGS OF LOVE

Jessica uses Lashings of Love!

Jessica uses Lashings of Love!

DESCRIPTION
Harness your inner passion to paralyse enemies.

NOTES
Replaces Whiplash. Deals 50% more damage than a normal attack, and paralyses targets more frequently.

Whip skill: 55
Target: Enemy group
MP Cost: 4
Tension Boost: Yes

TWIN DRAGON LASH

Jessica uses Twin Dragon Lash!

Inflicts an average of 47 points of damage on the tyrantosauruses.

DESCRIPTION
A double-strike that lashes a random group of enemies.

NOTES
Attacks twice, hitting two random enemies within the target group. Each hit deals more damage than a normal attack.

Whip skill: 23
Target: Random enemies
MP Cost: 3
Tension Boost: Yes

QUEEN'S THONG

Jessica uses Queen's Thong!

Jessica's wounds are healed!

DESCRIPTION
A fearsome attack that steals the HP of a group of enemies.

NOTES
Replaces Lady's Thong. Deals slightly more damage than a regular attack and user recovers 1/4 of the damage dealt to the first target in the group.

Whip skill: 82
Target: Enemy group
MP Cost: 2
Tension Boost: Yes

LADY'S THONG

Jessica uses Lady's Thong!

DESCRIPTION
A secret whip technique that steals HP as it damages an enemy.

NOTES
Deals normal damage. User recovers HP equal to 1/8 the damage dealt to the first target in the group.

Whip skill: 32
Target: Enemy group
MP Cost: 2
Tension Boost: Yes

SERPENT'S BITE

Jessica uses Serpent's Bite!

Jessica uses Serpent's Bite!

DESCRIPTION
A technique that transforms your whip into a snake that attacks a group of enemies.

NOTES
Deals 50% more damage than a normal attack. The amount of damage decreases as it goes down the line of enemies.

Whip skill: 100
Target: Enemy group
MP Cost: 8
Tension Boost: Yes

OTHER ABILITIES

Abilities

OTHER

CALL TEAM

HERO calls ? ? ? ? ? ? ? ? ? ?!

Does 157 points of damage to treeface
Treeface A is defeated.

DESCRIPTION

Call up your personal monster team.

NOTES

Summons one of your Monster Arena teams to replace all allies for three turns (duration may vary based on the monsters in your team). Each team can only be summoned once per fight.

Hero learns from story event

Target:	N/A
MP Cost:	10
Tension Boost:	No

GIGAGASH

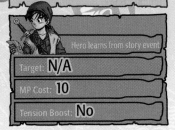

HERO uses Gigagash!

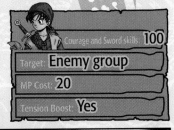

HERO uses Gigagash!

DESCRIPTION

The ultimate sword technique. Utterly destroys a group of enemies.

NOTES

Replaces Gigaslash after Hero masters both Courage and Sword skill sets. Deals base damage of 222-282 points to all enemies, and depending on the user's level, may deal up to 271-331 points of damage.

Courage and Sword skills: 100

Target:	Enemy group
MP Cost:	20
Tension Boost:	Yes

HERO uses Gigagash!

ITEMS

This section contains a comprehensive list of every item that can't be equipped. Many are used as recovery items, a few can be used offensively in combat, while others have no use at all. This last group exists simply as ingredients for advanced alchemy recipes.

A list of all the game's important items is at the end of this section. These items cannot be bought or sold, but instead must be delivered to certain characters or used in specific ways to advance the game. Most disappear from your inventory when they've served their purpose, but a few like the world map and Godbird's soulstone are essential tools you will use frequently throughout the game.

USABLE ITEMS

MEDICINAL HERB

| Buy: 8 |
| Sell: 4 |

Description: Restores 30 or more HP to a single ally.

Use: Combat or field

Function: Restores 30-40 HP to one ally.

Buy: Most item shops
Find: Farebury (bag, 3x pot, barrel), Waterfall Cave (chest), Alexandria (pot), Tower of Alexandra (2x barrel), Port Prospect (barrel), Ferry (pot, barrel), Peregrin Quay (barrel, pot), Ascantha (pot)
Obtain: Slime, Candy cat, Lips, Dracky, She-slime, Mischievous mole, Skipper, Drackmage, Beetleboy, Healslime, Frogface, Spiked hare, Chainine, Brownie, Pan piper, Treeface, Headhunter, Cureslime, Muddy hand, Mad mole, Dragonthorn, Great sabrecat, Puppet player, Orc, Skullrider, Notso macho, Woc, Swingin' hipster, Dark slime, Hellhound, Dark star, Bloody hand, Great troll, See urchin, Merman, Poison eveel, Merking, Tentacular

Recipe to Make: None

Use in Recipes:
Strong medicine = medicinal herb + medicinal herb
Rose-root = medicinal herb + medicinal herb + medicinal herb
Rose-root = strong medicine + medicinal herb
Strong antidote = medicinal herb + antidotal herb
Special antidote = medicinal herb + antidotal herb + antidotal herb
Rose-wort = medicinal herb + medicinal herb + moonwort bulb
Mystifying mixture = medicinal herb + antidotal herb + moonwort bulb

STRONG MEDICINE

| Buy: N/A |
| Sell: 88 |

Description: Restores 50 or more HP to a single ally.

Use: Combat or field

Function: Restores 50-68 HP to one ally.

Find: Baccarat (barrel), Argonia (barrel)
Obtain: Treeface, Treevil, Hades Condor, Gargoyle, Stone golem, Mucho macho, Dark macabour, King squid, Red horn

Recipe to Make:
Strong medicine = medicinal herb + medicinal herb

Use in Recipes:
Special medicine = strong medicine + strong medicine
Rose-root = strong medicine + medicinal herb
Amor seco essence = holy water + strong medicine
Rose-wort = strong medicine + moonwort bulb

SPECIAL MEDICINE

| Buy: N/A |
| Sell: 170 |

Description: Restores 90 or more HP to a single ally.

Use: Combat or field

Function: Restores 90-120 HP to one ally.

Find: Marta's Cottage (pot), Empycchu (chest)
Obtain: Jabberwockee, Boss troll

Recipe to Make:
Special medicine = strong medicine + strong medicine

Use in Recipes:
Lesser panacea = special medicine + special medicine
Greater panacea = special medicine + special medicine + special medicine

ROSE-ROOT

| Buy: N/A |
| Sell: 118 |

Description: Restores 70 or more HP to a single ally.

Use: Combat or field

Function: Restores 70-92 HP to one ally.

Find: Herb Grotto (pot)

Recipe to Make:
Rose-root = medicinal herb + medicinal herb + medicinal herb
Rose-root = strong medicine + medicinal herb

Use in Recipes:
Greater panacea = lesser panacea + rose-root + rose-wort

AMOR SECO ESSENCE

| Buy: 120 |
| Sell: 60 |

Description: Restores 60 or more HP to a single ally.

Use: Combat or field

Function: Restores 60-70 HP to one ally.

Buy: Pickham, Baccarat, Desert Chapel, Orkutsk, Tryan Gully
Find: Pickham (pot), Baccarat (barrel), Arcadia (barrel), Orkutsk (barrel)
Obtain: Slime, Firespirit, Healslime, Frogface, King cureslime, Phantom swordsman, Cyclops, Gigantes, See angel

Recipe to Make:
Amor seco essence = holy water + strong medicine

Use in Recipes:
Silver shield = mirror shield + amor seco essence + magic water
Holy water = amor seco essence + rock salt
Mild cheese = plain cheese + amor seco essence
Cured cheese = fresh milk + premium mould + amor seco essence

ANTIDOTAL HERB

| Buy: 10 |
| Sell: 5 |

Description: Cures a single ally of the effects of poison.

Use: Combat or field

Function: Cures effects of poison from one ally.

Buy: Most item shops
Find: Farebury (bag, cabinet, barrel), Tower of Alexandra (pot), Ferry (barrel), Peregrin Quay (barrel), Swordsman's Labyrinth (pot)
Obtain: Bubble slime, Funghoul, Scorpion, Walking corpse, Devilmoth, Bodkin fletcher, Toxic zombie, Ghoul, Killer moth, Kee, Death scorpion, Dark dullahan, Wild boarfish, Eveel, Pigmalion, Merking

Recipe to Make:
None

Use in Recipes:
Strong antidote = medicinal herb + antidotal herb
Special antidote = medicinal herb + antidotal herb + antidotal herb
Mystifying mixture = medicinal herb + antidotal herb + moonwort bulb

STRONG ANTIDOTE

Buy: N/A
Sell: 95

Description: Restores 30 or more HP to a single ally and cures the effects of poison.

Use: Combat or field

Function: Cures effects of poison and restores 30-40 HP to one ally.

Find: Argonia (barrel)
Obtain: Blue fang

Recipe to Make:
Strong antidote = medicinal herb + antidotal herb

Use in Recipes:
Special antidote = strong antidote + strong antidote

SPECIAL ANTIDOTE

Buy: N/A
Sell: 275

Description: Restores 60 or more HP to a single ally and cures the effects of poison.

Use: Combat or field

Function: Cures effects of poison and restores 60-80 HP to one ally.

Find: Marta's Cottage (pot), Dark Empycchu (chest)

Recipe to Make:
Special antidote = strong antidote + strong antidote
Special antidote = medicinal herb + antidotal herb + antidotal herb

Use in Recipes:
None

MOONWORT BULB

Buy: 30
Sell: 15

Description: Cures the entire party of the effects of paralysis.

Use: Combat only

Function: Cures effects of sleep or paralysis from all allies.

Buy: Ascantha, Savella Cathedral, Baccarat, Argonia, Arcadia, Peddler's Tent, Peddler in Neos (after certain events)
Find: Alexandria (barrel), Tower of Alexandra (barrel), Neos (pot)
Obtain: Lips, Bubble slime, Drackyma, Night sneaker, Hell hornet, Venom wasp, Jab, Soulspawn, Smacker, Dark skeleton, Solaris, Man o' war

Recipe to Make:
None

Use in Recipes:
Rose-wort = medicinal herb + medicinal herb + moonwort bulb
Rose-wort = strong medicine + moonwort bulb
Moon's mercy = moonwort bulb + moonwort bulb + moonwort bulb
Mystifying mixture = medicinal herb + antidotal herb + moonwort bulb

ITEMS

USABLE ITEMS

ROSE-WORT

Buy: N/A
Sell: 148

Description: Restores 60 or more HP to a single ally and cures the effects of paralysis.

Use: Combat or field

Function: Cures effects of paralysis and restores 60-80 HP to one ally.

Find: Herb Grotto (pot)

Recipe to Make:
Rose-wort = medicinal herb + medicinal herb + moonwort bulb
Rose-wort = strong medicine + moonwort bulb

Use in Recipes:
Greater panacea = lesser panacea + rose-root + rose-wort

MOON'S MERCY

Buy: N/A
Sell: 308

Description: Restores 110 or more HP to a single ally and cures the effects of paralysis.

Use: Combat or field

Function: Cures effects of paralysis and restores 110-120 HP to one ally.

Obtain: Cureslime, Spitnik, Hell hopper

Recipe to Make:
Moon's mercy = moonwort bulb + moonwort bulb + moonwort bulb

Use in Recipes:
Moon axe = golden axe + moon's mercy

LESSER PANACEA

Buy: N/A
Sell: 550

Description: Fully restores the HP of a single ally and cures the effects of poison and paralysis.

Use: Combat or field

Function: Cures effects of poison and paralysis and restores all HP to one ally.

Find: Kingdom of Trodain (chest), Isolated Plateau (chest), Arcadia (pot)

Recipe to Make:
Lesser panacea = special medicine + special medicine

Use in Recipes:
Greater panacea = lesser panacea + rose-root + rose-wort

GREATER PANACEA

Buy: N/A
Sell: 880

Description: Fully restores the HP of a single ally and cures a variety of status abnormalities.

Use: Combat or field

Function: Cures effects of poison, paralysis, sleep and confusion and restores all HP to one ally.

Obtain: Alchemy only

Recipe to Make:
Greater panacea = special medicine + special medicine + special medicine
Greater panacea = lesser panacea + rose-root + rose-wort

Use in Recipes:
None

YGGDRASIL LEAF

Buy: 1000
Sell: 500

Description: A mystical leaf that resurrects a single fallen ally.

Use: Combat or field

Function: Restores a fallen ally with full HP.

Buy: Argonia
Find: Egeus' Tablet (pot), E Argonia (chest), Blizzard Peaks (chest), Black Citadel (barrel)
Obtain: Treevil, Dark macarbour

Recipe to Make:
None

Use in Recipes:
Staff of resurrection = Yggdrasil leaf + rune staff + life bracer
Yggdrasil dew = Yggdrasil leaf + magic water
Premium mould = red mould + waterweed mould + Yggdrasil leaf

YGGDRASIL DEW

Buy: N/A
Sell: 1250

Description: Fully restores the HP of the entire party.

Use: Combat or field

Function: Restores all allies to full HP.

Find: Trodain Castle (chest), Kingdom of Ascantha on Unnamed Isle (chest), Tryan Gully (pot), Unknown... (pot)
Obtain: King cureslime, Megalodon

Recipe to Make:
Yggdrasil dew = Yggdrasil leaf + magic water

Use in Recipes:
Elfin elixir = Yggdrasil dew + magic water
Sage's stone = gold nugget + orichalcum + Yggdrasil dew
Angel cheese = fresh milk + premium mould + Yggdrasil dew

 **MAGIC WATER**

Buy: 300

Sell: 150

Description: Restores 30 or more MP to a single ally.

Use: Combat or field

Function: Restores 30-35 MP to one ally.

Buy: Tryan Gully, Unknown...
Find: Maella Region (chest), Pickham (cabinet), Baccarat (barrel), Argonia (cabinet), Arcadia (barrel, pot), Orkutsk (pot), Pirate's Cove (barrel), Savella Area (chest), Holy Isle of Neos (chest)
Obtain: Winky, Lost soul, Peeper, Hocus chimaera, Phantom swordsman, Frostburn, Hellstalker
Token Trade: Pickham (100 Tokens)

Recipe to Make: Magic water = holy water + seed of magic

Use in Recipes:
Crimson robe = sage's robe + magic water + nook grass
Silver shield = mirror shield + amor seco essence + magic water
Yggdrasil dew = Yggdrasil leaf + magic water
Elfin elixir = Yggdrasil dew + magic water
Chunky cheese = plain cheese + magic water

 **ELFIN ELIXIR**

Buy: N/A

Sell: 410

Description: Fully restores the MP of a single ally.

Use: Combat or field

Function: Restores one ally to full MP.

Find: Argonia (cabinet), Arcadia Region (chest), Herb Grotto (chest), Tryan Gully (barrel), Isolated Plateau (chest), Unknown... (chest)
Obtain: Soulspawn, Gigantes

Recipe to Make:
Elfin elixir = Yggdrasil dew + magic water

Use in Recipes:
None

 **SEED OF STRENGTH**

Buy: N/A

Sell: 15

Description: Permanently increases the strength of a single ally.

Use: Combat or field

Function: Permanently raises strength of one ally by 1-2 points.

Received: Troll's Maze
Find: Alexandria Region (chest), Tower of Alexandra (pot), Maella Region (chest), Pickham (bag), Baccarat (cabinet), Princess Minnie's Castle (chest), Argonia (cabinet), Arcadia (cabinet), Empycchu (pot), E Argonia (chest)
Obtain: Mimic, Geyzer, Red horn

Recipe to Make:
None

Use in Recipes:
Strength ring = prayer ring + seed of strength

 **SEED OF AGILITY**

Buy: N/A

Sell: 13

Description: Permanently increases the agility of a single ally.

Use: Combat or field

Function: Permanently raises agility of one ally by 1-2 points.

Find: Waterfall Hut (bag), Tower of Alexandra (chest), Ferry (pot), Kingdom of Ascantha (chest), Red's Den (chest), Baccarat Region (chest), W Argonia (chest), World of Darkness (chest)
Obtain: Metal slime, Liquid metal slime

Recipe to Make:
None

Use in Recipes:
Agility ring = prayer ring + seed of agility

 **SEED OF DEFENCE**

Buy: N/A

Sell: 15

Description: Permanently increases the resilience of a single ally.

Use: Combat or field

Function: Permanently raises resilience of one ally by 1-2 points.

Find: Farebury (pot), Peregrin Quay (barrel), Kingdom of Ascantha (chest), Pickham Region (chest), Kingdom of Trodain (chest), Mole Hole (pot), Baccarat (pot), Baccarat Region (barrel), Orkutsk (barrel), Tryan Gully (barrel), Black Citadel (barrel), Savella Area (chest)
Obtain: Metal slime

Recipe to Make:
None

Use in Recipes:
Ruby of protection = prayer ring + seed of defence

 **SEED OF WISDOM**

Buy: N/A

Sell: 10

Description: Permanently increases the wisdom of a single ally.

Use: Combat or field

Function: Permanently raises wisdom of one ally by 1-3 points.

Received: Farebury
Find: Port Prospect (pot), Maella Region (chest), Pickham (pot), Baccarat (pot), W Argonia (chest), Savella Cathedral (chest)
Obtain: Mimic king, Blue fang

Recipe to Make:
None

Use in Recipes:
Scholar's specs = ring of awakening + ring of clarity + seed of wisdom

SEED OF SKILL

Buy: 2000*

Sell: 50

Description: Permanently increases the skill points of a single ally.

Use: Field only

Function: One ally is given 5 skill points to distribute.

Buy: *Arcadia (once only)
Find: Pickham Region (chest), Seer's Retreat (cabinet), Empycchu (pot), Neos (chest), Unknown... (chest)
Obtain: Solaris, Great troll, Crocodog

Recipe to Make:
None

Use in Recipes:
None

 SEED OF LIFE

Buy: N/A

Sell: 18

Description: Permanently increases the maximum HP of a single ally.

Use: Combat or field

Function: Permanently raises max HP of one ally by 3-4 points.

Received: Troll's Maze
Find: Savella Area (bird), Farebury Region (chest), Alexandria Region (chest), Ferry (barrel), Kingdom of Ascantha (chest), Pickham (barrel), Princess Minnie's Castle (chest), Arcadia (pot), Herb Grotto (pot), Lord High Priest's Residence (barrel), Black Citadel (barrel), Cape West of Pickham (chest), Land of the Moles (chest)
Obtain: Mumboh-jumboo

Recipe to Make:
None

Use in Recipes:
Recovery ring = prayer ring + seed of life

 **SEED OF MAGIC**

Buy: N/A

Sell: 20

Description: Permanently increases the maximum MP of a single ally.

Use: Combat or field

Function: Permanently raises max MP of one ally by 3-4 points.

Find: Savella Area (bird), Alexandria (barrel), Peregrin Quay (cabinet), Maella Region (chest), Riverside Chapel (cabinet), Swordsman's Labyrinth (pot), Trodain Castle (chest), Neos (barrel), Argonia (after bazaar, barrel), Arcadia (chest), Pirate's Cove (pot), Dark Empycchu (pot), Kingdom of Trodain (chest)
Obtain: Democrobot

Recipe to Make:
None

Use in Recipes:
Magic water = holy water + seed of magic
Prayer ring = gold ring + seed of magic

HOLY WATER

A

Buy: 20
Sell: 10

Description: Temporarily prevents weaker monsters from attacking the party.

Use: Combat or field

Function: In the field, has the effect of Holy Protection spell; in combat, it deals 10-15 damage to one enemy.

Buy: Most item shops
Find: Farebury (cabinet), Waterfall Hut (bag), Alexandria (pot), Port Prospect (cabinet), Maella Abbey (barrel), Pickham (cabinet), Neos (barrel)
Obtain: Firespirit, Winky, Lost soul, Peeper, Lump wizard

Recipe to Make: Holy water = amor seco essence + rock salt

Use in Recipes:
Saintess shield = white shield + mirror shield + holy water
Holy talisman = tough guy tattoo + gold rosary + holy water
Amor seco essence = holy water + strong medicine
Magic water = holy water + seed of magic
Mystifying mixture = holy water + wing of bat + cowpat

CHIMAERA WING

A

Buy: 25
Sell: 13

Description: Allows you to warp instantly to a selection of places you have previously visited.

Use: Field only

Function: Has effect of Zoom spell.

Buy: Most item shops
Find: Farebury (chest), Waterfall Cave (chest), Alexandria (cabinet), Port Prospect (barrel), Peregrin Quay (barrel), Neos (pot), Orkutsk (pot), Empycchu (pot)
Obtain: Dracky, Mecha-mynah, Dancing devil, Drackmage, Imp, Diemon, Chimaera, Hawk man, Hocus chimaera, Puppet master, Gryphon, Dark condor, War gryphon

Recipe to Make: Chimaera wing = wing of bat + wing of bat

Use in Recipes:
Feathered cap = leather hat + chimaera wing

BAUMREN'S BELL

A ✓

Buy: N/A
Sell: N/A

Description: Summons a great sabrecat when rung.

Use: Combat or field

Function: Summons a sabrecat to ride (on field) or drives sabrecats away (in combat). Does not disappear when used. Cannot be sold or dropped.

Received: Chateau Felix

Recipe to Make:
None

Use in Recipes:
None

ITEMS

USABLE ITEMS

MYSTIFYING MIXTURE

Buy: N/A
Sell: 280

Description: Confuses a single enemy when used as an item during battle.

Use: Combat only

Function: Confuses one enemy.

Find: Arcadia (pot)

Recipe to Make:
Mystifying mixture = medicinal herb + antidotal herb + moonwort bulb
Mystifying mixture = holy water + wing of bat + cowpat

Use in Recipes:
Rusty old sword = liquid metal sword + mystifying mixture + cowpat

ROCKBOMB SHARD

 A ✓

Buy: 450
Sell: 225

Description: Explodes when thrown, damaging all enemies.

Use: Combat only

Function: Has effect of Bang spell. Deals 48-96 damage to all enemies.

Buy: Arcadia, Tryan Gully
Find: Orkutsk (barrel)
Obtain: Minidemon, Rockbomb, Bomboulder, Stone golem, Archdemon

Recipe to Make:
None

Use in Recipes:
Magma staff = wizard's staff + rockbomb shard

SAGE'S STONE

Buy: N/A
Sell: 20000

Description: Restores 100 or more HP to the entire party when used as an item in battle.

Use: Combat only

Function: Has effect of Midheal when used as an item in combat. Does not disappear when used.

Find: Black Citadel (chest)

Recipe to Make:
Sage's stone = gold nugget + orichalcum + Yggdrasil dew

Use in Recipes:
None

TIMBREL OF TENSION

Buy: N/A
Sell: N/A

Description: A musical instrument that raises the tension of the entire party.

Use: Combat only

Function: Raises tension of all allies by one level. Does not disappear when used. Cannot be sold or discarded.

Obtain: Alchemy only

Recipe to Make:
Timbrel of tension = sun crown + tough guy tattoo + magic beast hide

Use in Recipes:
None

PLAIN CHEESE

A

Buy: N/A
Sell: 25

Description: One of Munchie's favourites. Normal, everyday cheese.

Use: Combat only

Function: When fed to Munchie, Munchie deals 6-10 fire-based damage to all enemies.

Received: Waterfall Hut
Find: Alexandria (pot), Argonia (barrel)
Obtain: Bodkin archer, Funghoul, Jailcat, Morphean mushroom, Flyguy, Mumboh-jumboe, Mum, Boh, Jum, Boe, Bulldozer, Man o' war

Recipe to Make:
Plain cheese = scorching cheese + c-c-cold cheese
Plain cheese = fresh milk + rennet powder

Use in Recipes:
Spicy cheese = plain cheese + red mould
Cool cheese = plain cheese + waterweed mould
Mild cheese = plain cheese + amor seco essence
Hard cheese = plain cheese + rock salt
Chunky cheese = plain cheese + magic water

SPICY CHEESE

Buy: N/A
Sell: 250

Description: One of Munchie's favourites. Hot and spicy cheese.

Use: Combat only

Function: When fed to Munchie, Munchie deals 30-40 fire-based damage to all enemies.

Find: Neos (bag)
Obtain: Dancing flame, War gryphon, Abyss diver

Recipe to Make:
Spicy cheese = plain cheese + red mould

Use in Recipes:
Super spicy cheese = spicy cheese + nook grass
Super spicy cheese = spicy cheese + red mould + red mould

Super Spicy Cheese

Buy: N/A
Sell: 600

Description: One of Munchie's favourites. Really, really spicy cheese.

Use: Combat only

Function: When fed to Munchie, Munchie deals 65-85 fire-based damage to all enemies.

Find: Untrodden Groves (chest)

Recipe to Make:
Super spicy cheese = spicy cheese + nook grass
Super spicy cheese = spicy cheese + red mould + red mould

Use in Recipes:
Scorching cheese = super spicy cheese + premium mould + dragon dung
Highly-strung cheese = super spicy cheese + cold cheese + rock salt

Scorching Cheese

Buy: N/A
Sell: 1200

Description: One of Munchie's favourites. Spicy as hell.

Use: Combat only

Function: When fed to Munchie, Munchie deals 150-170 fire-based damage to all enemies.

Obtain: Alchemy only

Recipe to Make:
Scorching cheese = super spicy cheese + premium mould + dragon dung

Use in Recipes:
Plain cheese = scorching cheese + c-c-cold cheese

Cool Cheese

Buy: N/A
Sell: 88

Description: One of Munchie's favourites. Frosty cool cheese.

Use: Combat only

Function: When fed to Munchie, Munchie deals 13-16 ice-based damage to all enemies.

Find: Baccarat (barrel), Argonia (pot)
Obtain: Imp, Frogman, Demonrider

Recipe to Make:
Cool cheese = plain cheese + waterweed mould

Use in Recipes:
Chilly cheese = cool cheese + waterweed mould

Chilly Cheese

Buy: N/A
Sell: 300

Description: One of Munchie's favourites. Chilly cheese that's as cold as ice.

Use: Combat only

Function: When fed to Munchie, Munchie deals 50-60 ice-based damage to all enemies.

Find: Orkutsk (cabinet)
Obtain: Dead ringer, Frostburn, Abominape

Recipe to Make:
Chilly cheese = cool cheese + waterweed mould

Use in Recipes:
Cold cheese = chilly cheese + waterweed mould + waterweed mould

Cold Cheese

Buy: N/A
Sell: 550

Description: One of Munchie's favourites. Freezing cold cheese.

Use: Combat only

Function: When fed to Munchie, Munchie deals 120-140 ice-based damage to all enemies.

Find: Dark Empycchu (pot)

Recipe to Make:
Cold cheese = chilly cheese + waterweed mould + waterweed mould

Use in Recipes:
Blizzard blade = bastard sword + icicle dirk + cold cheese
C-c-cold cheese = cold cheese + premium mould + dragon dung
Highly-strung cheese = super spicy cheese + cold cheese + rock salt

C-C-Cold Cheese

Buy: N/A
Sell: 1400

Description: One of Munchie's f-f-favourites. Teeth ch-ch-chattering ch-ch-cheese that's as c-c-cold as w-w-winter in Orkutsk!

Use: Combat only

Function: When fed to Munchie, Munchie deals 210-230 ice-based damage to all enemies.

Obtain: Alchemy only

Recipe to Make:
C-c-cold cheese = cold cheese + premium mould + dragon dung

Use in Recipes:
Plain cheese = scorching cheese + c-c-cold cheese

Mild Cheese

Buy: N/A
Sell: 400

Description: One of Munchie's favourites. Cheese with healing properties.

Use: Combat only

Function: When fed to Munchie, Munchie restores 30-40 HP to all allies.

Received: Waterfall Hut

Recipe to Make:
Mild cheese = plain cheese + amor seco essence

Use in Recipes:
None

Cured Cheese

Buy: N/A
Sell: 800

Description: One of Munchie's favourites. Delicious cheese which makes the entire party feel better.

Use: Combat only

Function: When fed to Munchie, Munchie restores 100-120 HP to all allies.

Received: Waterfall Hut
Find: Black Citadel (barrel)

Recipe to Make:
Cured cheese = fresh milk + premium mould + amor seco essence

Use in Recipes:
Power shield = magic shield + strength ring + cured cheese

Angel Cheese

Buy: N/A
Sell: 2100

Description: One of Munchie's favourites. Blessed by an angel.

Use: Combat only

Function: When fed to Munchie, Munchie casts Zing on a randomly chosen fallen ally.

Find: Unknown... (pot)
Received: Waterfall Hut

Recipe to Make:
Angel cheese = fresh milk + premium mould + Yggdrasil dew

Use in Recipes:
None

HARD CHEESE

Buy: N/A
Sell: 500

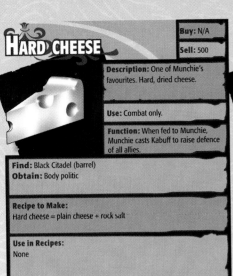

Description: One of Munchie's favourites. Hard, dried cheese.

Use: Combat only.

Function: When fed to Munchie, Munchie casts Kabuff to raise defence of all allies.

Find: Black Citadel (barrel)
Obtain: Body politic

Recipe to Make:
Hard cheese = plain cheese + rock salt

Use in Recipes:
None

SOFT CHEESE

Buy: N/A
Sell: 600

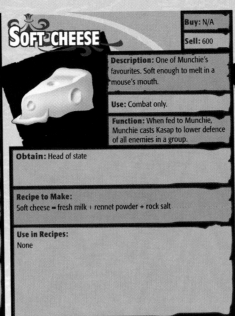

Description: One of Munchie's favourites. Soft enough to melt in a mouse's mouth.

Use: Combat only.

Function: When fed to Munchie, Munchie casts Kasap to lower defence of all enemies in a group.

Obtain: Head of state

Recipe to Make:
Soft cheese = fresh milk + rennet powder + rock salt

Use in Recipes:
None

CHUNKY CHEESE

Buy: N/A
Sell: 500

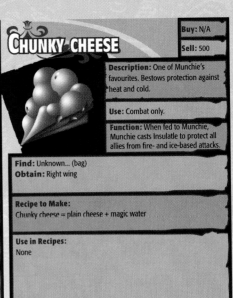

Description: One of Munchie's favourites. Bestows protection against heat and cold.

Use: Combat only.

Function: When fed to Munchie, Munchie casts Insulatle to protect all allies from fire- and ice-based attacks.

Find: Unknown... (bag)
Obtain: Right wing

Recipe to Make:
Chunky cheese = plain cheese + magic water

Use in Recipes:
None

HIGHLY-STRUNG CHEESE

Buy: N/A
Sell: 550

Description: One of Munchie's favourites. A tension-raising cheese.

Use: Combat only.

Function: When fed to Munchie, raises tension of all allies by one level.

Received: Waterfall Hut
Find: Unknown... (pot)
Obtain: Left wing

Recipe to Make:
Highly-strung cheese = super spicy cheese + cold cheese + rock salt

Use in Recipes:
None

INGREDIENTS AND OTHER ITEMS

IRON NAIL

Buy: N/A
Sell: 10

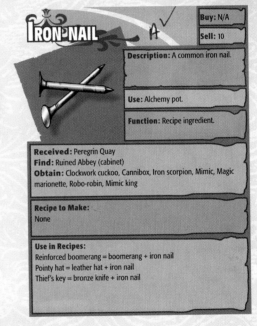

Description: A common iron nail.

Use: Alchemy pot.

Function: Recipe ingredient.

Received: Peregrin Quay
Find: Ruined Abbey (cabinet)
Obtain: Clockwork cuckoo, Cannibox, Iron scorpion, Mimic, Magic marionette, Robo-robin, Mimic king

Recipe to Make:
None

Use in Recipes:
Reinforced boomerang = boomerang + iron nail
Pointy hat = leather hat + iron nail
Thief's key = bronze knife + iron nail

ORICHALCUM

Buy: N/A
Sell: 5000

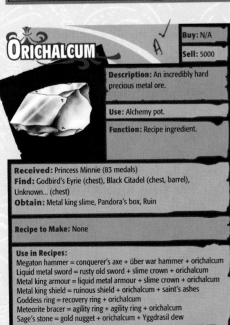

Description: An incredibly hard precious metal ore.

Use: Alchemy pot.

Function: Recipe ingredient.

Received: Princess Minnie (83 medals)
Find: Godbird's Eyrie (chest), Black Citadel (chest, barrel), Unknown... (chest)
Obtain: Metal king slime, Pandora's box, Ruin

Recipe to Make: None

Use in Recipes:
Megaton hammer = conquerer's axe + über war hammer + orichalcum
Liquid metal sword = rusty old sword + slime crown + orichalcum
Metal king armour = liquid metal armour + slime crown + orichalcum
Metal king shield = ruinous shield + orichalcum + saint's ashes
Goddess ring = recovery ring + orichalcum
Meteorite bracer = agility ring + agility ring + orichalcum
Sage's stone = gold nugget + orichalcum + Yggdrasil dew

GOLD NUGGET

Buy: N/A
Sell: 5000

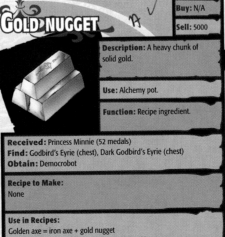

Description: A heavy chunk of solid gold.

Use: Alchemy pot.

Function: Recipe ingredient.

Received: Princess Minnie (52 medals)
Find: Godbird's Eyrie (chest), Dark Godbird's Eyrie (chest)
Obtain: Democrobot

Recipe to Make:
None

Use in Recipes:
Golden axe = iron axe + gold nugget
Golden tiara = silver tiara + thinking cap + gold nugget
Sage's stone = gold nugget + orichalcum + Yggdrasil dew

COWPAT

Buy: N/A
Sell: 3

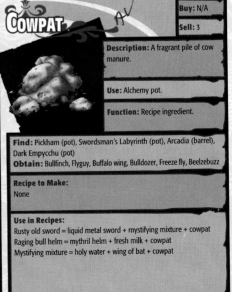

Description: A fragrant pile of cow manure.

Use: Alchemy pot.

Function: Recipe ingredient.

Find: Pickham (pot), Swordsman's Labyrinth (pot), Arcadia (barrel), Dark Empycchu (pot)
Obtain: Bullfinch, Flyguy, Buffalo wing, Bulldozer, Freeze fly, Beelzebuzz

Recipe to Make:
None

Use in Recipes:
Rusty old sword = liquid metal sword + mystifying mixture + cowpat
Raging bull helm = mythril helm + fresh milk + cowpat
Mystifying mixture = holy water + wing of bat + cowpat

DRAGON DUNG

Buy: 100
Sell: 50

Description: A smoking pile of dragon manure.

Use: Alchemy pot.

Function: Recipe ingredient.

Buy: Unknown...
Find: Arcadia (barrel), Dragon Graveyard (bag), Godbird's Eyrie (chest), Desert (chest)
Obtain: Hacksaurus, Freeze fly, Beelzebuzz, Dragurn, Bobonga

Recipe to Make:
None

Use in Recipes:
Scorching cheese = super spicy cheese + premium mould + dragon dung
C-c-cold cheese = cold cheese + premium mould + dragon dung

SAINT'S ASHES
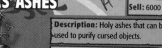

Buy: 12000
Sell: 6000

Description: Holy ashes that can be used to purify cursed objects.

Use: Alchemy pot.

Function: Recipe ingredient.

Buy: Unknown...
Trade Token: Baccarat (5000)
Received: Monster Arena Prize (Rank C)
Find: Dark Ruins (chest), Dark Godbird's Eyrie (chest), Black Citadel (barrel), Unknown... (bag)
Obtain: Dark minister, Dark moth, Dark gryphon, Dark sabrecat, Silhouette, Wight king

Recipe to Make: None

Use in Recipes: Sandstorm spear = partisan + saint's ashes
Über double-edge = double-edged sword + saint's ashes + saint's ashes
Leather whip = devil's tail + saint's ashes
Scourge whip = demon whip + saint's ashes
Platinum mail = zombie mail + saint's ashes
Metal king shield = ruinous shield + orichalcum + saint's ashes
Goddess shield = Thanatos' shield + saint's ashes
Mythril helm = Hades' helm + saint's ashes
Sun crown = skull helm + saint's ashes
Sorcerer's ring = skull ring + saint's ashes + saint's ashes

WING OF BAT

Buy: N/A
Sell: 16

Description: The large, black wing of a bat.

Use: Alchemy pot.

Function: Recipe ingredient

Find: Orkutsk (pot)
Obtain: Drackyma, Fat bat, Minidemon, Hipster, Night emperor, Redtail hipster, Shade, Dark condor

Recipe to Make: None

Use in Recipes:
Fallen angel rapier = holy silver rapier + devil's tail + wing of bat
Razor wing boomerang = edged boomerang + steel scythe + wing of bat
Dark robe = cloak of evasion + devil's tail + wing of bat
Chimaera wing = wing of bat + wing of bat
Mystifying mixture = holy water + wing of bat + cowpat

MAGIC BEAST HIDE

Buy: N/A
Sell: 70

Description: Sturdy hide obtained from an aggressive animal.

Use: Alchemy pot.

Function: Recipe ingredient

Find: Trodain Castle (barrel)
Obtain: Bullfinch, Diemon, Fat bat, Headhunter, Great sabrecat, Jumping jackal, Silenus, Orc king, Hellhound, Frou-frou

Recipe to Make:
None

Use in Recipes:
Leather armour = wayfarer's clothes + magic beast hide
Leather kilt = boxer shorts + magic beast hide
Leather dress = dancer's costume + magic beast hide
Fur poncho = magic beast hide + magic beast hide
Leather shield = pot lid + magic beast hide
Timbrel of tension = sun crown + tough guy tattoo + magic beast hide

RENNET POWDER

Buy: 10
Sell: 5

Description: A powder used to turn milk into cheese.

Use: Alchemy pot.

Function: Recipe ingredient

Buy: Ascantha, Argonia (during/after bazaar)
Find: Ascantha (pot), Pickham (pot), Baccarat (barrel), Argonia (2x pot), Arcadia (2x barrel), Empycchu (pot)
Obtain: Giant moth, Jargon, Devilmoth, Pink pongo, Shade, Killer moth, Golem, Dark moth, Silhouette

Recipe to Make:
None

Use in Recipes:
Plain cheese = fresh milk + rennet powder
Soft cheese = fresh milk + rennet powder + rock salt

ROCK SALT

Buy: N/A
Sell: 6

Description: A chunk of rock salt.

Use: Alchemy pot.

Function: Recipe ingredient

Find: Trodain Castle (pot), Argonia (barrel), Arcadia (2x barrel), Pirate's Cove (pot), Empycchu (pot), Dark Empycchu (pot), Black Citadel (barrel), Unknown... (pot)
Obtain: Mud mannequin, Rockbomb, Ber, Stone guardian

Recipe to Make:
None

Use in Recipes:
Holy water = amor seco essence + rock salt
Hard cheese = plain cheese + rock salt
Soft cheese = fresh milk + rennet powder + rock salt
Highly-strung cheese = super spicy cheese + cold cheese + rock salt

FRESH MILK

Buy: 30
Sell: 30

Description: Fresh cow's milk, straight from the udder!

Use: Alchemy pot.

Function: Recipe ingredient

Buy: Argonia (during/after bazaar)
Find: Field (cows), Pickham (barrel), Baccarat (pot), Arcadia (barrel), Empycchu (pot), Dark Empycchu (pot), Unknown... (2x pot)
Obtain: Jargon, Buffalo wing, Bobonga

Recipe to Make:
None

Use in Recipes:
White shield = light shield + fresh milk + fresh milk
Raging bull helm = mythril helm + fresh milk + cowpat
Plain cheese = fresh milk + rennet powder
Cured cheese = fresh milk + premium mould + amor seco essence
Angel cheese = fresh milk + premium mould + Yggdrasil dew
Soft cheese = fresh milk + rennet powder + rock salt

RED MOULD

Buy: 30
Sell: 15

Description: A chunk of mould with a fiery red colour.

Use: Alchemy pot.

Function: Recipe ingredient

Buy: Princess Minnie's Castle, Argonia (during/after bazaar)
Find: Ascantha (barrel), Pickham (barrel), Swordsman's Labyrinth (pot), Empycchu (pot)
Obtain: Giant moth, Morphean mushroom, Kisser, Paprikan, Hipster, Wailin' weed, Lump shaman, Mushroom mage, Lesser demon, Magic dumbbell, Blood mummy, Buffalogre

Recipe to Make:
None

Use in Recipes:
Spicy cheese = plain cheese + red mould
Super spicy cheese = spicy cheese + red mould + red mould
Premium mould = red mould + waterweed mould + Yggdrasil leaf

WATERWEED MOULD

Buy: 35
Sell: 18

Description: A chunk of mould that's as cold as ice.

Use: Alchemy pot.

Function: Recipe ingredient

Buy: Princess Minnie's Castle, Argonia (during/after bazaar)
Find: Ruined Abbey (barrel), Pickham (barrel), Trodain Castle (pot), Empycchu (pot)
Obtain: Kisser, Mushroom mage, Frogman, Smacker, Dark sea-diva, Killer croaker, Mohawker, Khalamari kid, King kelp, Pigmalion, Abyss diver

Recipe to Make:
None

Use in Recipes:
Cool cheese = plain cheese + waterweed mould
Chilly cheese = cool cheese + waterweed mould
Cold cheese = chilly cheese + waterweed mould + waterweed mould
Premium mould = red mould + waterweed mould + Yggdrasil leaf

PREMIUM MOULD

Buy: 500
Sell: 500

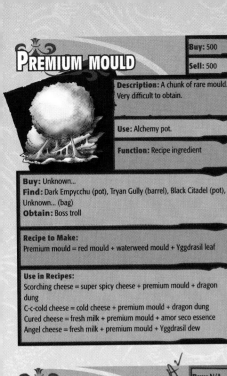

Description: A chunk of rare mould. Very difficult to obtain.

Use: Alchemy pot.

Function: Recipe ingredient

Buy: Unknown...
Find: Dark Empycchu (pot), Tryan Gully (barrel), Black Citadel (pot), Unknown... (bag)
Obtain: Boss troll

Recipe to Make:
Premium mould = red mould + waterweed mould + Yggdrasil leaf

Use in Recipes:
Scorching cheese = super spicy cheese + premium mould + dragon dung
C-c-cold cheese = cold cheese + premium mould + dragon dung
Cured cheese = fresh milk + premium mould + amor seco essence
Angel cheese = fresh milk + premium mould + Yggdrasil dew

NOOK GRASS

Buy: N/A
Sell: 600

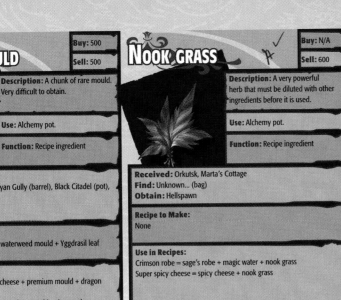

Description: A very powerful herb that must be diluted with other ingredients before it is used.

Use: Alchemy pot.

Function: Recipe ingredient

Received: Orkutsk, Marta's Cottage
Find: Unknown... (bag)
Obtain: Hellspawn

Recipe to Make:
None

Use in Recipes:
Crimson robe = sage's robe + magic water + nook grass
Super spicy cheese = spicy cheese + nook grass

MINI MEDAL

Buy: N/A
Sell: N/A

Description: A tiny medal. Gather enough and you can exchange them with Princess Minnie for prizes.

Use: Exchange with Princess Minnie for prizes.

Function: Bring these to Princess Minnie for rewards.

Find: See Side Quests part of this strategy guide for detailed locations.

Recipe to Make:
None

Use in Recipes:
None

ITEMS

INGREDIENTS AND OTHER ITEMS

COPPER MONSTER COIN

Buy: N/A
Sell: 200

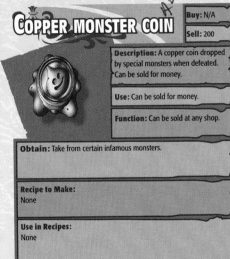

Description: A copper coin dropped by special monsters when defeated. Can be sold for money.

Use: Can be sold for money.

Function: Can be sold at any shop.

Obtain: Take from certain infamous monsters.

Recipe to Make:
None

Use in Recipes:
None

SILVER MONSTER COIN

Buy: N/A
Sell: 500

Description: A silver coin dropped by special monsters when defeated. Can be sold for money.

Use: Can be sold for money.

Function: Can be sold at any shop.

Obtain: Take from certain infamous monsters.

Recipe to Make:
None

Use in Recipes:
None

GOLD MONSTER COIN

Buy: N/A
Sell: 1000

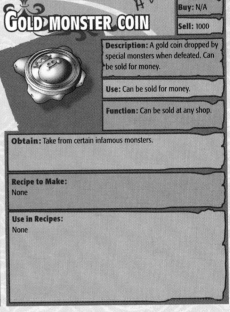

Description: A gold coin dropped by special monsters when defeated. Can be sold for money.

Use: Can be sold for money.

Function: Can be sold at any shop.

Obtain: Take from certain infamous monsters.

Recipe to Make:
None

Use in Recipes:
None

THIEF'S KEY

Buy: N/A
Sell: N/A

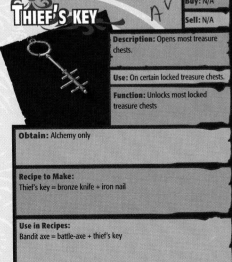

Description: Opens most treasure chests.

Use: On certain locked treasure chests.

Function: Unlocks most locked treasure chests

Obtain: Alchemy only

Recipe to Make:
Thief's key = bronze knife + iron nail

Use in Recipes:
Bandit axe = battle-axe + thief's key

MAGIC KEY

Buy: N/A
Sell: N/A

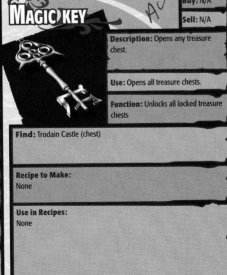

Description: Opens any treasure chest.

Use: Opens all treasure chests.

Function: Unlocks all locked treasure chests

Find: Trodain Castle (chest)

Recipe to Make:
None

Use in Recipes:
None

ULTIMATE KEY

Buy: N/A
Sell: N/A

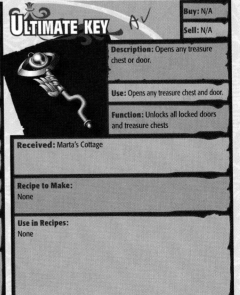

Description: Opens any treasure chest or door.

Use: Opens any treasure chest and door.

Function: Unlocks all locked doors and treasure chests

Received: Marta's Cottage

Recipe to Make:
None

Use in Recipes:
None

IMPORTANT ITEMS

GODBIRD'S SOULSTONE

Description: A sacred gem that allows the party to fly freely through the skies.

Function: Use in field areas to fly.

Received: Dark Godbird's Eyrie

CRYSTAL BALL

Description: The fortune-telling ball thrown into the waterfall by Kalderasha.

Function: Return this to Kalderasha's family.

Received: Waterfall Cave

TOOL BAG

Description: A tool bag left behind by the man who lives atop the waterfall.

Function: Return this to its owner for a reward.

Find: Farebury Region (on field)

JESSICA'S LETTER

Description: Jessica's letter to her family and friends, as retrieved by Munchie.

Function: Reveals Jessica's plans.

Find: Alexandria (examine)

WORLD MAP

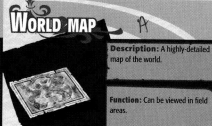

Description: A highly-detailed map of the world.

Function: Can be viewed in field areas.

Received: Maella Abbey

VENUS' TEAR

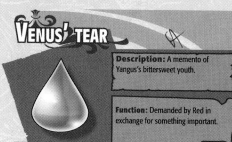

Description: A memento of Yangus's bittersweet youth.

Function: Demanded by Red in exchange for something important.

Find: Swordsman's Labyrinth (chest)

MOONSHADOW HARP

Description: A powerful instrument capable of calling forth a mysterious phantom ocean.

Function: Bring this to someone capable of playing it.

Received: Mole's Hole

SAND OF SERENITY

Description: A phial of mysterious powder received from Felix.

Function: Use this on a phantom sabrecat.

Received: Chateau Felix

LIZARD HUMOUR

Description: Powdered lizard extract. Used to disguise the odour of human hunters.

Function: Use this before entering Royal Hunting Ground.

Received: Argonia

ARGON HEART

Description: A crimson-coloured gemstone obtained by defeating an Argon lizard.

Function: Proof of a prince's valor.

Obtain: Royal Hunting Ground

GREAT BIG ARGON HEART

Description: A jumbo-sized Argon heart obtained through the party's hard work on the Royal Hunting Ground.

Function: Proof of a prince's valor.

Obtain: Royal Hunting Ground

MAGIC MIRROR

Description: A royal treasure of the Kingdom of Argonia.

Function: Must be restored through some process to the sun mirror.

Find: Argonia (examine)

SUN MIRROR

Description: The magic mirror restored to its true form by the power of the sea dragon.

Function: Set this in the pedestal at the Dark Ruins.

Obtain: Receive by recharging the magic mirror.

KRAN SPINELS

Description: A pair of precious jewels that were set into the eyes of the statue of Alexandra.

Function: Requested by Dominico in Arcadia.

Find: Tower of Alexandra (examine)

"THE BIG BOOK OF BARRIERS"

Description: An encyclopaedia of the world's magical barriers.

Function: Requested by Dominico in Arcadia.

Find: Arcadia (bookshelf)

MARTA'S BAG

Description: A pouch prepared by Marta for the medicine man, Marek.

Function: Marta asks you to take this to Marek.

Received: Marta's Cottage

ILLUMINATED SEA CHART

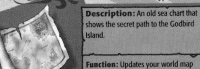

Description: An old sea chart that shows the secret path to the Godbird Island.

Function: Updates your world map with a secret path.

Obtain: Pirate's Cove

ITEMS

IMPORTANT ITEMS

DARKTREE LEAF

Description: Works like a compass, guiding the user to the source of evil.

Function: Guides user to a source of great evil.

Received: Tryan Gully

ECHO FLUTE

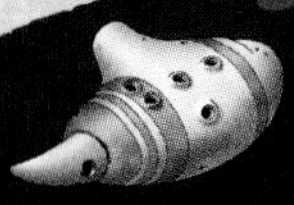

Description: A mysterious flute that locates orbs using echoes.

Function: Plays a special tone when an orb is nearby.

Received: Empycchu

GOLD ORB

Description: A gold orb that contains the soul of one of the great sages.

Function: Unknown…

Found: Unknown…

SILVER ORB

Description: A silver orb that contains the soul of one of the great sages.

Function: Unknown…

Found: Unknown…

RED ORB

Description: A red orb that contains the soul of one of the great sages.

Function: Unknown…

Found: Unknown…

BLUE ORB

Description: A blue orb that contains the soul of one of the great sages.

Function: Unknown…

Found: Unknown...

GREEN ORB

Description: A green orb that contains the soul of one of the great sages.

Function: Unknown…

Found: Unknown...

YELLOW ORB

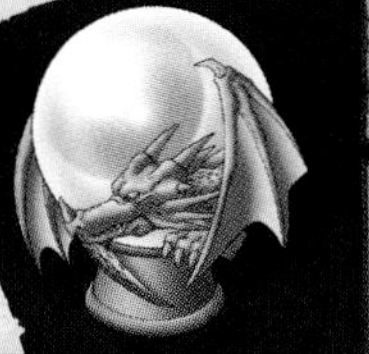

Description: A yellow orb that contains the soul of one of the great sages.

Function: Unknown…

Found: Unknown...

PURPLE ORB

Description: A purple orb that contains the soul of one of the great sages.

Function: Unknown…

Found: Unknown…

GODBIRD SCEPTRE

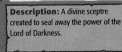

Description: A divine sceptre created to seal away the power of the Lord of Darkness.

Function: Has some significance in an important battle.

Received: Empycchu

THIEF'S KEY RECIPE

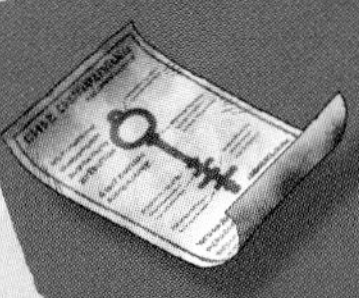

Description: A suspicious-looking document that contains tips on how to make a thief's key.

Function: Updates your recipe list.

Find: Farebury (on ground)

EROS' BOW RECIPE

Description: A strange document that contains tips on how to make Eros' bow.

Function: Updates your recipe list.

Find: Pickham (on ground)

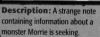

Description: A strange document that contains tips on how to make an imp knife.

Function: Updates your recipe list.

Find: Trodain Castle (on ground)

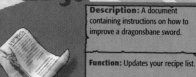

Description: A document containing instructions on how to improve a dragonsbane sword.

Function: Updates your recipe list.

Find: Savella Cathedral (on ground)

Description: A strange note containing information about a monster Morrie is seeking.

Function: Contains hint for quest.

Received: Monster Arena

MORRIE'S MEMO #2

Description: A strange note containing information about a monster Morrie is seeking.

Function: Contains hint for quest.

Received: Monster Arena

MORRIE'S MEMO #3

Description: A strange note containing information about a monster Morrie is seeking.

Function: Contains hint for quest.

Received: Monster Arena

MONSTER ARENA KEY

Description: A key received from Morrie that allows you to enter the Monster Arena.

Function: Unlocks Monster Arena main entrance.

Received: Monster Arena

ARMAMENTS

Each character can equip four armaments at once: armour, a shield, a helm, and an accessory. Basic armour provides most of the defensive boost, plus many types of armour have special properties that provide resistance to certain spells or improve the wearer's ability to dodge. Shields and helms provide a lesser defensive boost, although they too may have special defensive properties.

Accessories do all sorts of things. They may boost defence, but they're just as likely to boost attack, agility, or even wisdom stats. With many accessories, the stat boost pales in comparison to the special effect, which may restore HP or provide immunities to certain effects. Other accessories have little use as stat boosters, existing primarily as ingredients to create other items.

ITEMS

ARMOUR

Armour

DANGEROUS BUSTIER ✓

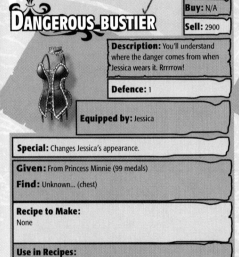

Buy: N/A
Sell: 2900

Description: You'll understand where the danger comes from when Jessica wears it. Rrrrrow!

Defence: 1

Equipped by: Jessica

Special: Changes Jessica's appearance.

Given: From Princess Minnie (99 medals)
Find: Unknown... (chest)

Recipe to Make:
None

Use in Recipes:
Divine bustier = dangerous bustier + shimmering dress

JESSICA'S OUTFIT ✓

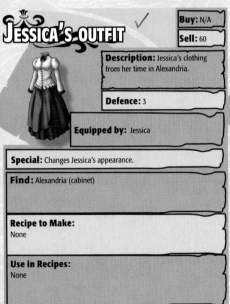

Buy: N/A
Sell: 60

Description: Jessica's clothing from her time in Alexandria.

Defence: 3

Equipped by: Jessica

Special: Changes Jessica's appearance.

Find: Alexandria (cabinet)

Recipe to Make:
None

Use in Recipes:
None

PLAIN CLOTHES ✓

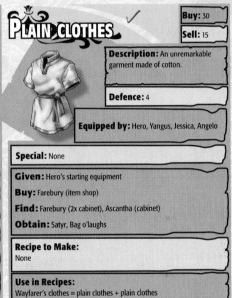

Buy: 30
Sell: 15

Description: An unremarkable garment made of cotton.

Defence: 4

Equipped by: Hero, Yangus, Jessica, Angelo

Special: None

Given: Hero's starting equipment
Buy: Farebury (item shop)
Find: Farebury (2x cabinet), Ascantha (cabinet)
Obtain: Satyr, Bag o'laughs

Recipe to Make:
None

Use in Recipes:
Wayfarer's clothes = plain clothes + plain clothes

BANDIT'S GRASS SKIRT ✓

Buy: 35
Sell: 18

Description: A rough grass kilt of the kind preferred by Yangus.

Defence: 5

Equipped by: Yangus

Special: None

Given: Yangus's starting equipment
Buy: Farebury
Find: Ruined Abbey (cabinet)
Obtain: Candy cat, Dancing flame, See urchin

Recipe to Make:
None

Use in Recipes:
Boxer shorts = bandit's grass skirt + bandanna
Magical skirt = magical mace + bandit's grass skirt + magical hat
Bandit mail = bandit's axe + bandit's grass skirt + heavy armour

WAYFARER'S CLOTHES ✓

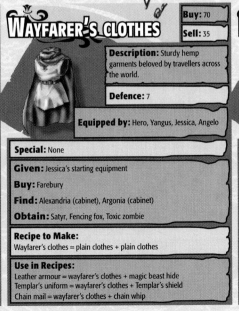

Buy: 70
Sell: 35

Description: Sturdy hemp garments beloved by travellers across the world.

Defence: 7

Equipped by: Hero, Yangus, Jessica, Angelo

Special: None

Given: Jessica's starting equipment
Buy: Farebury
Find: Alexandria (cabinet), Argonia (cabinet)
Obtain: Satyr, Fencing fox, Toxic zombie

Recipe to Make:
Wayfarer's clothes = plain clothes + plain clothes

Use in Recipes:
Leather armour = wayfarer's clothes + magic beast hide
Templar's uniform = wayfarer's clothes + Templar's shield
Chain mail = wayfarer's clothes + chain whip

BOXER SHORTS ✓

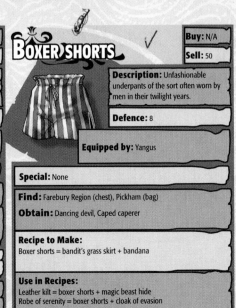

Buy: N/A
Sell: 50

Description: Unfashionable underpants of the sort often worn by men in their twilight years.

Defence: 8

Equipped by: Yangus

Special: None

Find: Farebury Region (chest), Pickham (bag)
Obtain: Dancing devil, Caped caperer

Recipe to Make:
Boxer shorts = bandit's grass skirt + bandana

Use in Recipes:
Leather kilt = boxer shorts + magic beast hide
Robe of serenity = boxer shorts + cloak of evasion

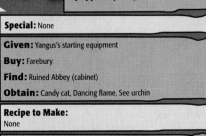

SILK ROBE

Buy: 420
Sell: 210

Description: A high-quality garment woven from pure silk.

Defence: 10

Equipped by: Jessica, Angelo

Special: None

Buy: Peregrin Quay

Find: Riverside Cottage (cabinet)

Obtain: Puppeteer, Bodkin bowyer

Recipe to Make:
None

Use in Recipes:
None

LEATHER ARMOUR

Buy: 180
Sell: 90

Description: Lightweight armour made of leather.

Defence: 11

Equipped by: Hero, Angelo

Special: None

Buy: Farebury

Obtain: Mum

Recipe to Make:
Leather armour = wayfarer's clothes + magic beast hide

Use in Recipes:
Scale armour = leather armour + dragon scale

LEATHER KILT

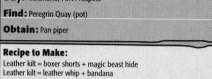

Buy: 220
Sell: 110

Description: A sturdy kilt fashioned from animal hide.

Defence: 12

Equipped by: Yangus

Special: None

Buy: Alexandria, Port Prospect

Find: Peregrin Quay (pot)

Obtain: Pan piper

Recipe to Make:
Leather kilt = boxer shorts + magic beast hide
Leather kilt = leather whip + bandana

Use in Recipes:
Titan belt = leather kilt + strength ring

TEMPLAR'S UNIFORM

Buy: N/A
Sell: 275

Description: The official uniform of the Templar Knights, whose sworn duty is to protect the church.

Defence: 13

Equipped by: Angelo

Special: None

Given: Angelo's starting equipment

Obtain: Skeleton

Recipe to Make:
Templar's uniform = wayfarer's clothes + Templar's shield

Use in Recipes:
Templar's shield = Templar's uniform + iron shield

LEATHER DRESS

Buy: 380
Sell: 190

Description: A sturdy suit of leather armour made for female adventurers.

Defence: 15

Equipped by: Jessica

Special: None

Buy: Ascantha

Find: Arcadia (cabinet)

Recipe to Make:
Leather dress = dancer's costume + magic beast hide

Use in Recipes:
None

SCALE ARMOUR

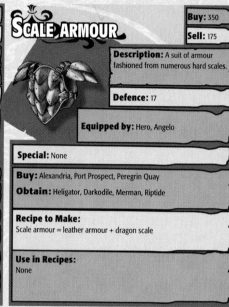

Buy: 350
Sell: 175

Description: A suit of armour fashioned from numerous hard scales.

Defence: 17

Equipped by: Hero, Angelo

Special: None

Buy: Alexandria, Port Prospect, Peregrin Quay

Obtain: Heligator, Darkodile, Merman, Riptide

Recipe to Make:
Scale armour = leather armour + dragon scale

Use in Recipes:
None

CHAIN MAIL

Buy: 500
Sell: 250

Description: A comfortable and lightweight suit of armour constructed from innumerable metal links.

Defence: 20

Equipped by: Yangus

Special: None

Buy: Peregrin Quay, Simpleton

Find: Kingdom of Ascantha (chest), Pickham (cabinet)

Obtain: Walking corpse

Recipe to Make:
Chain mail = wayfarer's clothes + chain whip

Use in Recipes:
Bronze armour = chain mail + bronze shield

LEATHER CAPE

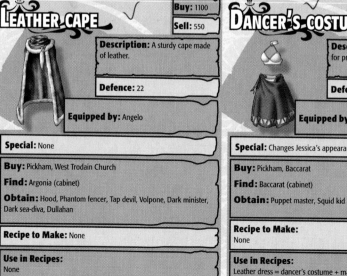

Buy: 1100
Sell: 550

Description: A sturdy cape made of leather.

Defence: 22

Equipped by: Angelo

Special: None

Buy: Pickham, West Trodain Church

Find: Argonia (cabinet)

Obtain: Hood, Phantom fencer, Tap devil, Volpone, Dark minister, Dark sea-diva, Dullahan

Recipe to Make: None

Use in Recipes:
None

DANCER'S COSTUME

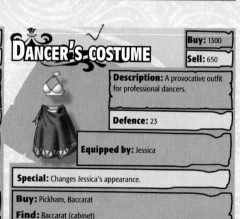

Buy: 1300
Sell: 650

Description: A provocative outfit for professional dancers.

Defence: 23

Equipped by: Jessica

Special: Changes Jessica's appearance.

Buy: Pickham, Baccarat

Find: Baccarat (cabinet)

Obtain: Puppet master, Squid kid

Recipe to Make:
None

Use in Recipes:
Leather dress = dancer's costume + magic beast hide
Dancer's mail = dancer's costume + silver mail

BRONZE ARMOUR ✓

Buy: 840
Sell: 420

Description: A suit of armour fashioned from forged bronze plates.

Defence: 24

Equipped by: Hero

Special: None

Buy: Ascantha, Pickham

Recipe to Make:
Bronze armour = chain mail + bronze shield

Use in Recipes:
None

IRON CUIRASS

Buy: 1000
Sell: 500

Description: Iron armour that only covers the wearer's chest.

Defence: 25

Equipped by: Yangus

Special: None

Buy: Ascantha

Obtain: Mars rover, Robo-robin, Killing machine, Buffalogre

Recipe to Make:
Iron cuirass = iron shield + iron shield

Use in Recipes:
Silver cuirass = iron cuirass + silver platter + silver platter

FUR PONCHO

Buy: N/A
Sell: 1100

Description: A sturdy fur garment capable of reducing damage from fire- and ice-based attacks by 20 points.

Defence: 29

Equipped by: Yangus

Special: Damage from fire- and ice-based attacks is reduced by 20.

Find: Empycchu (cabinet)

Recipe to Make:
Fur poncho = magic beast hide + magic beast hide

Use in Recipes:
Fur hood = fur poncho + feathered cap

ITEMS

ARMOUR

CLOAK OF EVASION ✓

Buy: 3000
Sell: 1500

Description: A magical cloak that makes it easier to dodge enemy attacks.

Defence: 29

Equipped by: Jessica, Angelo

Special: Increases ability to dodge enemy attacks.

Buy: Peddler's Tent, Arcadia, Peddler in Neos (after certain events)

Find: Argonia (chest), Arcadia (cabinet)

Obtain: Hellspawn

Recipe to Make:
None

Use in Recipes:
Robe of serenity = boxer shorts + cloak of evasion
Dark robe = cloak of evasion + devil's tail + wing of bat

IRON ARMOUR ✓

Buy: 1800
Sell: 900

Description: Heavy and sturdy iron armour.

Defence: 32

Equipped by: Hero, Yangus

Special: None

Buy: Baccarat

Find: Uncharted Island west of Maella Abbey (chest)

Obtain: Restless armour, Infernal armour, Ber

Recipe to Make:
None

Use in Recipes:
None

ROBE OF SERENITY

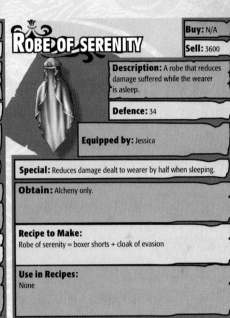

Buy: N/A
Sell: 3600

Description: A robe that reduces damage suffered while the wearer is asleep.

Defence: 34

Equipped by: Jessica

Special: Reduces damage dealt to wearer by half when sleeping.

Obtain: Alcheny only.

Recipe to Make:
Robe of serenity = boxer shorts + cloak of evasion

Use in Recipes:
None

TURTLE SHELL ✓

Buy: 2300
Sell: 1100

Description: A large tortoise shell worn in place of armour by those who don't mind looking silly.

Defence: 37

Equipped by: Yangus

Special: None

Buy: Peddler's Tent, Peddler in Neos (after certain events)

Obtain: Boh, Crayzee

Recipe to Make:
None

Use in Recipes:
None

BUNNY SUIT

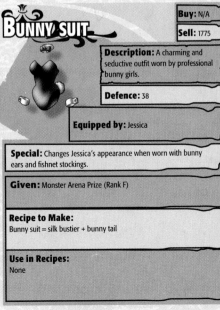

Buy: N/A
Sell: 1775

Description: A charming and seductive outfit worn by professional bunny girls.

Defence: 38

Equipped by: Jessica

Special: Changes Jessica's appearance when worn with bunny ears and fishnet stockings.

Given: Monster Arena Prize (Rank F)

Recipe to Make:
Bunny suit = silk bustier + bunny tail

Use in Recipes:
None

FULL-PLATE ARMOUR ✓

Buy: 2300
Sell: 1150

Description: Armour made from forged steel plates that cover the wearer's entire body.

Defence: 39

Equipped by: Hero

Special: None

Buy: Savella Cathedral, Neos

Recipe to Make:
None

Use in Recipes:
Magic armour = full plate armour + prayer ring + ruby of protection

MAGIC VESTMENT ✓

Buy: 4400
Sell: 2200

Description: An enchanted garment that reduces damage from spells by 2/3.

Defence: 39

Equipped by: Jessica, Angelo

Special: Damage from Frizz, Sizz, Crack, Bang, and Woosh-type spells is reduced by 2/3.

Buy: Argonia, Savella Cathedral

Find: Arcadia (chest)

Obtain: Fallen priest, Wight priest

Recipe to Make:
None

Use in Recipes:
Sage's robe = magic vestment + scholar's cap

ZOMBIE MAIL

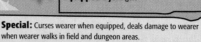

Buy: N/A
Sell: 250

Description: Ill-fated armour surrounded by an air of danger.

Defence: 42

Equipped by: Angelo

Special: Curses wearer when equipped, deals damage to wearer when wearer walks in field and dungeon areas.

Find: Northwest Isle (chest)

Obtain: Dark dullahan

Recipe to Make:
Zombie mail = zombiesbane + silver mail
Zombie mail = platinum mail + devil's tail

Use in Recipes:
Platinum mail = zombie mail + saint's ashes

SILVER CUIRASS

Buy: 3200
Sell: 1600

Description: Silver armour that covers the wearer's chest.

Defence: 44

Equipped by: Yangus

Special: None

Buy: Neos

Recipe to Make:
Silver cuirass = iron cuirass + silver platter + silver platter

Use in Recipes:
None

SILK BUSTIER ✓

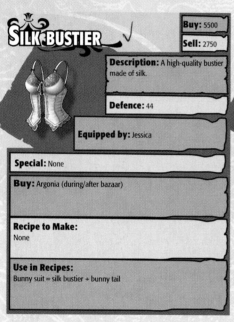

Buy: 5500
Sell: 2750

Description: A high-quality bustier made of silk.

Defence: 44

Equipped by: Jessica

Special: None

Buy: Argonia (during/after bazaar)

Recipe to Make:
None

Use in Recipes:
Bunny suit = silk bustier + bunny tail

SPANGLED DRESS ✓

Buy: N/A
Sell: 2350

Description: A chic dress worn by fashionable women-about-town.

Defence: 46

Equipped by: Jessica

Special: None

Token Trade: Baccarat (3000 tokens)

Find: Baccarat (cabinet)

Obtain: Swingin' hipster, Unholy bishop

Recipe to Make:
None

Use in Recipes:
Shimmering dress = spangled dress + gold bracer + ruby of protection

POSH WAISTCOAT ✓

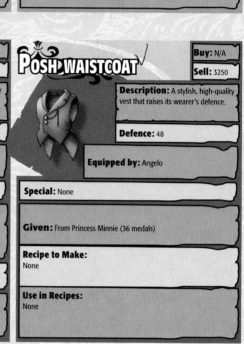

Buy: N/A
Sell: 3250

Description: A stylish, high-quality vest that raises its wearer's defence.

Defence: 48

Equipped by: Angelo

Special: None

Given: From Princess Minnie (36 medals)

Recipe to Make:
None

Use in Recipes:
None

SILVER MAIL ✓

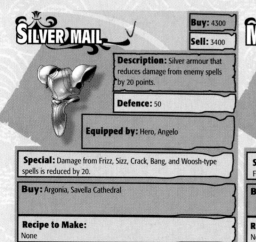

Buy: 4300
Sell: 3400

Description: Silver armour that reduces damage from enemy spells by 20 points.

Defence: 50

Equipped by: Hero, Angelo

Special: Damage from Frizz, Sizz, Crack, Bang, and Woosh-type spells is reduced by 20.

Buy: Argonia, Savella Cathedral

Recipe to Make:
None

Use in Recipes:
Dancer's mail = dancer's costume + silver mail
Zombie mail = zombiesbane + silver mail
Dragon mail = silver mail + dragon scale + dragon scale
Mirror armour = silver mail + mirror shield + mirror shield

MAGIC BIKINI ✓

Buy: 13,800
Sell: 6900

Description: An enchanted bikini that reduces damage from enemy spells by 15 points.

Defence: 50

Equipped by: Jessica

Special: Changes Jessica's appearance when worn. Damage from Frizz, Sizz, and Bang-type spells is reduced by 15.

Buy: Arcadia

Recipe to Make:
None

Use in Recipes:
None

HEAVY ARMOUR ✓

Buy: 5000
Sell: 2500

Description: Thick armour that reduces damage from fire- and ice-based spells by 15 points.

Defence: 52

Equipped by: Yangus

Special: Damage from fire- and ice-based spells is reduced by 15.

Buy: Argonia (during/after bazaar)

Obtain: Lethal armour

Recipe to Make:
None

Use in Recipes:
Bandit mail = bandit axe + bandit's grass skirt + heavy armour

SAGE'S ROBE

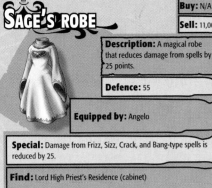

Buy: N/A
Sell: 11,000

Description: A magical robe that reduces damage from spells by 25 points.

Defence: 55

Equipped by: Angelo

Special: Damage from Frizz, Sizz, Crack, and Bang-type spells is reduced by 25.

Find: Lord High Priest's Residence (cabinet)

Recipe to Make:
Sage's robe = magic vestment + scholar's cap

Use in Recipes:
Crimson robe = sage's robe + magic water + nook grass

MAGICAL SKIRT

Buy: N/A
Sell: 3350

Description: An enchanted skirt that reduces damage from enemy spells by 2/3.

Defence: 55

Equipped by: Jessica

Special: Damage from Frizz, Sizz, Crack, Bang, and Woosh-type spells is reduced by 2/3.

Obtain: Alchemy only

Recipe to Make:
Magical skirt = magical mace + bandit's grass skirt + magical hat

Use in Recipes:
Angel's robe = magical skirt + flowing dress

MAGIC ARMOUR

Buy: 6100
Sell: 3750

Description: Enchanted armour that reduces damage from enemy spells by 15 points.

Defence: 55

Equipped by: Hero, Angelo

Special: Damage from Frizz, Sizz, Crack, Bang, and Woosh-type spells is reduced by 15.

Buy: Argonia (during/after bazaar), Arcadia

Obtain: Body politic

Recipe to Make:
Magic armour = full plate armour + prayer ring + ruby of protection

Use in Recipes:
Spiked armour = edged boomerang + magic armour

DANCER'S MAIL

Buy: N/A
Sell: 8200

Description: Lightweight and easy to move in, this armour allows the wearer to dodge enemy attacks more easily.

Defence: 57

Equipped by: Angelo

Special: Increases ability to dodge enemy attacks.

Obtain: Alchemy only

Recipe to Make:
Dancer's mail = dancer's costume + silver mail

Use in Recipes:
None

FLOWING DRESS ✓

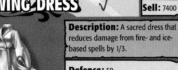

Buy: 14,800
Sell: 7400

Description: A sacred dress that reduces damage from fire- and ice-based spells by 1/3.

Defence: 59

Equipped by: Jessica

Special: Damage from fire- and ice-based attacks is reduced by 1/3.

Buy: Tryan Gully

Recipe to Make:
None

Use in Recipes:
Angel's robe = magical skirt + flowing dress

DRAGON MAIL

Buy: 12,000
Sell: 6000

Description: Armour fashioned from dragon scales. Provides excellent protection from fire- and ice-based spells.

Defence: 60

Equipped by: Hero, Yangus

Special: Damage from fire- and ice-based attacks is reduced by 20.

Buy: Orkutsk

Recipe to Make:
Dragon mail = silver mail + dragon scale + dragon scale

Use in Recipes:
None

VELVET CAPE ✓

Buy: 9400
Sell: 5300

Description: A durable cape made of velvet.

Defence: 60

Equipped by: Angelo

Special: None

Buy: Orkutsk

Obtain: Heavy hood, Unholy bishop

Recipe to Make:
None

Use in Recipes:
None

SHIMMERING DRESS

Buy: N/A
Sell: 8800

Description: A mysterious dress that occasionally reflects a spell cast on the wearer back at the caster.

Defence: 67

Equipped by: Jessica

Special: Sometimes reflects spells cast on wearer back to caster.

Obtain: Alchemy only

Recipe to Make:
Shimmering dress = spangled dress + gold bracer + ruby of protection

Use in Recipes:
Shamshir of light = rune staff + shimmering dress + light shield
Princess's robe = shimmering dress + angel's robe + gold rosary
Divine bustier = dangerous bustier + shimmering dress

SPIKED ARMOUR

Buy: N/A
Sell: 9500

Description: Mysterious armour that reflects damage back at the enemy who inflicted it.

Defence: 68

Equipped by: Hero, Yangus

Special: Sometimes reflects a percentage of damage dealt to wearer back to attacker.

Obtain: Alchemy only

Recipe to Make:
Spiked armour = edged boomerang + magic armour

Use in Recipes:
None

PLATINUM MAIL

Buy: N/A
Sell: 4900

Description: Platinum armour that reduces damage from enemy spells by 15 points.

Defence: 72

Equipped by: Hero, Angelo

Special: Damage from Frizz, Sizz, Crack, Bang, and Woosh-type spells is reduced by 15.

Obtain: Hell's gatekeeper

Recipe to Make:
Platinum mail = zombie mail + saint's ashes

Use in Recipes:
Zombie mail = platinum mail + devil's tail

ANGEL'S ROBE

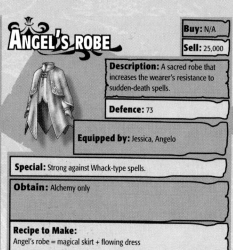

Buy: N/A
Sell: 25,000

Description: A sacred robe that increases the wearer's resistance to sudden-death spells.

Defence: 73

Equipped by: Jessica, Angelo

Special: Strong against Whack-type spells.

Obtain: Alchemy only

Recipe to Make:
Angel's robe = magical skirt + flowing dress

Use in Recipes:
Princess's robe = shimmering dress + angel's robe + gold rosary

BANDIT MAIL

Buy: 13,000
Sell: 7000

Description: Sturdy armour made from an exotic metal.

Defence: 80

Equipped by: Yangus

Special: None

Buy: Empycchu, Dark Empycchu

Recipe to Make:
Bandit mail = bandit axe + bandit's grass skirt + heavy armour

Use in Recipes:
Gigant armour = bandit mail + mighty armlet + mighty armlet

CRIMSON ROBE

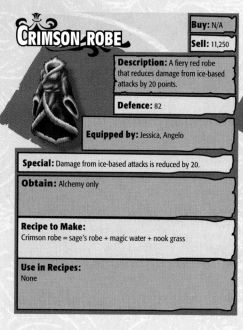

Buy: N/A
Sell: 11,250

Description: A fiery red robe that reduces damage from ice-based attacks by 20 points.

Defence: 82

Equipped by: Jessica, Angelo

Special: Damage from ice-based attacks is reduced by 20.

Obtain: Alchemy only

Recipe to Make:
Crimson robe = sage's robe + magic water + nook grass

Use in Recipes:
None

SACRED ARMOUR ✓

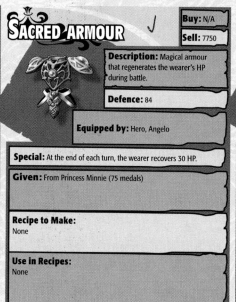

Buy: N/A
Sell: 7750

Description: Magical armour that regenerates the wearer's HP during battle.

Defence: 84

Equipped by: Hero, Angelo

Special: At the end of each turn, the wearer recovers 30 HP.

Given: From Princess Minnie (75 medals)

Recipe to Make:
None

Use in Recipes:
None

DARK ROBE

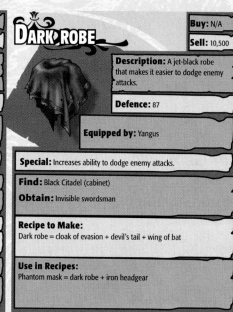

Buy: N/A
Sell: 10,500

Description: A jet-black robe that makes it easier to dodge enemy attacks.

Defence: 87

Equipped by: Yangus

Special: Increases ability to dodge enemy attacks.

Find: Black Citadel (cabinet)
Obtain: Invisible swordsman

Recipe to Make:
Dark robe = cloak of evasion + devil's tail + wing of bat

Use in Recipes:
Phantom mask = dark robe + iron headgear

MIRROR ARMOUR

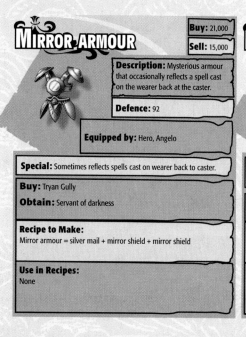

Buy: 21,000
Sell: 15,000

Description: Mysterious armour that occasionally reflects a spell cast on the wearer back at the caster.

Defence: 92

Equipped by: Hero, Angelo

Special: Sometimes reflects spells cast on wearer back to caster.

Buy: Tryan Gully
Obtain: Servant of darkness

Recipe to Make:
Mirror armour = silver mail + mirror shield + mirror shield

Use in Recipes:
None

PRINCESS'S ROBE

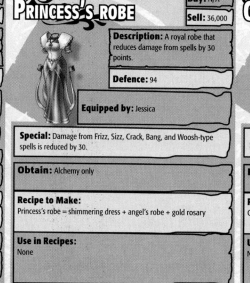

Buy: N/A
Sell: 36,000

Description: A royal robe that reduces damage from spells by 30 points.

Defence: 94

Equipped by: Jessica

Special: Damage from Frizz, Sizz, Crack, Bang, and Woosh-type spells is reduced by 30.

Obtain: Alchemy only

Recipe to Make:
Princess's robe = shimmering dress + angel's robe + gold rosary

Use in Recipes:
None

GIGANT ARMOUR

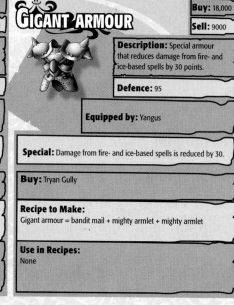

Buy: 18,000
Sell: 9000

Description: Special armour that reduces damage from fire- and ice-based spells by 30 points.

Defence: 95

Equipped by: Yangus

Special: Damage from fire- and ice-based spells is reduced by 30.

Buy: Tryan Gully

Recipe to Make:
Gigant armour = bandit mail + mighty armlet + mighty armlet

Use in Recipes:
None

LIQUID METAL ARMOUR ✓

Buy: N/A
Sell: 4750

Description: Metallic armour that reduces damage from curses by 2/3.

Defence: 101

Equipped by: Hero, Yangus, Jessica, Angelo

Special: Damage from Curse-type spells is reduced by 2/3.

Find: Unknown… (chest)
Token Trade: Baccarat (50,000 tokens)

Recipe to Make:
None

Use in Recipes:
Metal king armour = liquid metal armour + slime crown + orichalcum

DRAGON ROBE ✓

Buy: N/A
Sell: 7500

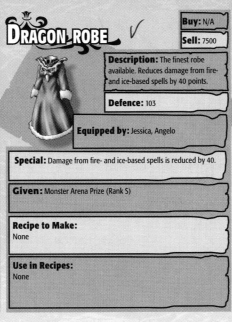

Description: The finest robe available. Reduces damage from fire- and ice-based spells by 40 points.

Defence: 103

Equipped by: Jessica, Angelo

Special: Damage from fire- and ice-based spells is reduced by 40.

Given: Monster Arena Prize (Rank S)

Recipe to Make:
None

Use in Recipes:
None

DIVINE BUSTIER

Buy: N/A
Sell: 37,000

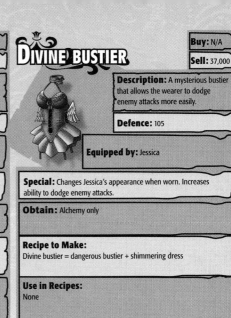

Description: A mysterious bustier that allows the wearer to dodge enemy attacks more easily.

Defence: 105

Equipped by: Jessica

Special: Changes Jessica's appearance when worn. Increases ability to dodge enemy attacks.

Obtain: Alchemy only

Recipe to Make:
Divine bustier = dangerous bustier + shimmering dress

Use in Recipes:
None

ITEMS

SHIELDS

METAL KING ARMOUR

Buy: N/A
Sell: 5000

Description: The ultimate suit of armour offering the strongest possible defence.

Defence: 120

Equipped by: Hero, Yangus, Jessica, Angelo

Special: Damage from fire- and ice-based attacks is reduced by 30.

Obtain: Alchemy only

Recipe to Make:
Metal king armour = liquid metal armour + slime crown + orichalcum

Use in Recipes:
None

SHIELDS

POT LID ✓

Buy: 40
Sell: 20

Description: The lid to a large cooking pot, commandeered to act as a makeshift shield of sorts.

Defence: 2

Equipped by: Yangus, Jessica

Special: None

Buy: Peregrin Quay
Find: Farebury (cabinet), Ferry (barrel)
Obtain: Mecha-mynah, Cannibox

Recipe to Make: None

Use in Recipes:
Leather shield = pot lid + magic beast hide

LEATHER SHIELD

Buy: 70
Sell: 35

Description: A simple shield made of leather stretched over wood.

Defence: 4

Equipped by: Hero, Yangus, Angelo

Special: None

Buy: Farebury
Find: Farebury (chest)
Obtain: Crocodog

Recipe to Make: Leather shield = pot lid + magic beast hide

Use in Recipes:
Scale shield = leather shield + dragon scale
Bronze shield = leather shield + bronze knife

SCALE SHIELD

Buy: 180
Sell: 90

Description: A shield made from extremely hard scales.

Defence: 7

Equipped by: Hero, Yangus, Jessica, Angelo

Special: None

Buy: Alexandria, Port Prospect, Peregrin Quay
Find: Tower of Alexandria (chest)
Obtain: Headhunter, Yabby, Wild boarfish

Recipe to Make: Scale shield = leather shield + dragon scale

Use in Recipes:
Snakeskin whip = leather whip + scale shield

SILVER PLATTER ✓

Buy: N/A
Sell: 100

Description: A silver serving platter large enough to serve as a makeshift shield.

Defence: 8

Equipped by: Jessica

Special: None

Token Trade: Pickham (500 tokens)

Find: Le Club Puff-Puff (cabinet)

Recipe to Make:
None

Use in Recipes:
Silver cuirass = iron cuirass + silver platter + silver platter
White shield = silver platter + iron shield
Silver tiara = silver platter + coral hairpin

BRONZE SHIELD ✓

Buy: 370
Sell: 185

Description: A large shield of beaten bronze.

Defence: 10

Equipped by: Hero, Yangus

Special: None

Buy: Ascantha

Find: Ruined Abbey (chest)

Obtain: Dark skeleton

Recipe to Make:
Bronze shield = leather shield + bronze knife

Use in Recipes:
Bronze armour = chain mail + bronze shield

KITTY SHIELD ✓

Buy: N/A
Sell: 550

Description: A light and durable shield sporting a cute kitty-cat motif.

Defence: 12

Equipped by: Jessica, Angelo

Special: None

Find: Swordsman's Labyrinth (chest)

Obtain: Metal slime knight, Berserker

Recipe to Make:
None

Use in Recipes:
None

TEMPLAR'S SHIELD

Buy: N/A
Sell: 875

Description: A shield used by Templar knights. Reduces the damage from certain fire- or ice-based attacks by 5 points.

Defence: 14

Equipped by: Angelo

Special: Damage from fire- and ice-based attacks is reduced by 5.

Find: Wisher's Peak (chest)

Obtain: Slime knight, Battle beetle

Recipe to Make:
Templar's shield = Templar's uniform + iron shield

Use in Recipes:
Templar's uniform = wayfarer's clothes + Templar's shield

IRON SHIELD ✓

Buy: 720
Sell: 360

Description: A forged iron shield. Reduces the damage from certain fire- or ice-based attacks by 5 points.

Defence: 15

Equipped by: Hero, Yangus

Special: Damage from fire- and ice-based attacks is reduced by 5.

Buy: Pickham

Find: Pickham Region (chest)

Obtain: Restless armour, Woc, Bone baron, Mohawker, Octavian pirate

Recipe to Make: None

Use in Recipes:
Iron cuirass = iron shield + iron shield
Templar's shield = Templar's uniform + iron shield
White shield = silver platter + iron shield

LIGHT SHIELD ✓

Buy: 2250
Sell: 1125

Description: A light and easy-to-handle shield that can be used by anyone.

Defence: 17

Equipped by: Hero, Yangus, Jessica, Angelo

Special: None

Buy: Baccarat, Argonia, Neos

Find: E Argonia (chest)

Recipe to Make:
None

Use in Recipes:
Shamshir of light = rune staff + light shield + shimmering dress
White shield = light shield + fresh milk + fresh milk

STEEL SHIELD ✓

Buy: 2500
Sell: 1250

Description: A steel shield that reduces the damage from fire- and ice-based attacks by 7 points.

Defence: 22

Equipped by: Hero, Yangus

Special: Damage from fire- and ice-based attacks is reduced by 7.

Buy: Savella Cathedral, Neos

Find: W Argonia (chest)

Obtain: Dullahan

Recipe to Make:
None

Use in Recipes:
Magic shield = steel shield + prayer ring + ruby of protection
Dragon shield = steel shield + dragon scale + dragon scale

WHITE SHIELD

Buy: N/A
Sell: 1800

Description: A sacred shield that reduces the damage from fire-based attacks by 10 points.

Defence: 24

Equipped by: Jessica, Angelo

Special: Damage from fire-based attacks is reduced by 10.

Obtain: Alchemy only

Recipe to Make:
White shield = silver platter + iron shield
White shield = light shield + fresh milk + fresh milk

Use in Recipes:
Saintess shield = white shield + mirror shield + holy water

MAGIC SHIELD

Buy: 5000
Sell: 2500

Description: An enchanted shield that reduces the damage from spells by 15 points.

Defence: 27

Equipped by: Hero, Angelo

Special: Damage from Frizz, Sizz, and Bang–type spells is reduced by 15.

Buy: Argonia (during/after bazaar), Arcadia

Recipe to Make:
Magic shield = steel shield + prayer ring + ruby of protection

Use in Recipes:
Flame shield = flametang boomerang + magic shield
Ice shield = icicle dirk + magic shield
Power shield = magic shield + strength ring + cured cheese

DRAGON SHIELD

Buy: 6900
Sell: 3450

Description: A shield fashioned from dragon scales. Boasts excellent resistance to fire- and ice-based attacks.

Defence: 30

Equipped by: Hero, Yangus

Special: Damage from fire- and ice-based attacks is reduced by 25.

Buy: Orkutsk

Find: Dragon Graveyard (chest)

Recipe to Make:
Dragon shield = steel shield + dragon scale + dragon scale

Use in Recipes:
None

ICE SHIELD

Buy: 8500
Sell: 4300

Description: A shield that increases the wielder's resistance to ice-based attacks when used as an item in battle.

Defence: 33

Equipped by: Hero, Angelo

Special: Damage from ice-based attacks is reduced by 5. When used in combat, all allies gain protection from ice-based spells and attacks.

Buy: Orkutsk

Recipe to Make:
Ice shield = icicle dirk + magic shield

Use in Recipes:
None

FLAME SHIELD

Buy: 7100
Sell: 3550

Description: A shield that increases the wielder's resistance to fire-based attacks when used as an item in battle.

Defence: 34

Equipped by: Yangus, Jessica

Special: Damage from fire-type attacks is reduced by 10. When used in combat, all allies gain protection from fire-based spells and attacks.

Buy: Empycchu, Dark Empycchu

Recipe to Make:
Flame shield = flametang boomerang + magic shield

Use in Recipes:
Flametang boomerang = swallowtail + flame shield

ITEMS

SHIELDS

BONE SHIELD ✓

Buy: N/A
Sell: 8750

Description: This handy monster-bone shield can also be boiled to make a delicious soup stock.

Defence: 36

Equipped by: Yangus

Special: None

Find: Pirate's Cove (chest)

Recipe to Make:
None

Use in Recipes:
None

POWER SHIELD

Buy: 18,000
Sell: 9000

Description: A shield that restores some of the user's HP when used as an item in battle.

Defence: 38

Equipped by: Hero, Yangus, Angelo

Special: Damage from fire- and ice-based attacks is reduced by 15. When used in combat, casts Midheal on wearer (recovers ~80 HP).

Buy: Tryan Gully

Find: Pickham (chest)

Obtain: Left wing

Recipe to Make:
Power shield = magic shield + strength ring + cured cheese

Use in Recipes:
Cheiron's bow = Eros' bow + power shield

MIRROR SHIELD ✓

Buy: 15,000
Sell: 7500

Description: A mysterious shield that occasionally reflects a spell cast on the wearer back at the caster.

Defence: 43

Equipped by: Hero, Angelo

Special: Sometimes reflects spells cast on wearer back to caster.

Buy: Tryan Gully

Recipe to Make:
None

Use in Recipes:
Mirror armour = silver mail + mirror shield + mirror shield
Saintess shield = white shield + mirror shield + holy water
Silver shield = mirror shield + amor seco essence + magic water

OGRE SHIELD ✓

Buy: N/A
Sell: 10,500

Description: A massive shield that reduces the damage from fire- and ice-based attacks by 10 points.

Defence: 45

Equipped by: Hero, Yangus

Special: Damage from fire- and ice-based attacks is reduced by 10.

Find: Desert (chest)

Recipe to Make:
None

Use in Recipes:
None

SAINTESS SHIELD

Buy: N/A
Sell: 28,000

Description: A holy shield that reduces the damage from fire- and ice-based attacks by 2/3.

Defence: 46

Equipped by: Jessica

Special: Damage from fire- and ice-based attacks is reduced by 2/3.

Obtain: Alchemy only

Recipe to Make:
Saintess shield = white shield + mirror shield + holy water

Use in Recipes:
None

SILVER SHIELD

Buy: N/A
Sell: 16,000

Description: Forged from mythril, a rare form of silver, this shield reduces the damage from fire-based attacks by 20 points.

Defence: 48

Equipped by: Hero, Yangus, Angelo

Special: Damage from fire-based attacks is reduced by 20.

Find: Black Citadel (chest)

Recipe to Make:
Silver shield = mirror shield + amor seco essence + magic water

Use in Recipes:
None

BIG BOSS SHIELD ✓

Buy: N/A
Sell: 12,000

Description: Lowers the enemy's defence when used as an item during battle.

Defence: 50

Equipped by: Yangus

Special: When used in combat casts the Kasap spell (lowers defence of enemies).

Given: From Dodgy Dave at Pickham Black Market (after certain accomplishments)

Recipe to Make:
None

Use in Recipes:
None

RUINOUS SHIELD

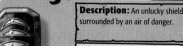

Buy: N/A
Sell: 2900

Description: An unlucky shield surrounded by an air of danger.

Defence: 50

Equipped by: Hero, Yangus, Angelo

Special: Curses wearer when equipped, damage from Frizz, Sizz, Crack, Bang, and Woosh-type spells and fire- and ice-based attacks is increased by 50.

Find: Northwest Isle (chest)
Obtain: Hell's gatekeeper

Recipe to Make:
Ruinous shield = metal king shield + devil's tail

Use in Recipes:
Metal king shield = ruinous shield + orichalcum + saint's ashes

THANATOS' SHIELD

Buy: N/A
Sell: 3650

Description: An ill-fated shield surrounded by an air of danger.

Defence: 55

Equipped by: Hero, Yangus, Angelo

Special: Curses wearer when equipped, wearer cannot act in first turn of combat.

Find: Unknown… (chest)

Recipe to Make:
Thanatos' shield = goddess shield + devil's tail

Use in Recipes:
Goddess shield = Thanatos' shield + saint's ashes

GODDESS SHIELD

Buy: N/A
Sell: 47,500

Description: A holy shield that reduces damage from fire- and ice-based spells by up to half.

Defence: 55

Equipped by: Jessica, Angelo

Special: Damage from fire- and ice-based spells is reduced by up to half.

Obtain: Alchemy only

Recipe to Make:
Goddess shield = Thanatos' shield + saint's ashes

Use in Recipes:
Thanatos' shield = goddess shield + devil's tail

METAL KING SHIELD

Buy: N/A
Sell: 5000

Description: The ultimate shield. Reduces damage from fire- and ice-based spells by 30 points.

Defence: 65

Equipped by: Hero, Yangus, Jessica, Angelo

Special: Damage from fire- and ice-based spells is reduced by 30.

Obtain: Alchemy only

Recipe to Make:
Metal king shield = ruinous shield + orichalcum + saint's ashes

Use in Recipes:
Ruinous shield = metal king shield + devil's tail

HELMETS

BANDANA ✓

Buy: 45
Sell: 23

Description: A normal cloth bandana. A favourite of Hero's.

Defence: 1

Equipped by: Hero

Special: None

Given: Hero's starting equipment
Buy: Peregrin Quay
Obtain: Bodkin archer, Jailcat, Mummy boy, Skullrider, Blood mummy, Killer croaker

Recipe to Make: None

Use in Recipes: Boxer shorts = bandit's grass skirt + bandana
Leather kilt = leather whip + bandana
Turban = bandana + bandana
Mercury's bandana = bandana + agility ring

LEATHER HAT ✓

Buy: 65
Sell: 33

Description: A popular hat made of leather.

Defence: 3

Equipped by: Hero, Yangus, Jessica, Angelo

Special: None

Given: Yangus's starting equipment
Buy: Farebury
Find: Waterfall Cave (chest)
Obtain: Bunicorn, Beetleboy, High roller, Dark sabrecat

Recipe to Make: None

Use in Recipes:
Pointy hat = leather hat + iron nail
Feathered cap = leather hat + chimaera wing

HAIRBAND ✓

Buy: 150
Sell: 75

Description: A cute and functional hairband for ladies.

Defence: 5

Equipped by: Jessica

Special: None

Given: Jessica's starting equipment
Buy: Peregrin Quay
Find: Red's Den (cabinet), Argonia (cabinet)
Obtain: Dingaling, Bag o' laughs, Chimaera, Garuda, Heligator, Darkodile

Recipe to Make: None

Use in Recipes:
Bunny ears = hairband + bunny tail

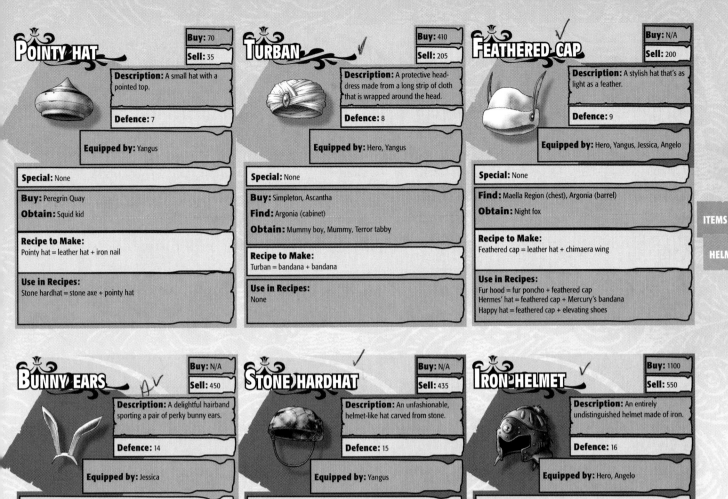

POINTY HAT

Buy: 70
Sell: 35

Description: A small hat with a pointed top.

Defence: 7

Equipped by: Yangus

Special: None

Buy: Peregrin Quay
Obtain: Squid kid

Recipe to Make:
Pointy hat = leather hat + iron nail

Use in Recipes:
Stone hardhat = stone axe + pointy hat

TURBAN ✓

Buy: 410
Sell: 205

Description: A protective head-dress made from a long strip of cloth that is wrapped around the head.

Defence: 8

Equipped by: Hero, Yangus

Special: None

Buy: Simpleton, Ascantha
Find: Argonia (cabinet)
Obtain: Mummy boy, Mummy, Terror tabby

Recipe to Make:
Turban = bandana + bandana

Use in Recipes:
None

FEATHERED CAP ✓

Buy: N/A
Sell: 200

Description: A stylish hat that's as light as a feather.

Defence: 9

Equipped by: Hero, Yangus, Jessica, Angelo

Special: None

Find: Maella Region (chest), Argonia (barrel)
Obtain: Night fox

Recipe to Make:
Feathered cap = leather hat + chimaera wing

Use in Recipes:
Fur hood = fur poncho + feathered cap
Hermes' hat = feathered cap + Mercury's bandana
Happy hat = feathered cap + elevating shoes

ITEMS

HELMETS

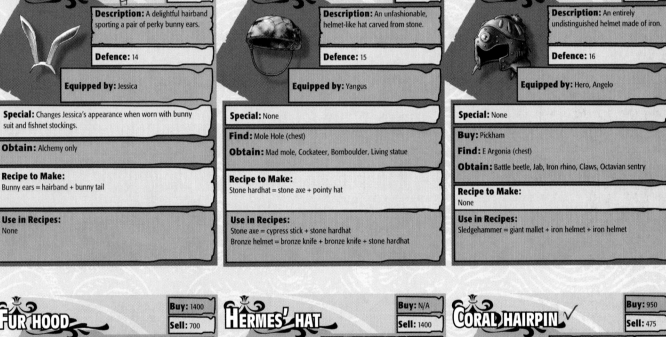

BUNNY EARS A✓

Buy: N/A
Sell: 450

Description: A delightful hairband sporting a pair of perky bunny ears.

Defence: 14

Equipped by: Jessica

Special: Changes Jessica's appearance when worn with bunny suit and fishnet stockings.

Obtain: Alchemy only

Recipe to Make:
Bunny ears = hairband + bunny tail

Use in Recipes:
None

STONE HARDHAT ✓

Buy: N/A
Sell: 435

Description: An unfashionable, helmet-like hat carved from stone.

Defence: 15

Equipped by: Yangus

Special: None

Find: Mole Hole (chest)
Obtain: Mad mole, Cockateer, Bomboulder, Living statue

Recipe to Make:
Stone hardhat = stone axe + pointy hat

Use in Recipes:
Stone axe = cypress stick + stone hardhat
Bronze helmet = bronze knife + bronze knife + stone hardhat

IRON HELMET ✓

Buy: 1100
Sell: 550

Description: An entirely undistinguished helmet made of iron.

Defence: 16

Equipped by: Hero, Angelo

Special: None

Buy: Pickham
Find: E Argonia (chest)
Obtain: Battle beetle, Jab, Iron rhino, Claws, Octavian sentry

Recipe to Make:
None

Use in Recipes:
Sledgehammer = giant mallet + iron helmet + iron helmet

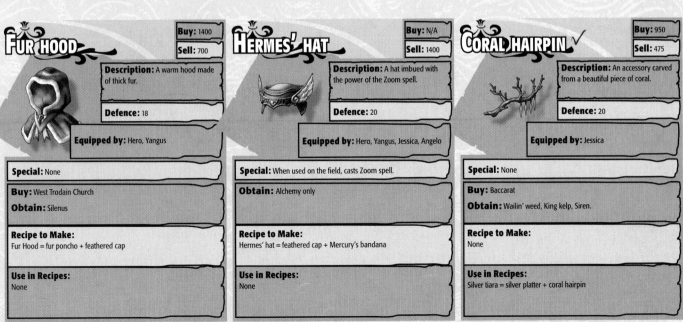

FUR HOOD

Buy: 1400
Sell: 700

Description: A warm hood made of thick fur.

Defence: 18

Equipped by: Hero, Yangus

Special: None

Buy: West Trodain Church
Obtain: Silenus

Recipe to Make:
Fur Hood = fur poncho + feathered cap

Use in Recipes:
None

HERMES' HAT

Buy: N/A
Sell: 1400

Description: A hat imbued with the power of the Zoom spell.

Defence: 20

Equipped by: Hero, Yangus, Jessica, Angelo

Special: When used on the field, casts Zoom spell.

Obtain: Alchemy only

Recipe to Make:
Hermes' hat = feathered cap + Mercury's bandana

Use in Recipes:
None

CORAL HAIRPIN ✓

Buy: 950
Sell: 475

Description: An accessory carved from a beautiful piece of coral.

Defence: 20

Equipped by: Jessica

Special: None

Buy: Baccarat
Obtain: Wailin' weed, King kelp, Siren.

Recipe to Make:
None

Use in Recipes:
Silver tiara = silver platter + coral hairpin

SLIME CROWN ✓

Buy: N/A
Sell: 6000

Description: The crown worn by a king slime.

Defence: 20

Equipped by: Yangus

Special: None

Find: Hilltop Hut (on the ground), Tryan Gully (barrel)
Obtain: King slime, Metal king slime.

Recipe to Make:
None

Use in Recipes:
Liquid metal sword = rusty old sword + slime crown + orichalcum
King axe = golden axe + slime crown
Metal king armour = liquid metal armour + slime crown + orichalcum

BRONZE HELMET

Buy: N/A
Sell: 825

Description: A helmet made from several bronze sheets hammered together.

Defence: 20

Equipped by: Hero, Angelo

Special: None

Obtain: Alchemy only

Recipe to Make:
Bronze helmet = bronze knife + bronze knife + stone hardhat

Use in Recipes:
None

MERCURY'S BANDANA

Buy: N/A
Sell: 2000

Description: A magical bandana that increases the wearer's agility.

Defence: 23

Equipped by: Hero

Special: Agility +15 while equipped.

Obtain: Seasaur

Recipe to Make:
Mercury's bandana = bandana + agility ring

Use in Recipes:
Mercury's rapier = fallen angel rapier + Mercury's bandana + Mercury's bandana
Hermes' hat = feathered cap + Mercury's bandana

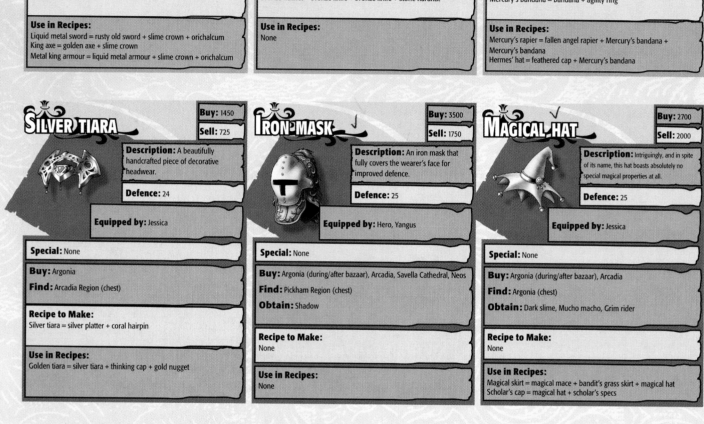

SILVER TIARA

Buy: 1450
Sell: 725

Description: A beautifully handcrafted piece of decorative headwear.

Defence: 24

Equipped by: Jessica

Special: None

Buy: Argonia

Find: Arcadia Region (chest)

Recipe to Make:
Silver tiara = silver platter + coral hairpin

Use in Recipes:
Golden tiara = silver tiara + thinking cap + gold nugget

IRON MASK ✓

Buy: 3500
Sell: 1750

Description: An iron mask that fully covers the wearer's face for improved defence.

Defence: 25

Equipped by: Hero, Yangus

Special: None

Buy: Argonia (during/after bazaar), Arcadia, Savella Cathedral, Neos

Find: Pickham Region (chest)
Obtain: Shadow

Recipe to Make:
None

Use in Recipes:
None

MAGICAL HAT ✓

Buy: 2700
Sell: 2000

Description: Intriguingly, and in spite of its name, this hat boasts absolutely no special magical properties at all.

Defence: 25

Equipped by: Jessica

Special: None

Buy: Argonia (during/after bazaar), Arcadia

Find: Argonia (chest)

Obtain: Dark slime, Mucho macho, Grim rider

Recipe to Make:
None

Use in Recipes:
Magical skirt = magical mace + bandit's grass skirt + magical hat
Scholar's cap = magical hat + scholar's specs

PIRATE'S HAT ✓

Buy: N/A
Sell: 1400

Description: An impressive hat worthy of a pirate captain.

Defence: 30

Equipped by: Hero

Special: None

Obtain: Heavy hood

Recipe to Make:
None

Use in Recipes:
None

PLATINUM HEADGEAR ✓

Buy: N/A
Sell: 2050

Description: A beautiful platinum helm.

Defence: 30

Equipped by: Hero, Angelo

Special: None

Token Trade: Pickham (5000 tokens)

Recipe to Make:
None

Use in Recipes:
None

HAPPY HAT

Buy: N/A
Sell: 10,000

Description: A magical hat that gradually restores MP as its wearer walks around.

Defence: 31

Equipped by: Jessica, Angelo

Special: Gradually restores MP as you walk in field and dungeon areas.

Given: From Dodgy Dave at Pickham Black Market (after certain accomplishments)

Recipe to Make:
Happy hat = feathered cap + elevating shoes

Use in Recipes:
Elevating shoes = happy hat + fishnet stockings

IRON HEADGEAR ✓

Buy: 5500
Sell: 2750

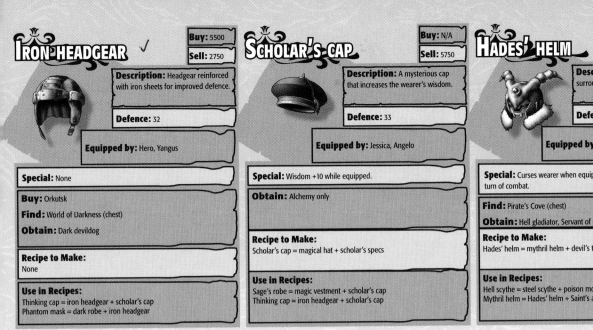

Description: Headgear reinforced with iron sheets for improved defence.

Defence: 32

Equipped by: Hero, Yangus

Special: None

Buy: Orkutsk

Find: World of Darkness (chest)

Obtain: Dark devildog

Recipe to Make:
None

Use in Recipes:
Thinking cap = iron headgear + scholar's cap
Phantom mask = dark robe + iron headgear

SCHOLAR'S CAP

Buy: N/A
Sell: 5750

Description: A mysterious cap that increases the wearer's wisdom.

Defence: 33

Equipped by: Jessica, Angelo

Special: Wisdom +10 while equipped.

Obtain: Alchemy only

Recipe to Make:
Scholar's cap = magical hat + scholar's specs

Use in Recipes:
Sage's robe = magic vestment + scholar's cap
Thinking cap = iron headgear + scholar's cap

HADES' HELM

Buy: N/A
Sell: 4250

Description: A strange helm surrounded by an air of danger.

Defence: 33

Equipped by: Hero, Yangus

Special: Curses wearer when equipped, wearer cannot act in first turn of combat.

Find: Pirate's Cove (chest)

Obtain: Hell gladiator, Servant of darkness

Recipe to Make:
Hades' helm = mythril helm + devil's tail

Use in Recipes:
Hell scythe = steel scythe + poison moth knife + Hades' helm
Mythril helm = Hades' helm + Saint's ashes

THINKING CAP

Buy: 13,000
Sell: 6500

Description: A magical helm that increases the wearer's wisdom.

Defence: 38

Equipped by: Jessica, Angelo

Special: Wisdom +15 while equipped.

Buy: Tryan Gully

Obtain: Head of state

Recipe to Make:
Thinking cap = iron headgear + scholar's cap

Use in Recipes:
Golden tiara = silver tiara + thinking cap + gold nugget

MYTHRIL HELM

Buy: 13,300
Sell: 8800

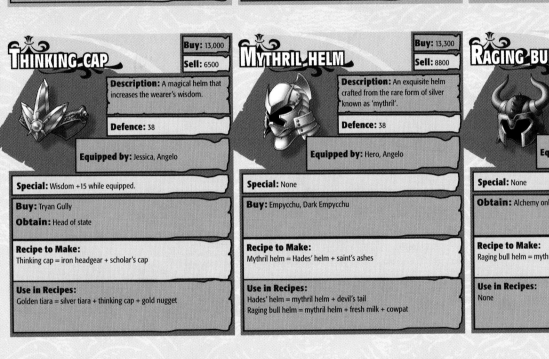

Description: An exquisite helm crafted from the rare form of silver known as 'mythril'.

Defence: 38

Equipped by: Hero, Angelo

Special: None

Buy: Empycchu, Dark Empycchu

Recipe to Make:
Mythril helm = Hades' helm + saint's ashes

Use in Recipes:
Hades' helm = mythril helm + devil's tail
Raging bull helm = mythril helm + fresh milk + cowpat

RAGING BULL HELM

Buy: N/A
Sell: 16,500

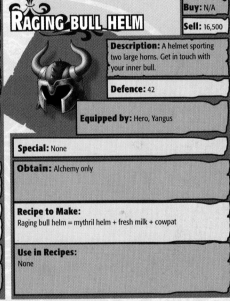

Description: A helmet sporting two large horns. Get in touch with your inner bull.

Defence: 42

Equipped by: Hero, Yangus

Special: None

Obtain: Alchemy only

Recipe to Make:
Raging bull helm = mythril helm + fresh milk + cowpat

Use in Recipes:
None

GOLDEN TIARA

Buy: N/A
Sell: 26,000

Description: A sacred tiara that makes its wearer more resistant to a variety of spells.

Defence: 43

Equipped by: Jessica

Special: Increases resistance to Whack, Snooze, Fizzle and Fuddle-type attacks.

Obtain: Alchemy only

Recipe to Make:
Golden tiara = silver tiara + thinking cap + gold nugget

Use in Recipes:
None

GREAT HELM ✓

Buy: 16,000
Sell: 8000

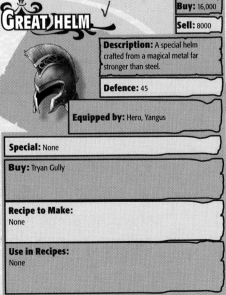

Description: A special helm crafted from a magical metal far stronger than steel.

Defence: 45

Equipped by: Hero, Yangus

Special: None

Buy: Tryan Gully

Recipe to Make:
None

Use in Recipes:
None

PHANTOM MASK

Buy: N/A
Sell: 29,000

Description: A mysterious mask that allows the wearer to dodge enemy attacks more easily.

Defence: 48

Equipped by: Angelo

Special: Increases ability to dodge enemy attacks.

Obtain: Alchemy only

Recipe to Make:
Phantom mask = dark robe + iron headgear

Use in Recipes:
None

SKULL HELM

Buy: N/A
Sell: 4500

Description: An eerie helm surrounded by an air of danger.

Defence: 49

Equipped by: Yangus

Special: Curses wearer when equipped, wearer's attack power is reduced to 0.

Find: Isolated Plateau (chest), Unknown... (chest)

Recipe to Make:
Skull helm = sun crown + devil's tail

Use in Recipes:
Sun crown = skull helm + saint's ashes

SUN CROWN

Buy: N/A
Sell: 37,000

Description: A special crown capable of nullifying spells which might otherwise confuse or put its wearer to sleep.

Defence: 52

Equipped by: Hero, Jessica

Special: Greatly increases resistance to Snooze and Fuddle-type attacks.

Obtain: Alchemy only

Recipe to Make:
Sun crown = skull helm + saint's ashes

Use in Recipes:
Skull helm = sun crown + devil's tail
Timbrel of tension = sun crown + tough guy tattoo + magic beast hide

METAL KING HELM
 ✓

Buy: N/A
Sell: 10,000

Description: The ultimate helm. Bestows a strong resistance to a variety of spells.

Defence: 55

Equipped by: Hero, Yangus, Jessica, Angelo

Special: Increases resistance to Whack, Snooze, Fuddle, and Fizzle-type attacks.

Given: From Princess Minnie (90 medals)

Recipe to Make:
None

Use in Recipes:
None

ACCESSORIES

STRENGTH RING

Buy: N/A
Sell: 325

Description: A magical ring that increases the wearer's attack power.

Attack: +5

Equipped by: Hero, Yangus, Jessica, Angelo

Special: None

Find: Arcadia (cabinet)

Given: Monster Arena Prize (Rank G)

Obtain: Muddy hand

Recipe to Make: Strength ring = prayer ring + seed of strength

Use in Recipes:
Hunter's bow = cypress stick + cypress stick + strength ring
Titan belt = leather kilt + strength ring
Power shield = magic shield + strength ring + cured cheese
Mighty armlet = strength ring + titan belt

TOUGH GUY TATTOO ✓

Buy: 2400
Sell: 1200

Description: A removable tattoo with a strange design. Increases attack power when worn.

Attack: +8

Equipped by: Hero, Yangus, Jessica, Angelo

Special: None

Buy: Argonia (during/after bazaar)

Find: Baccarat Region (chest)

Obtain: Hoodlum, Troll, Belial, Anchorman

Recipe to Make:
None

Use in Recipes:
Falcon knife = tough guy tattoo + slime earrings + agility ring
Timbrel of tension = sun crown + tough guy tattoo + magic beast hide
Holy talisman = tough guy tattoo + gold rosary + holy water

TEMPLAR CAPTAIN'S RING ✓

Buy: N/A
Sell: N/A

Description: The signet ring of the Captain of the Templars. Formerly belonged to Marcello.

Attack: +10   **Wisdom:** +10

Equipped by: Hero, Yangus, Jessica, Angelo

Special: Cannot be sold or dropped.

Given: From Marcello in Neos (after certain events)

Recipe to Make:
None

Use in Recipes:
None

TITAN BELT

Buy: N/A
Sell: 1500

Description: A magical belt that increases the wearer's attack power.

Attack: +10

Equipped by: Hero, Yangus, Jessica, Angelo

Special: None

Token Trade: Pickham (1500 tokens)

Find: Arcadia (chest), Arcadia Region (chest)

Obtain: Cockateer, Skeleton soldier, Jackal ripper, Golem, Icikiller

Recipe to Make:
Titan belt = leather kilt + strength ring

Use in Recipes:
Mighty armlet = strength ring + titan belt

MIGHTY ARMLET

Buy: N/A
Sell: 4500

Description: A magical bracer that increases the power of its wearer's attacks.

Attack: +15

Equipped by: Hero, Yangus, Jessica, Angelo

Special: None

Given: Monster Arena Prize (Rank D)

Find: Isolated Plateau (chest)

Obtain: Stone guardian

Recipe to Make:
Mighty armlet = strength ring + titan belt

Use in Recipes:
Dragon slayer = dragonsbane + mighty armlet
Über war hammer = war hammer + mighty armlet
Gigant armour = bandit mail + mighty armlet + mighty armlet

ARGON RING ✓

Buy: N/A
Sell: N/A

Description: A keepsake from Hero's parents.

Attack: +20   **Agility:** +20

Equipped by: Hero, Yangus, Jessica, Angelo

Special: Cannot be sold or dropped.

Given: Unknown...

Recipe to Make:
None

Use in Recipes:
None

LADY'S RING ✓

Buy: N/A
Sell: N/A

Description: An extravagant and expensive ring lost by a rich woman.

Defence: 2

Equipped by: Hero, Yangus, Jessica, Angelo

Special: Cannot be sold or dropped.

Find: Ascantha (on ground)

Recipe to Make:
None

Use in Recipes:
None

GOLD BRACER ✓

Buy: 350
Sell: 175

Description: A pure gold bracer that increases the wearer's defence.

Defence: 4

Equipped by: Hero, Yangus, Jessica, Angelo

Special: None

Buy: Argonia (during/after bazaar)

Given: Ferry

Find: Trodain Castle (bag), Arcadia (cabinet)

Obtain: Fencing fox, Chainine, Dingaling, Goodybag, Dieablo, Gold golem, Lesser demon, Notso macho

Recipe to Make: None

Use in Recipes:
Shimmering dress = spangled dress + gold bracer + ruby of protection
Life bracer = gold bracer + recovery ring

SLIME EARRINGS ✓

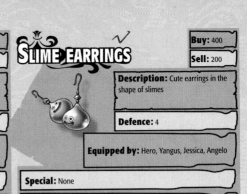

Buy: 400
Sell: 200

Description: Cute earrings in the shape of slimes

Defence: 4

Equipped by: Hero, Yangus, Jessica, Angelo

Special: None

Buy: Peregrin Quay, Ascantha

Find: Alexandria Region (chest)

Obtain: She-slime, Puppeteer, Slime knight, Metal slime knight, King slime, Magic marionette.

Recipe to Make:
None

Use in Recipes:
Falcon knife = tough guy tattoo + slime earrings + agility ring

LIFE BRACER

Buy: N/A
Sell: 7000

Description: A beautiful bracer that increases the wearer's maximum HP by 30.

Defence: 5

Equipped by: Hero, Yangus, Jessica, Angelo

Special: Max HP +30

Obtain: Dark devildog

Recipe to Make:
Life bracer = gold bracer + recovery ring

Use in Recipes:
Über miracle sword = miracle sword + life bracer
Staff of resurrection = Yggdrasil leaf + rune staff + life bracer

PRAYER RING

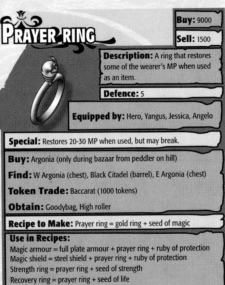

Buy: 9000
Sell: 1500

Description: A ring that restores some of the wearer's MP when used as an item.

Defence: 5

Equipped by: Hero, Yangus, Jessica, Angelo

Special: Restores 20-30 MP when used, but may break.

Buy: Argonia (only during bazaar from peddler on hill)

Find: W Argonia (chest), Black Citadel (barrel), E Argonia (chest)

Token Trade: Baccarat (1000 tokens)

Obtain: Goodybag, High roller

Recipe to Make: Prayer ring = gold ring + seed of magic

Use in Recipes:
Magic armour = full plate armour + prayer ring + ruby of protection
Magic shield = steel shield + prayer ring + ruby of protection
Strength ring = prayer ring + seed of strength
Recovery ring = prayer ring + seed of life
Ruby of protection = prayer ring + seed of defence
Agility ring = prayer ring + seed of agility

GOSPEL RING ✓

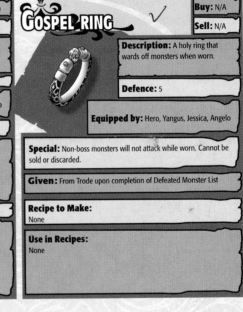

Buy: N/A
Sell: N/A

Description: A holy ring that wards off monsters when worn.

Defence: 5

Equipped by: Hero, Yangus, Jessica, Angelo

Special: Non-boss monsters will not attack while worn. Cannot be sold or discarded.

Given: From Trode upon completion of Defeated Monster List

Recipe to Make:
None

Use in Recipes:
None

TEMPLAR'S RING ✓

Buy: N/A
Sell: N/A

Description: A ring, engraved with a religious symbol, which Angelo gave to Jessica.

Defence: 5

Equipped by: Hero, Yangus, Jessica, Angelo

Special: Cannot be sold or discarded.

Given: From Angelo in Simpleton after certain events

Recipe to Make:
None

Use in Recipes:
None

DRAGON SCALE ✓

Buy: N/A
Sell: 240

Description: A warrior's lucky charm, made from a hand-worked dragon scale.

Defence: 5

Equipped by: Hero, Yangus, Jessica, Angelo

Special: None

Find: Royal Hunting Ground (chest), Dark Ruins (chest), Arcadia (cabinet), Dark Empycchu (pot), Desert (chest)

Obtain: Hacksaurus, Frost wyvine, Dragurn, Tyrantosaurus, Froufrou, Sea dragon, Seasaur

Recipe to Make: None

Use in Recipes:
Dragontail whip = snakeskin whip + dragon scale + dragon scale
Scale armour = leather armour + dragon scale
Dragon mail = silver mail + dragon scale + dragon scale
Scale shield = leather shield + dragon scale
Dragon shield = steel shield + dragon scale + dragon scale

GARTER ✓

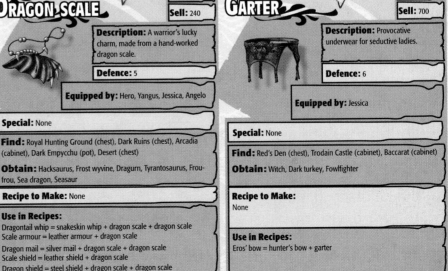

Buy: N/A
Sell: 700

Description: Provocative underwear for seductive ladies.

Defence: 6

Equipped by: Jessica

Special: None

Find: Red's Den (chest), Trodain Castle (cabinet), Baccarat (cabinet)

Obtain: Witch, Dark turkey, Fowlfighter

Recipe to Make:
None

Use in Recipes:
Eros' bow = hunter's bow + garter

FISHNET STOCKINGS

Buy: N/A
Sell: 900

Description: A pair of fishnet stockings. Perfect for bunny girls.

Defence: 8

Equipped by: Jessica

Special: Changes Jessica's appearance when worn with bunny ears and bunny tail.

Given: From Princess Minnie (28 medals)

Obtain: Ice queen

Recipe to Make:
None

Use in Recipes:
Elevating shoes = happy hat + fishnet stockings

GOLD RING ✓

Buy: 2000
Sell: 1000

Description: A ring that slightly increases the wearer's defence.

Defence: 10

Equipped by: Hero, Yangus, Jessica, Angelo

Special: None

Buy: Argonia (during/after bazaar)

Find: Pickham Region (chest), Baccarat (cabinet)

Obtain: Dieablo, Night emperor, Gold golem, Ghoul, Bloody hand

Recipe to Make: None

Use in Recipes:
Prayer ring = gold ring + seed of magic
Ring of truth = sandstorm spear + gold ring
Ring of immunity = poison needle + gold ring
Full moon ring = poison moth knife + gold ring
Ring of awakening = dream blade + gold ring
Ring of clarity = fallen angel rapier + gold ring

RING OF TRUTH

Buy: N/A
Sell: 700

Description: A ring that makes the wearer resistant to illusion attacks.

Defence: 10

Equipped by: Hero, Yangus, Jessica, Angelo

Special: Wearer is more resistant to Dazzle-type attacks.

Find: Dark Godbird's Eyrie (chest)

Recipe to Make:
Ring of truth = sandstorm spear + gold ring

Use in Recipes:
Catholicon ring = ring of truth + ring of immunity + full moon ring

RING OF IMMUNITY

Buy: N/A
Sell: 750

Description: A ring that makes the wearer resistant to poison attacks.

Defence: 10

Equipped by: Hero, Yangus, Jessica, Angelo

Special: Wearer is more resistant to poison-type attacks.

Obtain: Alchemy only

Recipe to Make:
Ring of immunity = poison needle + gold ring

Use in Recipes:
Catholicon ring = ring of truth + ring of immunity + full moon ring

HOLY TALISMAN

Buy: N/A
Sell: 2400

Description: A sacred talisman that increases the wearer's resistance to sudden-death spells.

Defence: 10

Equipped by: Hero, Yangus, Jessica, Angelo

Special: Wearer is more resistant to Whack-type spells.

Obtain: Alchemy only

Recipe to Make:
Holy talisman = tough guy tattoo + gold rosary + holy water

Use in Recipes:
Holy silver rapier = Templar's sword + holy talisman
Zombie slayer = zombiesbane + holy talisman

FULL MOON RING

Buy: N/A
Sell: 600

Description: A ring that makes the wearer resistant to paralysis attacks.

Defence: 10

Equipped by: Hero, Yangus, Jessica, Angelo

Special: Wearer is more resistant to paralysis-type attacks.

Obtain: Tentacular

Recipe to Make:
Full moon ring = poison moth knife + gold ring

Use in Recipes:
Catholicon ring = ring of truth + ring of immunity + full moon ring

RING OF AWAKENING

Buy: N/A
Sell: 550

Description: A ring that makes the wearer resistant to sleep attacks.

Defence: 10

Equipped by: Hero, Yangus, Jessica, Angelo

Special: Wearer is more resistant to Snooze-type attacks.

Obtain: Alchemy only

Recipe to Make:
Ring of awakening = dream blade + gold ring

Use in Recipes:
Scholar's specs = ring of awakening + ring of clarity + seed of wisdom

RING OF CLARITY

Buy: N/A
Sell: 650

Description: A ring that makes the wearer resistant to confusion attacks.

Defence: 10

Equipped by: Hero, Yangus, Jessica, Angelo

Special: Wearer is more resistant to Fuddle-type attacks.

Given: Monster Arena Prize (Rank E)

Recipe to Make:
Ring of clarity = fallen angel rapier + gold ring

Use in Recipes:
Scholar's specs = ring of awakening + ring of clarity + seed of wisdom

RECOVERY RING

Buy: N/A
Sell: 4800

Description: A wonderful ring that gradually restores HP as the wearer walks around.

Defence: 15

Equipped by: Hero, Yangus, Jessica, Angelo

Special: Wearer regains HP while walking in field and dungeon areas.

Find: Rydon's Tower (chest)

Obtain: Pandora's box

Recipe to Make:
Recovery ring = prayer ring + seed of life

Use in Recipes:
Life bracer = gold bracer + recovery ring
Goddess ring = recovery ring + orichalcum

CATHOLICON RING

Buy: N/A
Sell: 18,000

Description: A ring that makes the wearer resistant to a variety of attacks, including sleep, paralysis, and confusion.

Defence: 15

Equipped by: Hero, Yangus, Jessica, Angelo

Special: Wearer is more resistant to Snooze, Fuddle, Dazzle, poison and paralyzing attacks.

Obtain: Alchemy only

Recipe to Make:
Catholicon ring = ring of truth + ring of immunity + full moon ring

Use in Recipes:
None

RUBY OF PROTECTION

Buy: 3100
Sell: 1550

Description: A beautiful ruby that increases the wearer's defence.

Defence: 15

Equipped by: Hero, Yangus, Jessica, Angelo

Special: None

Buy: Argonia (during/after bazaar)

Find: Baccarat (chest), Orkutsk (pot)

Obtain: Living statue, Elysium bird

Recipe to Make:
Ruby of protection = prayer ring + seed of defence

Use in Recipes:
Magic armour = full plate armour + prayer ring + ruby of protection
Shimmering dress = spangled dress + gold bracer + ruby of protection
Magic shield = steel shield + prayer ring + ruby of protection

BUNNY TAIL ✓

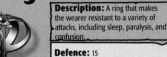

Buy: 50
Sell: 25

Description: A silky-soft and comfortable accessory.

Agility: +2

Equipped by: Hero, Yangus, Jessica, Angelo

Special: None

Buy: Argonia (during/after bazaar)

Find: Maella Region (chest), Pickham (cabinet), Baccarat (cabinet), Arcadia (cabinet)

Obtain: Bunicorn, Skipper, Spiked hare, Night sneaker, Dark gryphon, See angel

Recipe to Make: None

Use in Recipes:
Bunny ears = hairband + bunny tail
Bunny suit = silk bustier + bunny tail

ELEVATING SHOES

Buy: N/A
Sell: 50

Description: Wear them for a happily elevating experience!

Agility: +5

Equipped by: Hero, Yangus, Jessica, Angelo

Special: Wearer gains EXP while walking in field and dungeon areas.

Obtain: Liquid metal slime, Hell hopper

Recipe to Make:
Elevating shoes = happy hat + fishnet stockings

Use in Recipes:
Happy hat = feathered cap + elevating shoes

DEVIL'S TAIL ✓

Buy: 200
Sell: 100

Description: The tail of a demon. Surrounded by an air of danger.

Agility: +10

Equipped by: Hero, Yangus, Jessica, Angelo

Special: Curses wearer when equipped. Wearer's resistance to spell damage and effects is lowered.

Buy: Unknown...

Find: Argonia (chest), Herb Grotto (chest), World of Darkness (chest)

Obtain: Tap devil, Demon thunderer, Caped caperer

Recipe to Make: None

Use in Recipes:
Fallen angel rapier = holy silver rapier + devil's tail + wing of bat
Double-edged sword = über double-edge + devil's tail
Demon spear = battle fork + poison needle + devil's tail
Imp knife = assassin's dagger + devil's tail
Leather whip = devil's tail + saint's ashes
Demon whip = scourge whip + devil's tail
Dark robe = cloak of evasion + devil's tail + wing of bat
Zombie mail = platinum mail + devil's tail
Ruinous shield = metal king shield + devil's tail
Thanatos' shield = goddess shield + devil's tail
Hades' helm = mythril helm + devil's tail
Skull helm = sun crown + devil's tail
Skull ring = devil's tail + sorcerer's ring

AGILITY RING

Buy: N/A
Sell: 180

Description: A magical ring that increases the wearer's agility.

Agility: +15

Equipped by: Hero, Yangus, Jessica, Angelo

Special: None

Token Trade: Pickham (1000 tokens)

Find: Kingdom of Ascantha (chest), Blizzard Peaks (chest), Holy Isle of Neos (chest)

Recipe to Make:
Agility ring = prayer ring + seed of agility

Use in Recipes:
Falcon knife = tough guy tattoo + slime earrings + agility ring
Mercury's bandana = bandana + agility ring
Meteorite bracer = agility ring + agility ring + orichalcum

METEORITE BRACER

Buy: N/A
Sell: 2500

Description: A mystical bracer that allows the wearer to move at a blinding speed.

Agility: +50

Equipped by: Hero, Yangus, Jessica, Angelo

Special: None

Given: From Princess Minnie (60 medals)

Recipe to Make:
Meteorite bracer = agility ring + agility ring + orichalcum

Use in Recipes:
Über falcon blade = falcon blade + meteorite bracer

SKULL RING

Buy: N/A
Sell: 425

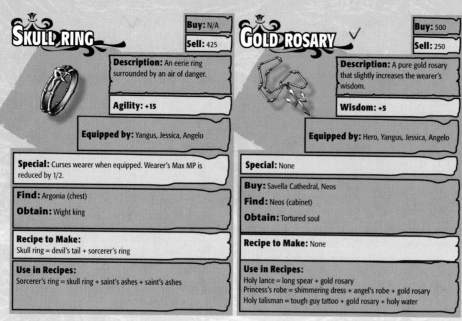

Description: An eerie ring surrounded by an air of danger.

Agility: +15

Equipped by: Yangus, Jessica, Angelo

Special: Curses wearer when equipped. Wearer's Max MP is reduced by 1/2.

Find: Argonia (chest)
Obtain: Wight king

Recipe to Make:
Skull ring = devil's tail + sorcerer's ring

Use in Recipes:
Sorcerer's ring = skull ring + saint's ashes + saint's ashes

GOLD ROSARY ✓

Buy: 500
Sell: 250

Description: A pure gold rosary that slightly increases the wearer's wisdom.

Wisdom: +5

Equipped by: Hero, Yangus, Jessica, Angelo

Special: None

Buy: Savella Cathedral, Neos
Find: Neos (cabinet)
Obtain: Tortured soul

Recipe to Make: None

Use in Recipes:
Holy lance = long spear + gold rosary
Princess's robe = shimmering dress + angel's robe + gold rosary
Holy talisman = tough guy tattoo + gold rosary + holy water

SORCERER'S RING

Buy: N/A
Sell: 7250

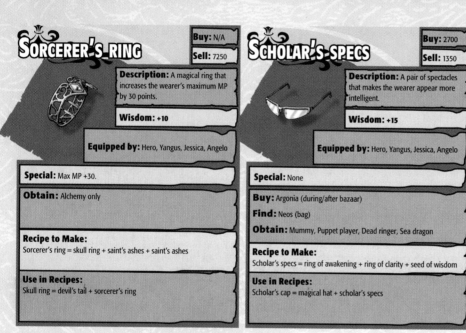

Description: A magical ring that increases the wearer's maximum MP by 30 points.

Wisdom: +10

Equipped by: Hero, Yangus, Jessica, Angelo

Special: Max MP +30.

Obtain: Alchemy only

Recipe to Make:
Sorcerer's ring = skull ring + saint's ashes + saint's ashes

Use in Recipes:
Skull ring = devil's tail + sorcerer's ring

SCHOLAR'S SPECS

Buy: 2700
Sell: 1350

Description: A pair of spectacles that makes the wearer appear more intelligent.

Wisdom: +15

Equipped by: Hero, Yangus, Jessica, Angelo

Special: None

Buy: Argonia (during/after bazaar)
Find: Neos (bag)
Obtain: Mummy, Puppet player, Dead ringer, Sea dragon

Recipe to Make:
Scholar's specs = ring of awakening + ring of clarity + seed of wisdom

Use in Recipes:
Scholar's cap = magical hat + scholar's specs

GODDESS RING

Buy: N/A
Sell: 25,500

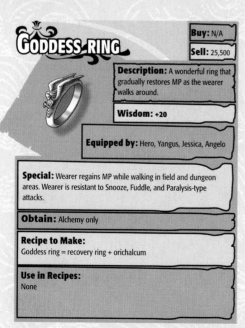

Description: A wonderful ring that gradually restores MP as the wearer walks around.

Wisdom: +20

Equipped by: Hero, Yangus, Jessica, Angelo

Special: Wearer regains MP while walking in field and dungeon areas. Wearer is resistant to Snooze, Fuddle, and Paralysis-type attacks.

Obtain: Alchemy only

Recipe to Make:
Goddess ring = recovery ring + orichalcum

Use in Recipes:
None

WEAPONS

There are 11 different types of weapon in *Dragon Quest VIII*. Each character can equip any of the weapons their skill sets give them access to, with the exception of flails, which are rare weapons for Yangus that are not associated with a particular skill set. Weapons are listed by type in order of their attack value. Attack power is important, but keep in mind that certain weapons have special traits that may make them much more powerful than their attack value suggests! Check the special field to see which weapons can hit multiple targets, strike multiple times, apply status effects to their targets or cast spells when used in combat!

JESSICA & SWORDS

Jessica can use swords after allocating 30 points to her Knife skill.

ITEMS

SWORDS

SWORDS

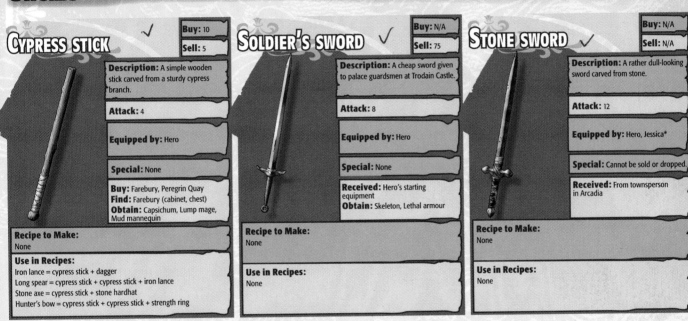

CYPRESS STICK ✓

Buy: 10
Sell: 5

Description: A simple wooden stick carved from a sturdy cypress branch.

Attack: 4

Equipped by: Hero

Special: None

Buy: Farebury, Peregrin Quay
Find: Farebury (cabinet, chest)
Obtain: Capsichum, Lump mage, Mud mannequin

Recipe to Make:
None

Use in Recipes:
Iron lance = cypress stick + dagger
Long spear = cypress stick + cypress stick + iron lance
Stone axe = cypress stick + stone hardhat
Hunter's bow = cypress stick + cypress stick + strength ring

SOLDIER'S SWORD ✓

Buy: N/A
Sell: 75

Description: A cheap sword given to palace guardsmen at Trodain Castle.

Attack: 8

Equipped by: Hero

Special: None

Received: Hero's starting equipment
Obtain: Skeleton, Lethal armour

Recipe to Make:
None

Use in Recipes:
None

STONE SWORD ✓

Buy: N/A
Sell: N/A

Description: A rather dull-looking sword carved from stone.

Attack: 12

Equipped by: Hero, Jessica*

Special: Cannot be sold or dropped.

Received: From townsperson in Arcadia

Recipe to Make:
None

Use in Recipes:
None

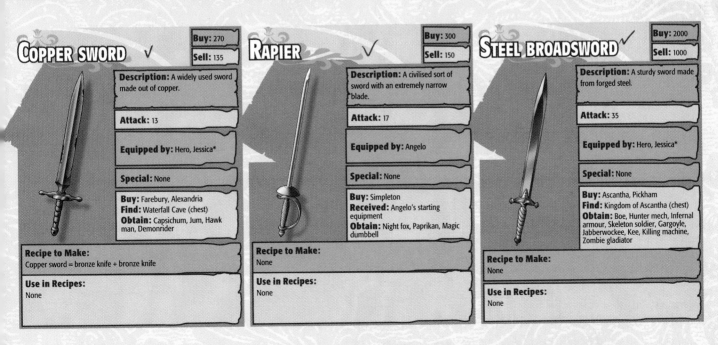

COPPER SWORD ✓

Buy: 270
Sell: 135

Description: A widely used sword made out of copper.

Attack: 13

Equipped by: Hero, Jessica*

Special: None

Buy: Farebury, Alexandria
Find: Waterfall Cave (chest)
Obtain: Capsichum, Jum, Hawk man, Demonrider

Recipe to Make:
Copper sword = bronze knife + bronze knife

Use in Recipes:
None

RAPIER ✓

Buy: 300
Sell: 150

Description: A civilised sort of sword with an extremely narrow blade.

Attack: 17

Equipped by: Angelo

Special: None

Buy: Simpleton
Received: Angelo's starting equipment
Obtain: Night fox, Paprikan, Magic dumbbell

Recipe to Make:
None

Use in Recipes:
None

STEEL BROADSWORD ✓

Buy: 2000
Sell: 1000

Description: A sturdy sword made from forged steel.

Attack: 35

Equipped by: Hero, Jessica*

Special: None

Buy: Ascantha, Pickham
Find: Kingdom of Ascantha (chest)
Obtain: Boe, Hunter mech, Infernal armour, Skeleton soldier, Gargoyle, Jabberwockee, Kee, Killing machine, Zombie gladiator

Recipe to Make:
None

Use in Recipes:
None

TEMPLAR'S SWORD ✓

Buy: N/A
Sell: 1175

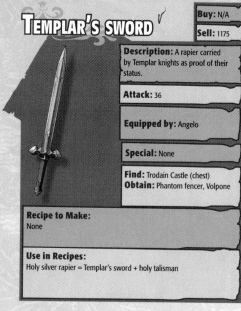

Description: A rapier carried by Templar knights as proof of their status.

Attack: 36

Equipped by: Angelo

Special: None

Find: Trodain Castle (chest)
Obtain: Phantom fencer, Volpone

Recipe to Make:
None

Use in Recipes:
Holy silver rapier = Templar's sword + holy talisman

FALCON BLADE ✓

Buy: N/A
Sell: 5000

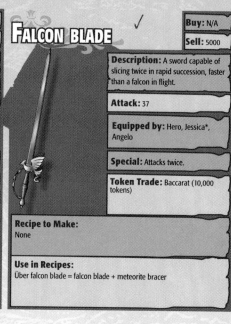

Description: A sword capable of slicing twice in rapid succession, faster than a falcon in flight.

Attack: 37

Equipped by: Hero, Jessica*, Angelo

Special: Attacks twice.

Token Trade: Baccarat (10,000 tokens)

Recipe to Make:
None

Use in Recipes:
Über falcon blade = falcon blade + meteorite bracer

RUSTY OLD SWORD

Buy: N/A
Sell: N/A

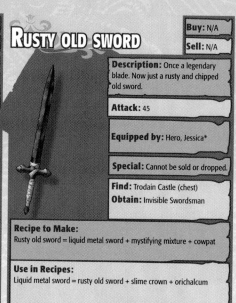

Description: Once a legendary blade. Now just a rusty and chipped old sword.

Attack: 45

Equipped by: Hero, Jessica*

Special: Cannot be sold or dropped.

Find: Trodain Castle (chest)
Obtain: Invisible Swordsman

Recipe to Make:
Rusty old sword = liquid metal sword + mystifying mixture + cowpat

Use in Recipes:
Liquid metal sword = rusty old sword + slime crown + orichalcum

HOLY SILVER RAPIER

Buy: 6600
Sell: 3300

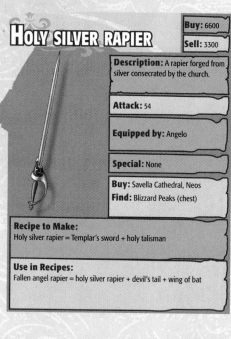

Description: A rapier forged from silver consecrated by the church.

Attack: 54

Equipped by: Angelo

Special: None

Buy: Savella Cathedral, Neos
Find: Blizzard Peaks (chest)

Recipe to Make:
Holy silver rapier = Templar's sword + holy talisman

Use in Recipes:
Fallen angel rapier = holy silver rapier + devil's tail + wing of bat

ZOMBIESBANE ✓

Buy: 6300
Sell: 3150

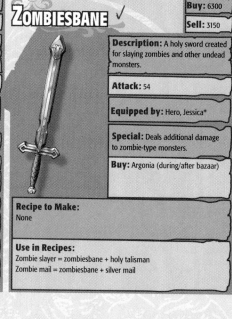

Description: A holy sword created for slaying zombies and other undead monsters.

Attack: 54

Equipped by: Hero, Jessica*

Special: Deals additional damage to zombie-type monsters.

Buy: Argonia (during/after bazaar)

Recipe to Make:
None

Use in Recipes:
Zombie slayer = zombiesbane + holy talisman
Zombie mail = zombiesbane + silver mail

ÜBER FALCON BLADE

Buy: N/A
Sell: 25000

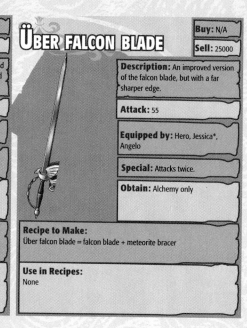

Description: An improved version of the falcon blade, but with a far sharper edge.

Attack: 55

Equipped by: Hero, Jessica*, Angelo

Special: Attacks twice.

Obtain: Alchemy only

Recipe to Make:
Über falcon blade = falcon blade + meteorite bracer

Use in Recipes:
None

DREAM BLADE ✓

Buy: 4700
Sell: 3150

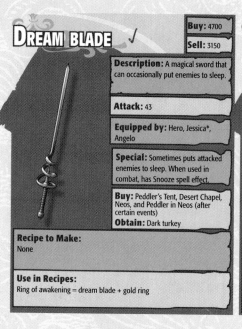

Description: A magical sword that can occasionally put enemies to sleep.

Attack: 43

Equipped by: Hero, Jessica*, Angelo

Special: Sometimes puts attacked enemies to sleep. When used in combat, has Snooze spell effect.

Buy: Peddler's Tent, Desert Chapel, Neos, and Peddler in Neos (after certain events)
Obtain: Dark turkey

Recipe to Make:
None

Use in Recipes:
Ring of awakening = dream blade + gold ring

PLATINUM SWORD ✓

Buy: N/A
Sell: 3000

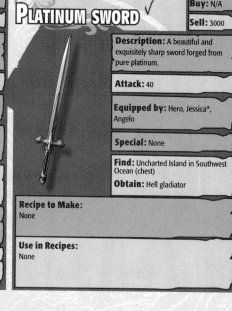

Description: A beautiful and exquisitely sharp sword forged from pure platinum.

Attack: 40

Equipped by: Hero, Jessica*, Angelo

Special: None

Find: Uncharted Island in Southwest Ocean (chest)
Obtain: Hell gladiator

Recipe to Make:
None

Use in Recipes:
None

FALLEN ANGEL RAPIER

Buy: N/A
Sell: 8500

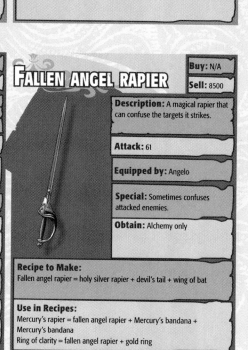

Description: A magical rapier that can confuse the targets it strikes.

Attack: 61

Equipped by: Angelo

Special: Sometimes confuses attacked enemies.

Obtain: Alchemy only

Recipe to Make:
Fallen angel rapier = holy silver rapier + devil's tail + wing of bat

Use in Recipes:
Mercury's rapier = fallen angel rapier + Mercury's bandana + Mercury's bandana
Ring of clarity = fallen angel rapier + gold ring

BASTARD SWORD ✓

Buy: 8800
Sell: 4400

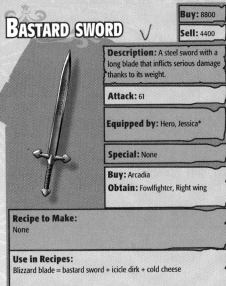

Description: A steel sword with a long blade that inflicts serious damage thanks to its weight.

Attack: 61

Equipped by: Hero, Jessica*

Special: None

Buy: Arcadia
Obtain: Fowlfighter, Right wing

Recipe to Make:
None

Use in Recipes:
Blizzard blade = bastard sword + icicle dirk + cold cheese

ZOMBIE SLAYER

Buy: N/A
Sell: 10000

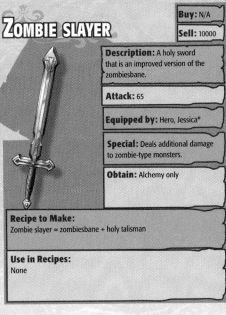

Description: A holy sword that is an improved version of the zombiesbane.

Attack: 65

Equipped by: Hero, Jessica*

Special: Deals additional damage to zombie-type monsters.

Obtain: Alchemy only

Recipe to Make:
Zombie slayer = zombiesbane + holy talisman

Use in Recipes:
None

DRAGONSBANE ✓

Buy: 11000
Sell: 6000

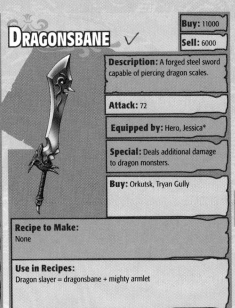

Description: A forged steel sword capable of piercing dragon scales.

Attack: 72

Equipped by: Hero, Jessica*

Special: Deals additional damage to dragon monsters.

Buy: Orkutsk, Tryan Gully

Recipe to Make:
None

Use in Recipes:
Dragon slayer = dragonsbane + mighty armlet

DOUBLE-EDGED SWORD

Buy: N/A
Sell: 2500

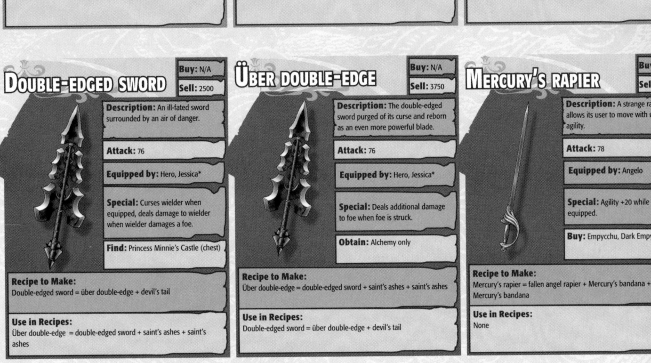

Description: An ill-fated sword surrounded by an air of danger.

Attack: 76

Equipped by: Hero, Jessica*

Special: Curses wielder when equipped, deals damage to wielder when wielder damages a foe.

Find: Princess Minnie's Castle (chest)

Recipe to Make:
Double-edged sword = über double-edge + devil's tail

Use in Recipes:
Über double-edge = double-edged sword + saint's ashes + saint's ashes

ÜBER DOUBLE-EDGE

Buy: N/A
Sell: 3750

Description: The double-edged sword purged of its curse and reborn as an even more powerful blade.

Attack: 76

Equipped by: Hero, Jessica*

Special: Deals additional damage to foe when foe is struck.

Obtain: Alchemy only

Recipe to Make:
Über double-edge = double-edged sword + saint's ashes + saint's ashes

Use in Recipes:
Double-edged sword = über double-edge + devil's tail

MERCURY'S RAPIER

Buy: 10500
Sell: 5100

Description: A strange rapier that allows its user to move with unnatural agility.

Attack: 78

Equipped by: Angelo

Special: Agility +20 while equipped.

Buy: Empycchu, Dark Empycchu

Recipe to Make:
Mercury's rapier = fallen angel rapier + Mercury's bandana + Mercury's bandana

Use in Recipes:
None

MIRACLE SWORD ✓

Buy: N/A
Sell: 1000

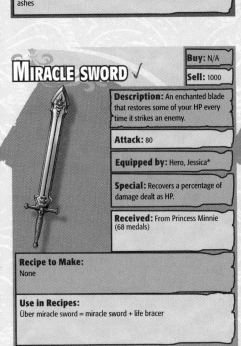

Description: An enchanted blade that restores some of your HP every time it strikes an enemy.

Attack: 80

Equipped by: Hero, Jessica*

Special: Recovers a percentage of damage dealt as HP.

Received: From Princess Minnie (68 medals)

Recipe to Make:
None

Use in Recipes:
Über miracle sword = miracle sword + life bracer

DRAGON SLAYER

Buy: N/A
Sell: 22500

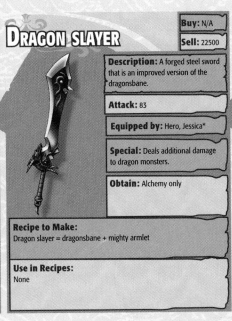

Description: A forged steel sword that is an improved version of the dragonsbane.

Attack: 83

Equipped by: Hero, Jessica*

Special: Deals additional damage to dragon monsters.

Obtain: Alchemy only

Recipe to Make:
Dragon slayer = dragonsbane + mighty armlet

Use in Recipes:
None

BLIZZARD BLADE

Buy: 21000
Sell: 10500

Description: An enchanted ice sword whose blade contains the power of a mighty snowstorm.

Attack: 90

Equipped by: Hero, Jessica*

Special: Deals additional ice-based damage to target.

Buy: Tryan Gully

Recipe to Make:
Blizzard blade = bastard sword + icicle dirk + cold cheese

Use in Recipes:
None

Über miracle sword

Buy: N/A
Sell: 1500

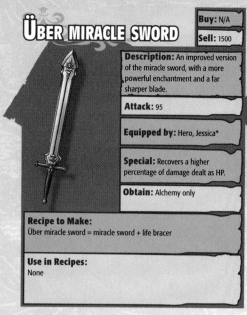

Description: An improved version of the miracle sword, with a more powerful enchantment and a far sharper blade.

Attack: 95

Equipped by: Hero, Jessica*

Special: Recovers a higher percentage of damage dealt as HP.

Obtain: Alchemy only

Recipe to Make:
Über miracle sword = miracle sword + life bracer

Use in Recipes:
None

Hell sabre ✓

Buy: N/A
Sell: 7300

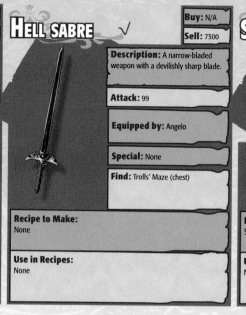

Description: A narrow-bladed weapon with a devilishly sharp blade.

Attack: 99

Equipped by: Angelo

Special: None

Find: Trolls' Maze (chest)

Recipe to Make:
None

Use in Recipes:
None

Shamshir of light

Buy: N/A
Sell: 9000

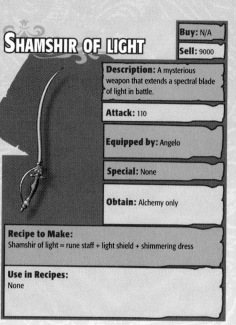

Description: A mysterious weapon that extends a spectral blade of light in battle.

Attack: 110

Equipped by: Angelo

Special: None

Obtain: Alchemy only

Recipe to Make:
Shamshir of light = rune staff + light shield + shimmering dress

Use in Recipes:
None

SPEARS

Liquid metal sword

Buy: N/A
Sell: 5000

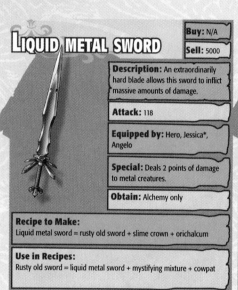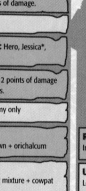

Description: An extraordinarily hard blade allows this sword to inflict massive amounts of damage.

Attack: 118

Equipped by: Hero, Jessica*, Angelo

Special: Deals 2 points of damage to metal creatures.

Obtain: Alchemy only

Recipe to Make:
Liquid metal sword = rusty old sword + slime crown + orichalcum

Use in Recipes:
Rusty old sword = liquid metal sword + mystifying mixture + cowpat

Iron lance

Buy: 750
Sell: 375

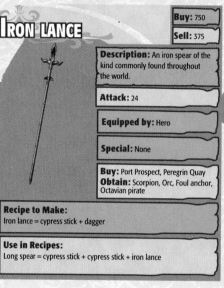

Description: An iron spear of the kind commonly found throughout the world.

Attack: 24

Equipped by: Hero

Special: None

Buy: Port Prospect, Peregrin Quay
Obtain: Scorpion, Orc, Foul anchor, Octavian pirate

Recipe to Make:
Iron lance = cypress stick + dagger

Use in Recipes:
Long spear = cypress stick + cypress stick + iron lance

Long spear

Buy: 1700
Sell: 850

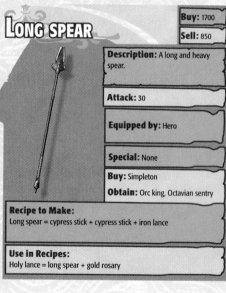

Description: A long and heavy spear.

Attack: 30

Equipped by: Hero

Special: None

Buy: Simpleton

Obtain: Orc king, Octavian sentry

Recipe to Make:
Long spear = cypress stick + cypress stick + iron lance

Use in Recipes:
Holy lance = long spear + gold rosary

Holy lance

Buy: 2700
Sell: 1350

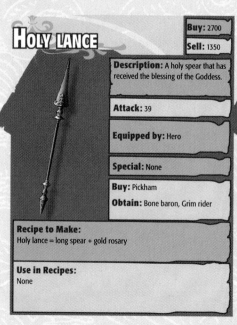

Description: A holy spear that has received the blessing of the Goddess.

Attack: 39

Equipped by: Hero

Special: None

Buy: Pickham

Obtain: Bone baron, Grim rider

Recipe to Make:
Holy lance = long spear + gold rosary

Use in Recipes:
None

Battle fork ✓

Buy: N/A
Sell: 3300

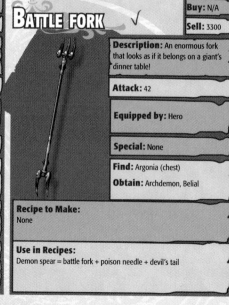

Description: An enormous fork that looks as if it belongs on a giant's dinner table!

Attack: 42

Equipped by: Hero

Special: None

Find: Argonia (chest)

Obtain: Archdemon, Belial

Recipe to Make:
None

Use in Recipes:
Demon spear = battle fork + poison needle + devil's tail

Partisan ✓

Buy: 4400
Sell: 2200

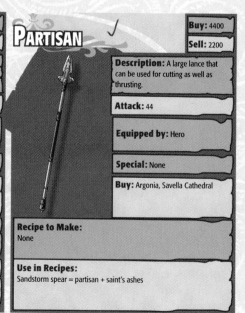

Description: A large lance that can be used for cutting as well as thrusting.

Attack: 44

Equipped by: Hero

Special: None

Buy: Argonia, Savella Cathedral

Recipe to Make:
None

Use in Recipes:
Sandstorm spear = partisan + saint's ashes

SANDSTORM SPEAR

Buy: N/A
Sell: 5300

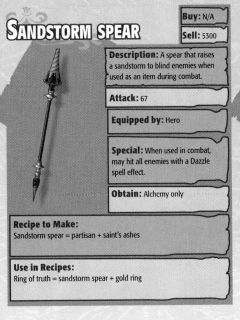

Description: A spear that raises a sandstorm to blind enemies when used as an item during combat.

Attack: 67

Equipped by: Hero

Special: When used in combat, may hit all enemies with a Dazzle spell effect.

Obtain: Alchemy only

Recipe to Make:
Sandstorm spear = partisan + saint's ashes

Use in Recipes:
Ring of truth = sandstorm spear + gold ring

DEMON SPEAR

Buy: N/A
Sell: 12500

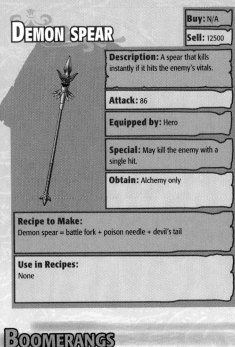

Description: A spear that kills instantly if it hits the enemy's vitals.

Attack: 86

Equipped by: Hero

Special: May kill the enemy with a single hit.

Obtain: Alchemy only

Recipe to Make:
Demon spear = battle fork + poison needle + devil's tail

Use in Recipes:
None

HERO SPEAR

Buy: N/A
Sell: 15000

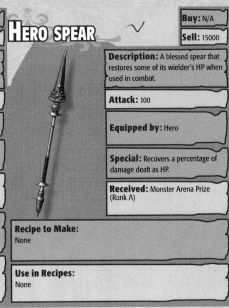
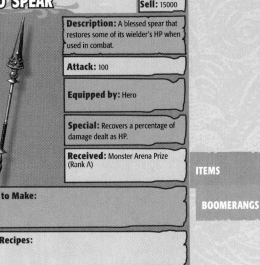

Description: A blessed spear that restores some of its wielder's HP when used in combat.

Attack: 100

Equipped by: Hero

Special: Recovers a percentage of damage dealt as HP.

Received: Monster Arena Prize (Rank A)

Recipe to Make:
None

Use in Recipes:
None

ITEMS

BOOMERANGS

BOOMERANGS

METAL KING SPEAR

Buy: N/A
Sell: 24000

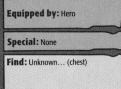
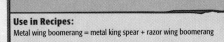
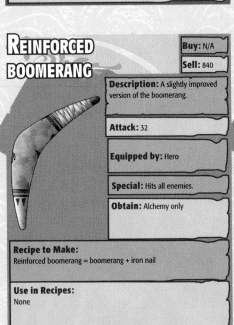

Description: The most powerful spear. Capable of penetrating almost any material.

Attack: 120

Equipped by: Hero

Special: None

Find: Unknown… (chest)

Recipe to Make:
None

Use in Recipes:
Metal wing boomerang = metal king spear + razor wing boomerang

BOOMERANG

Buy: 420
Sell: 210

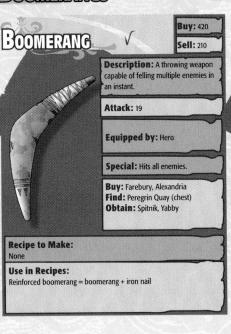

Description: A throwing weapon capable of felling multiple enemies in an instant.

Attack: 19

Equipped by: Hero

Special: Hits all enemies.

Buy: Farebury, Alexandria
Find: Peregrin Quay (chest)
Obtain: Spitnik, Yabby

Recipe to Make:
None

Use in Recipes:
Reinforced boomerang = boomerang + iron nail

EDGED BOOMERANG

Buy: 1360
Sell: 680

Description: A metal boomerang with knife-like edges.

Attack: 27

Equipped by: Hero

Special: Hits all enemies.

Buy: Ascantha, Neos
Find: Orkutsk (chest)
Obtain: Dark star, Crayzee

Recipe to Make:
None

Use in Recipes:
Razor wing boomerang = edged boomerang + steel scythe + wing of bat
Spiked armour = edged boomerang + magic armour

REINFORCED BOOMERANG

Buy: N/A
Sell: 840

Description: A slightly improved version of the boomerang.

Attack: 32

Equipped by: Hero

Special: Hits all enemies.

Obtain: Alchemy only

Recipe to Make:
Reinforced boomerang = boomerang + iron nail

Use in Recipes:
None

RAZOR WING BOOMERANG

Buy: 3800
Sell: 1900

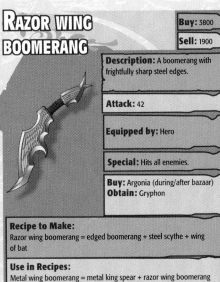

Description: A boomerang with frightfully sharp steel edges.

Attack: 42

Equipped by: Hero

Special: Hits all enemies.

Buy: Argonia (during/after bazaar)
Obtain: Gryphon

Recipe to Make:
Razor wing boomerang = edged boomerang + steel scythe + wing of bat

Use in Recipes:
Metal wing boomerang = metal king spear + razor wing boomerang

SWALLOWTAIL

Buy: 6800
Sell: 3400

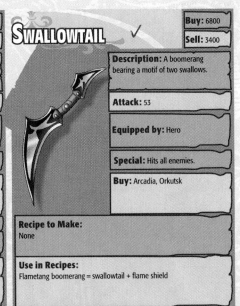

Description: A boomerang bearing a motif of two swallows.

Attack: 53

Equipped by: Hero

Special: Hits all enemies.

Buy: Arcadia, Orkutsk

Recipe to Make:
None

Use in Recipes:
Flametang boomerang = swallowtail + flame shield

185

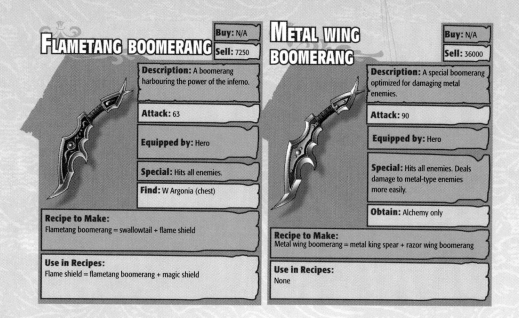

FLAMETANG BOOMERANG

Buy: N/A
Sell: 7250

Description: A boomerang harbouring the power of the inferno.

Attack: 63

Equipped by: Hero

Special: Hits all enemies.

Find: W Argonia (chest)

Recipe to Make:
Flametang boomerang = swallowtail + flame shield

Use in Recipes:
Flame shield = flametang boomerang + magic shield

METAL WING BOOMERANG

Buy: N/A
Sell: 36000

Description: A special boomerang optimized for damaging metal enemies.

Attack: 90

Equipped by: Hero

Special: Hits all enemies. Deals damage to metal-type enemies more easily.

Obtain: Alchemy only

Recipe to Make:
Metal wing boomerang = metal king spear + razor wing boomerang

Use in Recipes:
None

AXES

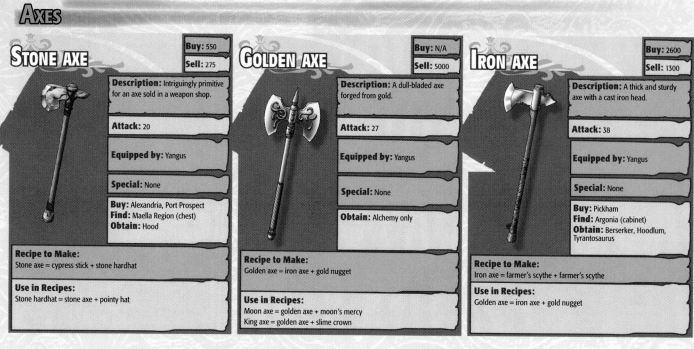

STONE AXE

Buy: 550
Sell: 275

Description: Intriguingly primitive for an axe sold in a weapon shop.

Attack: 20

Equipped by: Yangus

Special: None

Buy: Alexandria, Port Prospect
Find: Maella Region (chest)
Obtain: Hood

Recipe to Make:
Stone axe = cypress stick + stone hardhat

Use in Recipes:
Stone hardhat = stone axe + pointy hat

GOLDEN AXE

Buy: N/A
Sell: 5000

Description: A dull-bladed axe forged from gold.

Attack: 27

Equipped by: Yangus

Special: None

Obtain: Alchemy only

Recipe to Make:
Golden axe = iron axe + gold nugget

Use in Recipes:
Moon axe = golden axe + moon's mercy
King axe = golden axe + slime crown

IRON AXE

Buy: 2600
Sell: 1300

Description: A thick and sturdy axe with a cast iron head.

Attack: 38

Equipped by: Yangus

Special: None

Buy: Pickham
Find: Argonia (cabinet)
Obtain: Berserker, Hoodlum, Tyrantosaurus

Recipe to Make:
Iron axe = farmer's scythe + farmer's scythe

Use in Recipes:
Golden axe = iron axe + gold nugget

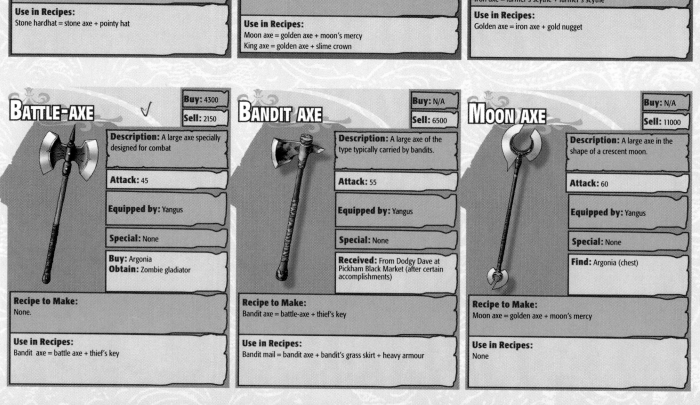

BATTLE-AXE ✓

Buy: 4300
Sell: 2150

Description: A large axe specially designed for combat

Attack: 45

Equipped by: Yangus

Special: None

Buy: Argonia
Obtain: Zombie gladiator

Recipe to Make:
None.

Use in Recipes:
Bandit axe = battle axe + thief's key

BANDIT AXE

Buy: N/A
Sell: 6500

Description: A large axe of the type typically carried by bandits.

Attack: 55

Equipped by: Yangus

Special: None

Received: From Dodgy Dave at Pickham Black Market (after certain accomplishments)

Recipe to Make:
Bandit axe = battle-axe + thief's key

Use in Recipes:
Bandit mail = bandit axe + bandit's grass skirt + heavy armour

MOON AXE

Buy: N/A
Sell: 11000

Description: A large axe in the shape of a crescent moon.

Attack: 60

Equipped by: Yangus

Special: None

Find: Argonia (chest)

Recipe to Make:
Moon axe = golden axe + moon's mercy

Use in Recipes:
None

King axe

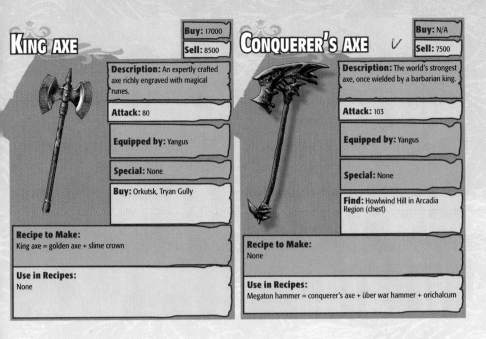

Buy: 17000
Sell: 8500

Description: An expertly crafted axe richly engraved with magical runes.

Attack: 80

Equipped by: Yangus

Special: None

Buy: Orkutsk, Tryan Gully

Recipe to Make:
King axe = golden axe + slime crown

Use in Recipes:
None

Conquerer's axe ✓

Buy: N/A
Sell: 7500

Description: The world's strongest axe, once wielded by a barbarian king.

Attack: 103

Equipped by: Yangus

Special: None

Find: Howlwind Hill in Arcadia Region (chest)

Recipe to Make:
None

Use in Recipes:
Megaton hammer = conquerer's axe + über war hammer + orichalcum

---

Clubs

Oaken club ✓

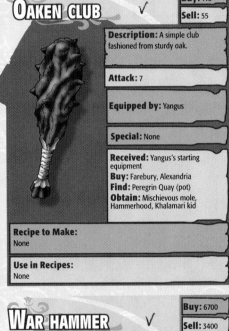

Buy: 110
Sell: 55

Description: A simple club fashioned from sturdy oak.

Attack: 7

Equipped by: Yangus

Special: None

Received: Yangus's starting equipment
Buy: Farebury, Alexandria
Find: Peregrin Quay (pot)
Obtain: Mischievous mole, Hammerhood, Khalamari kid

Recipe to Make:
None

Use in Recipes:
None

Giant mallet ✓

Buy: 240
Sell: 120

Description: A giant wooden hammer of the sort often carried by monsters as well as humans.

Attack: 13

Equipped by: Yangus

Special: None

Buy: Farebury, Alexandria
Find: Arcadia (chest)
Obtain: Hammerhood, Brownie, Gorerilla, Pink pongo, Abominape, Cyclops

Recipe to Make:
None

Use in Recipes:
Sledgehammer = giant mallet + iron helmet + iron helmet

Sledgehammer

Buy: 1700
Sell: 1000

Description: An enormous hammer made of iron.

Attack: 33

Equipped by: Yangus

Special: None

Buy: Simpleton
Find: Kingdom of Trodain (chest)

Obtain: Troll

Recipe to Make:
Sledgehammer = giant mallet + iron helmet + iron helmet

Use in Recipes:
None

War hammer ✓

Buy: 6700
Sell: 3400

Description: A steel hammer specially designed for combat.

Attack: 51

Equipped by: Yangus

Special: None

Buy: Argonia (during/after bazaar)

Recipe to Make:
None

Use in Recipes:
Über war hammer = war hammer + mighty armlet

Über war hammer

Buy: N/A
Sell: 16000

Description: An improved version of the war hammer conveying even greater attack power.

Attack: 69

Equipped by: Yangus

Special: None

Obtain: Alchemy only

Recipe to Make:
Über war hammer = war hammer + mighty armlet

Use in Recipes:
Megaton hammer = conquerer's axe + über war hammer + orichalcum

Megaton hammer

Buy: N/A
Sell: 55500

Description: A giant hammer that improves your chances of landing a critical hit.

Attack: 108

Equipped by: Yangus

Special: Increases odds of critical hits.

Obtain: Alchemy only

Recipe to Make:
Megaton hammer = conquerer's axe + über war hammer + orichalcum

Use in Recipes:
None

SCYTHES

FARMER'S SCYTHE ✓

Buy: 910
Sell: 460

Description: A large iron scythe of the type often used to cut grass and straw.

Attack: 28

Equipped by: Yangus

Special: None

Buy: Port Prospect, Peregrin Quay
Find: Pickham Region (chest)
Obtain: Iron scorpion, Iron rhino, Foul anchor

Recipe to Make:
None

Use in Recipes:
Iron axe = farmer's scythe + farmer's scythe

STEEL SCYTHE ✓

Buy: 3700
Sell: 1650

Description: A scythe designed specifically for combat.

Attack: 42

Equipped by: Yangus

Special: None

Buy: Baccarat, Savella Cathedral, Neos
Obtain: Fallen priest

Recipe to Make:
None

Use in Recipes:
Razor wing boomerang = edged boomerang + steel scythe + wing of bat
Hell scythe = steel scythe + poison moth knife + Hades' helm

HELL SCYTHE

Buy: 9500
Sell: 5000

Description: An enormous scythe that may paralyse the enemies that it strikes.

Attack: 65

Equipped by: Yangus

Special: May paralyse enemies it hits.

Buy: Arcadia

Recipe to Make:
Hell scythe = steel scythe + poison moth knife + Hades' helm

Use in Recipes:
None

BARDICHE OF BINDING ✓

Buy: N/A
Sell: 12000

Description: An enchanted weapon that can deprive its target of the ability to cast spells.

Attack: 83

Equipped by: Yangus

Special: Deals additional damage to demon enemies. May silence enemies it hits.

Received: Monster Arena Prize (Rank B)

Recipe to Make:
None

Use in Recipes:
None

HEAVY HATCHET ✓

Buy: 29000
Sell: 15000

Description: An enormous hatchet capable of cutting down enemies where they stand.

Attack: 110

Equipped by: Yangus

Special: None

Buy: Tryan Gully

Recipe to Make:
None

Use in Recipes:
None

FLAILS

FLAIL OF FURY ✓

Buy: N/A
Sell: N/A

Description: A present from Red, this flail is capable of hitting multiple enemies in a single swing.

Attack: 93

Equipped by: Yangus

Special: Hits each enemy in a group. Cannot be sold or dropped.

Received: Red's Den (after certain events)

Recipe to Make:
None

Use in Recipes:
None

FLAIL OF DESTRUCTION ✓

Buy: N/A
Sell: 22500

Description: Scourges all enemies with a power beyond imagination.

Attack: 125

Equipped by: Yangus

Special: Hits all enemies.

Received: From Princess Minnie (110 medals)

Recipe to Make:
None

Use in Recipes:
None

KNIVES

POISON NEEDLE ✓

Buy: 1900
Sell: 1000

Description: Capable of felling an enemy with a single well-aimed strike.

Attack: 0

Equipped by: Jessica

Special: Always deals only 1 damage to foes, but may kill non-boss foes in a single hit.

Buy: Baccarat
Obtain: Venom wasp, Death scorpion

Recipe to Make:
None

Use in Recipes:
Demon spear = battle fork + poison needle + devil's tail
Assassin's dagger = poison needle + eagle dagger
Ring of immunity = poison needle + gold ring

BRONZE KNIFE ✓

Buy: 150
Sell: 75

Description: A small knife forged from bronze.

Attack: 9

Equipped by: Jessica

Special: None

Buy: Peregrin Quay
Find: Ferry (chest), Uncharted Island west of Maella Abbey (chest)
Obtain: Shadow

Recipe to Make: None

Use in Recipes:
Thief's key = bronze knife + iron nail
Copper sword = bronze knife + bronze knife
Bronze shield = bronze knife + leather shield
Bronze helmet = bronze knife + bronze knife + stone hardhat

DAGGER ✓

Buy: 350
Sell: 175

Description: A long-bladed knife designed for combat.

Attack: 18

Equipped by: Jessica

Special: None

Buy: Ascantha
Find: Farebury (chest)
Obtain: Clockwork cuckoo, Riptide

Recipe to Make:
None

Use in Recipes:
Iron lance = cypress stick + dagger

POISON MOTH KNIFE ✓

Buy: 950
Sell: 475

Description: Features a blade coated with the poison of a moth that can paralyse enemies.

Attack: 29

Equipped by: Jessica

Special: May paralyse enemies it hits.

Buy: Pickham
Find: Arcadia (cabinet)
Obtain: Hell hornet, Garuda, Icikiller

Recipe to Make:
None

Use in Recipes:
Hell scythe = steel scythe + poison moth knife + Hades' helm
Full moon ring = poison moth knife + gold ring

FALCON KNIFE

Buy: 7700
Sell: 4400

Description: A magical dagger that lends its user the agility to attack twice in rapid succession.

Attack: 34

Equipped by: Jessica

Special: Attacks twice.

Buy: Argonia (during/after bazaar), Orkutsk

Recipe to Make:
Falcon knife = tough guy tattoo + slime earrings + agility ring

Use in Recipes:
None

ASSASSIN'S DAGGER

Buy: N/A
Sell: 1250

Description: A compact knife made especially for assassins.

Attack: 37

Equipped by: Jessica

Special: None

Find: Arcadia Region (chest)
Obtain: Jumping jackal, Jackal ripper, Claws, Anchorman

Recipe to Make:
Assassin's dagger = poison needle + eagle dagger

Use in Recipes:
Imp knife = assassin's dagger + devil's tail

EAGLE DAGGER ✓

Buy: 3900
Sell: 1950

Description: A short sword with a blade as sharp as an eagle's talons.

Attack: 39

Equipped by: Jessica

Special: None

Buy: Savella Cathedral
Find: W Argonia (chest)
Obtain: Hades condor, Elysium bird

Recipe to Make:
None

Use in Recipes:
Assassin's dagger = poison needle + eagle dagger

IMP KNIFE

Buy: N/A
Sell: 2250

Description: A knife capable of stealing MP from the targets it strikes.

Attack: 52

Equipped by: Jessica

Special: May absorb MP from enemies you hit.

Obtain: Alchemy only

Recipe to Make:
Imp knife = assassin's dagger + devil's tail

Use in Recipes:
None

ICICLE DIRK ✓

Buy: N/A
Sell: 4000

Description: A short sword with a blade of ice. Generates a blizzard when used as an item during battle.

Attack: 52

Equipped by: Jessica

Special: Deals additional ice-type damage to target. When used in combat, casts Crackle on enemy group.

Find: Herb Grotto (chest), Black Citadel (barrel)

Recipe to Make:
None

Use in Recipes:
Blizzard blade = bastard sword + icicle dirk + cold cheese
Ice shield = icicle dirk + magic shield

SWORD BREAKER ✓

Buy: 5500
Sell: 2750

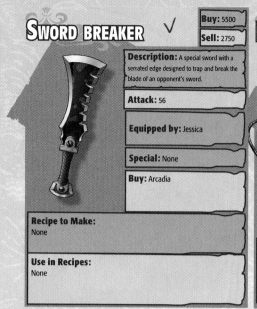

Description: A special sword with a serrated edge designed to trap and break the blade of an opponent's sword.

Attack: 56

Equipped by: Jessica

Special: None

Buy: Arcadia

Recipe to Make:
None

Use in Recipes:
None

LEATHER WHIP

Buy: N/A
Sell: 85

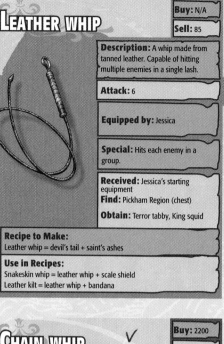

Description: A whip made from tanned leather. Capable of hitting multiple enemies in a single lash.

Attack: 6

Equipped by: Jessica

Special: Hits each enemy in a group.

Received: Jessica's starting equipment
Find: Pickham Region (chest)
Obtain: Terror tabby, King squid

Recipe to Make:
Leather whip = devil's tail + saint's ashes

Use in Recipes:
Snakeskin whip = leather whip + scale shield
Leather kilt = leather whip + bandana

THORN WHIP ✓

Buy: 350
Sell: 175

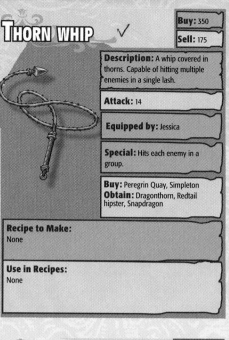

Description: A whip covered in thorns. Capable of hitting multiple enemies in a single lash.

Attack: 14

Equipped by: Jessica

Special: Hits each enemy in a group.

Buy: Peregrin Quay, Simpleton
Obtain: Dragonthorn, Redtail hipster, Snapdragon

Recipe to Make:
None

Use in Recipes:
None

SNAKESKIN WHIP ✓

Buy: N/A
Sell: 1250

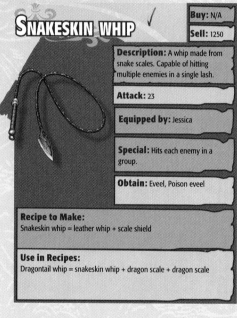

Description: A whip made from snake scales. Capable of hitting multiple enemies in a single lash.

Attack: 23

Equipped by: Jessica

Special: Hits each enemy in a group.

Obtain: Eveel, Poison eveel

Recipe to Make:
Snakeskin whip = leather whip + scale shield

Use in Recipes:
Dragontail whip = snakeskin whip + dragon scale + dragon scale

CHAIN WHIP ✓

Buy: 2200
Sell: 1100

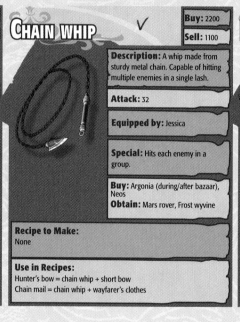

Description: A whip made from sturdy metal chain. Capable of hitting multiple enemies in a single lash.

Attack: 32

Equipped by: Jessica

Special: Hits each enemy in a group.

Buy: Argonia (during/after bazaar), Neos
Obtain: Mars rover, Frost wyvine

Recipe to Make:
None

Use in Recipes:
Hunter's bow = chain whip + short bow
Chain mail = chain whip + wayfarer's clothes

DRAGONTAIL WHIP

Buy: N/A
Sell: 7400

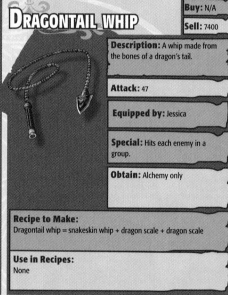

Description: A whip made from the bones of a dragon's tail.

Attack: 47

Equipped by: Jessica

Special: Hits each enemy in a group.

Obtain: Alchemy only

Recipe to Make:
Dragontail whip = snakeskin whip + dragon scale + dragon scale

Use in Recipes:
None

SPIKED STEEL WHIP ✓

Buy: 8300
Sell: 4300

Description: A powerful whip covered in painful-looking steel barbs.

Attack: 62

Equipped by: Jessica

Special: Hits each enemy in a group.

Buy: Orkutsk
Find: Red's Den (chest)
Obtain: Snapdragon

Recipe to Make
None

Use in Recipes
None

DEMON WHIP

Buy: N/A
Sell: 3500

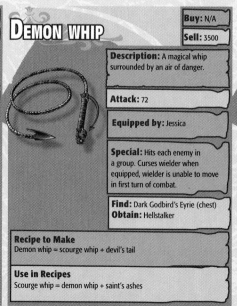

Description: A magical whip surrounded by an air of danger.

Attack: 72

Equipped by: Jessica

Special: Hits each enemy in a group. Curses wielder when equipped, wielder is unable to move in first turn of combat.

Find: Dark Godbird's Eyrie (chest)
Obtain: Hellstalker

Recipe to Make
Demon whip = scourge whip + devil's tail

Use in Recipes
Scourge whip = demon whip + saint's ashes

SCOURGE WHIP

Buy: N/A
Sell: 9250

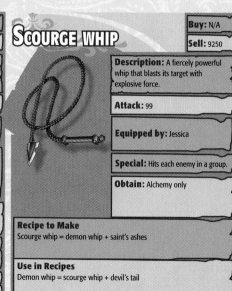

Description: A fiercely powerful whip that blasts its target with explosive force.

Attack: 99

Equipped by: Jessica

Special: Hits each enemy in a group.

Obtain: Alchemy only

Recipe to Make
Scourge whip = demon whip + saint's ashes

Use in Recipes
Demon whip = scourge whip + devil's tail

GRINGHAM WHIP ✓

Buy: N/A
Sell: 10000

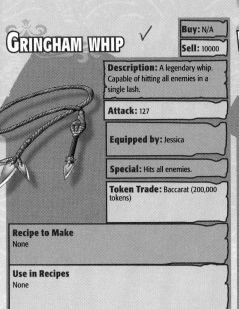

Description: A legendary whip. Capable of hitting all enemies in a single lash.

Attack: 127

Equipped by: Jessica

Special: Hits all enemies.

Token Trade: Baccarat (200,000 tokens)

Recipe to Make
None

Use in Recipes
None

WIZARD'S STAFF ✓

Buy: 1300
Sell: 650

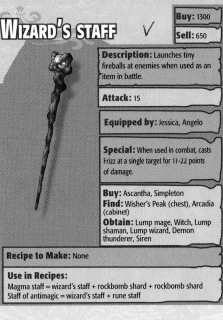

Description: Launches tiny fireballs at enemies when used as an item in battle.

Attack: 15

Equipped by: Jessica, Angelo

Special: When used in combat, casts Frizz at a single target for 11-22 points of damage.

Buy: Ascantha, Simpleton
Find: Wisher's Peak (chest), Arcadia (cabinet)
Obtain: Lump mage, Witch, Lump shaman, Lump wizard, Demon thunderer, Siren

Recipe to Make: None

Use in Recipes:
Magma staff = wizard's staff + rockbomb shard + rockbomb shard
Staff of antimagic = wizard's staff + rune staff

LIGHTNING STAFF ✓

Buy: N/A
Sell: 2300

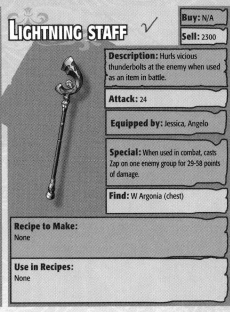

Description: Hurls vicious thunderbolts at the enemy when used as an item in battle.

Attack: 24

Equipped by: Jessica, Angelo

Special: When used in combat, casts Zap on one enemy group for 29-58 points of damage.

Find: W Argonia (chest)

Recipe to Make:
None

Use in Recipes:
None

ITEMS

STAVES

MAGMA STAFF

Buy: N/A
Sell: 2500

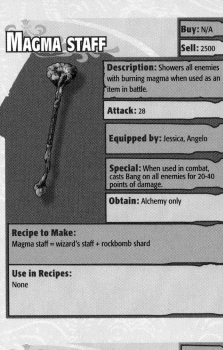

Description: Showers all enemies with burning magma when used as an item in battle.

Attack: 28

Equipped by: Jessica, Angelo

Special: When used in combat, casts Bang on all enemies for 20-40 points of damage.

Obtain: Alchemy only

Recipe to Make:
Magma staff = wizard's staff + rockbomb shard

Use in Recipes:
None

RUNE STAFF ✓

Buy: N/A
Sell: 3150

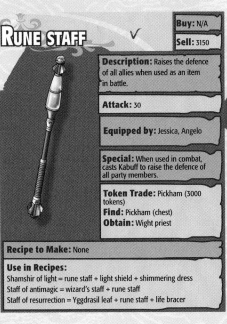

Description: Raises the defence of all allies when used as an item in battle.

Attack: 30

Equipped by: Jessica, Angelo

Special: When used in combat, casts Kabuff to raise the defence of all party members.

Token Trade: Pickham (3000 tokens)
Find: Pickham (chest)
Obtain: Wight priest

Recipe to Make: None

Use in Recipes:
Shamshir of light = rune staff + light shield + shimmering dress
Staff of antimagic = wizard's staff + rune staff
Staff of resurrection = Yggdrasil leaf + rune staff + life bracer

STAFF OF DIVINE WRATH ✓

Buy: N/A
Sell: 2500

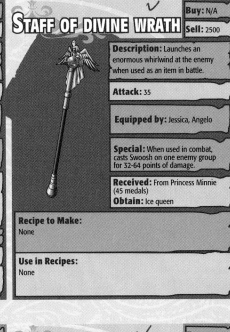

Description: Launches an enormous whirlwind at the enemy when used as an item in battle.

Attack: 35

Equipped by: Jessica, Angelo

Special: When used in combat, casts Swoosh on one enemy group for 32-64 points of damage.

Received: From Princess Minnie (45 medals)
Obtain: Ice queen

Recipe to Make:
None

Use in Recipes:
None

STAFF OF ANTIMAGIC

Buy: N/A
Sell: 3000

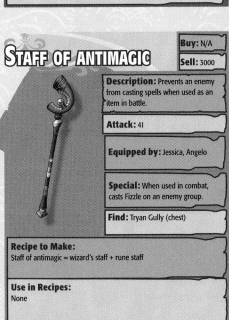

Description: Prevents an enemy from casting spells when used as an item in battle.

Attack: 41

Equipped by: Jessica, Angelo

Special: When used in combat, casts Fizzle on an enemy group.

Find: Tryan Gully (chest)

Recipe to Make:
Staff of antimagic = wizard's staff + rune staff

Use in Recipes:
None

STAFF OF RESURRECTION

Buy: 45000
Sell: 22500

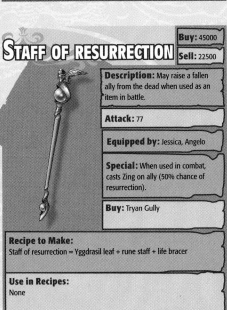

Description: May raise a fallen ally from the dead when used as an item in battle.

Attack: 77

Equipped by: Jessica, Angelo

Special: When used in combat, casts Zing on ally (50% chance of resurrection).

Buy: Tryan Gully

Recipe to Make:
Staff of resurrection = Yggdrasil leaf + rune staff + life bracer

Use in Recipes:
None

MAGICAL MACE ✓

Buy: 9000
Sell: 4500

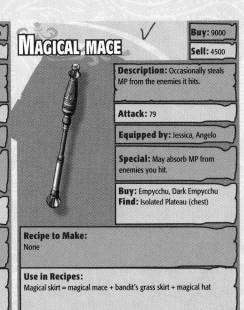

Description: Occasionally steals MP from the enemies it hits.

Attack: 79

Equipped by: Jessica, Angelo

Special: May absorb MP from enemies you hit.

Buy: Empycchu, Dark Empycchu
Find: Isolated Plateau (chest)

Recipe to Make:
None

Use in Recipes:
Magical skirt = magical mace + bandit's grass skirt + magical hat

Bows

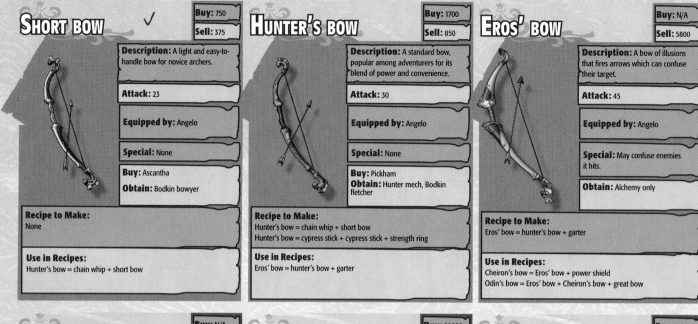

SHORT BOW ✓

Buy: 750
Sell: 375

Description: A light and easy-to-handle bow for novice archers.

Attack: 23

Equipped by: Angelo

Special: None

Buy: Ascantha
Obtain: Bodkin bowyer

Recipe to Make:
None

Use in Recipes:
Hunter's bow = chain whip + short bow

HUNTER'S BOW

Buy: 1700
Sell: 850

Description: A standard bow, popular among adventurers for its blend of power and convenience.

Attack: 30

Equipped by: Angelo

Special: None

Buy: Pickham
Obtain: Hunter mech, Bodkin fletcher

Recipe to Make:
Hunter's bow = chain whip + short bow
Hunter's bow = cypress stick + cypress stick + strength ring

Use in Recipes:
Eros' bow = hunter's bow + garter

EROS' BOW

Buy: N/A
Sell: 5800

Description: A bow of illusions that fires arrows which can confuse their target.

Attack: 45

Equipped by: Angelo

Special: May confuse enemies it hits.

Obtain: Alchemy only

Recipe to Make:
Eros' bow = hunter's bow + garter

Use in Recipes:
Cheiron's bow = Eros' bow + power shield
Odin's bow = Eros' bow + Cheiron's bow + great bow

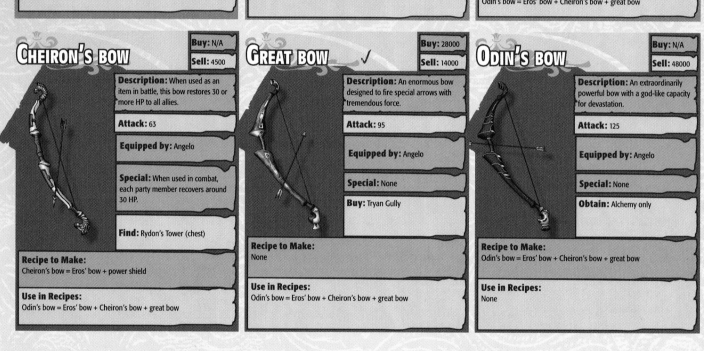

CHEIRON'S BOW

Buy: N/A
Sell: 4500

Description: When used as an item in battle, this bow restores 30 or more HP to all allies.

Attack: 63

Equipped by: Angelo

Special: When used in combat, each party member recovers around 30 HP.

Find: Rydon's Tower (chest)

Recipe to Make:
Cheiron's bow = Eros' bow + power shield

Use in Recipes:
Odin's bow = Eros' bow + Cheiron's bow + great bow

GREAT BOW ✓

Buy: 28000
Sell: 14000

Description: An enormous bow designed to fire special arrows with tremendous force.

Attack: 95

Equipped by: Angelo

Special: None

Buy: Tryan Gully

Recipe to Make:
None

Use in Recipes:
Odin's bow = Eros' bow + Cheiron's bow + great bow

ODIN'S BOW

Buy: N/A
Sell: 48000

Description: An extraordinarily powerful bow with a god-like capacity for devastation.

Attack: 125

Equipped by: Angelo

Special: None

Obtain: Alchemy only

Recipe to Make:
Odin's bow = Eros' bow + Cheiron's bow + great bow

Use in Recipes:
None

ALCHEMY POT RECIPES

It takes King Trode time to work out the kinks in the alchemy pot, so it doesn't become available until you've completed the first couple of tasks. When you get it, the "Alchemy Pot" option is added to the list in the Misc. menu tab. From the alchemy screen, you can scroll through each character's personal inventory as well as the contents of the bag in search of ingredients. Usable items are displayed normally. If an item's name is grayed out, it is unavailable either because the item is equipped by a character or unusable in any recipes.

When you first receive the alchemy pot, it can only handle two ingredients. At a later point in the quest, it is upgraded to handle three items, allowing for more complex recipes.

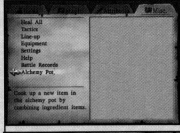

THE MIXING PROCESS

If the chosen ingredients don't form a working recipe, the pot spits them back out. If the ingredients can form a new item, however, the pot will require time to work. The amount of time varies, based primarily on the value of the item being created. It won't take long to turn a pair of medicinal herbs into strong medicine, but making a weapon or armament worth 10,000+ gold coins will take much longer.

You won't always have access to the alchemy pot. For example, the wagon stays behind when you enter a dungeon. Additionally, you won't have access to it at certain points in the storyline. The mixing continues whether you're near the pot or not, so put in more time-consuming recipes before entering dungeon areas.

The duration of the alchemical process is based not on actual time, but on the number of footsteps you take. Travelling by sabrecat or ship will not speed up the process, but walking on the field will make the mixing process go about 50% faster than it does when walking in towns or dungeons. Note that you just need to walk; you don't actually have to go anywhere.

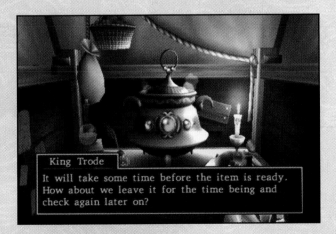

King Trode

It will take some time before the item is ready. How about we leave it for the time being and check again later on?

FINDING RECIPE HINTS

You can craft new items from all sorts of different ingredients. Occasionally, it's as simple as mixing two weapons to make a more powerful weapon of the same type, but you'll usually need to think a little more creatively. Try combining weapons with armour and accessories for better results.

For the most part, recovery items can only be combined with other recovery items but there are a few times when a recovery item can be mixed with a weapon or armament. Also, pay special attention to items that have no function; these may exist solely as alchemy pot ingredients and are often a requirement for the game's best recipes.

It is not possible to make every item in a single game. Some recipes require unique ingredients, of which only one may exist. Before you make a recipe that includes an ingredient that can't be easily purchased or remade from available ingredients, you may want to save your game just in case the resultant item is not worth the sacrifice.

NOTEWORTHY INGREDIENTS

Fresh milk and rennet powder: These are the basic ingredients for making cheese.

Moulds: These are used exclusively to flavour cheeses.

Metals and minerals: Rare materials like gold nuggets and orichalcum are used primarily for making exceptional weapons and armaments.

Monster parts: Items like magic beast hides, wings of bat and dragon scales add a touch of their source's nature to recipes.

Dung: Cowpats and dragon dung may ruin some recipes, but they occasionally work to your advantage.

CURSING AND PURIFYING ITEMS

Saint's ashes and devil's tails appear frequently in recipes. These items work to purify cursed items and curse purified items, respectively. Whenever an item has an air of danger around it, you can try dropping it in the alchemy pot with saint's ashes to remove the curse and reveal a new item. You'll find more cursed items than saint's ashes, however, so use them sparingly.

Devil's tails are a bit harder to use. Just because you can use them in a recipe doesn't mean you should; they'll often ruin perfectly good items by cursing them. But certain weapons and types of armour can benefit from the taint of evil. As a general rule, the devil's tail will have a positive effect when it's one of three ingredients, but not when it's one of two (the imp knife is an exception).

POTENTIAL PERILS OF ALCHEMY

Just because a recipe works doesn't mean it will work to your advantage. While most recipes create an item that is better than its constituent ingredients, this is not always the case. Be very careful of recipes that involve magic beast hides or devil's tails, since these can often ruin or curse items. However, either can be a great asset when used in the right recipe.

ARTISAN CHEESES AND FOR-PROFIT ALCHEMY

Once you get the hang of alchemy, you should keep the alchemy pot running full time, even if you don't particularly want the items it produces. Many items are worth more than the sum of their ingredients, so you can purchase cheap ingredients, whip up items and sell them for gold coins.

This is true of many weapons and armaments, but no item is as profitable as cheese. The constituent ingredients in cheese are fresh milk, rennet powder, rock salt, and moulds, all of which can be found frequently and, later on, purchased for small sums. Hard cheese, soft cheese, and chunky cheese all sell for around 500 gold coins and require ingredients with barely one-tenth of that cost.

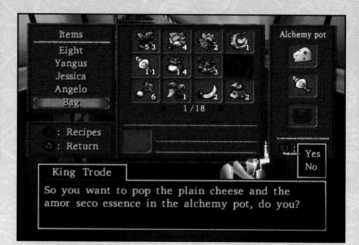

Other highly profitable items, which require easily purchasable ingredients to make, include strong medicines, mystifying mixtures, and turbans. Much later in the game, you can clear a 10,000 gold coins profit from a two-stage recipe: Make white shields out of light shield and fresh milk, then buy mirror shields in Tryan Gully to make high value saintess shields.

Plain cheese = fresh milk + rennet powder

Hard cheese = plain cheese + rock salt

Soft cheese = fresh milk + rennet powder + rock salt

Chunky cheese = plain cheese + magic water

Strong medicine = medicinal herb + medicinal herb

INGREDIENT COST: 16 GOLD COINS
RESALE VALUE: 88 GOLD COINS

Turban = bandana + bandana

INGREDIENT COST: 90 GOLD COINS
RESALE VALUE: 205 GOLD COINS

Mystifying mixture = medicinal herb + antidotal herb + moonwort bulb

INGREDIENT COST: 48 GOLD COINS
RESALE VALUE: 280 GOLD COINS

Saintess shield = white shield + mirror shield + holy water

INGREDIENT COST: 17330 GOLD COINS
RESALE VALUE: 28000 GOLD COINS

RECIPE LIST

USABLE ITEMS

 Strong medicine = medicinal herb + medicinal herb

 Special medicine = strong medicine + strong medicine

 Rose-root = medicinal herb + medicinal herb + medicinal herb

 Rose-root = strong medicine + medicinal herb

 Amor seco essence = holy water + strong medicine

 Strong antidote = medicinal herb + antidotal herb

 Special antidote = strong antidote + strong antidote

 Special antidote = medicinal herb + antidotal herb + antidotal herb

 Rose-wort = medicinal herb + medicinal herb + moonwort bulb

 Rose-wort = strong medicine + moonwort bulb

 Moon's mercy = moonwort bulb + moonwort bulb + moonwort bulb

 Lesser panacea = special medicine + special medicine

 Greater panacea = special medicine + special medicine + special medicine

 Greater panacea = lesser panacea + rose-root + rose-wort

 Yggdrasil dew = Yggdrasil leaf + magic water

 Magic water = holy water + seed of magic

 Elfin elixir = Yggdrasil dew + magic water

 Holy water = amor seco essence + rock salt

 Chimaera wing = wing of bat + wing of bat

 Mystifying mixture = holy water + wing of bat + cowpat

 Mystifying mixture = medicinal herb + antidotal herb + moonwort bulb

 Sage's stone = gold nugget + orichalcum + Yggdrasil dew

 Timbrel of tension = sun crown + tough guy tattoo + magic beast hide

CHEESES

 Plain cheese = fresh milk + rennet powder

 Plain cheese = scorching cheese + c-c-cold cheese

 Spicy cheese = plain cheese + red mould

 Super spicy cheese = spicy cheese + nook grass

 Super spicy cheese = spicy cheese + red mould + red mould

 Scorching cheese = super spicy cheese + premium mould + dragon dung

 Cool cheese = plain cheese + waterweed mould

 Chilly cheese = cool cheese + waterweed mould

 Cold cheese = chilly cheese + waterweed mould + waterweed mould

 C-c-cold cheese = cold cheese + premium mould + dragon dung

 Mild cheese = plain cheese + amor seco essence

 Cured cheese = fresh milk + premium mould + amor seco essence

 Angel cheese = fresh milk + premium mould + Yggdrasil dew

 Hard cheese = plain cheese + rock salt

 Soft cheese = fresh milk + rennet powder + rock salt

 Chunky cheese = plain cheese + magic water

 Highly-strung cheese = super spicy cheese + cold cheese + rock salt

INGREDIENTS

 Premium mould = red mould + waterweed mould + Yggdrasil leaf

 Thief's key = bronze knife + iron nail

SWORDS

Copper sword = bronze knife + bronze knife

Rusty old sword = liquid metal sword + mystifying mixture + cowpat

Holy silver rapier = Templar's sword + holy talisman

Über falcon blade = falcon blade + meteorite bracer

Fallen angel rapier = holy silver rapier + devil's tail + wing of bat

Zombie slayer = zombiesbane + holy talisman

Double-edged sword = über double-edge + devil's tail

Über double-edge = double-edged sword + saint's ashes + saint's ashes

Mercury's rapier = fallen angel rapier + Mercury's bandana + Mercury's bandana

Dragon slayer = dragonsbane + mighty armlet

Blizzard blade = bastard sword + icicle dirk + cold cheese

Über miracle sword = miracle sword + life bracer

Shamshir of light = rune staff + light shield + shimmering dress

Liquid metal sword = rusty old sword + slime crown + orichalcum

SPEARS

Iron lance = cypress stick + dagger

Long spear = cypress stick + cypress stick + iron lance

Holy lance = long spear + gold rosary

Sandstorm spear = partisan + saint's ashes

Demon spear = battle fork + poison needle + devil's tail

BOOMERANGS

Reinforced boomerang = boomerang + iron nail

Razor wing boomerang = edged boomerang + wing of bat + steel scythe

Flametang boomerang = swallowtail + flame shield

Metal wing boomerang = razor wing boomerang + metal king spear

AXES

Stone axe = stone hardhat + cypress stick

Golden axe = iron axe + gold nugget

Iron axe = farmer's scythe + farmer's scythe

Bandit axe = battle-axe + thief's key

Moon axe = golden axe + moon's mercy

King axe = golden axe + slime crown

HAMMERS

Sledgehammer = giant mallet + iron helmet + iron helmet

Über war hammer = war hammer + mighty armlet

Megaton hammer = über war hammer + conquerer's axe + orichalcum

SCYTHES

Hell scythe = steel scythe + poison moth knife + Hades' helm

DAGGERS

Falcon knife = slime earrings + tough guy tattoo + agility ring

Assassin's dagger = eagle dagger + poison needle

Imp knife = assassin's dagger + devil's tail

WHIPS

Leather whip = devil's tail + saint's ashes

Snakeskin whip = leather whip + scale shield

Dragontail whip = snakeskin whip + dragon scale + dragon scale

Demon whip = scourge whip + devil's tail

Scourge whip = demon whip + saint's ashes

STAVES

Magma staff = wizard's staff + rockbomb shard

Staff of antimagic = wizard's staff + rune staff

Staff of resurrection = rune staff + life bracer + Yggdrasil leaf

BOWS

 Hunter's bow = short bow + chain whip

 Hunter's bow = cypress stick + cypress stick + strength ring

 Eros' bow = hunter's bow + garter

 Cheiron's bow = Eros' bow + power shield

 Odin's bow = Cheiron's bow + Eros' bow + great bow

ARMOUR

 Wayfarer's clothes = plain clothes + plain clothes

 Boxer shorts = bandit's grass skirt + bandana

 Leather armour = wayfarer's clothes + magic beast hide

 Leather kilt = leather whip + bandana

 Leather kilt = boxer shorts + magic beast hide

 Templar's uniform = wayfarer's clothes + Templar's shield

 Leather dress = dancer's costume + magic beast hide

 Scale armour = leather armour + dragon scale

 Chain mail = wayfarer's clothes + chain whip

 Bronze armour = chain mail + bronze shield

 Iron cuirass = iron shield + iron shield

 Fur poncho = magic beast hide + magic beast hide

 Robe of serenity = cloak of evasion + boxer shorts

 Bunny suit = silk bustier + bunny tail

 Zombie mail = silver mail + zombiesbane

 Zombie mail = platinum mail + devil's tail

 Silver cuirass = iron cuirass + silver platter + silver platter

 Sage's robe = magic vestment + scholar's cap

 Magical skirt = bandit's grass skirt + magical hat + magical mace

 Magic armour = full plate armour + prayer ring + ruby of protection

 Dancer's mail = silver mail + dancer's costume

 Dragon mail = silver mail + dragon scale + dragon scale

 Shimmering dress = spangled dress + ruby of protection + gold bracer

ARMOUR (CONT.)

 Spiked armour = magic armour + edged boomerang

 Platinum mail = zombie mail + saint's ashes

 Angel's robe = flowing dress + magical skirt

 Bandit mail = heavy armour + bandit axe + bandit's grass skirt

 Crimson robe = sage's robe + magic water + nook grass

 Dark robe = cloak of evasion + devil's tail + wing of bat

 Mirror armour = silver mail + mirror shield + mirror shield

 Princess's robe = angel's robe + gold rosary + shimmering dress

 Gigant armour = bandit mail + mighty armlet + mighty armlet

 Divine bustier = dangerous bustier + shimmering dress

 Metal king armour = liquid metal armour + slime crown + orichalcum

SHIELDS

 Leather shield = pot lid + magic beast hide

 Scale shield = leather shield + dragon scale

 Bronze shield = leather shield + bronze knife

 Templar's shield = iron shield + Templar's uniform

 White shield = light shield + fresh milk + fresh milk

 White shield = iron shield + silver platter

 Magic shield = steel shield + prayer ring + ruby of protection

 Dragon shield = steel shield + dragon scale + dragon scale

 Ice shield = magic shield + icicle dirk

 Flame shield = magic shield + flametang boomerang

 Power shield = magic shield + strength ring + cured cheese

 Saintess shield = mirror shield + white shield + holy water

 Silver shield = mirror shield + amor seco essence + magic water

 Ruinous shield = metal king shield + devil's tail

 Thanatos' shield = goddess shield + devil's tail

 Goddess shield = Thanatos' shield + saint's ashes

Metal king shield = ruinous shield + saint's ashes + orichalcum

197

HELMETS

Pointy hat = leather hat + iron nail

Turban = bandana + bandana

Feathered cap = leather hat + chimaera wing

Bunny ears = hairband + bunny tail

Stone hardhat = stone axe + pointy hat

Fur hood = feathered cap + fur poncho

Hermes' hat = feathered cap + Mercury's bandana

Bronze helmet = stone hardhat + bronze knife + bronze knife

Mercury's bandana = bandana + agility ring

Silver tiara = coral hairpin + silver platter

Happy hat = feathered cap + elevating shoes

Scholar's cap = magical hat + scholar's specs

Hades' helm = mythril helm + devil's tail

Thinking cap = scholar's cap + iron headgear

Mythril helm = Hades' helm + saint's ashes

Raging bull helm = mythril helm + cowpat + fresh milk

Golden tiara = thinking cap + silver tiara + gold nugget

Phantom mask = iron headgear + dark robe

Skull helm = sun crown + devil's tail

Sun crown = skull helm + saint's ashes

ACCESSORIES

 Strength ring = prayer ring + seed of strength

 Titan belt = leather kilt + strength ring

 Mighty armlet = strength ring + titan belt

 Life bracer = recovery ring + gold bracer

 Prayer ring = gold ring + seed of magic

 Ring of truth = gold ring + sandstorm spear

 Ring of immunity = gold ring + poison needle

 Holy talisman = tough guy tattoo + holy water + gold rosary

 Full moon ring = gold ring + poison moth knife

 Ring of awakening = gold ring + dream blade

 Ring of clarity = gold ring + fallen angel rapier

 Recovery ring = prayer ring + seed of life

 Catholicon ring = full moon ring + ring of truth + ring of immunity

 Ruby of protection = prayer ring + seed of defence

 Elevating shoes = fishnet stockings + happy hat

 Agility ring = prayer ring + seed of agility

 Meteorite bracer = agility ring + agility ring + orichalcum

 Skull ring = sorcerer's ring + devil's tail

 Sorcerer's ring = skull ring + saint's ashes + saint's ashes

 Scholar's specs = ring of awakening + ring of clarity + seed of wisdom

 Goddess ring = recovery ring + orichalcum

IS THAT ALL?

For those who are willing to experiment, there may just be some other recipes available. Invest some time with the alchemy pot and you may uncover something special!

MONSTER APPENDIX

This appendix contains detailed statistical information for each of the game's 260 normal monsters. They're presented in numerical order, as in the game's Battle Records menu. If you can find and defeat all of them, you'll complete the Battle Records screen and earn a prize. Note that we can't show certain bosses here, lest we spoil the surprise.

1: SLIME
FAMILY: SLIME

HP: 7
MP: 0
Attack: 10
Defence: 8
Agility: 6

Description: A well-known monster commonly encountered throughout the world. Quite intelligent. Some have even managed to learn the human tongue.

GOLD	1	EXP	1

NORMAL ITEM	Medicinal herb
RARE ITEM	Amor seco essence
REGIONS	Farebury Region, Kingdom of Trodain, Waterfall Cave, Isolated Plateau, Unnamed Isle, Baccarat Region, Areas Accessible By Air

2: CANDY CAT
FAMILY: BEAST

HP: 10
MP: 0
Attack: 11
Defence: 9
Agility: 6

Description: A happy-go-lucky, good-natured monster. Born with only one stripe, it grows another with each passing year.

GOLD	2	EXP	2

NORMAL ITEM	Medicinal herb
RARE ITEM	Bandit's grass skirt
REGIONS	Farebury Region, Kingdom of Trodain, Areas Accessible By Air

3: LIPS
FAMILY: BUG

HP: 11
MP: 0
Attack: 12
Defence: 8
Agility: 5

Description: A slug-like creature with distinctively large lips. They seem to greet one another with big, sloppy kisses!

GOLD	3	EXP	2

NORMAL ITEM	Medicinal herb
RARE ITEM	Moonwort bulb
REGIONS	Farebury Region

4: DRACKY
FAMILY: BIRD

HP: 10
MP: 0
Attack: 12
Defence: 9
Agility: 8

Description: A bat-like monster that flies freely through the night sky. According to one account, they're born in a world without light.

GOLD	3	EXP	2

NORMAL ITEM	Medicinal herb
RARE ITEM	Chimaera wing
REGIONS	Farebury Region, Kingdom of Trodain, Waterfall Cave, Isolated Plateau, Godbird's Eyrie

5: SATYR
FAMILY: HUMANOID

HP: 13
MP: 0
Attack: 14
Defence: 9
Agility: 7

Description: The large horns above each ear fall off and grow back every year. The hornpipes they carry are carved from their old horns.

GOLD	4	EXP	3

NORMAL ITEM	Plain clothes
RARE ITEM	Wayfarer's clothes
REGIONS	Farebury Region

6: CAPSICHUM
FAMILY: PLANT

HP: 15
MP: 4
Attack: 12
Defence: 9
Agility: 6

Description: A distinctive monster shaped like a pepper. In their culture, two is always better than one, so they stick together with the help of a large skewer!

GOLD	3	EXP	3

NORMAL ITEM	Cypress stick
RARE ITEM	Copper sword
REGIONS	Farebury Region

7: BUNICORN
FAMILY: BEAST

HP: 16
MP: 0
Attack: 13
Defence: 8
Agility: 10

Description: A rabbit-like monster with a distinctive single horn growing from the middle of its forehead. Unlike normal rabbits, they are determinedly carnivorous, using their sharp horns to spear prey.

GOLD	5	EXP	5

NORMAL ITEM	Leather hat
RARE ITEM	Bunny tail
REGIONS	Farebury Region

8: SHE-SLIME
FAMILY: SLIME

HP: 18
MP: 0
Attack: 16
Defence: 15
Agility: 25

Description: Slimes of a different colour, apparently due to a sudden mutation. Although commonly referred to as 'she-slimes', their true gender remains unknown.

GOLD	6	EXP	8

NORMAL ITEM	Medicinal herb
RARE ITEM	Slime earrings
REGIONS	Maella Region, Kingdom of Ascantha, Areas Accessible By Air

9: FIRESPIRIT
FAMILY: ELEMENTAL

HP: 14
MP: 3
Attack: 9
Defence: 9
Agility: 9

Description: A physical manifestation of fire magic. As this monster lacks a material body, most physical attacks pass right through it. Try raising your tension when fighting them.

GOLD	4	EXP	5

NORMAL ITEM	Holy water
RARE ITEM	Amor seco essence
REGIONS	Farebury Region, Waterfall Cave

10: MISCHIEVOUS MOLE
FAMILY: BEAST

HP: 15
MP: 0
Attack: 14
Defence: 12
Agility: 6

Description: Small but seriously strong. Once they psyche themselves up, these pint-sized pests can inflict some serious damage.

GOLD	5	EXP	4

NORMAL ITEM	Medicinal herb
RARE ITEM	Oaken club
REGIONS	Land of the Moles, Waterfall Cave, Beneath Ascantha, Mole Hole

11: MECHA-MYNAH
FAMILY: MACHINE

HP: 9
MP: 4
Attack: 16
Defence: 27
Agility: 9

Description: The mechanical bodies of these birds weigh more than Yangus after a big dinner! They have a tendency to snap the tree branches where they roost and fall to earth with a metallic clunk.

GOLD	8	EXP	5

NORMAL ITEM	Pot lid
RARE ITEM	Chimaera wing
REGIONS	Farebury Region, Alexandria Region, Waterfall Cave

12: BUBBLE SLIME
FAMILY: SLIME

HP: 20
MP: 0
Attack: 13
Defence: 10
Agility: 8

Description: These sticky masses of muck are poisonous to the touch. Once a traveller comes into contact with a bubble slime's body in battle, the effects of the poison will persist until the individual is cured.

GOLD	7	EXP	5

NORMAL ITEM	Antidotal herb
RARE ITEM	Moonwort bulb
REGIONS	Farebury Region, Waterfall Cave, Tower of Alexandra, Areas Accessible By Air

13: DANCING DEVIL
FAMILY: DEMON

HP: 20
MP: 0
Attack: 16
Defence: 14
Agility: 14

GOLD 10 · EXP 7

Description: A race of demons wearing what appear to be bright blue pants. They are rumoured to drop them when defeated.

NORMAL ITEM	Chimaera wing
RARE ITEM	Boxer shorts
REGIONS	Farebury Region, Kingdom of Trodain, Waterfall Cave

14: BODKIN ARCHER
FAMILY: HUMANOID

HP: 21
MP: 2
Attack: 22
Defence: 18
Agility: 12

GOLD 8 · EXP 10

Description: Diminutive but resourceful monsters. Upon encountering an enemy, they keep their distance and let fly with long-range bow and arrow attacks.

NORMAL ITEM	Bandana
RARE ITEM	Plain cheese
REGIONS	Alexandria Region, Kingdom of Trodain

15: SKIPPER
FAMILY: MATERIAL

HP: 21
MP: 5
Attack: 20
Defence: 17
Agility: 22

GOLD 10 · EXP 12

Description: A hairy fur ball of a monster whose love for unwanted old boots manifests itself in much the same way as a hermit crab's love for discarded shells.

NORMAL ITEM	Medicinal herb
RARE ITEM	Bunny tail
REGIONS	Alexandria Region, Waterfall Cave

16: DRACKMAGE
FAMILY: BIRD

HP: 19
MP: 6
Attack: 20
Defence: 16
Agility: 10

GOLD 7 · EXP 9

Description: Related to the dracky, these monsters have evolved a green colouration to match their woodland habitat. They remain constantly airborne, smoothly dodging attacks whilst casting spells on their opponents.

NORMAL ITEM	Medicinal herb
RARE ITEM	Chimaera wing
REGIONS	Alexandria Region, Kingdom of Ascantha, Tower of Alexandra, Pickham Region, Kingdom of Trodain

17: BEETLEBOY
FAMILY: BUG

HP: 16
MP: 0
Attack: 26
Defence: 36
Agility: 16

GOLD 10 · EXP 12

Description: Despite their weighty appearance, these insectoid monsters are quite swift. They like to tackle their opponents head-on with the help of their huge horns.

NORMAL ITEM	Medicinal herb
RARE ITEM	Leather hat
REGIONS	Farebury Region, Alexandria Region, Tower of Alexandra, Kingdom of Trodain

18: IMP
FAMILY: DEMON

HP: 28
MP: 0
Attack: 21
Defence: 21
Agility: 18

GOLD 11 · EXP 15

Description: Juvenile forms of elite magical monsters. Imps try to cast spells which are far too powerful for them and fail every time.

NORMAL ITEM	Chimaera wing
RARE ITEM	Cool cheese
REGIONS	Tower of Alexandra

19: FUNGHOUL
FAMILY: PLANT

HP: 22
MP: 0
Attack: 21
Defence: 18
Agility: 14

GOLD 12 · EXP 13

Description: Mushroom-shaped monsters with a sweet breath that puts enemies to sleep. They grow in humid areas like grasslands and deep forests.

NORMAL ITEM	Antidotal herb
RARE ITEM	Plain cheese
REGIONS	Alexandria Region, Tower of Alexandra

20: FENCING FOX
FAMILY: BEAST

HP: 25
MP: 8
Attack: 28
Defence: 20
Agility: 16

GOLD 16 · EXP 20

Description: These foppish fiends leave foes floundering with their flamboyant foil-work. When not showing off their skill with a sword, they like to demonstrate their dazzling dancing.

NORMAL ITEM	Wayfarer's clothes
RARE ITEM	Gold bracer
REGIONS	Alexandria Region

21: HEALSLIME
FAMILY: SLIME

HP: 24
MP: 12
Attack: 19
Defence: 21
Agility: 15

GOLD 13 · EXP 18

Description: A kindly slime that never hesitates to help comrades by casting healing spells, even when in danger itself. All in all, a supportive little monster.

NORMAL ITEM	Medicinal herb
RARE ITEM	Amor seco essence
REGIONS	Kingdom of Ascantha, Kingdom of Trodain, Tower of Alexandra, Wishers' Peak, Areas Accessible By Air

22: HAMMERHOOD
FAMILY: HUMANOID

HP: 33
MP: 0
Attack: 32
Defence: 16
Agility: 10

GOLD 9 · EXP 21

Description: Not the largest monster in the world, but amongst the strongest. Their bodies seem even smaller next to the massive wooden mallets they carry. The unwieldiness of these weapons means they frequently miss.

NORMAL ITEM	Oaken club
RARE ITEM	Giant mallet
REGIONS	Alexandria Region, Waterfall Cave

23: JAILCAT
FAMILY: BEAST

HP: 29
MP: 6
Attack: 27
Defence: 18
Agility: 19

GOLD 8 · EXP 19

Description: A feline monster with stripes reminiscent of a jailhouse convict. Strangely popular among cat lovers. Usually quite playful, but capable of casting spells when provoked.

NORMAL ITEM	Bandana
RARE ITEM	Plain cheese
REGIONS	Alexandria Region

24: FROGFACE
FAMILY: BUG

HP: 36
MP: 6
Attack: 20
Defence: 23
Agility: 13

GOLD 13 · EXP 20

Description: Although quite weak in frog form, their attacks become far more dangerous when they reveal the human faces on their backs.

NORMAL ITEM	Medicinal herb
RARE ITEM	Amor seco essence
REGIONS	Alexandria Region, Tower of Alexandra

25: LUMP MAGE
FAMILY: HUMANOID

HP: 38
MP: 12
Attack: 18
Defence: 24
Agility: 21

GOLD 18 · EXP 31

Description: Physically quite weak, but capable of wearing enemies down by repeatedly casting unpleasant spells. Occasionally splits into two when losing a battle.

NORMAL ITEM	Cypress stick
RARE ITEM	Wizard's staff
REGIONS	Maella Region

26: WINKY
FAMILY: DEMON

HP: 40
MP: 0
Attack: 22
Defence: 25
Agility: 24

GOLD 12 · EXP 32

Description: An odd monster in the form of an eyeball with arms and legs. Said to turn red and become very strong when angered.

NORMAL ITEM	Holy water
RARE ITEM	Magic water
REGIONS	Maella Region, Kingdom of Ascantha

27: SPIKED HARE
FAMILY: BEAST

HP: 42
MP: 0
Attack: 34
Defence: 24
Agility: 26

GOLD 13 EXP 30

NORMAL ITEM	Medicinal herb
RARE ITEM	Bunny tail
REGIONS	Alexandria Region, Kingdom of Ascantha

Description: Ignore their cuddly appearance. These monsters are actually ruthless adversaries, capable of decreasing an enemy's tension whilst raising their own.

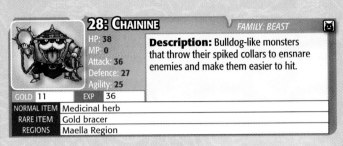

28: CHAININE
FAMILY: BEAST

HP: 38
MP: 0
Attack: 36
Defence: 27
Agility: 25

GOLD 11 EXP 36

NORMAL ITEM	Medicinal herb
RARE ITEM	Gold bracer
REGIONS	Maella Region

Description: Bulldog-like monsters that throw their spiked collars to ensnare enemies and make them easier to hit.

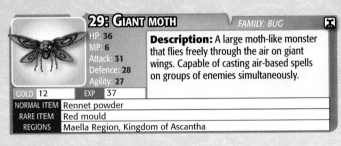

29: GIANT MOTH
FAMILY: BUG

HP: 36
MP: 6
Attack: 31
Defence: 28
Agility: 27

GOLD 12 EXP 37

NORMAL ITEM	Rennet powder
RARE ITEM	Red mould
REGIONS	Maella Region, Kingdom of Ascantha

Description: A large moth-like monster that flies freely through the air on giant wings. Capable of casting air-based spells on groups of enemies simultaneously.

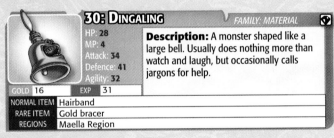

30: DINGALING
FAMILY: MATERIAL

HP: 28
MP: 4
Attack: 34
Defence: 41
Agility: 32

GOLD 16 EXP 31

NORMAL ITEM	Hairband
RARE ITEM	Gold bracer
REGIONS	Maella Region

Description: A monster shaped like a large bell. Usually does nothing more than watch and laugh, but occasionally calls jargons for help.

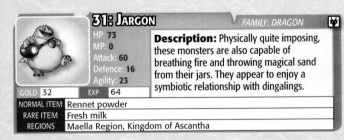

31: JARGON
FAMILY: DRAGON

HP: 73
MP: 0
Attack: 60
Defence: 16
Agility: 23

GOLD 32 EXP 64

NORMAL ITEM	Rennet powder
RARE ITEM	Fresh milk
REGIONS	Maella Region, Kingdom of Ascantha

Description: Physically quite imposing, these monsters are also capable of breathing fire and throwing magical sand from their jars. They appear to enjoy a symbiotic relationship with dingalings.

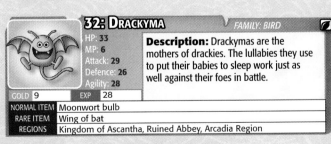

32: DRACKYMA
FAMILY: BIRD

HP: 33
MP: 6
Attack: 29
Defence: 26
Agility: 28

GOLD 9 EXP 28

NORMAL ITEM	Moonwort bulb
RARE ITEM	Wing of bat
REGIONS	Kingdom of Ascantha, Ruined Abbey, Arcadia Region

Description: Drackymas are the mothers of drackies. The lullabies they use to put their babies to sleep work just as well against their foes in battle.

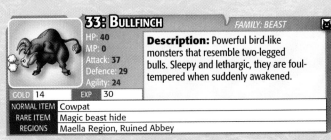

33: BULLFINCH
FAMILY: BEAST

HP: 40
MP: 0
Attack: 37
Defence: 29
Agility: 24

GOLD 14 EXP 30

NORMAL ITEM	Cowpat
RARE ITEM	Magic beast hide
REGIONS	Maella Region, Ruined Abbey

Description: Powerful bird-like monsters that resemble two-legged bulls. Sleepy and lethargic, they are foul-tempered when suddenly awakened.

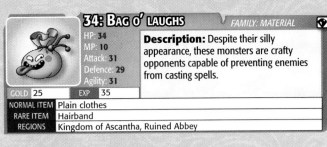

34: BAG O' LAUGHS
FAMILY: MATERIAL

HP: 34
MP: 10
Attack: 31
Defence: 29
Agility: 31

GOLD 25 EXP 35

NORMAL ITEM	Plain clothes
RARE ITEM	Hairband
REGIONS	Kingdom of Ascantha, Ruined Abbey

Description: Despite their silly appearance, these monsters are crafty opponents capable of preventing enemies from casting spells.

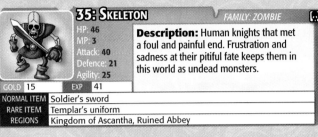

35: SKELETON
FAMILY: ZOMBIE

HP: 46
MP: 3
Attack: 40
Defence: 21
Agility: 25

GOLD 15 EXP 41

NORMAL ITEM	Soldier's sword
RARE ITEM	Templar's uniform
REGIONS	Kingdom of Ascantha, Ruined Abbey

Description: Human knights that met a foul and painful end. Frustration and sadness at their pitiful fate keeps them in this world as undead monsters.

36: METAL SLIME
FAMILY: SLIME

HP: 4
MP: Infinite
Attack: 30
Defence: 4096
Agility: 65

GOLD 5 EXP 1350

NORMAL ITEM	Seed of defence
RARE ITEM	Seed of agility
REGIONS	Kingdom of Ascantha, East Argonia, Unnamed Isle, Ruined Abbey, Areas Accessible By Air

Description: Popular among adventurers for the inordinately large number of experience points they bestow. Although not particularly dangerous, their tendency to flee at the first sign of trouble makes them quite difficult to defeat.

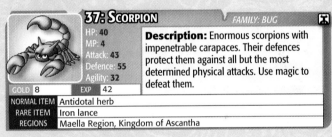

37: SCORPION
FAMILY: BUG

HP: 40
MP: 4
Attack: 43
Defence: 55
Agility: 32

GOLD 8 EXP 42

NORMAL ITEM	Antidotal herb
RARE ITEM	Iron lance
REGIONS	Maella Region, Kingdom of Ascantha

Description: Enormous scorpions with impenetrable carapaces. Their defences protect them against all but the most determined physical attacks. Use magic to defeat them.

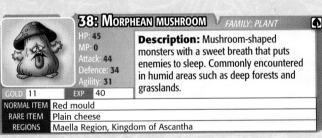

38: MORPHEAN MUSHROOM
FAMILY: PLANT

HP: 45
MP: 0
Attack: 44
Defence: 34
Agility: 31

GOLD 11 EXP 40

NORMAL ITEM	Red mould
RARE ITEM	Plain cheese
REGIONS	Maella Region, Kingdom of Ascantha

Description: Mushroom-shaped monsters with a sweet breath that puts enemies to sleep. Commonly encountered in humid areas such as deep forests and grasslands.

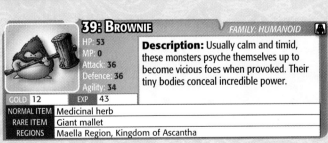

39: BROWNIE
FAMILY: HUMANOID

HP: 53
MP: 0
Attack: 36
Defence: 36
Agility: 34

GOLD 12 EXP 43

NORMAL ITEM	Medicinal herb
RARE ITEM	Giant mallet
REGIONS	Maella Region, Kingdom of Ascantha

Description: Usually calm and timid, these monsters psyche themselves up to become vicious foes when provoked. Their tiny bodies conceal incredible power.

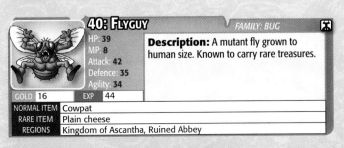

40: FLYGUY
FAMILY: BUG

HP: 39
MP: 8
Attack: 42
Defence: 35
Agility: 34

GOLD 16 EXP 44

NORMAL ITEM	Cowpat
RARE ITEM	Plain cheese
REGIONS	Kingdom of Ascantha, Ruined Abbey

Description: A mutant fly grown to human size. Known to carry rare treasures.

41: PUPPETEER — FAMILY: HUMANOID

HP: 75	MP: 12	Attack: 41	Defence: 38	Agility: 38

Description: A unique monster that delights in telling its opponents stories using hand-puppets.

GOLD	21	EXP	45

NORMAL ITEM	Silk robe
RARE ITEM	Slime earrings
REGIONS	Kingdom of Ascantha

42: BODKIN BOWYER — FAMILY: HUMANOID

HP: 48	MP: Infinite	Attack: 46	Defence: 36	Agility: 37

Description: Great archers in spite of their size. Capable of surrounding opponents and unleashing a fusillade of arrows upon them. When trouble beckons, they swiftly call for reinforcements.

GOLD	17	EXP	43

NORMAL ITEM	Silk robe
RARE ITEM	Short bow
REGIONS	Kingdom of Ascantha, Wishers' Peak

43: NIGHT SNEAKER — FAMILY: MATERIAL

HP: 52	MP: 12	Attack: 42	Defence: 43	Agility: 30

Description: Monsters that skulk around in the dead of night. They are masters of defensive magic and can deflect enemy spells.

GOLD	20	EXP	52

NORMAL ITEM	Moonwort bulb
RARE ITEM	Bunny tail
REGIONS	Kingdom of Ascantha

44: MUMMY BOY — FAMILY: ZOMBIE

HP: 73	MP: 0	Attack: 37	Defence: 30	Agility: 25

Description: A monster wrapped from head to toe in filthy old bandages. Capable of spitting curses that envelop and immobilize enemies.

GOLD	9	EXP	55

NORMAL ITEM	Bandana
RARE ITEM	Turban
REGIONS	Kingdom of Ascantha, Ruined Abbey, Wishers' Peak, Dark Ruins, Swordman's Labyrinth

45: HELL HORNET — FAMILY: BUG

HP: 37	MP: 0	Attack: 43	Defence: 38	Agility: 34

Description: A monster hornet with a paralysing sting. Be sure to carry moonwort bulbs with you if you think you will encounter these vicious monsters.

GOLD	12	EXP	51

NORMAL ITEM	Moonwort bulb
RARE ITEM	Poison moth knife
REGIONS	Maella Region, Kingdom of Ascantha, Wishers' Peak

46: PAN PIPER — FAMILY: HUMANOID

HP: 48	MP: 0	Attack: 32	Defence: 42	Agility: 30

Description: Half man, half goat, and the worst of both. Usually timid, they turn red if provoked and call for fellow pan pipers to join the fray.

GOLD	18	EXP	54

NORMAL ITEM	Medicinal herb
RARE ITEM	Leather kilt
REGIONS	Kingdom of Ascantha

47: SLIME KNIGHT — FAMILY: SLIME

HP: 52	MP: 4	Attack: 49	Defence: 45	Agility: 32

Description: Angry at seeing their slime-friends bullied by swaggering adventurers, these courageous little monsters swore an oath to defend them. Now they roam the land as knights on slime steeds!

GOLD	22	EXP	55

NORMAL ITEM	Slime earrings
RARE ITEM	Templar's shield
REGIONS	Kingdom of Ascantha, Wishers' Peak

48: CLOCKWORK CUCKOO — FAMILY: MACHINE

HP: 32	MP: 0	Attack: 43	Defence: 111	Agility: 44

Description: These mechanical birds are the result of a mad scientist's twisted experiment. When they detect a target, they become a deadly whirlwind of razor-sharp blades.

GOLD	31	EXP	56

NORMAL ITEM	Iron nail
RARE ITEM	Dagger
REGIONS	Kingdom of Ascantha, Pickham Region

49: TREEFACE — FAMILY: PLANT

HP: 64	MP: 0	Attack: 56	Defence: 49	Agility: 38

Description: Rightly feared for their habit of hiding in forests and ambushing travellers. When hurt, they pluck leaves from their own branches to use as healing herbs.

GOLD	23	EXP	67

NORMAL ITEM	Medicinal herb
RARE ITEM	Strong medicine
REGIONS	Maella Region, Kingdom of Ascantha, Wishers' Peak, Pickham Region, Baccarat Region

50: KISSER — FAMILY: BUG

HP: 49	MP: 0	Attack: 46	Defence: 39	Agility: 42

Description: Wet and glistening monsters said to carry various moulds that can be used to make special cheeses.

GOLD	15	EXP	53

NORMAL ITEM	Waterweed mould
RARE ITEM	Red mould
REGIONS	Kingdom of Ascantha, Pickham Region

51: DIEMON — FAMILY: BEAST

HP: 64	MP: 10	Attack: 31	Defence: 44	Agility: 43

Description: Mysterious monsters known for wearing eerie masks. Their real faces are said to be even scarier.

GOLD	19	EXP	58

NORMAL ITEM	Chimaera wing
RARE ITEM	Magic beast hide
REGIONS	Kingdom of Ascantha, Wishers' Peak

52: WALKING CORPSE — FAMILY: ZOMBIE

HP: 94	MP: 0	Attack: 39	Defence: 9	Agility: 10

Description: As the name implies, a monstrous rotten corpse. Their foul appearance can cause your tension to decrease suddenly.

GOLD	11	EXP	59

NORMAL ITEM	Antidotal herb
RARE ITEM	Chain mail
REGIONS	Pickham Region, Ruined Abbey, Wishers' Peak

53: FAT BAT — FAMILY: BIRD

HP: 52	MP: 5	Attack: 53	Defence: 42	Agility: 41

Description: Heavyweight monsters that dive-bomb opponents, body-slamming them to the ground.

GOLD	9	EXP	61

NORMAL ITEM	Wing of bat
RARE ITEM	Magic beast hide
REGIONS	Kingdom of Ascantha, Wishers' Peak

54: NIGHT FOX — FAMILY: HUMANOID

HP: 56	MP: 6	Attack: 54	Defence: 44	Agility: 64

Description: Extremely agile, these monsters are feared for their skilful rapier-work and Mercurial Thrusts.

GOLD	16	EXP	56

NORMAL ITEM	Rapier
RARE ITEM	Feathered cap
REGIONS	Pickham Region

55: PAPRIKAN
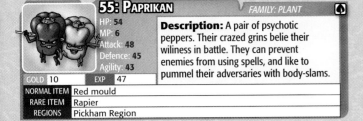
FAMILY: PLANT

HP: 54
MP: 6
Attack: 48
Defence: 45
Agility: 43

GOLD 10   EXP 47

Description: A pair of psychotic peppers. Their crazed grins belie their wiliness in battle. They can prevent enemies from using spells, and like to pummel their adversaries with body-slams.

NORMAL ITEM	Red mould
RARE ITEM	Rapier
REGIONS	Pickham Region

56: CHIMAERA
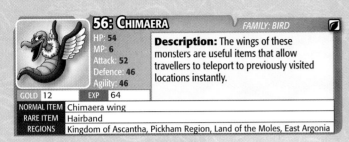
FAMILY: BIRD

HP: 54
MP: 6
Attack: 52
Defence: 46
Agility: 46

GOLD 12   EXP 64

Description: The wings of these monsters are useful items that allow travellers to teleport to previously visited locations instantly.

NORMAL ITEM	Chimaera wing
RARE ITEM	Hairband
REGIONS	Kingdom of Ascantha, Pickham Region, Land of the Moles, East Argonia

57: HOOD

FAMILY: HUMANOID

HP: 60
MP: 0
Attack: 54
Defence: 40
Agility: 38

GOLD 14   EXP 66

Description: Mysterious masked monsters with a nasty habit of hacking down unwary travellers. These vain creatures love to flex their muscles and psyche up in front of their enemies.

NORMAL ITEM	Stone axe
RARE ITEM	Leather cape
REGIONS	Pickham Region

58: HEADHUNTER
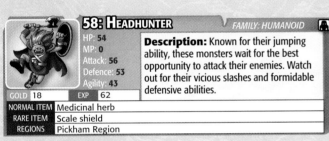
FAMILY: HUMANOID

HP: 54
MP: 0
Attack: 56
Defence: 53
Agility: 43

GOLD 18   EXP 62

Description: Known for their jumping ability, these monsters wait for the best opportunity to attack their enemies. Watch out for their vicious slashes and formidable defensive abilities.

NORMAL ITEM	Medicinal herb
RARE ITEM	Scale shield
REGIONS	Pickham Region

59: MINIDEMON

FAMILY: DEMON

HP: 58
MP: 5
Attack: 40
Defence: 52
Agility: 45

GOLD 11   EXP 59

Description: A surprisingly powerful monster. Its cute looks betray no hint that it is skilled at both fire and ice magic.

NORMAL ITEM	Wing of bat
RARE ITEM	Rockbomb shard
REGIONS	Pickham Region

60: GORERILLA
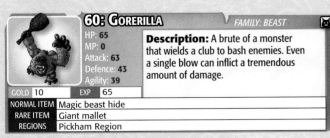
FAMILY: BEAST

HP: 65
MP: 0
Attack: 63
Defence: 43
Agility: 39

GOLD 10   EXP 65

Description: A brute of a monster that wields a club to bash enemies. Even a single blow can inflict a tremendous amount of damage.

NORMAL ITEM	Magic beast hide
RARE ITEM	Giant mallet
REGIONS	Pickham Region

61: MUD MANNEQUIN

FAMILY: MATERIAL

HP: 63
MP: 0
Attack: 63
Defence: 66
Agility: 50

GOLD 15   EXP 69

Description: A crude figure fashioned out of mud and animated with a magical spell. Dances a strange dance that lowers the MP of opponents.

NORMAL ITEM	Rock salt
RARE ITEM	Cypress stick
REGIONS	Kingdom of Trodain

62: CANNIBOX
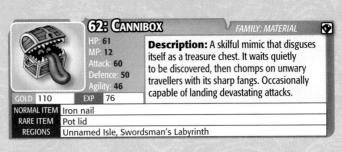
FAMILY: MATERIAL

HP: 61
MP: 12
Attack: 60
Defence: 50
Agility: 46

GOLD 110   EXP 76

Description: A skilful mimic that disguises itself as a treasure chest. It waits quietly to be discovered, then chomps on unwary travellers with its sharp fangs. Occasionally capable of landing devastating attacks.

NORMAL ITEM	Iron nail
RARE ITEM	Pot lid
REGIONS	Unnamed Isle, Swordsman's Labyrinth

63: GOODYBAG
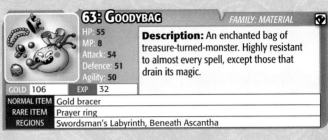
FAMILY: MATERIAL

HP: 55
MP: 8
Attack: 54
Defence: 51
Agility: 50

GOLD 106   EXP 32

Description: An enchanted bag of treasure-turned-monster. Highly resistant to almost every spell, except those that drain its magic.

NORMAL ITEM	Gold bracer
RARE ITEM	Prayer ring
REGIONS	Swordsman's Labyrinth, Beneath Ascantha

64: WITCH
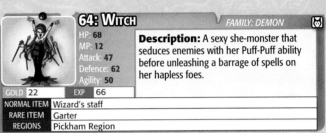
FAMILY: DEMON

HP: 68
MP: 12
Attack: 47
Defence: 62
Agility: 50

GOLD 22   EXP 66

Description: A sexy she-monster that seduces enemies with her Puff-Puff ability before unleashing a barrage of spells on her hapless foes.

NORMAL ITEM	Wizard's staff
RARE ITEM	Garter
REGIONS	Pickham Region

65: MUMMY
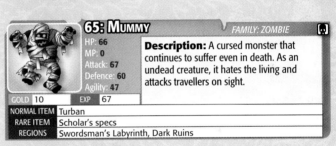
FAMILY: ZOMBIE

HP: 66
MP: 0
Attack: 67
Defence: 60
Agility: 47

GOLD 10   EXP 67

Description: A cursed monster that continues to suffer even in death. As an undead creature, it hates the living and attacks travellers on sight.

NORMAL ITEM	Turban
RARE ITEM	Scholar's specs
REGIONS	Swordsman's Labyrinth, Dark Ruins

66: CURESLIME
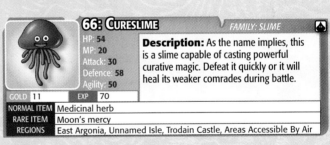
FAMILY: SLIME

HP: 54
MP: 20
Attack: 30
Defence: 58
Agility: 50

GOLD 11   EXP 70

Description: As the name implies, this is a slime capable of casting powerful curative magic. Defeat it quickly or it will heal its weaker comrades during battle.

NORMAL ITEM	Medicinal herb
RARE ITEM	Moon's mercy
REGIONS	East Argonia, Unnamed Isle, Trodain Castle, Areas Accessible By Air

67: RESTLESS ARMOUR
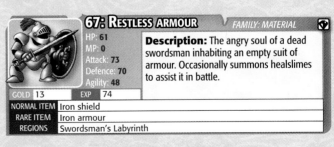
FAMILY: MATERIAL

HP: 61
MP: 0
Attack: 73
Defence: 70
Agility: 48

GOLD 13   EXP 74

Description: The angry soul of a dead swordsman inhabiting an empty suit of armour. Occasionally summons healslimes to assist it in battle.

NORMAL ITEM	Iron shield
RARE ITEM	Iron armour
REGIONS	Swordsman's Labyrinth

68: LOST SOUL
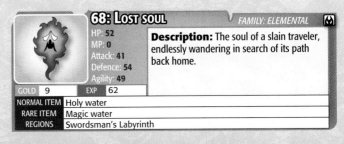
FAMILY: ELEMENTAL

HP: 52
MP: 0
Attack: 41
Defence: 50
Agility: 49

GOLD 9   EXP 62

Description: The soul of a slain traveler, endlessly wandering in search of its path back home.

NORMAL ITEM	Holy water
RARE ITEM	Magic water
REGIONS	Swordsman's Labyrinth

69: PHANTOM FENCER
FAMILY: ZOMBIE

HP: 65
MP: 0
Attack: 71
Defence: 62
Agility: 50

Description: A ragged cape enchanted by powerful magic. Invulnerable to air-based spells.

GOLD	12	EXP	68

NORMAL ITEM	Leather cape
RARE ITEM	Templar's sword
REGIONS	Swordsman's Labyrinth

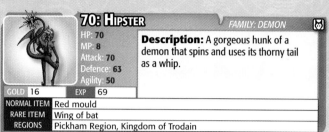

70: HIPSTER
FAMILY: DEMON

HP: 70
MP: 8
Attack: 70
Defence: 63
Agility: 50

Description: A gorgeous hunk of a demon that spins and uses its thorny tail as a whip.

GOLD	16	EXP	69

NORMAL ITEM	Red mould
RARE ITEM	Wing of bat
REGIONS	Pickham Region, Kingdom of Trodain

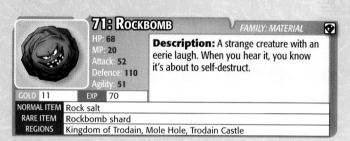

71: ROCKBOMB
FAMILY: MATERIAL

HP: 68
MP: 20
Attack: 52
Defence: 110
Agility: 51

Description: A strange creature with an eerie laugh. When you hear it, you know it's about to self-destruct.

GOLD	11	EXP	70

NORMAL ITEM	Rock salt
RARE ITEM	Rockbomb shard
REGIONS	Kingdom of Trodain, Mole Hole, Trodain Castle

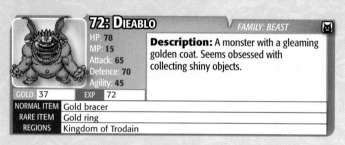

72: DIEABLO
FAMILY: BEAST

HP: 78
MP: 15
Attack: 65
Defence: 70
Agility: 45

Description: A monster with a gleaming golden coat. Seems obsessed with collecting shiny objects.

GOLD	37	EXP	72

NORMAL ITEM	Gold bracer
RARE ITEM	Gold ring
REGIONS	Kingdom of Trodain

73: MUDDY HAND
FAMILY: ZOMBIE

HP: 49
MP: 0
Attack: 61
Defence: 64
Agility: 52

Description: A horrifying mud-monster that lives in the depths of the earth. Extends a hand above ground to pull travellers to their doom.

GOLD	8	EXP	45

NORMAL ITEM	Medicinal herb
RARE ITEM	Strength ring
REGIONS	Kingdom of Trodain, Desert, Beneath Ascantha, Mole Hole, Areas Accessible By Air

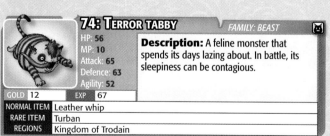

74: TERROR TABBY
FAMILY: BEAST

HP: 56
MP: 10
Attack: 65
Defence: 63
Agility: 52

Description: A feline monster that spends its days lazing about. In battle, its sleepiness can be contagious.

GOLD	12	EXP	67

NORMAL ITEM	Leather whip
RARE ITEM	Turban
REGIONS	Kingdom of Trodain

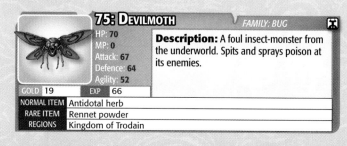

75: DEVILMOTH
FAMILY: BUG

HP: 70
MP: 0
Attack: 67
Defence: 64
Agility: 52

Description: A foul insect-monster from the underworld. Spits and sprays poison at its enemies.

GOLD	19	EXP	66

NORMAL ITEM	Antidotal herb
RARE ITEM	Rennet powder
REGIONS	Kingdom of Trodain

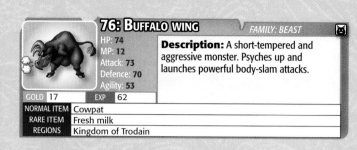

76: BUFFALO WING
FAMILY: BEAST

HP: 74
MP: 12
Attack: 73
Defence: 70
Agility: 53

Description: A short-tempered and aggressive monster. Psyches up and launches powerful body-slam attacks.

GOLD	17	EXP	62

NORMAL ITEM	Cowpat
RARE ITEM	Fresh milk
REGIONS	Kingdom of Trodain

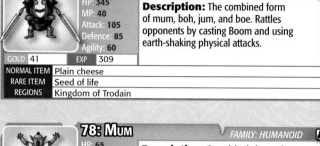

77: MUMBOH-JUMBOE
FAMILY: HUMANOID

HP: 345
MP: 40
Attack: 105
Defence: 85
Agility: 60

Description: The combined form of mum, boh, jum, and boe. Rattles opponents by casting Boom and using earth-shaking physical attacks.

GOLD	41	EXP	309

NORMAL ITEM	Plain cheese
RARE ITEM	Seed of life
REGIONS	Kingdom of Trodain

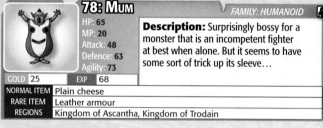

78: MUM
FAMILY: HUMANOID

HP: 65
MP: 20
Attack: 48
Defence: 63
Agility: 73

Description: Surprisingly bossy for a monster that is an incompetent fighter at best when alone. But it seems to have some sort of trick up its sleeve…

GOLD	25	EXP	68

NORMAL ITEM	Plain cheese
RARE ITEM	Leather armour
REGIONS	Kingdom of Ascantha, Kingdom of Trodain

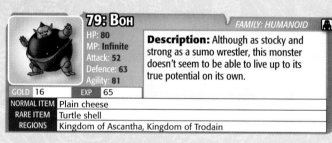

79: BOH
FAMILY: HUMANOID

HP: 80
MP: Infinite
Attack: 52
Defence: 63
Agility: 81

Description: Although as stocky and strong as a sumo wrestler, this monster doesn't seem to be able to live up to its true potential on its own.

GOLD	16	EXP	65

NORMAL ITEM	Plain cheese
RARE ITEM	Turtle shell
REGIONS	Kingdom of Ascantha, Kingdom of Trodain

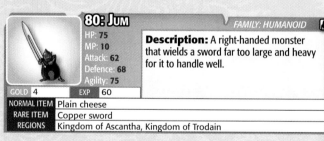

80: JUM
FAMILY: HUMANOID

HP: 75
MP: 10
Attack: 62
Defence: 68
Agility: 75

Description: A right-handed monster that wields a sword far too large and heavy for it to handle well.

GOLD	4	EXP	60

NORMAL ITEM	Plain cheese
RARE ITEM	Copper sword
REGIONS	Kingdom of Ascantha, Kingdom of Trodain

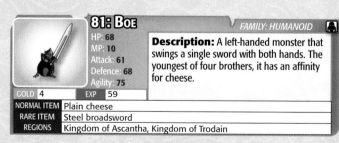

81: BOE
FAMILY: HUMANOID

HP: 68
MP: 10
Attack: 61
Defence: 68
Agility: 75

Description: A left-handed monster that swings a single sword with both hands. The youngest of four brothers, it has an affinity for cheese.

GOLD	4	EXP	59

NORMAL ITEM	Plain cheese
RARE ITEM	Steel broadsword
REGIONS	Kingdom of Ascantha, Kingdom of Trodain

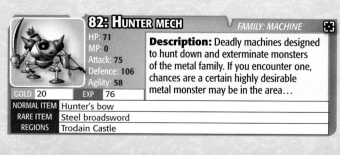

82: HUNTER MECH
FAMILY: MACHINE

HP: 71
MP: 0
Attack: 75
Defence: 106
Agility: 58

Description: Deadly machines designed to hunt down and exterminate monsters of the metal family. If you encounter one, chances are a certain highly desirable metal monster may be in the area…

GOLD	20	EXP	76

NORMAL ITEM	Hunter's bow
RARE ITEM	Steel broadsword
REGIONS	Trodain Castle

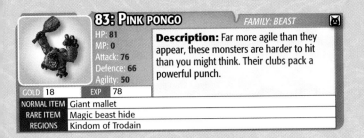

83: Pink Pongo
FAMILY: BEAST

HP: 81
MP: 0
Attack: 76
Defence: 66
Agility: 50

GOLD 18   EXP 78

NORMAL ITEM	Giant mallet
RARE ITEM	Magic beast hide
REGIONS	Kindom of Trodain

Description: Far more agile than they appear, these monsters are harder to hit than you might think. Their clubs pack a powerful punch.

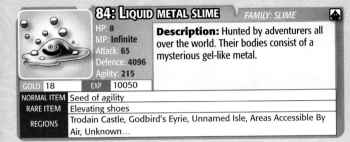

90: Mars rover
FAMILY: BEAST

HP: 78
MP: 0
Attack: 77
Defence: 63
Agility: 58

GOLD 17   EXP 56

NORMAL ITEM	Iron cuirass
RARE ITEM	Chain whip
REGIONS	Land of the Moles, Mole Hole, Beneath Ascantha

Description: Quick-witted dog monsters. Their loud barks serve to intimidate the enemy and summon allies.

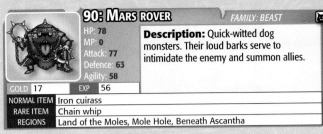

84: Liquid metal slime
FAMILY: SLIME

HP: 8
MP: Infinite
Attack: 65
Defence: 4096
Agility: 215

GOLD 18   EXP 10050

NORMAL ITEM	Seed of agility
RARE ITEM	Elevating shoes
REGIONS	Trodain Castle, Godbird's Eyrie, Unnamed Isle, Areas Accessible By Air, Unknown…

Description: Hunted by adventurers all over the world. Their bodies consist of a mysterious gel-like metal.

91: Peeper
FAMILY: DEMON

HP: 55
MP: 32
Attack: 55
Defence: 73
Agility: 73

GOLD 14   EXP 75

NORMAL ITEM	Holy water
RARE ITEM	Magic water
REGIONS	Mole Hole

Description: Mysterious and unpredictable monsters. Don't let their small size fool you. They are more powerful than they appear.

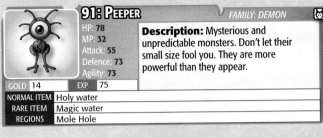

85: Mad mole
FAMILY: BEAST

HP: 65
MP: 0
Attack: 75
Defence: 65
Agility: 62

GOLD 16   EXP 68

NORMAL ITEM	Medicinal herb
RARE ITEM	Stone hardhat
REGIONS	Land of the Moles, Mole Hole, Beneath Ascantha

Description: Capable of extremely powerful attacks when psyched up. Beware of mad moles who are in a state of high tension!

92: Cockateer
FAMILY: BIRD

HP: 105
MP: 0
Attack: 96
Defence: 92
Agility: 59

GOLD 28   EXP 90

NORMAL ITEM	Stone hardhat
RARE ITEM	Titan belt
REGIONS	Baccarat Region

Description: A race of swordsmen… or should that be 'swordchickens'? They boast powerful sword skills and mastery of the Wind Sickles attack.

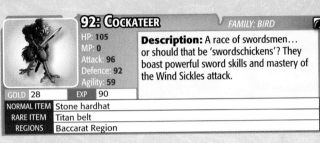

86: Wailin' weed
FAMILY: PLANT

HP: 59
MP: 0
Attack: 72
Defence: 59
Agility: 61

GOLD 17   EXP 73

NORMAL ITEM	Red mould
RARE ITEM	Coral hairpin
REGIONS	Trodain Castle

Description: Flower-monsters nourished by the anguish of those unfortunate enough to be turned into thorny vines, such as the residents of Trodain Castle.

93: Great sabrecat
FAMILY: BEAST

HP: 95
MP: 0
Attack: 110
Defence: 84
Agility: 72

GOLD 31   EXP 120

NORMAL ITEM	Medicinal herb
RARE ITEM	Magic beast hide
REGIONS	Baccarat Region

Description: Fearless, highly agile predators with sharp fangs. Rumour has it that they can be tamed, but the truth remains unknown.

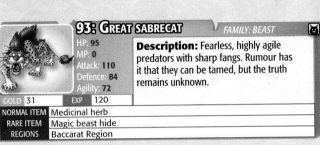

87: Garuda
FAMILY: BIRD

HP: 80
MP: 21
Attack: 74
Defence: 71
Agility: 56

GOLD 12   EXP 75

NORMAL ITEM	Hairband
RARE ITEM	Poison moth knife
REGIONS	Kingdom of Trodain, Trodain Castle

Description: Monsters that attack their enemies from the sky. Rumour has it that they can cast spells capable of wiping out entire parties, but the truth remains unknown.

94: Metal slime knight
FAMILY: SLIME

HP: 90
MP: 8
Attack: 78
Defence: 145
Agility: 64

GOLD 33   EXP 91

NORMAL ITEM	Slime earrings
RARE ITEM	Kitty shield
REGIONS	Baccarat Region

Description: Brave slime-knights who live for a fight. Although resistant to attack spells, they are susceptible to support spells.

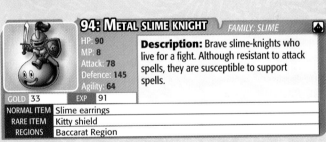

88: Infernal armour
FAMILY: MATERIAL

HP: 88
MP: 0
Attack: 83
Defence: 86
Agility: 47

GOLD 19   EXP 90

NORMAL ITEM	Iron armour
RARE ITEM	Steel broadsword
REGIONS	Trodain Castle

Description: Ambulatory suits of cursed armour. Beware their swords. When driven into the ground, they can stun a group of adversaries with powerful lightning bolts.

95: Puppet player
FAMILY: HUMANOID

HP: 100
MP: 15
Attack: 72
Defence: 92
Agility: 58

GOLD 41   EXP 90

NORMAL ITEM	Medicinal herb
RARE ITEM	Scholar's specs
REGIONS	Baccarat Region, East Argonia, Unnamed Isle

Description: A strangely theatrical monster. Performs a carefully prepared puppet show, entitled 'Love Story', that stirs up the enemy in all sorts of ways.

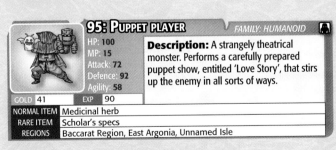

89: Dragonthorn
FAMILY: DRAGON

HP: 164
MP: 0
Attack: 90
Defence: 55
Agility: 57

GOLD 25   EXP 101

NORMAL ITEM	Medicinal herb
RARE ITEM	Thorn whip
REGIONS	Trodain Castle

Description: Thorny rose bushes turned into monsters by Dhoulmagus. Whenever one is killed, another is born to take its place.

96: Spitnik
FAMILY: ELEMENTAL

HP: 108
MP: 0
Attack: 88
Defence: 90
Agility: 58

GOLD 18   EXP 92

NORMAL ITEM	Boomerang
RARE ITEM	Moon's mercy
REGIONS	Baccarat Region

Description: The dazzling bodies of these monsters burn as fiercely as the surface of the sun. They spew fire at their enemies.

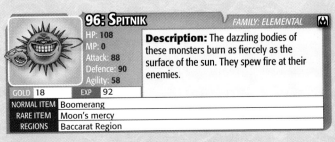

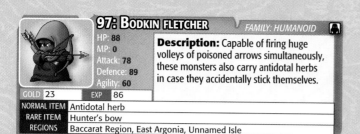

97: Bodkin Fletcher
FAMILY: HUMANOID

HP: 88
MP: 0
Attack: 78
Defence: 89
Agility: 60

GOLD 23 | EXP 86

NORMAL ITEM: Antidotal herb
RARE ITEM: Hunter's bow
REGIONS: Baccarat Region, East Argonia, Unnamed Isle

Description: Capable of firing huge volleys of poisoned arrows simultaneously, these monsters also carry antidotal herbs in case they accidentally stick themselves.

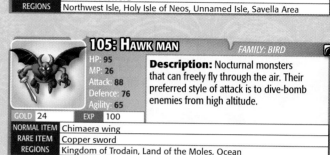

104: Skeleton Soldier
FAMILY: ZOMBIE

HP: 94
MP: 12
Attack: 93
Defence: 95
Agility: 62

GOLD 26 | EXP 93

NORMAL ITEM: Titan belt
RARE ITEM: Steel broadsword
REGIONS: Northwest Isle, Holy Isle of Neos, Unnamed Isle, Savella Area

Description: Former knights enslaved by the power of the Lord of Darkness. Loyal to the core, they continue to fight even in death.

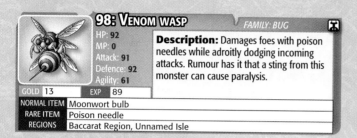

98: Venom Wasp
FAMILY: BUG

HP: 92
MP: 0
Attack: 91
Defence: 92
Agility: 61

GOLD 13 | EXP 89

NORMAL ITEM: Moonwort bulb
RARE ITEM: Poison needle
REGIONS: Baccarat Region, Unnamed Isle

Description: Damages foes with poison needles while adroitly dodging incoming attacks. Rumour has it that a sting from this monster can cause paralysis.

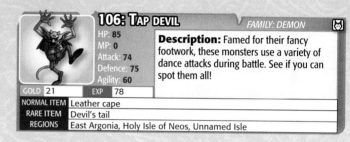

105: Hawk Man
FAMILY: BIRD

HP: 95
MP: 26
Attack: 88
Defence: 76
Agility: 65

GOLD 24 | EXP 100

NORMAL ITEM: Chimaera wing
RARE ITEM: Copper sword
REGIONS: Kingdom of Trodain, Land of the Moles, Ocean

Description: Nocturnal monsters that can freely fly through the air. Their preferred style of attack is to dive-bomb enemies from high altitude.

99: Orc
FAMILY: BEAST

HP: 105
MP: Infinite
Attack: 99
Defence: 88
Agility: 45

GOLD 31 | EXP 94

NORMAL ITEM: Medicinal herb
RARE ITEM: Iron lance
REGIONS: Baccarat Region, Unnamed Isle

Description: Boar-like monsters with masterful spear technique. Their Achilles heel is their low agility.

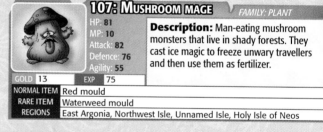

106: Tap Devil
FAMILY: DEMON

HP: 85
MP: 0
Attack: 74
Defence: 75
Agility: 60

GOLD 21 | EXP 78

NORMAL ITEM: Leather cape
RARE ITEM: Devil's tail
REGIONS: East Argonia, Holy Isle of Neos, Unnamed Isle

Description: Famed for their fancy footwork, these monsters use a variety of dance attacks during battle. See if you can spot them all!

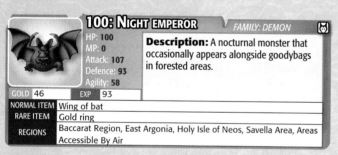

100: Night Emperor
FAMILY: DEMON

HP: 100
MP: 0
Attack: 107
Defence: 93
Agility: 58

GOLD 46 | EXP 93

NORMAL ITEM: Wing of bat
RARE ITEM: Gold ring
REGIONS: Baccarat Region, East Argonia, Holy Isle of Neos, Savella Area, Areas Accessible By Air

Description: A nocturnal monster that occasionally appears alongside goodybags in forested areas.

107: Mushroom Mage
FAMILY: PLANT

HP: 81
MP: 10
Attack: 82
Defence: 76
Agility: 60

GOLD 13 | EXP 75

NORMAL ITEM: Red mould
RARE ITEM: Waterweed mould
REGIONS: East Argonia, Northwest Isle, Unnamed Isle, Holy Isle of Neos

Description: Man-eating mushroom monsters that live in shady forests. They cast ice magic to freeze unwary travellers and then use them as fertilizer.

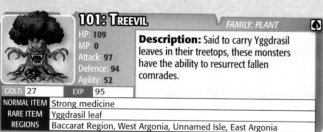

101: Treevil
FAMILY: PLANT

HP: 109
MP: 0
Attack: 97
Defence: 94
Agility: 52

GOLD 27 | EXP 95

NORMAL ITEM: Strong medicine
RARE ITEM: Yggdrasil leaf
REGIONS: Baccarat Region, West Argonia, Unnamed Isle, East Argonia

Description: Said to carry Yggdrasil leaves in their treetops, these monsters have the ability to resurrect fallen comrades.

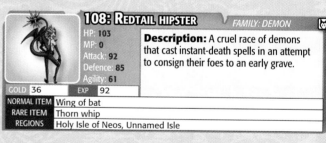

108: Redtail Hipster
FAMILY: DEMON

HP: 103
MP: 0
Attack: 92
Defence: 85
Agility: 61

GOLD 36 | EXP 92

NORMAL ITEM: Wing of bat
RARE ITEM: Thorn whip
REGIONS: Holy Isle of Neos, Unnamed Isle

Description: A cruel race of demons that cast instant-death spells in an attempt to consign their foes to an early grave.

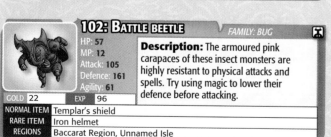

102: Battle Beetle
FAMILY: BUG

HP: 57
MP: 12
Attack: 105
Defence: 161
Agility: 61

GOLD 22 | EXP 96

NORMAL ITEM: Templar's shield
RARE ITEM: Iron helmet
REGIONS: Baccarat Region, Unnamed Isle

Description: The armoured pink carapaces of these insect monsters are highly resistant to physical attacks and spells. Try using magic to lower their defence before attacking.

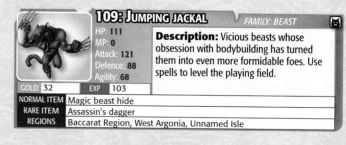

109: Jumping Jackal
FAMILY: BEAST

HP: 111
MP: 0
Attack: 121
Defence: 88
Agility: 68

GOLD 32 | EXP 103

NORMAL ITEM: Magic beast hide
RARE ITEM: Assassin's dagger
REGIONS: Baccarat Region, West Argonia, Unnamed Isle

Description: Vicious beasts whose obsession with bodybuilding has turned them into even more formidable foes. Use spells to level the playing field.

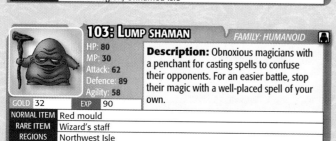

103: Lump Shaman
FAMILY: HUMANOID

HP: 80
MP: 30
Attack: 62
Defence: 89
Agility: 58

GOLD 32 | EXP 90

NORMAL ITEM: Red mould
RARE ITEM: Wizard's staff
REGIONS: Northwest Isle

Description: Obnoxious magicians with a penchant for casting spells to confuse their opponents. For an easier battle, stop their magic with a well-placed spell of your own.

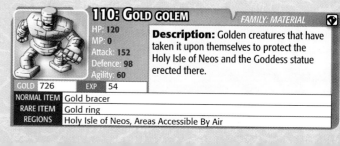

110: Gold Golem
FAMILY: MATERIAL

HP: 120
MP: 0
Attack: 152
Defence: 98
Agility: 60

GOLD 726 | EXP 54

NORMAL ITEM: Gold bracer
RARE ITEM: Gold ring
REGIONS: Holy Isle of Neos, Areas Accessible By Air

Description: Golden creatures that have taken it upon themselves to protect the Holy Isle of Neos and the Goddess statue erected there.

111: KING SLIME
FAMILY: SLIME

HP: 210
MP: 25
Attack: 150
Defence: 75
Agility: 62

Description: The result of many small slimes fusing together and bestowing themselves with a crown. A slime with royal aspirations!

GOLD	51	EXP	110

NORMAL ITEM	Slime earrings
RARE ITEM	Slime crown
REGIONS	Baccarat Region, Unnamed Isle, Areas Accessible By Air

112: IRON SCORPION
FAMILY: BUG

HP: 64
MP: 21
Attack: 105
Defence: 152
Agility: 63

Description: The iron carapaces of these fearsome creatures are virtually impervious to sword attacks, but they are susceptible to explosive spells.

GOLD	21	EXP	82

NORMAL ITEM	Iron nail
RARE ITEM	Farmer's scythe
REGIONS	West Argonia, East Argonia, Unnamed Isle, Desert

113: TOXIC ZOMBIE
FAMILY: ZOMBIE

HP: 116
MP: 0
Attack: 75
Defence: 48
Agility: 51

Description: Undead corpses that live in poisonous swamps. If you have a hard time hitting them, try psyching up first.

GOLD	17	EXP	75

NORMAL ITEM	Antidotal herb
RARE ITEM	Wayfarer's clothes
REGIONS	Holy Isle of Neos, Northwest Isle, Unnamed Isle, West Argonia

114: LESSER DEMON
FAMILY: DEMON

HP: 119
MP: 0
Attack: 101
Defence: 77
Agility: 64

Description: Fearsome demons capable of channeling the power of the underworld into a dazzling light attack.

GOLD	38	EXP	107

NORMAL ITEM	Red mould
RARE ITEM	Gold bracer
REGIONS	Northwest Isle

115: VOLPONE
FAMILY: BEAST

HP: 107
MP: 24
Attack: 114
Defence: 100
Agility: 64

Description: Aristocrats of the monster world. Famed for doing the Hustle Dance when in dire trouble to tip the balance of a battle in their favour.

GOLD	43	EXP	102

NORMAL ITEM	Leather cape
RARE ITEM	Templar's sword
REGIONS	Holy Isle of Neos, Unnamed Isle

116: BOMBOULDER
FAMILY: MATERIAL

HP: 115
MP: 10
Attack: 80
Defence: 111
Agility: 80

Description: They often appear uninterested when first encountered, but, in reality, they are merely biding their time, waiting for the best moment to attack.

GOLD	11	EXP	111

NORMAL ITEM	Stone hardhat
RARE ITEM	Rockbomb shard
REGIONS	Baccarat Region, West Argonia, Unnamed Isle, Cape West of Pickham, Areas Accessible By Air

117: SKULLRIDER
FAMILY: DEMON

HP: 109
MP: 0
Attack: 110
Defence: 101
Agility: 77

Description: Ninja-like monsters that execute rapid turns and rush their opponents' legs in an attempt to trip them up.

GOLD	32	EXP	97

NORMAL ITEM	Medicinal herb
RARE ITEM	Bandana
REGIONS	West Argonia, East Argonia, Unnamed Isle

118: HADES CONDOR
FAMILY: BIRD

HP: 102
MP: 16
Attack: 107
Defence: 98
Agility: 72

Description: A crafty monster that quietly observes its enemies to determine the weakest member of a party. Beware its talons.

GOLD	22	EXP	99

NORMAL ITEM	Strong medicine
RARE ITEM	Eagle dagger
REGIONS	West Argonia, Ocean, Holy Isle of Neos

119: FROGMAN
FAMILY: BUG

HP: 116
MP: 16
Attack: 83
Defence: 99
Agility: 47

Description: Frog-monsters with strange patterns covering their bodies. When provoked to reveal the human faces on their backs, they can use powerful spells and ice attacks which damage the whole party.

GOLD	18	EXP	88

NORMAL ITEM	Waterweed mould
RARE ITEM	Cool cheese
REGIONS	West Argonia, East Argonia, Unnamed Isle

120: MIMIC
FAMILY: MATERIAL

HP: 144
MP: Infinite
Attack: 160
Defence: 100
Agility: 65

Description: To all appearances, these monsters look like nothing more than normal treasure chests. Try to open one, however, and the joke's on you. Beware the fearsome mimic!

GOLD	72	EXP	128

NORMAL ITEM	Iron nail
RARE ITEM	Seed of strength
REGIONS	Unnamed Isle, Pirate's Cove

121: MAGIC DUMBBELL
FAMILY: MATERIAL

HP: 78
MP: 14
Attack: 84
Defence: 90
Agility: 60

Description: In groups, these otherwise silly-looking monsters are capable of playing melodies that can lay low even experienced adventurers.

GOLD	9	EXP	41

NORMAL ITEM	Red mould
RARE ITEM	Rapier
REGIONS	Savella Area, West Argonia, Cape West of Pickham, East Argonia

122: GARGOYLE
FAMILY: BIRD

HP: 120
MP: 0
Attack: 112
Defence: 102
Agility: 71

Description: Masters of the air, these monsters take flight on their leathery wings and attack foes from above.

GOLD	36	EXP	114

NORMAL ITEM	Strong medicine
RARE ITEM	Steel broadsword
REGIONS	West Argonia, East Argonia

123: MAGIC MARIONETTE
FAMILY: MATERIAL

HP: 117
MP: 0
Attack: 97
Defence: 92
Agility: 64

Description: Famed for launching into a strange dance that steals opponents' MP before running off. Although not particularly strong, these monsters can be quite annoying.

GOLD	27	EXP	108

NORMAL ITEM	Iron nail
RARE ITEM	Slime earrings
REGIONS	West Argonia, East Argonia

124: NOTSO MACHO
FAMILY: HUMANOID

HP: 147
MP: 12
Attack: 135
Defence: 80
Agility: 66

Description: A monster whose enormous, flabby body and lolling tongue belie its intelligence. Generally uses spells to raise its attack power before unleashing a powerful strike.

GOLD	38	EXP	120

NORMAL ITEM	Medicinal herb
RARE ITEM	Gold bracer
REGIONS	East Argonia

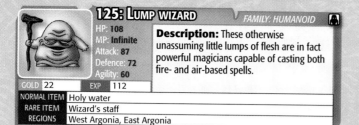

125: LUMP WIZARD
FAMILY: HUMANOID

HP: 108
MP: Infinite
Attack: 87
Defence: 72
Agility: 60

GOLD 22　　EXP 112

NORMAL ITEM	Holy water
RARE ITEM	Wizard's staff
REGIONS	West Argonia, East Argonia

Description: These otherwise unassuming little lumps of flesh are in fact powerful magicians capable of casting both fire- and air-based spells.

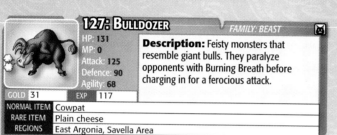

126: BERSERKER
FAMILY: HUMANOID

HP: 120
MP: 0
Attack: 119
Defence: 106
Agility: 67

GOLD 19　　EXP 118

NORMAL ITEM	Kitty shield
RARE ITEM	Iron axe
REGIONS	West Argonia

Description: Hyperactive monsters that live deep in forests. They swing their axes wildly as they charge their enemies.

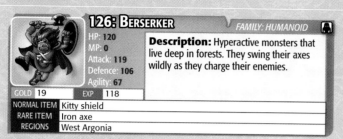

127: BULLDOZER
FAMILY: BEAST

HP: 131
MP: 0
Attack: 125
Defence: 90
Agility: 68

GOLD 31　　EXP 117

NORMAL ITEM	Cowpat
RARE ITEM	Plain cheese
REGIONS	East Argonia, Savella Area

Description: Feisty monsters that resemble giant bulls. They paralyze opponents with Burning Breath before charging in for a ferocious attack.

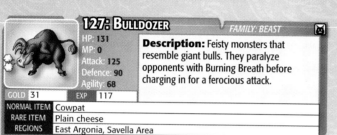

128: GHOUL
FAMILY: ZOMBIE

HP: 182
MP: 0
Attack: 102
Defence: 42
Agility: 66

GOLD 17　　EXP 98

NORMAL ITEM	Antidotal herb
RARE ITEM	Gold ring
REGIONS	East Argonia

Description: Strike or slice these monsters all you want; their undead flesh feels no pain. Beware of their tendency to call in fellow ghouls to sway the odds in their favour.

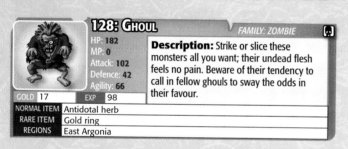

129: SHADE
FAMILY: ELEMENTAL

HP: 86
MP: 0
Attack: 95
Defence: 70
Agility: 68

GOLD 14　　EXP 78

NORMAL ITEM	Rennet powder
RARE ITEM	Wings of bat
REGIONS	East Argonia, Savella Area, Ocean

Description: It is said that these terrifying apparitions are born when the restless shadows of fallen monsters coalesce.

130: LETHAL ARMOUR
FAMILY: MATERIAL

HP: 145
MP: 20
Attack: 151
Defence: 136
Agility: 70

GOLD 52　　EXP 124

NORMAL ITEM	Soldier's sword
RARE ITEM	Heavy armour
REGIONS	East Argonia, Desert

Description: A killer suit of armour with a grudge against humanity. This monster boasts high offensive and defensive capabilities. Use support magic to subdue it before it uses its own magic to put everyone to sleep.

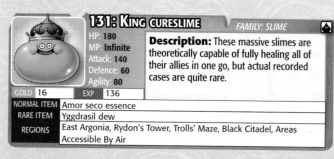

131: KING CURESLIME
FAMILY: SLIME

HP: 180
MP: Infinite
Attack: 140
Defence: 60
Agility: 80

GOLD 16　　EXP 136

NORMAL ITEM	Amor seco essence
RARE ITEM	Yggdrasil dew
REGIONS	East Argonia, Rydon's Tower, Trolls' Maze, Black Citadel, Areas Accessible By Air

Description: These massive slimes are theoretically capable of fully healing all of their allies in one go, but actual recorded cases are quite rare.

132: HOODLUM
FAMILY: HUMANOID

HP: 123
MP: 0
Attack: 126
Defence: 97
Agility: 69

GOLD 32　　EXP 106

NORMAL ITEM	Tough guy tattoo
RARE ITEM	Iron axe
REGIONS	East Argonia, Savella Area, Cape West of Pickham

Description: Humanoid nightstalkers that prowl the paths of the world, preying upon unwary travellers. Beware their dazzling light attacks and huge axes.

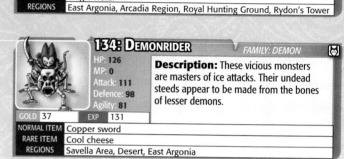

133: HOCUS CHIMAERA
FAMILY: BIRD

HP: 108
MP: 8
Attack: 106
Defence: 108
Agility: 98

GOLD 35　　EXP 115

NORMAL ITEM	Chimaera wing
RARE ITEM	Magic water
REGIONS	East Argonia, Arcadia Region, Royal Hunting Ground, Rydon's Tower

Description: Though they are capable of casting spells, these monsters are rather more hocus-pocus than proper magicians.

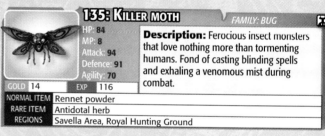

134: DEMONRIDER
FAMILY: DEMON

HP: 126
MP: 0
Attack: 111
Defence: 98
Agility: 81

GOLD 37　　EXP 131

NORMAL ITEM	Copper sword
RARE ITEM	Cool cheese
REGIONS	Savella Area, Desert, East Argonia

Description: These vicious monsters are masters of ice attacks. Their undead steeds appear to be made from the bones of lesser demons.

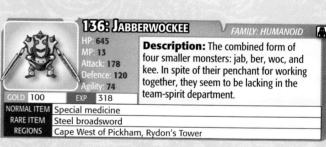

135: KILLER MOTH
FAMILY: BUG

HP: 84
MP: 8
Attack: 94
Defence: 91
Agility: 70

GOLD 14　　EXP 116

NORMAL ITEM	Rennet powder
RARE ITEM	Antidotal herb
REGIONS	Savella Area, Royal Hunting Ground

Description: Ferocious insect monsters that love nothing more than tormenting humans. Fond of casting blinding spells and exhaling a venomous mist during combat.

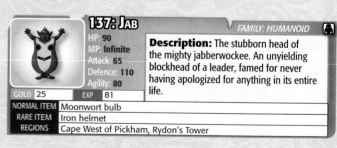

136: JABBERWOCKEE
FAMILY: HUMANOID

HP: 645
MP: 13
Attack: 178
Defence: 120
Agility: 74

GOLD 100　　EXP 318

NORMAL ITEM	Special medicine
RARE ITEM	Steel broadsword
REGIONS	Cape West of Pickham, Rydon's Tower

Description: The combined form of four smaller monsters: jab, ber, woc, and kee. In spite of their penchant for working together, they seem to be lacking in the team-spirit department.

137: JAB
FAMILY: HUMANOID

HP: 90
MP: Infinite
Attack: 65
Defence: 110
Agility: 80

GOLD 25　　EXP 81

NORMAL ITEM	Moonwort bulb
RARE ITEM	Iron helmet
REGIONS	Cape West of Pickham, Rydon's Tower

Description: The stubborn head of the mighty jabberwockee. An unyielding blockhead of a leader, famed for never having apologized for anything in its entire life.

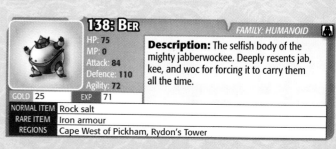

138: BER
FAMILY: HUMANOID

HP: 75
MP: 0
Attack: 84
Defence: 110
Agility: 72

GOLD 25　　EXP 71

NORMAL ITEM	Rock salt
RARE ITEM	Iron armour
REGIONS	Cape West of Pickham, Rydon's Tower

Description: The selfish body of the mighty jabberwockee. Deeply resents jab, kee, and woc for forcing it to carry them all the time.

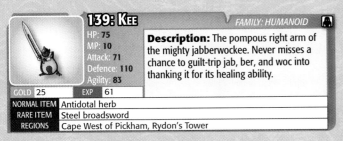

139: KEE
FAMILY: HUMANOID

HP: 75
MP: 10
Attack: 71
Defence: 110
Agility: 83

Description: The pompous right arm of the mighty jabberwockee. Never misses a chance to guilt-trip jab, ber, and woc into thanking it for its healing ability.

GOLD	25	EXP	61
NORMAL ITEM	Antidotal herb		
RARE ITEM	Steel broadsword		
REGIONS	Cape West of Pickham, Rydon's Tower		

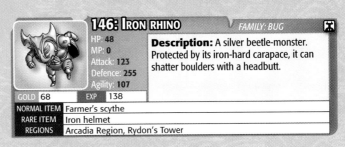

146: IRON RHINO
FAMILY: BUG

HP: 48
MP: 0
Attack: 123
Defence: 255
Agility: 107

Description: A silver beetle-monster. Protected by its iron-hard carapace, it can shatter boulders with a headbutt.

GOLD	68	EXP	138
NORMAL ITEM	Farmer's scythe		
RARE ITEM	Iron helmet		
REGIONS	Arcadia Region, Rydon's Tower		

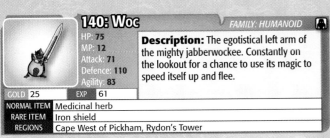

140: WOC
FAMILY: HUMANOID

HP: 75
MP: 12
Attack: 71
Defence: 110
Agility: 83

Description: The egotistical left arm of the mighty jabberwockee. Constantly on the lookout for a chance to use its magic to speed itself up and flee.

GOLD	25	EXP	61
NORMAL ITEM	Medicinal herb		
RARE ITEM	Iron shield		
REGIONS	Cape West of Pickham, Rydon's Tower		

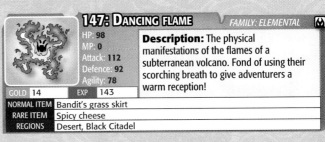

147: DANCING FLAME
FAMILY: ELEMENTAL

HP: 98
MP: 0
Attack: 112
Defence: 92
Agility: 78

Description: The physical manifestations of the flames of a subterranean volcano. Fond of using their scorching breath to give adventurers a warm reception!

GOLD	14	EXP	143
NORMAL ITEM	Bandit's grass skirt		
RARE ITEM	Spicy cheese		
REGIONS	Desert, Black Citadel		

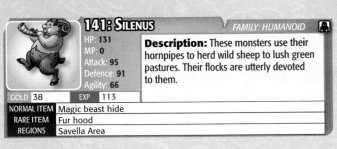

141: SILENUS
FAMILY: HUMANOID

HP: 131
MP: 0
Attack: 95
Defence: 91
Agility: 65

Description: These monsters use their hornpipes to herd wild sheep to lush green pastures. Their flocks are utterly devoted to them.

GOLD	38	EXP	113
NORMAL ITEM	Magic beast hide		
RARE ITEM	Fur hood		
REGIONS	Savella Area		

148: BLOOD MUMMY
FAMILY: ZOMBIE

HP: 138
MP: 0
Attack: 118
Defence: 75
Agility: 65

Description: Recent converts to the cult of the Lord of Darkness. Use magic to fell them quickly before they have a chance to curse you.

GOLD	16	EXP	125
NORMAL ITEM	Bandana		
RARE ITEM	Red mould		
REGIONS	Dark Ruins		

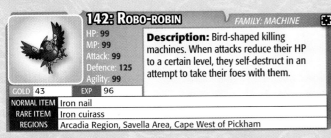

142: ROBO-ROBIN
FAMILY: MACHINE

HP: 99
MP: 99
Attack: 99
Defence: 125
Agility: 99

Description: Bird-shaped killing machines. When attacks reduce their HP to a certain level, they self-destruct in an attempt to take their foes with them.

GOLD	43	EXP	96
NORMAL ITEM	Iron nail		
RARE ITEM	Iron cuirass		
REGIONS	Arcadia Region, Savella Area, Cape West of Pickham		

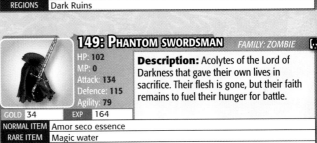

149: PHANTOM SWORDSMAN
FAMILY: ZOMBIE

HP: 102
MP: 0
Attack: 134
Defence: 115
Agility: 79

Description: Acolytes of the Lord of Darkness that gave their own lives in sacrifice. Their flesh is gone, but their faith remains to fuel their hunger for battle.

GOLD	34	EXP	164
NORMAL ITEM	Amor seco essence		
RARE ITEM	Magic water		
REGIONS	Dark Ruins		

143: PUPPET MASTER
FAMILY: HUMANOID

HP: 130
MP: 8
Attack: 120
Defence: 112
Agility: 75

Description: The undisputed master of puppeteers. The distinctive fire-spewing chimaera puppet is an original creation.

GOLD	51	EXP	132
NORMAL ITEM	Chimaera wing		
RARE ITEM	Dancer's costume		
REGIONS	Arcadia Region, Cape West of Pickham		

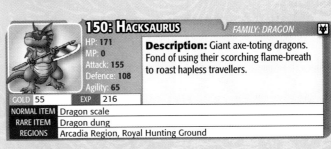

150: HACKSAURUS
FAMILY: DRAGON

HP: 171
MP: 0
Attack: 155
Defence: 108
Agility: 65

Description: Giant axe-toting dragons. Fond of using their scorching flame-breath to roast hapless travellers.

GOLD	55	EXP	216
NORMAL ITEM	Dragon scale		
RARE ITEM	Dragon dung		
REGIONS	Arcadia Region, Royal Hunting Ground		

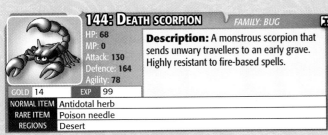

144: DEATH SCORPION
FAMILY: BUG

HP: 68
MP: 0
Attack: 130
Defence: 164
Agility: 78

Description: A monstrous scorpion that sends unwary travellers to an early grave. Highly resistant to fire-based spells.

GOLD	14	EXP	99
NORMAL ITEM	Antidotal herb		
RARE ITEM	Poison needle		
REGIONS	Desert		

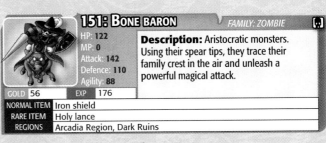

151: BONE BARON
FAMILY: ZOMBIE

HP: 122
MP: 0
Attack: 142
Defence: 110
Agility: 88

Description: Aristocratic monsters. Using their spear tips, they trace their family crest in the air and unleash a powerful magical attack.

GOLD	56	EXP	176
NORMAL ITEM	Iron shield		
RARE ITEM	Holy lance		
REGIONS	Arcadia Region, Dark Ruins		

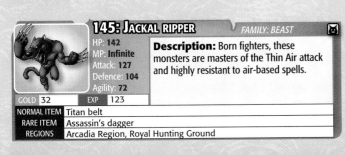

145: JACKAL RIPPER
FAMILY: BEAST

HP: 142
MP: Infinite
Attack: 127
Defence: 104
Agility: 72

Description: Born fighters, these monsters are masters of the Thin Air attack and highly resistant to air-based spells.

GOLD	32	EXP	123
NORMAL ITEM	Titan belt		
RARE ITEM	Assassin's dagger		
REGIONS	Arcadia Region, Royal Hunting Ground		

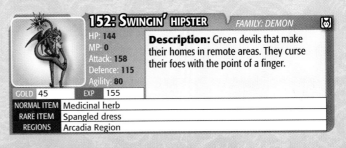

152: SWINGIN' HIPSTER
FAMILY: DEMON

HP: 144
MP: 0
Attack: 158
Defence: 115
Agility: 80

Description: Green devils that make their homes in remote areas. They curse their foes with the point of a finger.

GOLD	45	EXP	155
NORMAL ITEM	Medicinal herb		
RARE ITEM	Spangled dress		
REGIONS	Arcadia Region		

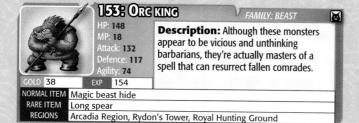

153: ORC KING
FAMILY: BEAST

HP: 148
MP: 18
Attack: 132
Defence: 117
Agility: 74

GOLD 38 | EXP 154

NORMAL ITEM	Magic beast hide
RARE ITEM	Long spear
REGIONS	Arcadia Region, Rydon's Tower, Royal Hunting Ground

Description: Although these monsters appear to be vicious and unthinking barbarians, they're actually masters of a spell that can resurrect fallen comrades.

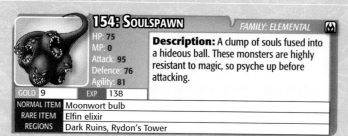

154: SOULSPAWN
FAMILY: ELEMENTAL

HP: 75
MP: 0
Attack: 95
Defence: 76
Agility: 81

GOLD 9 | EXP 138

NORMAL ITEM	Moonwort bulb
RARE ITEM	Elfin elixir
REGIONS	Dark Ruins, Rydon's Tower

Description: A clump of souls fused into a hideous ball. These monsters are highly resistant to magic, so psyche up before attacking.

155: GRYPHON
FAMILY: BIRD

HP: 161
MP: 16
Attack: 141
Defence: 107
Agility: 91

GOLD 32 | EXP 167

NORMAL ITEM	Chimaera wing
RARE ITEM	Razor wing boomerang
REGIONS	Arcadia Region, Rydon's Tower

Description: Silent and intimidating bird-creatures that like to prevent their foes from using magic before attacking them with their razor-sharp talons.

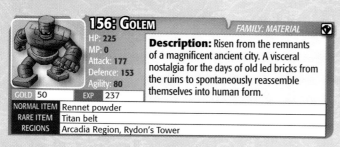

156: GOLEM
FAMILY: MATERIAL

HP: 225
MP: 0
Attack: 177
Defence: 153
Agility: 80

GOLD 50 | EXP 237

NORMAL ITEM	Rennet powder
RARE ITEM	Titan belt
REGIONS	Arcadia Region, Rydon's Tower

Description: Risen from the remnants of a magnificent ancient city. A visceral nostalgia for the days of old led bricks from the ruins to spontaneously reassemble themselves into human form.

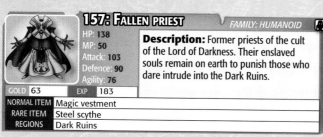

157: FALLEN PRIEST
FAMILY: HUMANOID

HP: 138
MP: 50
Attack: 103
Defence: 90
Agility: 76

GOLD 63 | EXP 183

NORMAL ITEM	Magic vestment
RARE ITEM	Steel scythe
REGIONS	Dark Ruins

Description: Former priests of the cult of the Lord of Darkness. Their enslaved souls remain on earth to punish those who dare intrude into the Dark Ruins.

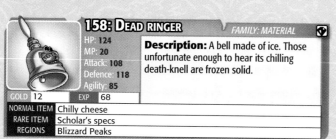

158: DEAD RINGER
FAMILY: MATERIAL

HP: 124
MP: 20
Attack: 108
Defence: 118
Agility: 85

GOLD 12 | EXP 68

NORMAL ITEM	Chilly cheese
RARE ITEM	Scholar's specs
REGIONS	Blizzard Peaks

Description: A bell made of ice. Those unfortunate enough to hear its chilling death-knell are frozen solid.

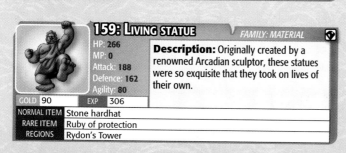

159: LIVING STATUE
FAMILY: MATERIAL

HP: 266
MP: 0
Attack: 188
Defence: 162
Agility: 80

GOLD 90 | EXP 306

NORMAL ITEM	Stone hardhat
RARE ITEM	Ruby of protection
REGIONS	Rydon's Tower

Description: Originally created by a renowned Arcadian sculptor, these statues were so exquisite that they took on lives of their own.

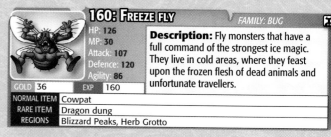

160: FREEZE FLY
FAMILY: BUG

HP: 126
MP: 30
Attack: 107
Defence: 120
Agility: 86

GOLD 36 | EXP 160

NORMAL ITEM	Cowpat
RARE ITEM	Dragon dung
REGIONS	Blizzard Peaks, Herb Grotto

Description: Fly monsters that have a full command of the strongest ice magic. They live in cold areas, where they feast upon the frozen flesh of dead animals and unfortunate travellers.

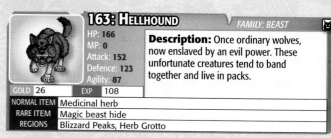

161: DARK SLIME
FAMILY: SLIME

HP: 97
MP: 16
Attack: 138
Defence: 97
Agility: 87

GOLD 12 | EXP 87

NORMAL ITEM	Medicinal herb
RARE ITEM	Magical hat
REGIONS	Godbird's Eyrie (Dark), Farebury Region, Unnamed Isle, Untrodden Groves, Pickham Region, Maella Region, Baccarat Region, Arcadia Region, East Argonia, Areas Accessible By Air, World of Darkness

Description: A slime from the World of Darkness who has mastered the Slime Spank, a secret attack technique used only by slimes. A fearsome foe indeed.

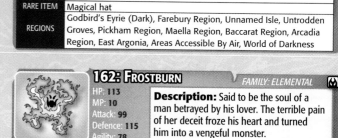

162: FROSTBURN
FAMILY: ELEMENTAL

HP: 113
MP: 10
Attack: 99
Defence: 115
Agility: 78

GOLD 16 | EXP 199

NORMAL ITEM	Magic water
RARE ITEM	Chilly cheese
REGIONS	Blizzard Peaks, Herb Grotto

Description: Said to be the soul of a man betrayed by his lover. The terrible pain of her deceit froze his heart and turned him into a vengeful monster.

163: HELLHOUND
FAMILY: BEAST

HP: 166
MP: 0
Attack: 152
Defence: 123
Agility: 87

GOLD 26 | EXP 108

NORMAL ITEM	Medicinal herb
RARE ITEM	Magic beast hide
REGIONS	Blizzard Peaks, Herb Grotto

Description: Once ordinary wolves, now enslaved by an evil power. These unfortunate creatures tend to band together and live in packs.

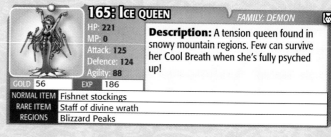

164: TROLL
FAMILY: DEMON

HP: 423
MP: 0
Attack: 210
Defence: 66
Agility: 51

GOLD 46 | EXP 210

NORMAL ITEM	Tough guy tattoo
RARE ITEM	Sledgehammer
REGIONS	Arcadia Region, Isolated Plateau, Dark Ruins, Trolls' Maze

Description: Gruesome giants with grotesque smiles. They love to pound the enemy with their massive clubs, and, with their high HP, can take just as much damage as they deal.

165: ICE QUEEN
FAMILY: DEMON

HP: 221
MP: 0
Attack: 125
Defence: 124
Agility: 88

GOLD 56 | EXP 186

NORMAL ITEM	Fishnet stockings
RARE ITEM	Staff of divine wrath
REGIONS	Blizzard Peaks

Description: A tension queen found in snowy mountain regions. Few can survive her Cool Breath when she's fully psyched up!

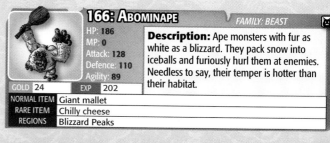

166: ABOMINAPE
FAMILY: BEAST

HP: 186
MP: 0
Attack: 128
Defence: 110
Agility: 89

GOLD 24 | EXP 202

NORMAL ITEM	Giant mallet
RARE ITEM	Chilly cheese
REGIONS	Blizzard Peaks

Description: Ape monsters with fur as white as a blizzard. They pack snow into iceballs and furiously hurl them at enemies. Needless to say, their temper is hotter than their habitat.

167: BEELZEBUZZ
FAMILY: BUG

HP: 154
MP: 16
Attack: 121
Defence: 128
Agility: 95

GOLD 21 EXP 165

Description: Fly monsters that feast upon the flesh of fallen dragons. They are rightly feared as insect versions of bomboulders.

NORMAL ITEM	Cowpat
RARE ITEM	Dragon dung
REGIONS	Dragon Graveyard

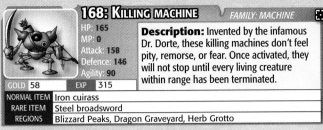

168: KILLING MACHINE
FAMILY: MACHINE

HP: 165
MP: 0
Attack: 158
Defence: 146
Agility: 90

GOLD 58 EXP 315

Description: Invented by the infamous Dr. Dorte, these killing machines don't feel pity, remorse, or fear. Once activated, they will not stop until every living creature within range has been terminated.

NORMAL ITEM	Iron cuirass
RARE ITEM	Steel broadsword
REGIONS	Blizzard Peaks, Dragon Graveyard, Herb Grotto

169: ICIKILLER
FAMILY: HUMANOID

HP: 198
MP: 24
Attack: 182
Defence: 130
Agility: 91

GOLD 78 EXP 221

Description: Ferocious ice-warriors born and raised in the deep mountain snow. Said to display a chilling hatred of all things warm.

NORMAL ITEM	Titan belt
RARE ITEM	Poison moth knife
REGIONS	Blizzard Peaks, Herb Grotto

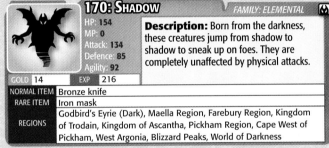

170: SHADOW
FAMILY: ELEMENTAL

HP: 154
MP: 0
Attack: 134
Defence: 85
Agility: 92

GOLD 14 EXP 216

Description: Born from the darkness, these creatures jump from shadow to shadow to sneak up on foes. They are completely unaffected by physical attacks.

NORMAL ITEM	Bronze knife
RARE ITEM	Iron mask
REGIONS	Godbird's Eyrie (Dark), Maella Region, Farebury Region, Kingdom of Trodain, Kingdom of Ascantha, Pickham Region, Cape West of Pickham, West Argonia, Blizzard Peaks, World of Darkness

171: METAL KING SLIME
FAMILY: SLIME

HP: 20
MP: 66
Attack: 166
Defence: 4096
Agility: 255

GOLD 240 EXP 30010

Description: Travellers who happen to encounter this monster can't help chuckling. And if they're fortunate enough to defeat it, they can't stop smiling.

NORMAL ITEM	Slime crown
RARE ITEM	Orichalcum
REGIONS	Untrodden Groves, Dragon Graveyard, Black Citadel, Areas Accessible By Air, Unknown…

172: FROST WYVINE
FAMILY: DRAGON

HP: 286
MP: 30
Attack: 190
Defence: 130
Agility: 86

GOLD 62 EXP 326

Description: Born from silver frost, these ice-monsters live to punish those who hate snow and blizzards.

NORMAL ITEM	Dragon scale
RARE ITEM	Chain whip
REGIONS	Blizzard Peaks, Herb Grotto

173: ELYSIUM BIRD
FAMILY: BIRD

HP: 173
MP: 32
Attack: 113
Defence: 99
Agility: 92

GOLD 43 EXP 163

Description: Beautiful masters of the skies. Beware their resistance to support spells and their ability to heal multiple allies simultaneously.

NORMAL ITEM	Eagle dagger
RARE ITEM	Ruby of protection
REGIONS	Isolated Plateau, Godbird's Eyrie, Areas Accessible By Air

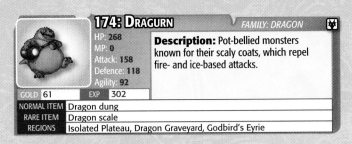

174: DRAGURN
FAMILY: DRAGON

HP: 268
MP: 0
Attack: 158
Defence: 118
Agility: 95

GOLD 61 EXP 302

Description: Pot-bellied monsters known for their scaly coats, which repel fire- and ice-based attacks.

NORMAL ITEM	Dragon dung
RARE ITEM	Dragon scale
REGIONS	Isolated Plateau, Dragon Graveyard, Godbird's Eyrie

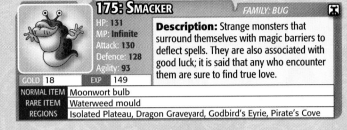

175: SMACKER
FAMILY: BUG

HP: 131
MP: Infinite
Attack: 130
Defence: 128
Agility: 149

GOLD 18 EXP 149

Description: Strange monsters that surround themselves with magic barriers to deflect spells. They are also associated with good luck; it is said that any who encounter them are sure to find true love.

NORMAL ITEM	Moonwort bulb
RARE ITEM	Waterweed mould
REGIONS	Isolated Plateau, Dragon Graveyard, Godbird's Eyrie, Pirate's Cove

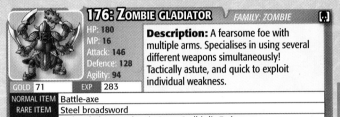

176: ZOMBIE GLADIATOR
FAMILY: ZOMBIE

HP: 180
MP: 16
Attack: 146
Defence: 128
Agility: 94

GOLD 71 EXP 283

Description: A fearsome foe with multiple arms. Specialises in using several different weapons simultaneously! Tactically astute, and quick to exploit individual weakness.

NORMAL ITEM	Battle-axe
RARE ITEM	Steel broadsword
REGIONS	Isolated Plateau, Pirate's Cove, Godbird's Eyrie

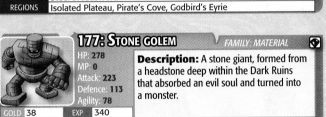

177: STONE GOLEM
FAMILY: MATERIAL

HP: 278
MP: 0
Attack: 223
Defence: 113
Agility: 78

GOLD 38 EXP 340

Description: A stone giant, formed from a headstone deep within the Dark Ruins that absorbed an evil soul and turned into a monster.

NORMAL ITEM	Strong medicine
RARE ITEM	Rockbomb shard
REGIONS	Isolated Plateau, Godbird's Eyrie

178: DARK CONDOR
FAMILY: BIRD

HP: 163
MP: 36
Attack: 170
Defence: 130
Agility: 98

GOLD 26 EXP 224

Description: An evil bird-monster that flies through the skies of the World of Darkness. Casts powerful healing magic on itself and its allies when close to defeat.

NORMAL ITEM	Chimaera wing
RARE ITEM	Wing of bat
REGIONS	Godbird's Eyrie (Dark), Desert, Farebury Region, Blizzard Peaks, Unnamed Isle, World of Darkness

179: MUCHO MACHO
FAMILY: HUMANOID

HP: 316
MP: 24
Attack: 189
Defence: 107
Agility: 96

GOLD 51 EXP 318

Description: An overweight warrior with a penchant for using magic to double its attack power. Fights like a real mucho macho man.

NORMAL ITEM	Strong medicine
RARE ITEM	Magical hat
REGIONS	Isolated Plateau, Godbird's Eyrie

180: DARK SKELETON
FAMILY: ZOMBIE

HP: 240
MP: 0
Attack: 186
Defence: 132
Agility: 95

GOLD 31 EXP 304

Description: These dedicated and fiercely loyal monsters stand against humanity.

NORMAL ITEM	Moonwort bulb
RARE ITEM	Bronze shield
REGIONS	Godbird's Eyrie (Dark), World of Darkness, Farebury Region, Unnamed Isle, Areas Accessible By Air

181: DARK MACARBOUR — FAMILY: PLANT

HP: 334
MP: 0
Attack: 188
Defence: 126
Agility: 84

Description: A fearsome tree of death. In the World of Darkness, trees grow from leaves rather than seeds, sprouting branches first and roots last.

GOLD	56	EXP	333

NORMAL ITEM	Strong medicine
RARE ITEM	Yggdrasil leaf
REGIONS	World of Darkness, Kingdom of Trodain, Kingdom of Ascantha, Arcadia Region, Baccarat Region

---

182: TYRANTOSAURUS — FAMILY: DRAGON

HP: 208
MP: 0
Attack: 187
Defence: 146
Agility: 108

Description: A dragon warrior. Use magic to defend yourself against fire, lest you be consumed by their searing flame breath.

GOLD	57	EXP	283

NORMAL ITEM	Dragon scale
RARE ITEM	Iron axe
REGIONS	Isolated Plateau, Dragon Graveyard, Godbird's Eyrie

183: DEMON THUNDERER — FAMILY: DEMON

HP: 179
MP: 0
Attack: 132
Defence: 138
Agility: 97

Description: This foul demon is completely resistant to thunder-based attacks. Said to be a physical form of thunder itself.

GOLD	48	EXP	250

NORMAL ITEM	Devil's tail
RARE ITEM	Wizard's staff
REGIONS	Isolated Plateau, Pirate's Cove, Godbird's Eyrie

184: DARK STAR — FAMILY: ELEMENTAL

HP: 236
MP: 12
Attack: 196
Defence: 135
Agility: 99

Description: A tiny star system from the World of Darkness. Emits an eerie light that makes enemies more vulnerable to spells.

GOLD	66	EXP	301

NORMAL ITEM	Medicinal herb
RARE ITEM	Edged boomerang
REGIONS	Godbird's Eyrie (Dark), Pickham Region, Alexandria Region, Land of the Moles, Untrodden Groves, East Argonia, Blizzard Peaks

---

185: DARK MINISTER — FAMILY: DEMON

HP: 193
MP: 16
Attack: 163
Defence: 177
Agility: 108

Description: Loyal creatures that have dedicated their lives to evil.

GOLD	101	EXP	316

NORMAL ITEM	Leather cape
RARE ITEM	Saint's ashes
REGIONS	Godbird's Eyrie (Dark), Alexandria Region, Farebury Region

---

186: GRIM RIDER — FAMILY: ZOMBIE

HP: 236
MP: 9
Attack: 184
Defence: 110
Agility: 98

Description: They may not look it, but the grim riders' donkeys are monsters in their own right. They are utterly dedicated to their riders.

GOLD	72	EXP	304

NORMAL ITEM	Holy lance
RARE ITEM	Magical hat
REGIONS	Isolated Plateau, Godbird's Eyrie

187: DARK SEA-DIVA — FAMILY: DEMON

HP: 236
MP: 25
Attack: 188
Defence: 98
Agility: 99

Description: Born from the toxic sludge of the dark seas. Prevents foes from attacking by singing funny songs and making them laugh.

GOLD	61	EXP	287

NORMAL ITEM	Waterweed mould
RARE ITEM	Leather cape
REGIONS	World of Darkness, Godbird's Eyrie (Dark)

188: WAR GRYPHON — FAMILY: BIRD

HP: 249
MP: 20
Attack: 172
Defence: 118
Agility: 99

Description: These monsters combine the strengths of four-legged and winged creatures. Use physical attacks to defeat them as they are highly resistant to spells.

GOLD	59	EXP	305

NORMAL ITEM	Chimaera wing
RARE ITEM	Spicy cheese
REGIONS	Isolated Plateau, Areas Accessible By Air

189: DARK TURKEY — FAMILY: BIRD

HP: 214
MP: 12
Attack: 158
Defence: 129
Agility: 110

Description: Once able to fly freely, these fearsome birds descended from the skies long ago to become swordsmen on terra firma. They taunt their foes by calling them 'chickens'.

GOLD	73	EXP	309

NORMAL ITEM	Garter
RARE ITEM	Dream blade
REGIONS	Godbird's Eyrie (Dark), World of Darkness, Farebury Region, Kingdom of Ascantha, Kingdom of Trodain, Pickham Region, East Argonia, Baccarat Region, Alexandria Region, Areas Accessible By Air

---

190: HELIGATOR — FAMILY: BEAST

HP: 512
MP: 0
Attack: 223
Defence: 96
Agility: 75

Description: A flying alligator creature that uses its enormous weight to body-slam unwary foes into submission.

GOLD	138	EXP	617

NORMAL ITEM	Hairband
RARE ITEM	Scale armour
REGIONS	Isolated Plateau, Areas Accessible By Air

191: DARK DULLAHAN — FAMILY: ZOMBIE

HP: 292
MP: 0
Attack: 195
Defence: 242
Agility: 105

Description: A warrior beheaded in battle and risen again as a monster. Said to occasionally summon dark condors.

GOLD	138	EXP	326

NORMAL ITEM	Antidotal herb
RARE ITEM	Zombie mail
REGIONS	Godbird's Eyrie (Dark), Maella Region, Farebury Region, Arcadia Region, East Argonia, Kingdom of Trodain

---

192: KILLER CROAKER — FAMILY: BUG

HP: 183
MP: 14
Attack: 102
Defence: 126
Agility: 100

Description: Frog monsters with two faces. The sight of the demonic faces on their backs is widely regarded as an omen of death by adventurers.

GOLD	16	EXP	166

NORMAL ITEM	Waterweed mould
RARE ITEM	Bandana
REGIONS	Untrodden Groves, Godbird's Eyrie, Areas Accessible By Air

---

193: HIGH ROLLER — FAMILY: BEAST

HP: 284
MP: 28
Attack: 148
Defence: 118
Agility: 101

Description: The number of eyes hidden underneath their masks constantly changes during battle. When they roll a six, expect to see a bomboulder join the fray.

GOLD	87	EXP	245

NORMAL ITEM	Leather hat
RARE ITEM	Prayer ring
REGIONS	Untrodden Groves, Godbird's Eyrie, Areas Accessible By Air

---

194: DARKODILE — FAMILY: BEAST

HP: 593
MP: 0
Attack: 243
Defence: 96
Agility: 68

Description: A heligator that somehow lost its way, ended up in the World of Darkness, and began a new life as a darkodile.

GOLD	138	EXP	637

NORMAL ITEM	Hairband
RARE ITEM	Scale armour
REGIONS	Godbird's Eyrie (Dark), World of Darkness, Alexandria Region, West Argonia, Kingdom of Ascantha, Maella Region, Baccarat Region

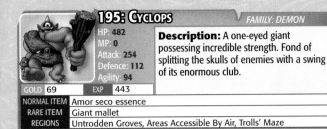

195: CYCLOPS
FAMILY: DEMON

HP: 482
MP: 0
Attack: 254
Defence: 112
Agility: 94

GOLD 69 | EXP 443

NORMAL ITEM	Amor seco essence
RARE ITEM	Giant mallet
REGIONS	Untrodden Groves, Areas Accessible By Air, Trolls' Maze

Description: A one-eyed giant possessing incredible strength. Fond of splitting the skulls of enemies with a swing of its enormous club.

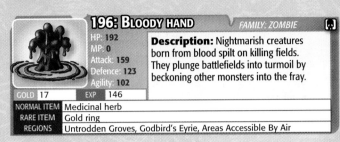

196: BLOODY HAND
FAMILY: ZOMBIE

HP: 192
MP: 0
Attack: 159
Defence: 123
Agility: 102

GOLD 17 | EXP 146

NORMAL ITEM	Medicinal herb
RARE ITEM	Gold ring
REGIONS	Untrodden Groves, Godbird's Eyrie, Areas Accessible By Air

Description: Nightmarish creatures born from blood spilt on killing fields. They plunge battlefields into turmoil by beckoning other monsters into the fray.

197: SNAPDRAGON
FAMILY: DRAGON

HP: 436
MP: 30
Attack: 171
Defence: 116
Agility: 102

GOLD 63 | EXP 356

NORMAL ITEM	Thorn whip
RARE ITEM	Spiked steel whip
REGIONS	Untrodden Groves, Areas Accessible By Air, Trolls' Maze

Description: Strange monsters that are animated forms of cursed rose bushes. They entwine enemies in thorny vines, then incinerate them with powerful fire spells.

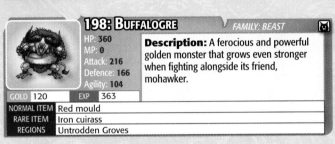

198: BUFFALOGRE
FAMILY: BEAST

HP: 360
MP: 0
Attack: 216
Defence: 166
Agility: 104

GOLD 120 | EXP 363

NORMAL ITEM	Red mould
RARE ITEM	Iron cuirass
REGIONS	Untrodden Groves

Description: A ferocious and powerful golden monster that grows even stronger when fighting alongside its friend, mohawker.

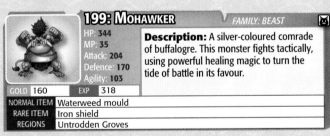

199: MOHAWKER
FAMILY: BEAST

HP: 344
MP: 35
Attack: 204
Defence: 170
Agility: 103

GOLD 160 | EXP 318

NORMAL ITEM	Waterweed mould
RARE ITEM	Iron shield
REGIONS	Untrodden Groves

Description: A silver-coloured comrade of buffalogre. This monster fights tactically, using powerful healing magic to turn the tide of battle in its favour.

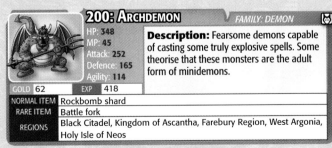

200: ARCHDEMON
FAMILY: DEMON

HP: 348
MP: 45
Attack: 252
Defence: 165
Agility: 114

GOLD 62 | EXP 418

NORMAL ITEM	Rockbomb shard
RARE ITEM	Battle fork
REGIONS	Black Citadel, Kingdom of Ascantha, Farebury Region, West Argonia, Holy Isle of Neos

Description: Fearsome demons capable of casting some truly explosive spells. Some theorise that these monsters are the adult form of minidemons.

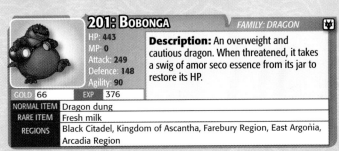

201: BOBONGA
FAMILY: DRAGON

HP: 443
MP: 0
Attack: 249
Defence: 148
Agility: 90

GOLD 66 | EXP 376

NORMAL ITEM	Dragon dung
RARE ITEM	Fresh milk
REGIONS	Black Citadel, Kingdom of Ascantha, Farebury Region, East Argonia, Arcadia Region

Description: An overweight and cautious dragon. When threatened, it takes a swig of amor seco essence from its jar to restore its HP.

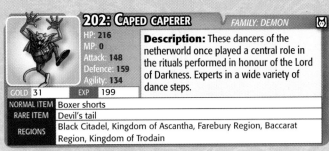

202: CAPED CAPERER
FAMILY: DEMON

HP: 216
MP: 0
Attack: 148
Defence: 159
Agility: 134

GOLD 31 | EXP 199

NORMAL ITEM	Boxer shorts
RARE ITEM	Devil's tail
REGIONS	Black Citadel, Kingdom of Ascantha, Farebury Region, Baccarat Region, Kingdom of Trodain

Description: These dancers of the netherworld once played a central role in the rituals performed in honour of the Lord of Darkness. Experts in a wide variety of dance steps.

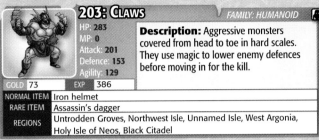

203: CLAWS
FAMILY: HUMANOID

HP: 283
MP: 0
Attack: 201
Defence: 153
Agility: 129

GOLD 73 | EXP 386

NORMAL ITEM	Iron helmet
RARE ITEM	Assassin's dagger
REGIONS	Untrodden Groves, Northwest Isle, Unnamed Isle, West Argonia, Holy Isle of Neos, Black Citadel

Description: Aggressive monsters covered from head to toe in hard scales. They use magic to lower enemy defences before moving in for the kill.

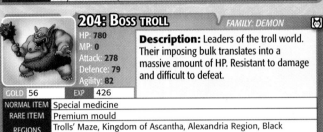

204: BOSS TROLL
FAMILY: DEMON

HP: 780
MP: 0
Attack: 278
Defence: 79
Agility: 82

GOLD 56 | EXP 426

NORMAL ITEM	Special medicine
RARE ITEM	Premium mould
REGIONS	Trolls' Maze, Kingdom of Ascantha, Alexandria Region, Black Citadel, Arcadia Region, Desert

Description: Leaders of the troll world. Their imposing bulk translates into a massive amount of HP. Resistant to damage and difficult to defeat.

205: MIMIC KING
FAMILY: MATERIAL

HP: 340
MP: Infinite
Attack: 231
Defence: 224
Agility: 135

GOLD 71 | EXP 402

NORMAL ITEM	Iron nail
RARE ITEM	Seed of wisdom
REGIONS	Farebury Region, Kingdom of Ascantha, Kingdom of Trodain, Blizzard Peaks, Arcadia Region, Black Citadel

Description: Treasure chests brought as tribute to the Black Citadel, transformed by the power of the Lord of Darkness into vicious monsters.

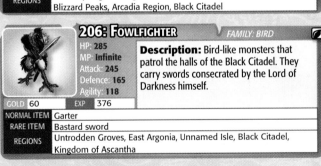

206: FOWLFIGHTER
FAMILY: BIRD

HP: 285
MP: Infinite
Attack: 245
Defence: 165
Agility: 118

GOLD 60 | EXP 376

NORMAL ITEM	Garter
RARE ITEM	Bastard sword
REGIONS	Untrodden Groves, East Argonia, Unnamed Isle, Black Citadel, Kingdom of Ascantha

Description: Bird-like monsters that patrol the halls of the Black Citadel. They carry swords consecrated by the Lord of Darkness himself.

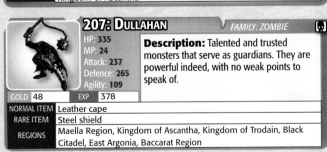

207: DULLAHAN
FAMILY: ZOMBIE

HP: 335
MP: 24
Attack: 237
Defence: 265
Agility: 109

GOLD 48 | EXP 378

NORMAL ITEM	Leather cape
RARE ITEM	Steel shield
REGIONS	Maella Region, Kingdom of Ascantha, Kingdom of Trodain, Black Citadel, East Argonia, Baccarat Region

Description: Talented and trusted monsters that serve as guardians. They are powerful indeed, with no weak points to speak of.

208: GIGANTES
FAMILY: DEMON

HP: 710
MP: 0
Attack: 285
Defence: 148
Agility: 99

GOLD 36 | EXP 511

NORMAL ITEM	Amor seco essence
RARE ITEM	Elfin elixir
REGIONS	Black Citadel, Areas Accessible By Air, Maella Region

Description: The fury of the Lord of Darkness taken physical form as a powerful monster. Combines sheer size and strength with an overwhelming hatred for anything human.

209: FROU-FROU — FAMILY: DRAGON

HP: 510
MP: 0
Attack: 254
Defence: 180
Agility: 111

GOLD 57 | EXP 396

NORMAL ITEM	Magic beast hide
RARE ITEM	Dragon scale
REGIONS	Black Citadel, Alexandria Region, Maella Region, Northwest Isle, Baccarat Region

Description: This giant dragon swings its enormous tail to wallop multiple foes simultaneously.

210: STONE GUARDIAN — FAMILY: MATERIAL

HP: 450
MP: 0
Attack: 246
Defence: 287
Agility: 73

GOLD 80 | EXP 422

NORMAL ITEM	Rock salt
RARE ITEM	Mighty armlet
REGIONS	Black Citadel, Maella Region, Alexandria Region, East Argonia, Pickham Region

Description: A statue from the Black Citadel, risen to protect the Lord of Darkness in answer to devout believers' prayers.

211: WIGHT PRIEST — FAMILY: ZOMBIE

HP: 258
MP: Infinite
Attack: 169
Defence: 198
Agility: 126

GOLD 57 | EXP 398

NORMAL ITEM	Magic vestment
RARE ITEM	Rune staff
REGIONS	Black Citadel, Alexandria Region, Farebury Region, Arcadia Region, Kingdom of Ascantha

Description: An apostle of the Lord of Darkness who sacrificed his own life in order to serve his master. Calls upon other monsters to fight alongside him during difficult battles.

212: HELL GLADIATOR — FAMILY: ZOMBIE

HP: 276
MP: 0
Attack: 256
Defence: 167
Agility: 112

GOLD 94 | EXP 416

NORMAL ITEM	Hades' helm
RARE ITEM	Platinum sword
REGIONS	Black Citadel, Baccarat Region, Pickham Region

Description: Powerful warriors, enslaved and imprisoned by the power of the Lord of Darkness long ago.

213: DARK MOTH — FAMILY: BUG

HP: 286
MP: 100
Attack: 170
Defence: 136
Agility: 118

GOLD 15 | EXP 226

NORMAL ITEM	Rennet powder
RARE ITEM	Saint's ashes
REGIONS	Farebury Region, Alexandria Region, Kingdom of Trodain, Maella Region, Land of the Moles, Pickham Region, Baccarat Region, Arcadia Region

Description: Few travellers survive an encounter with these foul monsters, as every beat of their dark wings fills the air with a poisonous powder.

214: DARK GRYPHON — FAMILY: BIRD

HP: 349
MP: 16
Attack: 273
Defence: 186
Agility: 119

GOLD 61 | EXP 411

NORMAL ITEM	Bunny tail
RARE ITEM	Saint's ashes
REGIONS	Alexandria Region, Kingdom of Ascantha, Unnamed Isle, East Argonia, Holy Isle of Neos, Pickham Region

Description: Firebirds born phoenix-like from raging infernos. Capable of exhaling an incinerating breath. Totally resistant to any fire-based attack.

215: DARK SABRECAT — FAMILY: BEAST

HP: 372
MP: 0
Attack: 261
Defence: 177
Agility: 128

GOLD 103 | EXP 507

NORMAL ITEM	Leather hat
RARE ITEM	Saint's ashes
REGIONS	Farebury Region, Kingdom of Ascantha, Unnamed Isle, Arcadia Region, East Argonia, Pickham Region, Areas Accessible By Air

Description: Ferocious shadowcats that prowl through the darkness. It is said that no one who set eyes on a dark sabrecat ever lives to tell the tale.

216: HELL HOPPER — FAMILY: MATERIAL

HP: 263
MP: 255
Attack: 279
Defence: 166
Agility: 130

GOLD 66 | EXP 379

NORMAL ITEM	Moon's mercy
RARE ITEM	Elevating shoes
REGIONS	Unknown...

Description: A strange pair of monsters living together in a symbiotic relationship. Said to drop an exceedingly rare pair of shoes when defeated.

217: DARK DEVILDOG — FAMILY: BEAST

HP: 397
MP: 0
Attack: 312
Defence: 153
Agility: 105

GOLD 71 | EXP 398

NORMAL ITEM	Iron headgear
RARE ITEM	Life bracer
REGIONS	Unknown...

Description: These powerful dog-monsters are a handful in their own right, but become even more difficult to defeat when they call upon hell's gatekeepers for help.

218: HEAVY HOOD — FAMILY: HUMANOID

HP: 438
MP: 0
Attack: 348
Defence: 156
Agility: 127

GOLD 53 | EXP 423

NORMAL ITEM	Velvet cape
RARE ITEM	Pirate's hat
REGIONS	Unknown...

Description: Murderous monsters that slipped into another world during their search for prey. When in a state of high tension, they can fell even experienced adventurers with a single chop of their axes.

219: HELL STALKER — FAMILY: DEMON

HP: 405
MP: 0
Attack: 336
Defence: 144
Agility: 123

GOLD 46 | EXP 408

NORMAL ITEM	Magic water
RARE ITEM	Demon whip
REGIONS	Unknown...

Description: Fearsome demon-creatures belched from the depths of hell. It is said that they leave an eternal killing field in their bloody wake.

220: SILHOUETTE — FAMILY: ELEMENTAL

HP: 156
MP: 0
Attack: 169
Defence: 101
Agility: 118

GOLD 32 | EXP 376

NORMAL ITEM	Rennet powder
RARE ITEM	Saint's ashes
REGIONS	Unknown...

Description: Almost nothing is known about these mysterious and phantasmal monsters who have a penchant for luring travellers to their death with an evil dance.

221: DEMOCROBOT — FAMILY: HUMANOID

HP: 1520
MP: 255
Attack: 378
Defence: 185
Agility: 128

GOLD 380 | EXP 1830

NORMAL ITEM	Seed of magic
RARE ITEM	Gold nugget
REGIONS	Unknown...

Description: The mighty combined form of the head of state, the body politic, the right wing, and the other right wing... er, left wing. Feared for its mastery of lightning magic.

222: HEAD OF STATE — FAMILY: HUMANOID

HP: 412
MP: 255
Attack: 155
Defence: 152
Agility: 162

GOLD 60 | EXP 320

NORMAL ITEM	Soft cheese
RARE ITEM	Thinking cap
REGIONS	Unknown...

Description: The self-proclaimed brains of the team. Capable of casting both lightning-based and healing spells. Boasts of being elected by its fellow party members. In reality, it was handed the position by its father.

223: BODY POLITIC
FAMILY: HUMANOID

HP: 564
MP: 0
Attack: 185
Defence: 170
Agility: 104

GOLD 30 | EXP 310

NORMAL ITEM	Hard cheese
RARE ITEM	Magic armour
REGIONS	Unknown…

Description: The huge and sluggish body politic resists all but the most dedicated attacks.

224: RIGHT WING
FAMILY: HUMANOID

HP: 508
MP: 0
Attack: 180
Defence: 164
Agility: 115

GOLD 20 | EXP 290

NORMAL ITEM	Chunky cheese
RARE ITEM	Bastard sword
REGIONS	Unknown…

Description: Famed for chuckling evilly during battle. In reality, chuckles evilly all the time.

225: LEFT WING
FAMILY: HUMANOID

HP: 396
MP: 0
Attack: 163
Defence: 159
Agility: 115

GOLD 20 | EXP 280

NORMAL ITEM	Highly-strung cheese
RARE ITEM	Power shield
REGIONS	Unknown…

Description: Incessantly complains about the activities of the right wing, body politic, and head of state, but lacks the motivation to actually do anything about it.

226: PANDORA'S BOX
FAMILY: MATERIAL

HP: 405
MP: 255
Attack: 369
Defence: 210
Agility: 130

GOLD 184 | EXP 560

NORMAL ITEM	Recovery ring
RARE ITEM	Orichalcum
REGIONS	Unknown…

Description: Like a demented jack-in-the-box, this well-camouflaged monster lives to surprise unwary travellers. Often carries precious materials that can be used in the alchemy pot.

227: WIGHT KING
FAMILY: ZOMBIE

HP: 456
MP: 64
Attack: 194
Defence: 136
Agility: 125

GOLD 72 | EXP 477

NORMAL ITEM	Saint's ashes
RARE ITEM	Skull ring
REGIONS	Unknown…

Description: Once a king amongst men. Killed during a crusade. His bitter soul bears a grudge to this very day.

228: INVISIBLE SWORDSMAN
FAMILY: ZOMBIE

HP: 511
MP: 0
Attack: 314
Defence: 178
Agility: 128

GOLD 55 | EXP 502

NORMAL ITEM	Dark robe
RARE ITEM	Rusty old sword
REGIONS	Unknown…

Description: A knight that traded his physical body for the power of the Lord of Darkness. Lofts his sword high in the air to call down a divine punishment upon his foes.

229: HELLSPAWN
FAMILY: ELEMENTAL

HP: 107
MP: 0
Attack: 156
Defence: 54
Agility: 121

GOLD 42 | EXP 389

NORMAL ITEM	Nook grass
RARE ITEM	Cloak of evasion
REGIONS	Unknown…

Description: Undead creatures that torment enemies with an array of powerful and destructive breath attacks. Psyche up if you want any hope of landing a solid hit.

230: BELIAL
FAMILY: DEMON

HP: 720
MP: 60
Attack: 389
Defence: 168
Agility: 124

GOLD 156 | EXP 523

NORMAL ITEM	Tough guy tattoo
RARE ITEM	Battle fork
REGIONS	Unknown…

Description: A general in the army of the underworld. Already powerful in its own right, after psyching up its attacks can injure entire parties with a single strike.

231: SOLARIS
FAMILY: ELEMENTAL

HP: 457
MP: 0
Attack: 331
Defence: 203
Agility: 129

GOLD 86 | EXP 468

NORMAL ITEM	Moonwort bulb
RARE ITEM	Seed of skill
REGIONS	Unknown…

Description: A mad planet with evil ambitions. Calls forth meteor storms to destroy any who dare oppose it.

232: GREAT TROLL
FAMILY: DEMON

HP: 1010
MP: 0
Attack: 415
Defence: 66
Agility: 101

GOLD 68 | EXP 679

NORMAL ITEM	Medicinal herb
RARE ITEM	Seed of skill
REGIONS	Trolls' Maze, Unknown…

Description: An incredibly destructive monster with an attack power almost beyond imagination. Said to carry extremely rare seeds.

233: UNHOLY BISHOP
FAMILY: HUMANOID

HP: 412
MP: 58
Attack: 153
Defence: 180
Agility: 102

GOLD 73 | EXP 619

NORMAL ITEM	Spangled dress
RARE ITEM	Velvet cape
REGIONS	Unknown…

Description: Fearsome magicians who hold the power of life and death in their cruel hands. Masters of magic, they are adept at casting every form of spell.

234: HELL'S GATEKEEPER
FAMILY: ZOMBIE

HP: 625
MP: 0
Attack: 354
Defence: 225
Agility: 105

GOLD 68 | EXP 662

NORMAL ITEM	Platinum mail
RARE ITEM	Ruinous shield
REGIONS	Unknown…

Description: A monster that stands guard at the gates to the netherworld. Calls forth an elysium bird to drive your monster team back into reserve.

235: CROCODOG
FAMILY: BEAST

HP: 1070
MP: 0
Attack: 386
Defence: 168
Agility: 108

GOLD 82 | EXP 718

NORMAL ITEM	Leather shield
RARE ITEM	Seed of skill
REGIONS	Unknown…

Description: An enormous, airborne alligator creature with a cruel smile and a vicious chuckle. Beware its powerful body-slam attack.

236: KHALAMARI KID
FAMILY: AQUATIC

HP: 44
MP: 0
Attack: 44
Defence: 31
Agility: 42

GOLD 9 | EXP 37

NORMAL ITEM	Waterweed mould
RARE ITEM	Oaken club
REGIONS	Kingdom of Ascantha, Pickham Region, Ocean

Description: The juvenile form of the same type of monsters as Khalamari. Often tries to play with the enemy instead of attacking them.

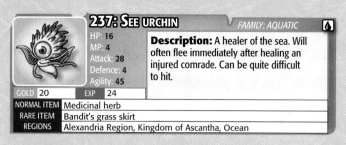

237: SEE URCHIN
FAMILY: AQUATIC

HP: 16
MP: 4
Attack: 28
Defence: 4
Agility: 45

Description: A healer of the sea. Will often flee immediately after healing an injured comrade. Can be quite difficult to hit.

GOLD	20
EXP	24

NORMAL ITEM	Medicinal herb
RARE ITEM	Bandit's grass skirt
REGIONS	Alexandria Region, Kingdom of Ascantha, Ocean

244: SQUID KID
FAMILY: AQUATIC

HP: 74
MP: 0
Attack: 71
Defence: 68
Agility: 48

Description: The juvenile form of the king squid. Not particularly interested in fighting. Think of them as the mascots of the sea!

GOLD	15
EXP	74

NORMAL ITEM	Pointy hat
RARE ITEM	Dancer's costume
REGIONS	East Argonia

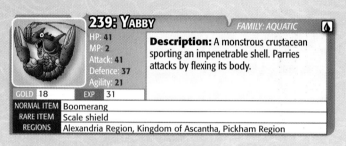

238: MAN O' WAR
FAMILY: AQUATIC

HP: 35
MP: 0
Attack: 34
Defence: 22
Agility: 23

Description: Their cute appearance belies the ferocity of their attacks. Known for preying upon ships at sea, which they surround and subdue with powerful paralysis spells.

GOLD	12
EXP	23

NORMAL ITEM	Moonwort bulb
RARE ITEM	Plain cheese
REGIONS	Alexandria Region, Ocean, Pirate's Cove

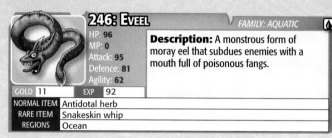

245: CRAYZEE
FAMILY: AQUATIC

HP: 91
MP: 16
Attack: 86
Defence: 85
Agility: 64

Description: Crayfish monsters covered in ultra-hard armour plates. Particularly resistant to air-based spells.

GOLD	25
EXP	94

NORMAL ITEM	Edged boomerang
RARE ITEM	Turtle shell
REGIONS	East Argonia, Pirate's Cove

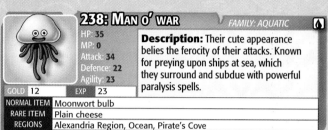

239: YABBY
FAMILY: AQUATIC

HP: 41
MP: 2
Attack: 41
Defence: 37
Agility: 21

Description: A monstrous crustacean sporting an impenetrable shell. Parries attacks by flexing its body.

GOLD	18
EXP	31

NORMAL ITEM	Boomerang
RARE ITEM	Scale shield
REGIONS	Alexandria Region, Kingdom of Ascantha, Pickham Region

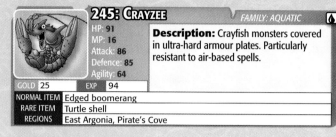

246: EVEEL
FAMILY: AQUATIC

HP: 96
MP: 0
Attack: 95
Defence: 81
Agility: 62

Description: A monstrous form of moray eel that subdues enemies with a mouth full of poisonous fangs.

GOLD	11
EXP	92

NORMAL ITEM	Antidotal herb
RARE ITEM	Snakeskin whip
REGIONS	Ocean

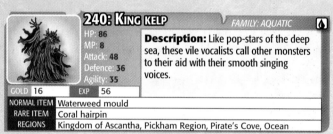

240: KING KELP
FAMILY: AQUATIC

HP: 86
MP: 8
Attack: 48
Defence: 36
Agility: 35

Description: Like pop-stars of the deep sea, these vile vocalists call other monsters to their aid with their smooth singing voices.

GOLD	16
EXP	56

NORMAL ITEM	Waterweed mould
RARE ITEM	Coral hairpin
REGIONS	Kingdom of Ascantha, Pickham Region, Pirate's Cove, Ocean

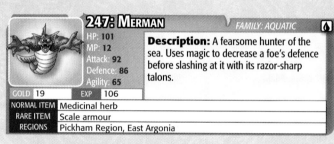

247: MERMAN
FAMILY: AQUATIC

HP: 101
MP: 12
Attack: 92
Defence: 86
Agility: 65

Description: A fearsome hunter of the sea. Uses magic to decrease a foe's defence before slashing at it with its razor-sharp talons.

GOLD	19
EXP	106

NORMAL ITEM	Medicinal herb
RARE ITEM	Scale armour
REGIONS	Pickham Region, East Argonia

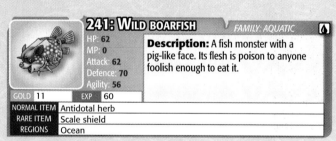

241: WILD BOARFISH
FAMILY: AQUATIC

HP: 62
MP: 0
Attack: 62
Defence: 70
Agility: 56

Description: A fish monster with a pig-like face. Its flesh is poison to anyone foolish enough to eat it.

GOLD	11
EXP	60

NORMAL ITEM	Antidotal herb
RARE ITEM	Scale shield
REGIONS	Ocean

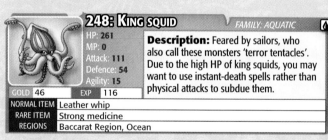

248: KING SQUID
FAMILY: AQUATIC

HP: 261
MP: 0
Attack: 111
Defence: 54
Agility: 15

Description: Feared by sailors, who also call these monsters 'terror tentacles'. Due to the high HP of king squids, you may want to use instant-death spells rather than physical attacks to subdue them.

GOLD	46
EXP	116

NORMAL ITEM	Leather whip
RARE ITEM	Strong medicine
REGIONS	Baccarat Region, Ocean

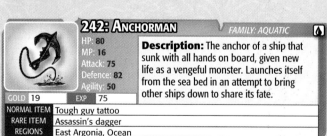

242: ANCHORMAN
FAMILY: AQUATIC

HP: 80
MP: 16
Attack: 75
Defence: 82
Agility: 50

Description: The anchor of a ship that sunk with all hands on board, given new life as a vengeful monster. Launches itself from the sea bed in an attempt to bring other ships down to share its fate.

GOLD	19
EXP	75

NORMAL ITEM	Tough guy tattoo
RARE ITEM	Assassin's dagger
REGIONS	East Argonia, Ocean

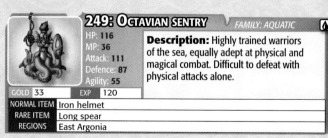

249: OCTAVIAN SENTRY
FAMILY: AQUATIC

HP: 116
MP: 36
Attack: 111
Defence: 87
Agility: 55

Description: Highly trained warriors of the sea, equally adept at physical and magical combat. Difficult to defeat with physical attacks alone.

GOLD	33
EXP	120

NORMAL ITEM	Iron helmet
RARE ITEM	Long spear
REGIONS	East Argonia

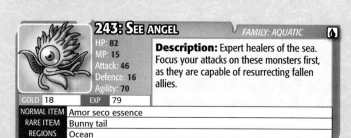

243: SEE ANGEL
FAMILY: AQUATIC

HP: 82
MP: 15
Attack: 46
Defence: 16
Agility: 70

Description: Expert healers of the sea. Focus your attacks on these monsters first, as they are capable of resurrecting fallen allies.

GOLD	18
EXP	79

NORMAL ITEM	Amor seco essence
RARE ITEM	Bunny tail
REGIONS	Ocean

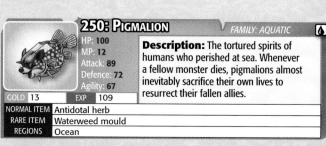

250: PIGMALION
FAMILY: AQUATIC

HP: 100
MP: 12
Attack: 89
Defence: 72
Agility: 67

Description: The tortured spirits of humans who perished at sea. Whenever a fellow monster dies, pigmalions almost inevitably sacrifice their own lives to resurrect their fallen allies.

GOLD	13
EXP	109

NORMAL ITEM	Antidotal herb
RARE ITEM	Waterweed mould
REGIONS	Ocean

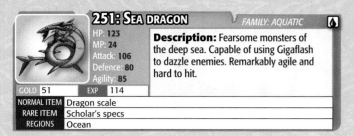

251: SEA DRAGON
FAMILY: AQUATIC

HP: 123
MP: 24
Attack: 106
Defence: 80
Agility: 85

GOLD 51 | EXP 114

NORMAL ITEM	Dragon scale
RARE ITEM	Scholar's specs
REGIONS	Ocean

Description: Fearsome monsters of the deep sea. Capable of using Gigaflash to dazzle enemies. Remarkably agile and hard to hit.

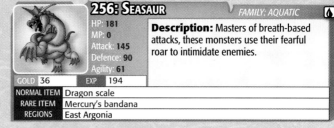

256: SEASAUR
FAMILY: AQUATIC

HP: 181
MP: 0
Attack: 145
Defence: 90
Agility: 61

GOLD 36 | EXP 194

NORMAL ITEM	Dragon scale
RARE ITEM	Mercury's bandana
REGIONS	East Argonia

Description: Masters of breath-based attacks, these monsters use their fearful roar to intimidate enemies.

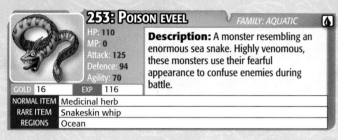

252: FOUL ANCHOR
FAMILY: AQUATIC

HP: 47
MP: 16
Attack: 109
Defence: 184
Agility: 68

GOLD 33 | EXP 121

NORMAL ITEM	Iron lance
RARE ITEM	Farmer's scythe
REGIONS	Ocean

Description: Fearsome and angry wharf-monsters. Use spells to attack them, as weapons have little or no effect on their tough steel bodies.

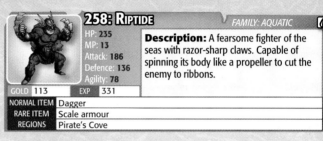

257: OCTAVIAN PIRATE
FAMILY: AQUATIC

HP: 205
MP: 16
Attack: 153
Defence: 128
Agility: 89

GOLD 63 | EXP 290

NORMAL ITEM	Iron shield
RARE ITEM	Iron lance
REGIONS	Pirate's Cove

Description: Long feared by sailors, these monsters use their vicious lances and lightning-fast reflexes to deprive unwary ships of treasure.

253: POISON EVEEL
FAMILY: AQUATIC

HP: 110
MP: 0
Attack: 125
Defence: 94
Agility: 70

GOLD 16 | EXP 116

NORMAL ITEM	Medicinal herb
RARE ITEM	Snakeskin whip
REGIONS	Ocean

Description: A monster resembling an enormous sea snake. Highly venomous, these monsters use their fearful appearance to confuse enemies during battle.

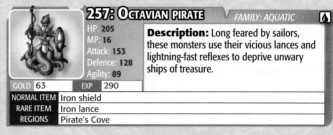

258: RIPTIDE
FAMILY: AQUATIC

HP: 235
MP: 13
Attack: 186
Defence: 136
Agility: 78

GOLD 113 | EXP 331

NORMAL ITEM	Dagger
RARE ITEM	Scale armour
REGIONS	Pirate's Cove

Description: A fearsome fighter of the seas with razor-sharp claws. Capable of spinning its body like a propeller to cut the enemy to ribbons.

BESTIARY

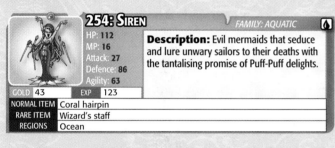

254: SIREN
FAMILY: AQUATIC

HP: 112
MP: 16
Attack: 27
Defence: 86
Agility: 63

GOLD 43 | EXP 123

NORMAL ITEM	Coral hairpin
RARE ITEM	Wizard's staff
REGIONS	Ocean

Description: Evil mermaids that seduce and lure unwary sailors to their deaths with the tantalising promise of Puff-Puff delights.

259: TENTACULAR
FAMILY: AQUATIC

HP: 502
MP: 20
Attack: 174
Defence: 40
Agility: 45

GOLD 52 | EXP 303

NORMAL ITEM	Medicinal herb
RARE ITEM	Full moon ring
REGIONS	Ocean

Description: Rulers of the deep sea, these monsters boast incredible vitality. Generally speaking, they are nearly impossible to defeat with physical attacks alone.

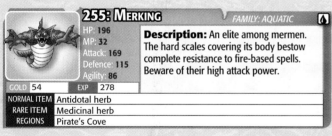

255: MERKING
FAMILY: AQUATIC

HP: 196
MP: 32
Attack: 169
Defence: 115
Agility: 86

GOLD 54 | EXP 278

NORMAL ITEM	Antidotal herb
RARE ITEM	Medicinal herb
REGIONS	Pirate's Cove

Description: An elite among mermen. The hard scales covering its body bestow complete resistance to fire-based spells. Beware of their high attack power.

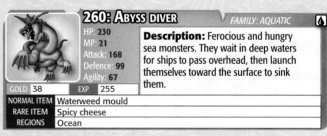

260: ABYSS DIVER
FAMILY: AQUATIC

HP: 230
MP: 21
Attack: 168
Defence: 99
Agility: 67

GOLD 38 | EXP 255

NORMAL ITEM	Waterweed mould
RARE ITEM	Spicy cheese
REGIONS	Ocean

Description: Ferocious and hungry sea monsters. They wait in deep waters for ships to pass overhead, then launch themselves toward the surface to sink them.

SELECTED BOSS MONSTERS

The following section contains just a smattering of the bosses in the game. Part of the enjoyment of playing this game is deciphering the strengths and weaknesses of the bosses, so be cautious when entering any boss fight!

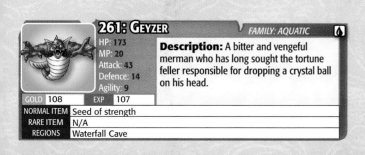

261: GEYZER
FAMILY: AQUATIC

HP: 173
MP: 20
Attack: 43
Defence: 14
Agility: 9

GOLD 108 | EXP 107

NORMAL ITEM	Seed of strength
RARE ITEM	N/A
REGIONS	Waterfall Cave

Description: A bitter and vengeful merman who has long sought the tortune feller responsible for dropping a crystal ball on his head.

262: KHALAMARI
FAMILY: AQUATIC

HP: 360
MP: 255
Attack: 63
Defence: 16
Agility: 17

GOLD 230 | EXP 311

NORMAL ITEM	N/A
RARE ITEM	N/A
REGIONS	Ocean

Description: Although temporarily transformed into a ferocious brute by Dhoulmagus's enchantments, Khalamari is actually quite a kind fellow at heart. At one time he planned to open his own comedy club.

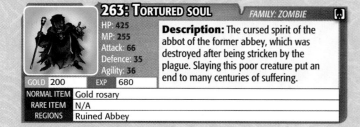

263: TORTURED SOUL
FAMILY: ZOMBIE

HP: 425
MP: 255
Attack: 66
Defence: 35
Agility: 36

Description: The cursed spirit of the abbot of the former abbey, which was destroyed after being stricken by the plague. Slaying this poor creature put an end to many centuries of suffering.

GOLD	200
EXP	680

NORMAL ITEM	Gold rosary
RARE ITEM	N/A
REGIONS	Ruined Abbey

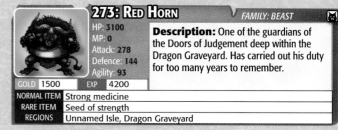

273: RED HORN
FAMILY: BEAST

HP: 3100
MP: 0
Attack: 278
Defence: 144
Agility: 93

Description: One of the guardians of the Doors of Judgement deep within the Dragon Graveyard. Has carried out his duty for too many years to remember.

GOLD	1500
EXP	4200

NORMAL ITEM	Strong medicine
RARE ITEM	Seed of strength
REGIONS	Unnamed Isle, Dragon Graveyard

264: TRAP BOX
FAMILY: MATERIAL

HP: 1100
MP: 255
Attack: 92
Defence: 60
Agility: 50

Description: A monster that carries the precious Venus' tear in its mouth. Its guiding motivation appears to be its obsession with priceless jewels and treasures.

GOLD	660
EXP	1020

NORMAL ITEM	Venus' tear
RARE ITEM	N/A
REGIONS	Swordsman's Labyrinth

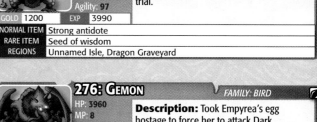

274: BLUE FANG
FAMILY: BEAST

HP: 2630
MP: 16
Attack: 243
Defence: 173
Agility: 97

Description: One of the guardians of the Dragon Graveyard. Attacks candidates to test their worthiness to undertake the trial.

GOLD	1200
EXP	3990

NORMAL ITEM	Strong antidote
RARE ITEM	Seed of wisdom
REGIONS	Unnamed Isle, Dragon Graveyard

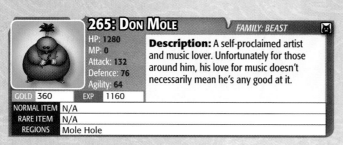

265: DON MOLE
FAMILY: BEAST

HP: 1280
MP: 0
Attack: 132
Defence: 76
Agility: 64

Description: A self-proclaimed artist and music lover. Unfortunately for those around him, his love for music doesn't necessarily mean he's any good at it.

GOLD	360
EXP	1160

NORMAL ITEM	N/A
RARE ITEM	N/A
REGIONS	Mole Hole

276: GEMON
FAMILY: BIRD

HP: 3960
MP: 8
Attack: 328
Defence: 152
Agility: 99

Description: Took Empyrea's egg hostage to force her to attack Dark Empycchu.

GOLD	0
EXP	8600

NORMAL ITEM	Seed of skill
RARE ITEM	N/A
REGIONS	World of Darkness

266: SOUL MOLE
FAMILY: BEAST

HP: 88
MP: 0
Attack: 80
Defence: 80
Agility: 55

Description: Don Mole's loyal henchmen. Willing to endure anything for their boss… Except listening to his music, that is.

GOLD	16
EXP	68

NORMAL ITEM	N/A
RARE ITEM	N/A
REGIONS	Mole Hole

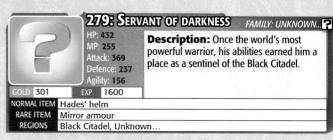

279: SERVANT OF DARKNESS
FAMILY: UNKNOWN…

HP: 432
MP: 255
Attack: 369
Defence: 237
Agility: 156

Description: Once the world's most powerful warrior, his abilities earned him a place as a sentinel of the Black Citadel.

GOLD	301
EXP	1600

NORMAL ITEM	Hades' helm
RARE ITEM	Mirror armour
REGIONS	Black Citadel, Unknown…

267: ARGON LIZARD
FAMILY: DRAGON

HP: 472
MP: 0
Attack: 168
Defence: 155
Agility: 90

Description: Long hunted for their precious Argon hearts, these monsters run at the first sight of humans.

GOLD	102
EXP	650

NORMAL ITEM	Argon heart
RARE ITEM	N/A
REGIONS	Royal Hunting Ground

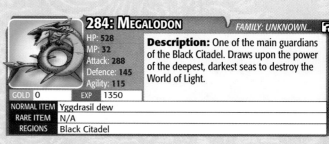

284: MEGALODON
FAMILY: UNKNOWN…

HP: 528
MP: 32
Attack: 288
Defence: 145
Agility: 115

Description: One of the main guardians of the Black Citadel. Draws upon the power of the deepest, darkest seas to destroy the World of Light.

GOLD	0
EXP	1350

NORMAL ITEM	Yggdrasil dew
RARE ITEM	N/A
REGIONS	Black Citadel

268: GREAT ARGON LIZARD
FAMILY: DRAGON

HP: 1390
MP: 0
Attack: 195
Defence: 160
Agility: 54

Description: The largest and most impressive Argon lizard. Its Argon heart is said to be pretty huge!

GOLD	520
EXP	2830

NORMAL ITEM	Great big Argon heart
RARE ITEM	N/A
REGIONS	Royal Hunting Ground

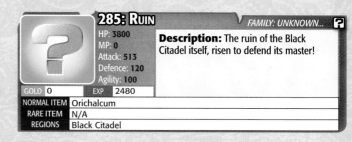

285: RUIN
FAMILY: UNKNOWN…

HP: 3800
MP: 0
Attack: 513
Defence: 120
Agility: 100

Description: The ruin of the Black Citadel itself, risen to defend its master!

GOLD	0
EXP	2480

NORMAL ITEM	Orichalcum
RARE ITEM	N/A
REGIONS	Black Citadel

Here are all the monsters you can find, recruit, and add to your Monster Arena teams. Consider the following when putting together a team:

Many monsters have stats that are not fixed because they rise along with the level of your party leader. Note that these stats reflect the stats they will bring to your team; many Team Monsters have higher stats when they fight your party during the scouting process.

Turns in combat is only relevant when you use the Call Team command in a normal battle. Add together the Turns in Combat field for all three numbers, then round off to the nearest whole number. This determines how long your team will stay on the field. The wait extra turn team bonus adds 1 to this number.

The Teams are special monster teams to which the monster belongs. See the "Special Monster Teams" chapter to find out what other monsters are needed to fill out the team and unlock the bonuses.

BESTIARY

Infamous Monsters

ARCHER

TITLE: SHARPSHOOTER
SPECIES: BODKIN BOWYER
FAMILY: HUMANOID

HP: 88-193
MP: 15-32
Attack: 58-154
Defence: 50-190
Agility: 38-231
Turns in Combat: 0.7

GOLD	17	EXP	46
MONSTER COIN	Copper		
TEAM	The Angry Archers		
DEATHMOVE	Harrowing Arrow		
TEAM BONUSES	Team Max HP +15		
TEAM	Not Quite Human		
DEATHMOVE	N/A		
TEAM BONUSES	Team Max HP +15		
LOCATION	Kingdom of Ascantha	CONDITION	None

Comments: Sharpshooter a.k.a. Archer has a more useful selection of attacks than its kin, including Snooze spells and the Multishot ability. However, it is still hampered by low HP.

ARCHFIEND

TITLE: ARCH-ARCHDEMON
SPECIES: ARCHDEMON
FAMILY: DEMON

HP: 926
MP: 38-74
Attack: 304-335
Defence: 132-168
Agility: 102-190
Turns in Combat: 0.9

GOLD	31	EXP	466
MONSTER COIN	Gold		
TEAM	Far From Heaven		
DEATHMOVE	N/A		
TEAM BONUSES	Wait Extra Turn		
LOCATION	Untrodden Groves	CONDITION	None

Comments: Arch-archdemon a.k.a. Archfiend has 926 HP, a high attack score, and the useful Kaboom spell (as well as Insulatle). It doesn't play well with other monsters, but is a great addition to any team.

ARGES

TITLE: BIG BLUE BULLY
SPECIES: CYCLOPS
FAMILY: DEMON

HP: 671-760
MP: 0
Attack: 238-255
Defence: 112-124
Agility: 94-159
Turns in Combat: 0.9

GOLD	66	EXP	346
MONSTER COIN	Silver		
TEAM	Club Club		
DEATHMOVE	Mind Breaker		
TEAM BONUSES	N/A		
TEAM	Far From Heaven		
DEATHMOVE	N/A		
TEAM BONUSES	Wait Extra Turn		
LOCATION	Untrodden Groves in Areas Accessible By Air	CONDITION	None

Comments: Big Blue Bully a.k.a. Arges is a heavy hitter with a lot of HP, but it's a bit below the power curve by the time you can scout it. Brontes, for example, is a very similar monster that has better stats and works in a larger combination of teams.

BIG AL

TITLE: AL GEE
SPECIES: KING KELP
FAMILY: AQUATIC

HP: 226-327
MP: 16-22
Attack: 126-203
Defence: 89-113
Agility: 72-183
Turns in Combat: 1

GOLD	33	EXP	181
MONSTER COIN	Copper		
TEAM	The Psyche Wards		
DEATHMOVE	Tension Boost		
TEAM BONUSES	N/A		
TEAM	The Aqua Marines		
DEATHMOVE	N/A		
TEAM BONUSES	Team Defence +30		
LOCATION	E Argonia	CONDITION	None

Comments: Al Gee a.k.a. Big Al's Silly Song only hits one target. He also suffers from a lack of defence, although he can shore up this weakness to some extent with his Midheal spell.

BLADEWOLF

TITLE: LOOPY LUPUS
SPECIES: JUMPING JACKAL
FAMILY: BEAST

HP: 441-541
MP: 0
Attack: 208-278
Defence: 101-238
Agility: 90-168
Turns in Combat: 1.2

GOLD	43	EXP	216
MONSTER COIN	Silver		
TEAM	Just Beastly		
DEATHMOVE	N/A		
TEAM BONUSES	Team Attack +15		
LOCATION	Uncharted Isle on the southwest part of the world map	CONDITION	After defeating Monster Arena Rank D

Comments: Loopy Lupus a.k.a. Bladewolf will add some offensive mights to any mid-level team with its powerful and consistent attacks. But first you must find it; it prowls around on a small island that doesn't even appear on the world map!

BLIZAG JR.

TITLE: COLD FIRE
SPECIES: FROSTBURN
FAMILY: ELEMENTAL

HP: 199-223
MP: 12-16
Attack: 118-190
Defence: 82-155
Agility: 93-134
Turns in Combat: 0.8

GOLD	63	EXP	224
MONSTER COIN	Copper		
TEAM	Demented Elements		
DEATHMOVE	Elemental Storm		
TEAM BONUSES	N/A		
LOCATION	Blizzard Peaks	CONDITION	None

Comments: Cold Fire a.k.a. Blizag Jr. can be a dangerous monster to scout, because it can use the Thwack spell to score instant-kills. Thwack can work in the Monster Arena too, but it is less effective because it can only target one enemy at a time.

BONES

TITLE: OLD SOLDIER
SPECIES: SKELETON
FAMILY: ZOMBIE

HP: 271
MP: 10-29
Attack: 148-187
Defence: 81-208
Agility: 90-217
Turns in Combat: 0.6

GOLD	26	EXP	173
MONSTER COIN	Copper		
TEAM	The Blade Runners		
DEATHMOVE	Triple Swords		
TEAM BONUSES	N/A		
TEAM	The Zombebops		
DEATHMOVE	N/A		
TEAM BONUSES	Team Max HP +30		
LOCATION	Northwest Isle	CONDITION	None

Comments: Old Soldier a.k.a. Bones is a decent warrior that alternates between sword strikes and casting Kasap. If you're looking for a third swordsman, Bones will fit the bill. When fighting solo, though, Bones has too few HP to last.

BRICKMAN

TITLE: BRICKLAYER
SPECIES: GOLEM
FAMILY: MATERIAL

HP: 260-743
MP: 0
Attack: 132-297
Defence: 89-302
Agility: 37-165
Turns in Combat: 0.7

Comments: Bricklayer a.k.a. Brickman is unique among the Golems, as its stats don't increase like the others. Like the other Golems, Brickman is a solid attacker and a key part of the all-Golem team, but it will spend some of its turns psyching up instead of attacking.

GOLD	55	EXP	275
MONSTER COIN	Silver		
TEAM	My Three Golems		
DEATHMOVE	The Golemator		
TEAM BONUSES	N/A		
TEAM	Materialistic		
DEATHMOVE	N/A		
TEAM BONUSES	Wait Extra Turn		
LOCATION	Maella Region	CONDITION	None

BRONTES

TITLE: GIGANTES GUARDSMAN
SPECIES: GIGANTES
FAMILY: DEMON

HP: 764-864
MP: 0
Attack: 274-282
Defence: 141-166
Agility: 88-99
Turns in Combat: 1

Comments: Gigantes Guardsman a.k.a. Brontes is a top-class monster that delivers consistently powerful attacks. Like Steropes, its partner in team Two Eyes, Brontes is a bit of a marshmallow with lots of HP but only average defence.

GOLD	75	EXP	381
MONSTER COIN	Gold		
TEAM	Two Eyes		
DEATHMOVE	Sapper Slappers		
TEAM BONUSES	Wait Extra Turn		
TEAM	Club Club	TEAM	Far From Heaven
DEATHMOVE	Mind Breaker	DEATHMOVE	N/A
TEAM BONUSES	N/A	TEAM BONUSES	Wait Extra Turn
LOCATION	Isolated Plateau	CONDITION	Day only

BUSH-W.

TITLE: BUSHWHACKER
SPECIES: BERSERKER
FAMILY: HUMANOID

HP: 563-611
MP: 0
Attack: 189-232
Defence: 138-176
Agility: 100-240
Turns in Combat: 0.9

Comments: Bushwhacker a.k.a. Bush-W. is a powerful, quick, and reliable attacker. Bush-W. is also a particularly good choice in combination with other axe-wielding monsters.

GOLD	83	EXP	326
MONSTER COIN	Silver		
TEAM	The Hackers		
DEATHMOVE	Typhoeus' Maul		
TEAM BONUSES	N/A		
TEAM	Not Quite Human		
DEATHMOVE	N/A		
TEAM BONUSES	Team Max HP +15		
LOCATION	Kingdom of Ascantha on small isle	CONDITION	None

CAPERS

TITLE: FANTOM OF CHOPERA
SPECIES: PHANTOM FENCER
FAMILY: ZOMBIE

HP: 281-665
MP: 0
Attack: 196-303
Defence: 83-205
Agility: 90-227
Turns in Combat: 1

Comments: Fantom of Chopera a.k.a. Capers is a deadly attacker that can be scouted early in the game. It attacks reliably, often using a sword attack that causes good damage. As a sword-wielding, zombie/nocturnal creature, it fits into three special teams.

GOLD	Team	EXP	Max
MONSTER COIN	HP +30		
TEAM			
DEATHMOVE	Team Goodnight		
TEAM BONUSES	Dirge		
TEAM	N/A	TEAM	N/A
DEATHMOVE	The Blade Runners	DEATHMOVE	The Zombebops
TEAM BONUSES	Triple Swords	TEAM BONUSES	N/A
LOCATION	Kingdom of Ascantha	CONDITION	Night only; appears after beating Monster Arena Rank F

CLIO

TITLE: COLOSSAL CLIONE
SPECIES: SEE ANGEL
FAMILY: AQUATIC

HP: 131-284
MP: 48-89
Attack: 36-50
Defence: 83-131
Agility: 163-233
Turns in Combat: 0.6

Comments: With recovery spells like Zing and Multiheal and a naturally high agility (further boosted by Acceleratle), Colossal Clione a.k.a. Clio can be a very effective healer. However, this monster doesn't have enough HP to survive for long in any Monster Arena battles beyond the first few ranks.

GOLD	40	EXP	120
MONSTER COIN	Silver		
TEAM	The Aqua Marines		
DEATHMOVE	N/A		
TEAM BONUSES	Team Defence +30		
LOCATION	Unnamed Isle	CONDITION	None

COWBOY

TITLE: BUFFALO BILL
SPECIES: BULLFINCH
FAMILY: BEAST

HP: 181-764
MP: 0
Attack: 61-196
Defence: 21-124
Agility: 20-195
Turns in Combat: 0.8

Comments: Buffalo Bill a.k.a. Cowboy is a simple and straightforward attacker. Its attacks grow significantly along with your Hero's level, but they'll always be at the low end of the scale.

GOLD	21	EXP	42
MONSTER COIN	Copper		
TEAM	Just Beastly		
DEATHMOVE	N/A		
TEAM BONUSES	Team Attack +15		
LOCATION	Alexandria Region	CONDITION	None

CURER

TITLE: ANGEL OF CURING
SPECIES: CURESLIME
FAMILY: SLIME

HP: 369-384
MP: 32-47
Attack: 76-95
Defence: 128-188
Agility: 93-229
Turns in Combat: 1.2

Comments: Angel of Curing a.k.a. Curer is an enhanced version of Healer who uses Fullheal and Multiheal instead of the weaker versions. It is quite resilient for a healer, and can function well solo or in a wide variety of teams with Healer and other slimes.

GOLD	72	EXP	309
MONSTER COIN	Silver		
TEAM	Slime Therapy		
DEATHMOVE	Multiheal		
TEAM BONUSES	Team Max HP x2		
TEAM	Trauma Centre	TEAM	Wizards o' Z
DEATHMOVE	Omniheal	DEATHMOVE	Zingslinger
TEAM BONUSES	Team Max HP x2	TEAM BONUSES	Team Max HP x2
TEAM	The King and Us	TEAM	Slime Power
DEATHMOVE	Maximaster	DEATHMOVE	N/A
TEAM BONUSES	Team Max HP x2	TEAM BONUSES	Team Max HP x2
LOCATION	Two areas in Arcadia Region	CONDITION	After defeating Monster Arena Rank F

CYBOT

TITLE: ATTACK BOT MK II
SPECIES: KILLING MACHINE
FAMILY: MACHINE

HP: 525-635
MP: 0
Attack: 210-250
Defence: 175-275
Agility: 125-225
Turns in Combat: 1.2

Comments: Attack Bot Mk II a.k.a. Cybot is virtually identical to Roborg, but with slightly better stats. Still, if one Killing Machine is good, two are better, and three are nearly unstoppable!

GOLD	121	EXP	336
MONSTER COIN	Silver		
TEAM	The Blade Runners		
DEATHMOVE	Triple Swords		
TEAM BONUSES	N/A		
TEAM	Clank and Spank	TEAM	Triple Trouble
DEATHMOVE	Metal Panic	DEATHMOVE	Stream Killer Attack
TEAM BONUSES	N/A	TEAM BONUSES	N/A
LOCATION	Blizzard Peaks	CONDITION	After defeating Monster Arena Rank D

DEADNOBLE

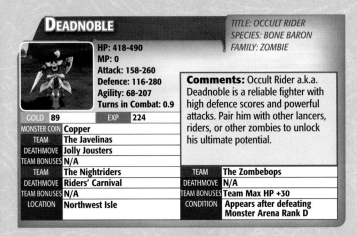

TITLE: OCCULT RIDER
SPECIES: BONE BARON
FAMILY: ZOMBIE

HP: 418-490
MP: 0
Attack: 158-260
Defence: 116-280
Agility: 68-207
Turns in Combat: 0.9

GOLD	89	EXP	224
MONSTER COIN	Copper		
TEAM	The Javelinas		
DEATHMOVE	Jolly Jousters		
TEAM BONUSES	N/A		
TEAM	The Nightriders		
DEATHMOVE	Riders' Carnival		
TEAM BONUSES	N/A		
LOCATION	Northwest Isle		

TEAM	The Zombebops
DEATHMOVE	N/A
TEAM BONUSES	Team Max HP +30
CONDITION	Appears after defeating Monster Arena Rank D

Comments: Occult Rider a.k.a. Deadnoble is a reliable fighter with high defence scores and powerful attacks. Pair him with other lancers, riders, or other zombies to unlock his ultimate potential.

DOLLDRUMS

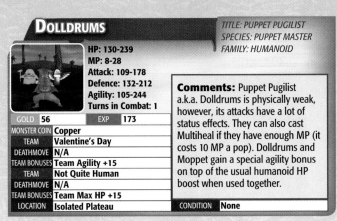

TITLE: PUPPET PUGILIST
SPECIES: PUPPET MASTER
FAMILY: HUMANOID

HP: 130-239
MP: 8-28
Attack: 109-178
Defence: 132-212
Agility: 105-244
Turns in Combat: 1

GOLD	56	EXP	173
MONSTER COIN	Copper		
TEAM	Valentine's Day		
DEATHMOVE	N/A		
TEAM BONUSES	Team Agility +15		
TEAM	Not Quite Human		
DEATHMOVE	N/A		
TEAM BONUSES	Team Max HP +15		
LOCATION	Isolated Plateau	CONDITION	None

Comments: Puppet Pugilist a.k.a. Dolldrums is physically weak, however, its attacks have a lot of status effects. They can also cast Multiheal if they have enough MP (it costs 10 MP a pop). Dolldrums and Moppet gain a special agility bonus on top of the usual humanoid HP boost when used together.

DOUG

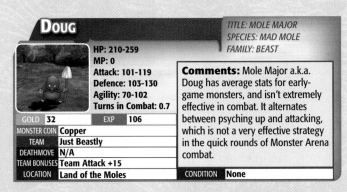

TITLE: MOLE MAJOR
SPECIES: MAD MOLE
FAMILY: BEAST

HP: 210-259
MP: 0
Attack: 101-119
Defence: 103-130
Agility: 70-102
Turns in Combat: 0.7

GOLD	32	EXP	106
MONSTER COIN	Copper		
TEAM	Just Beastly		
DEATHMOVE	N/A		
TEAM BONUSES	Team Attack +15		
LOCATION	Land of the Moles	CONDITION	None

Comments: Mole Major a.k.a. Doug has average stats for early-game monsters, and isn't extremely effective in combat. It alternates between psyching up and attacking, which is not a very effective strategy in the quick rounds of Monster Arena combat.

DUMBKING

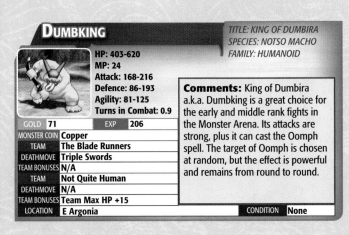

TITLE: KING OF DUMBIRA
SPECIES: NOTSO MACHO
FAMILY: HUMANOID

HP: 403-620
MP: 24
Attack: 168-216
Defence: 86-193
Agility: 81-125
Turns in Combat: 0.9

GOLD	71	EXP	206
MONSTER COIN	Copper		
TEAM	The Blade Runners		
DEATHMOVE	Triple Swords		
TEAM BONUSES	N/A		
TEAM	Not Quite Human		
DEATHMOVE	N/A		
TEAM BONUSES	Team Max HP +15		
LOCATION	E Argonia	CONDITION	None

Comments: King of Dumbira a.k.a. Dumbking is a great choice for the early and middle rank fights in the Monster Arena. Its attacks are strong, plus it can cast the Oomph spell. The target of Oomph is chosen at random, but the effect is powerful and remains from round to round.

FAT CAT

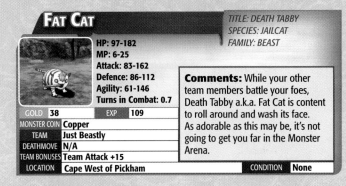

TITLE: DEATH TABBY
SPECIES: JAILCAT
FAMILY: BEAST

HP: 97-182
MP: 6-25
Attack: 83-162
Defence: 86-112
Agility: 61-146
Turns in Combat: 0.7

GOLD	38	EXP	109
MONSTER COIN	Copper		
TEAM	Just Beastly		
DEATHMOVE	N/A		
TEAM BONUSES	Team Attack +15		
LOCATION	Cape West of Pickham	CONDITION	None

Comments: While your other team members battle your foes, Death Tabby a.k.a. Fat Cat is content to roll around and wash its face. As adorable as this may be, it's not going to get you far in the Monster Arena.

FAUNUS

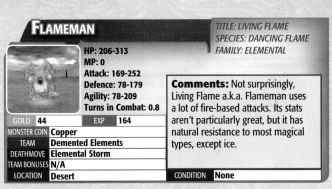

TITLE: FERTILISER
SPECIES: SILENUS
FAMILY: HUMANOID

HP: 252-329
MP: 0
Attack: 116-142
Defence: 99-182
Agility: 76-124
Turns in Combat: 0.8

GOLD	66	EXP	136
MONSTER COIN	Copper		
TEAM	The Fatal Attraction		
DEATHMOVE	Love Typhoon		
TEAM BONUSES	N/A		
TEAM	Not Quite Human		
DEATHMOVE	N/A		
TEAM BONUSES	Team Max HP +15		
LOCATION	Baccarat Region	CONDITION	None

Comments: When you add Fertiliser a.k.a. Faunus to your team, you get its entire flock of sheep to boot. The Counting Sheep attack can put enemy parties to sleep, while Sheep Call can inflict heavy damage (regardless of enemy defence) to a target. Faunus is a decent early-game choice.

FLAMEMAN

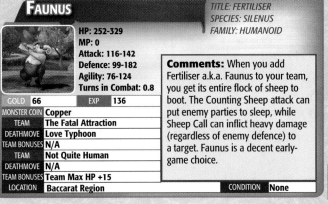

TITLE: LIVING FLAME
SPECIES: DANCING FLAME
FAMILY: ELEMENTAL

HP: 206-313
MP: 0
Attack: 169-252
Defence: 78-179
Agility: 78-209
Turns in Combat: 0.8

GOLD	44	EXP	164
MONSTER COIN	Copper		
TEAM	Demented Elements		
DEATHMOVE	Elemental Storm		
TEAM BONUSES	N/A		
LOCATION	Desert	CONDITION	None

Comments: Not surprisingly, Living Flame a.k.a. Flameman uses a lot of fire-based attacks. Its stats aren't particularly great, but it has natural resistance to most magical types, except ice.

FLETCH

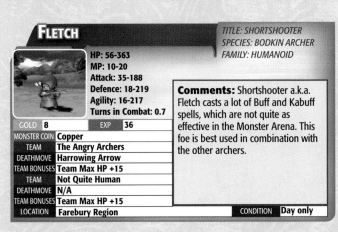

TITLE: SHORTSHOOTER
SPECIES: BODKIN ARCHER
FAMILY: HUMANOID

HP: 56-363
MP: 10-20
Attack: 35-188
Defence: 18-219
Agility: 16-217
Turns in Combat: 0.7

GOLD	8	EXP	36
MONSTER COIN	Copper		
TEAM	The Angry Archers		
DEATHMOVE	Harrowing Arrow		
TEAM BONUSES	Team Max HP +15		
TEAM	Not Quite Human		
DEATHMOVE	N/A		
TEAM BONUSES	Team Max HP +15		
LOCATION	Farebury Region	CONDITION	Day only

Comments: Shortshooter a.k.a. Fletch casts a lot of Buff and Kabuff spells, which are not quite as effective in the Monster Arena. This foe is best used in combination with the other archers.

FOUL FOWL

TITLE: RAGING ROOSTER
SPECIES: FOWLFIGHTER
FAMILY: BIRD

HP: 381
MP: 0
Attack: 143
Defence: 116
Agility: 64-115
Turns in Combat: 1.1

GOLD	33		EXP	181
MONSTER COIN	Copper			
TEAM	The Blade Runners			
DEATHMOVE	Triple Swords			
TEAM BONUSES	N/A			
TEAM	The Avian Attackers			
DEATHMOVE	N/A			
TEAM BONUSES	Team Agility +30			
LOCATION	Baccarat Region			

Comments: There is nothing exceptional about Raging Rooster a.k.a. Foul Fowl, except perhaps the ease with which you can find and capture it. This is a fine choice for filling out the third sword-wielder slot in your version of the Blade Runners team.

CONDITION	Day only

GOLDMAN

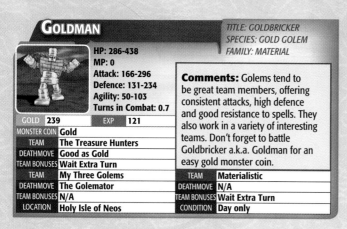

TITLE: GOLDBRICKER
SPECIES: GOLD GOLEM
FAMILY: MATERIAL

HP: 286-438
MP: 0
Attack: 166-296
Defence: 131-234
Agility: 50-103
Turns in Combat: 0.7

GOLD	239		EXP	121
MONSTER COIN	Gold			
TEAM	The Treasure Hunters			
DEATHMOVE	Good as Gold			
TEAM BONUSES	Wait Extra Turn			
TEAM	My Three Golems		TEAM	Materialistic
DEATHMOVE	The Golemator		DEATHMOVE	N/A
TEAM BONUSES	N/A		TEAM BONUSES	Wait Extra Turn
LOCATION	Holy Isle of Neos		CONDITION	Day only

Comments: Golems tend to be great team members, offering consistent attacks, high defence and good resistance to spells. They also work in a variety of interesting teams. Don't forget to battle Goldbricker a.k.a. Goldman for an easy gold monster coin.

HACKZILLA

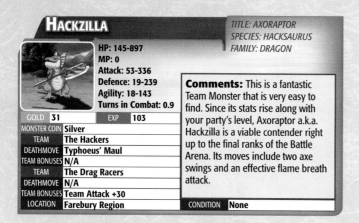

TITLE: AXORAPTOR
SPECIES: HACKSAURUS
FAMILY: DRAGON

HP: 145-897
MP: 0
Attack: 53-336
Defence: 19-239
Agility: 18-143
Turns in Combat: 0.9

GOLD	31		EXP	103
MONSTER COIN	Silver			
TEAM	The Hackers			
DEATHMOVE	Typhoeus' Maul			
TEAM BONUSES	N/A			
TEAM	The Drag Racers			
DEATHMOVE	N/A			
TEAM BONUSES	Team Attack +30			
LOCATION	Farebury Region		CONDITION	None

Comments: This is a fantastic Team Monster that is very easy to find. Since its stats rise along with your party's level, Axoraptor a.k.a. Hackzilla is a viable contender right up to the final ranks of the Battle Arena. Its moves include two axe swings and an effective flame breath attack.

HAZEL

TITLE: FEMME FATALE
SPECIES: WITCH
FAMILY: DEMON

HP: 268-296
MP: 47-64
Attack: 65-71
Defence: 102-120
Agility: 104-132
Turns in Combat: 0.9

GOLD	68		EXP	188
MONSTER COIN	Copper			
TEAM	The Fatal Attraction			
DEATHMOVE	Love Typhoon			
TEAM BONUSES	N/A			
TEAM	The Psyche Wards		TEAM	Far From Heaven
DEATHMOVE	Tension Boost		DEATHMOVE	N/A
TEAM BONUSES	N/A		TEAM BONUSES	Wait Extra Turn
LOCATION	Pickham Region		CONDITION	After defeating Monster Arena Rank F

Comments: Femme Fatale a.k.a. Hazel has a wide variety of moves to utilize. Its ability to raise itself to max tension is great, but not when it's followed by Puff-Puff, Fizzle, or some other non-attack move. Hazel does complete several interesting teams, however.

HEALER

TITLE: FAMILY DOCTOR
SPECIES: HEALSLIME
FAMILY: SLIME

HP: 48-245
MP: 12-95
Attack: 27-152
Defence: 26-248
Agility: 20-242
Turns in Combat: 1.3

GOLD	26		EXP	44
MONSTER COIN	Copper			
TEAM	Slime Therapy			
DEATHMOVE	Multiheal			
TEAM BONUSES	Team Max HP x2			
TEAM	Trauma Centre		TEAM	Wizards o' Z
DEATHMOVE	Multiheal, Omniheal		DEATHMOVE	Zingslinger
TEAM BONUSES	Team Max HP x2		TEAM BONUSES	Team Max HP x2
TEAM	The King and Us		TEAM	Slime Power
DEATHMOVE	Maximaster		DEATHMOVE	N/A
TEAM BONUSES	Team Max HP x2		TEAM BONUSES	Team Max HP x2
LOCATION	Alexandria Region		CONDITION	None

Comments: As the name implies, Family Doctor a.k.a. Healer is primarily a healer that will cast Heal or Midheal as often as it attacks. When combined with other slimes, its healing abilities can become supercharged and many of them affect your party.

HOODWINK

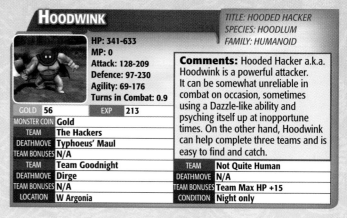

TITLE: HOODED HACKER
SPECIES: HOODLUM
FAMILY: HUMANOID

HP: 341-633
MP: 0
Attack: 128-209
Defence: 97-230
Agility: 69-176
Turns in Combat: 0.9

GOLD	56		EXP	213
MONSTER COIN	Gold			
TEAM	The Hackers			
DEATHMOVE	Typhoeus' Maul			
TEAM BONUSES	N/A			
TEAM	Team Goodnight		TEAM	Not Quite Human
DEATHMOVE	Dirge		DEATHMOVE	N/A
TEAM BONUSES	N/A		TEAM BONUSES	Team Max HP +15
LOCATION	W Argonia		CONDITION	Night only

Comments: Hooded Hacker a.k.a. Hoodwink is a powerful attacker. It can be somewhat unreliable in combat on occasion, sometimes using a Dazzle-like ability and psyching itself up at inopportune times. On the other hand, Hoodwink can help complete three teams and is easy to find and catch.

HORI

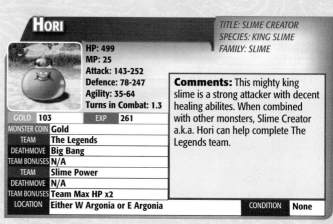

TITLE: SLIME CREATOR
SPECIES: KING SLIME
FAMILY: SLIME

HP: 499
MP: 25
Attack: 143-252
Defence: 78-247
Agility: 35-64
Turns in Combat: 1.3

GOLD	103		EXP	261
MONSTER COIN	Gold			
TEAM	The Legends			
DEATHMOVE	Big Bang			
TEAM BONUSES	N/A			
TEAM	Slime Power			
DEATHMOVE	N/A			
TEAM BONUSES	Team Max HP x2			
LOCATION	Either W Argonia or E Argonia		CONDITION	None

Comments: This mighty king slime is a strong attacker with decent healing abilites. When combined with other monsters, Slime Creator a.k.a. Hori can help complete The Legends team.

HORK

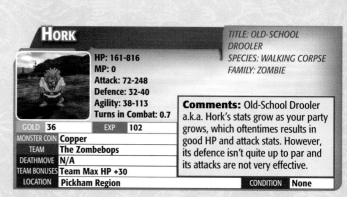

TITLE: OLD-SCHOOL DROOLER
SPECIES: WALKING CORPSE
FAMILY: ZOMBIE

HP: 161-816
MP: 0
Attack: 72-248
Defence: 32-40
Agility: 38-113
Turns in Combat: 0.7

GOLD	36		EXP	102
MONSTER COIN	Copper			
TEAM	The Zombebops			
DEATHMOVE	N/A			
TEAM BONUSES	Team Max HP +30			
LOCATION	Pickham Region		CONDITION	None

Comments: Old-School Drooler a.k.a. Hork's stats grow as your party grows, which oftentimes results in good HP and attack stats. However, its defence isn't quite up to par and its attacks are not very effective.

JACK FROST

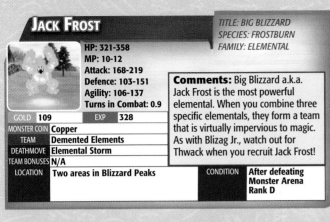

TITLE: BIG BLIZZARD
SPECIES: FROSTBURN
FAMILY: ELEMENTAL

HP: 321-358
MP: 10-12
Attack: 168-219
Defence: 103-151
Agility: 106-137
Turns in Combat: 0.9

GOLD	109	EXP	328
MONSTER COIN	Copper		
TEAM	Demented Elements		
DEATHMOVE	Elemental Storm		
TEAM BONUSES	N/A		
LOCATION	Two areas in Blizzard Peaks	CONDITION	After defeating Monster Arena Rank D

Comments: Big Blizzard a.k.a. Jack Frost is the most powerful elemental. When you combine three specific elementals, they form a team that is virtually impervious to magic. As with Blizag Jr., watch out for Thwack when you recruit Jack Frost!

JEWELBAG

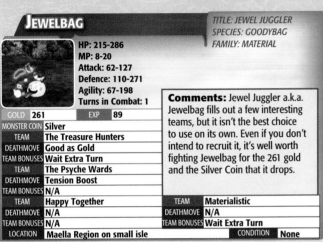

TITLE: JEWEL JUGGLER
SPECIES: GOODYBAG
FAMILY: MATERIAL

HP: 215-286
MP: 8-20
Attack: 62-127
Defence: 110-271
Agility: 67-198
Turns in Combat: 1

GOLD	261	EXP	89
MONSTER COIN	Silver		
TEAM	The Treasure Hunters		
DEATHMOVE	Good as Gold		
TEAM BONUSES	Wait Extra Turn		
TEAM	The Psyche Wards		
DEATHMOVE	Tension Boost		
TEAM BONUSES	N/A		
TEAM	Happy Together	TEAM	Materialistic
DEATHMOVE	N/A	DEATHMOVE	N/A
TEAM BONUSES	N/A	TEAM BONUSES	Wait Extra Turn
LOCATION	Maella Region on small isle	CONDITION	None

Comments: Jewel Juggler a.k.a. Jewelbag fills out a few interesting teams, but it isn't the best choice to use on its own. Even if you don't intend to recruit it, it's well worth fighting Jewelbag for the 261 gold and the Silver Coin that it drops.

JOCKEY

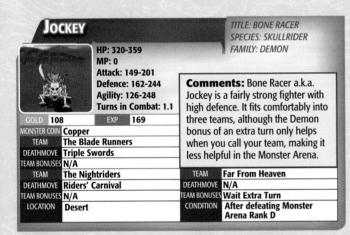

TITLE: BONE RACER
SPECIES: SKULLRIDER
FAMILY: DEMON

HP: 320-359
MP: 0
Attack: 149-201
Defence: 162-244
Agility: 126-248
Turns in Combat: 1.1

GOLD	108	EXP	169
MONSTER COIN	Copper		
TEAM	The Blade Runners		
DEATHMOVE	Triple Swords		
TEAM BONUSES	N/A		
TEAM	The Nightriders	TEAM	Far From Heaven
DEATHMOVE	Riders' Carnival	DEATHMOVE	N/A
TEAM BONUSES	N/A	TEAM BONUSES	Wait Extra Turn
LOCATION	Desert	CONDITION	After defeating Monster Arena Rank D

Comments: Bone Racer a.k.a. Jockey is a fairly strong fighter with high defence. It fits comfortably into three teams, although the Demon bonus of an extra turn only helps when you call your team, making it less helpful in the Monster Arena.

KLUB KONG

TITLE: ABOMINABLE APE
SPECIES: GORERILLA
FAMILY: BEAST

HP: 162-349
MP: 0
Attack: 109-267
Defence: 53-211
Agility: 81-150
Turns in Combat: 0.9

GOLD	22	EXP	128
MONSTER COIN	Copper		
TEAM	Club Club		
DEATHMOVE	Mind Breaker		
TEAM BONUSES	N/A		
TEAM	Just Beastly		
DEATHMOVE	N/A		
TEAM BONUSES	Team Attack +15		
LOCATION	Baccarat Region	CONDITION	None

Comments: Abominable Ape a.k.a. Klub Kong has some very strong attacks, but occasionally wastes a turn doing nothing or using a power attack that frequently misses.

LONELY JOE

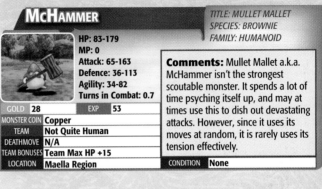

TITLE: HOLLOW KNIGHT
SPECIES: RESTLESS ARMOUR
FAMILY: MATERIAL

HP: 78-266
MP: 0
Attack: 71-328
Defence: 37-262
Agility: 29-153
Turns in Combat: 0.9

GOLD	34	EXP	56
MONSTER COIN	Copper	
TEAM	The Blade Runners	
DEATHMOVE	Triple Swords	
TEAM BONUSES	Materialistic	
DEATHMOVE	N/A	
TEAM BONUSES	Wait Extra Turn	
LOCATION	Maella Region	CONDITION	None

Comments:
If your party is at a high enough level when you begin to pursue the Monster Arena side quest, Hollow Knight a.k.a. Lonely Joe can be a potent fighter. It's one member of your starting party that you may not need to replace for the first couple of Monster Arena rank fights.

McHAMMER

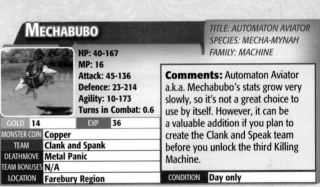

TITLE: MULLET MALLET
SPECIES: BROWNIE
FAMILY: HUMANOID

HP: 83-179
MP: 0
Attack: 65-163
Defence: 36-113
Agility: 34-82
Turns in Combat: 0.7

GOLD	28	EXP	53
MONSTER COIN	Copper	
TEAM	Not Quite Human	
DEATHMOVE	N/A	
TEAM BONUSES	Team Max HP +15	
LOCATION	Maella Region	CONDITION	None

Comments: Mullet Mallet a.k.a. McHammer isn't the strongest scoutable monster. It spends a lot of time psyching itself up, and may at times use this to dish out devastating attacks. However, since it uses its moves at random, it is rarely uses its tension effectively.

MECHABUBO

TITLE: AUTOMATON AVIATOR
SPECIES: MECHA-MYNAH
FAMILY: MACHINE

HP: 40-167
MP: 16
Attack: 45-136
Defence: 23-214
Agility: 10-173
Turns in Combat: 0.6

GOLD	14	EXP	36
MONSTER COIN	Copper	
TEAM	Clank and Spank	
DEATHMOVE	Metal Panic	
TEAM BONUSES	N/A	
LOCATION	Farebury Region	CONDITION	Day only

Comments: Automaton Aviator a.k.a. Mechabubo's stats grow very slowly, so it's not a great choice to use by itself. However, it can be a valuable addition if you plan to create the Clank and Speak team before you unlock the third Killing Machine.

METABBLE

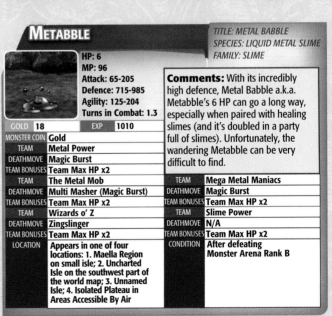

TITLE: METAL BABBLE
SPECIES: LIQUID METAL SLIME
FAMILY: SLIME

HP: 6
MP: 96
Attack: 65-205
Defence: 715-985
Agility: 125-204
Turns in Combat: 1.3

GOLD	18	EXP	1010
MONSTER COIN	Gold			
TEAM	Metal Power			
DEATHMOVE	Magic Burst			
TEAM BONUSES	Team Max HP x2			
TEAM	The Metal Mob		TEAM	Mega Metal Maniacs
DEATHMOVE	Multi Masher (Magic Burst)		DEATHMOVE	Magic Burst
TEAM BONUSES	Team Max HP x2		TEAM BONUSES	Team Max HP x2
TEAM	Wizards o' Z		TEAM	Slime Power
DEATHMOVE	Zingslinger		DEATHMOVE	N/A
TEAM BONUSES	Team Max HP x2		TEAM BONUSES	Team Max HP x2
LOCATION	Appears in one of four locations: 1. Maella Region on small isle; 2. Uncharted Isle on the southwest part of the world map; 3. Unnamed Isle; 4. Isolated Plateau in Areas Accessible By Air		CONDITION	After defeating Monster Arena Rank B

Comments: With its incredibly high defence, Metal Babble a.k.a. Metabble's 6 HP can go a long way, especially when paired with healing slimes (and it's doubled in a party full of slimes). Unfortunately, the wandering Metabble can be very difficult to find.

METALY

TITLE: QUICK SILVER
SPECIES: METAL SLIME
FAMILY: SLIME

HP: 3
MP: 64
Attack: 36-129
Defence: 499-970
Agility: 65-122
Turns in Combat: 1.2

GOLD	5	EXP	135
MONSTER COIN	Gold		
TEAM	Slime Time		
DEATHMOVE	Slime Spank		
TEAM BONUSES	Team Max HP x2		
TEAM	Slime Therapy		
DEATHMOVE	Multiheal		
TEAM BONUSES	Team Max HP x2		
TEAM	Metal Power		
DEATHMOVE	Magic Burst		
TEAM BONUSES	Team Max HP x2		
LOCATION	Appears in one of four locations in Alexandria Region		

Comments: Metal slimes can be difficult opponents in the Monster Arena for your foes. A mere 3 HP doesn't provide a large margin of error, but it gets doubled in a party full of slimes. Quick Silver a.k.a. Metaly can make a good special team with nearly any combination of slimes!

TEAM	Trauma Centre
DEATHMOVE	Omniheal
TEAM BONUSES	Team Max HP x2
TEAM	The Metal Mob
DEATHMOVE	Multi Masher (Magic Burst)
TEAM BONUSES	Team Max HP x2
TEAM	Full Metal Power
DEATHMOVE	Magic Burst
TEAM BONUSES	Team Max HP x2
TEAM	Slime Power
DEATHMOVE	N/A
TEAM BONUSES	Team Max HP x2
CONDITION	After defeating Monster Arena Rank F

MOPPET

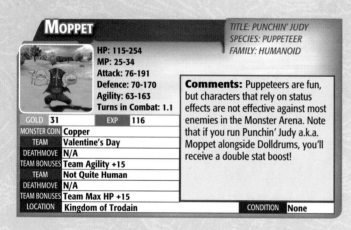

TITLE: PUNCHIN' JUDY
SPECIES: PUPPETEER
FAMILY: HUMANOID

HP: 115-254
MP: 25-34
Attack: 76-191
Defence: 70-170
Agility: 63-163
Turns in Combat: 1.1

GOLD	31	EXP	116
MONSTER COIN	Copper		
TEAM	Valentine's Day		
DEATHMOVE	N/A		
TEAM BONUSES	Team Agility +15		
TEAM	Not Quite Human		
DEATHMOVE	N/A		
TEAM BONUSES	Team Max HP +15		
LOCATION	Kingdom of Trodain		

Comments: Puppeteers are fun, but characters that rely on status effects are not effective against most enemies in the Monster Arena. Note that if you run Punchin' Judy a.k.a. Moppet alongside Dolldrums, you'll receive a double stat boost!

CONDITION	None

NIGHTWING

TITLE: NIGHTSTALKER
SPECIES: NIGHT EMPEROR
FAMILY: DEMON

HP: 271-312
MP: 0
Attack: 90-191
Defence: 81-167
Agility: 55-85
Turns in Combat: 0.8

GOLD	89	EXP	166
MONSTER COIN	Copper		
TEAM	Team Goodnight		
DEATHMOVE	Dirge		
TEAM BONUSES	N/A		
TEAM	Far From Heaven		
DEATHMOVE	N/A		
TEAM BONUSES	Wait Extra Turn		
LOCATION	Unnamed Isle		

Comments: Nightstalker a.k.a. Nightwing is one of the weaker demons due to its low HP, but its Sweet Breath attack (which puts foes to sleep) can be useful in early ranks. Nightwing can unleash the risky Dirge deathmove when matched with Capers and Hoodwink.

CONDITION	Night only

NOHI

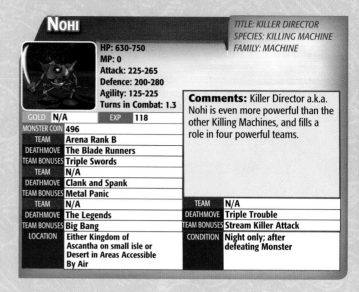

TITLE: KILLER DIRECTOR
SPECIES: KILLING MACHINE
FAMILY: MACHINE

HP: 630-750
MP: 0
Attack: 225-265
Defence: 200-280
Agility: 125-225
Turns in Combat: 1.3

GOLD	N/A	EXP	118
MONSTER COIN	496		
TEAM	Arena Rank B		
DEATHMOVE	The Blade Runners		
TEAM BONUSES	Triple Swords		
TEAM	N/A		
DEATHMOVE	Clank and Spank		
TEAM BONUSES	Metal Panic		
TEAM	N/A		
DEATHMOVE	The Legends		
TEAM BONUSES	Big Bang		
LOCATION	Either Kingdom of Ascantha on small isle or Desert in Areas Accessible By Air		

Comments: Killer Director a.k.a. Nohi is even more powerful than the other Killing Machines, and fills a role in four powerful teams.

TEAM	N/A
DEATHMOVE	Triple Trouble
TEAM BONUSES	Stream Killer Attack
CONDITION	Night only; after defeating Monster

OCTURION

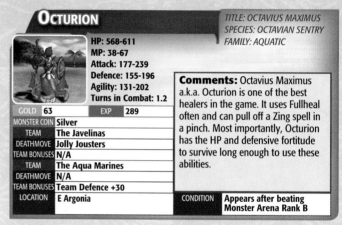

TITLE: OCTAVIUS MAXIMUS
SPECIES: OCTAVIAN SENTRY
FAMILY: AQUATIC

HP: 568-611
MP: 38-67
Attack: 177-239
Defence: 155-196
Agility: 131-202
Turns in Combat: 1.2

GOLD	63	EXP	289
MONSTER COIN	Silver		
TEAM	The Javelinas		
DEATHMOVE	Jolly Jousters		
TEAM BONUSES	N/A		
TEAM	The Aqua Marines		
DEATHMOVE	N/A		
TEAM BONUSES	Team Defence +30		
LOCATION	E Argonia		

Comments: Octavius Maximus a.k.a. Octurion is one of the best healers in the game. It uses Fullheal often and can pull off a Zing spell in a pinch. Most importantly, Octurion has the HP and defensive fortitude to survive long enough to use these abilities.

CONDITION	Appears after beating Monster Arena Rank B

ORCUS

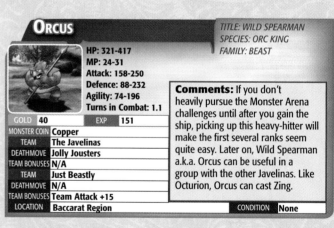

TITLE: WILD SPEARMAN
SPECIES: ORC KING
FAMILY: BEAST

HP: 321-417
MP: 24-31
Attack: 158-250
Defence: 88-232
Agility: 74-196
Turns in Combat: 1.1

GOLD	40	EXP	151
MONSTER COIN	Copper		
TEAM	The Javelinas		
DEATHMOVE	Jolly Jousters		
TEAM BONUSES	N/A		
TEAM	Just Beastly		
DEATHMOVE	N/A		
TEAM BONUSES	Team Attack +15		
LOCATION	Baccarat Region		

Comments: If you don't heavily pursue the Monster Arena challenges until after you gain the ship, picking up this heavy-hitter will make the first several ranks seem quite easy. Later on, Wild Spearman a.k.a. Orcus can be useful in a group with the other Javelinas. Like Octurion, Orcus can cast Zing.

CONDITION	None

ORRID

TITLE: OCHRE OGRE
SPECIES: BUFFALOGRE
FAMILY: BEAST

HP: 613-634
MP: 0
Attack: 244-249
Defence: 138-150
Agility: 104-114
Turns in Combat: 1.1

GOLD	103	EXP	261
MONSTER COIN	Silver		
TEAM	The Dynamic Duo		
DEATHMOVE	Sapper Slapper		
TEAM BONUSES	Team Attack +15		
TEAM	Just Beastly		
DEATHMOVE	N/A		
TEAM BONUSES	Team Attack +15		
LOCATION	Isolated Plateau		

Comments: Ochre Ogre a.k.a. Orrid is quite powerful and has the ability to psyche up quickly and unleash devastating attacks. In combination with Spike, Orrid is even stronger and the pair form a two-monster team that will serve you well in the high rank fights of the Monster Arena competition.

CONDITION	After defeating Monster Arena Rank F

PA TROLL

TITLE: TROLL PATROLLER
SPECIES: BOSS TROLL
FAMILY: DEMON

HP: 999
MP: 0
Attack: 321-348
Defence: 63-74
Agility: 84-90
Turns in Combat: 1

GOLD	79	EXP	466
MONSTER COIN	Gold		
TEAM	Club Club		
DEATHMOVE	Mind Breaker		
TEAM BONUSES	N/A		
TEAM	Far From Heaven		
DEATHMOVE	N/A		
TEAM BONUSES	Wait Extra Turn		
LOCATION	Northwest Isle in Areas Accessible By Air		
CONDITION	None		

Comments: Troll Patroller a.k.a. Pa Troll's power comes at a cost, which is a serious lack of defence and agility. That's a high hurdle to leap, but if you're starting the Monster Arena late in the game or if you're at a low level, Pa Troll could be an effective member of your team.

POTBELLY

TITLE: POTTY DRAGON
SPECIES: JARGON
FAMILY: DRAGON

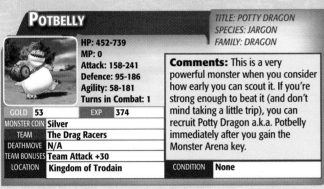

HP: 452-739
MP: 0
Attack: 158-241
Defence: 95-186
Agility: 58-181
Turns in Combat: 1

GOLD	53	EXP	374
MONSTER COIN	Silver		
TEAM	The Drag Racers		
DEATHMOVE	N/A		
TEAM BONUSES	Team Attack +30		
LOCATION	Kingdom of Trodain		
CONDITION	None		

Comments: This is a very powerful monster when you consider how early you can scout it. If you're strong enough to beat it (and don't mind taking a little trip) you can recruit Potty Dragon a.k.a. Potbelly immediately after you gain the Monster Arena key.

ROBORG

TITLE: ROBSTER MK I
SPECIES: KILLING MACHINE
FAMILY: MACHINE

HP: 432-586
MP: 0
Attack: 173-222
Defence: 168-238
Agility: 120-251
Turns in Combat: 1

GOLD	35	EXP	351
MONSTER COIN	Silver		
TEAM	The Blade Runners		
DEATHMOVE	Triple Swords		
TEAM BONUSES	N/A		
TEAM	Clank and Spank		
DEATHMOVE	Metal Panic		
TEAM BONUSES	N/A		
LOCATION	Blizzard Peaks		
TEAM	Triple Trouble		
DEATHMOVE	Stream Killer Attack		
TEAM BONUSES	N/A		
CONDITION	None		

Comments: Killing machines make for fantastic team members, offering a wide variety of useful attacks, filling slots in three different teams and boasting impressive attack and defence stats. Since Robster Mk I a.k.a. Roborg has no prerequisites, you should grab it as soon as possible.

ROBSTER

TITLE: LITTLE NIPPER
SPECIES: YABBY
FAMILY: AQUATIC

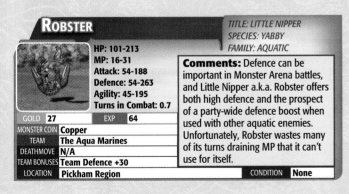

HP: 101-213
MP: 16-31
Attack: 54-188
Defence: 54-263
Agility: 45-195
Turns in Combat: 0.7

GOLD	27	EXP	64
MONSTER COIN	Copper		
TEAM	The Aqua Marines		
DEATHMOVE	N/A		
TEAM BONUSES	Team Defence +30		
LOCATION	Pickham Region		
CONDITION	None		

Comments: Defence can be important in Monster Arena battles, and Little Nipper a.k.a. Robster offers both high defence and the prospect of a party-wide defence boost when used with other aquatic enemies. Unfortunately, Robster wastes many of its turns draining MP that it can't use for itself.

SAGITTARI

TITLE: POISONOUS SNIPER
SPECIES: BODKIN FLETCHER
FAMILY: HUMANOID

HP: 238-353
MP: 32
Attack: 160-170
Defence: 120-170
Agility: 80-100
Turns in Combat: 0.8

GOLD	26	EXP	83
MONSTER COIN	Copper		
TEAM	The Angry Archers		
DEATHMOVE	Harrowing Arrow		
TEAM BONUSES	Team Max HP +15		
TEAM	Not Quite Human		
DEATHMOVE	N/A		
TEAM BONUSES	Team Max HP +15		
LOCATION	Arcadia Region		
CONDITION	None		

Comments: A reliable fighter that uses standard arrow shots and occasional poisonous multishot attacks that can inflict long-term damage to foes. Poisonous Sniper a.k.a. Sagittari is very easy to find, located on the path just north of Arcadia.

SALSA

TITLE: PELVIC THRUSTER
SPECIES: REDTAIL HIPSTER
FAMILY: DEMON

HP: 266-330
MP: 0
Attack: 128-232
Defence: 91-180
Agility: 61-170
Turns in Combat: 1

GOLD	49	EXP	116
MONSTER COIN	Copper		
TEAM	Far From Heaven		
DEATHMOVE	N/A		
TEAM BONUSES	Wait Extra Turn		
LOCATION	Pickham Region		
CONDITION	None		

Comments: Pelvic Thruster a.k.a. Salsa can be a powerful addition to your team, but it depends on which random moves it dishes out. Spin Attack is fantastic, but the tension-lowering Foxtrot dance isn't nearly as effective against many foes.

SCORPIUS

TITLE: SAND SLAYER
SPECIES: SCORPION
FAMILY: BUG

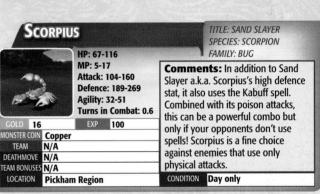

HP: 67-116
MP: 5-17
Attack: 104-160
Defence: 189-269
Agility: 32-51
Turns in Combat: 0.6

GOLD	16	EXP	100
MONSTER COIN	Copper		
TEAM	N/A		
DEATHMOVE	N/A		
TEAM BONUSES	N/A		
LOCATION	Pickham Region		
CONDITION	Day only		

Comments: In addition to Sand Slayer a.k.a. Scorpius's high defence stat, it also uses the Kabuff spell. Combined with its poison attacks, this can be a powerful combo but only if your opponents don't use spells! Scorpius is a fine choice against enemies that use only physical attacks.

SEASAW

TITLE: TERROR TALONS
SPECIES: RIPTIDE
FAMILY: HUMANOID

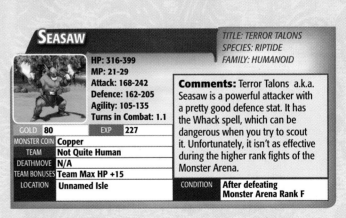

HP: 316-399
MP: 21-29
Attack: 168-242
Defence: 162-205
Agility: 105-135
Turns in Combat: 1.1

GOLD	80	EXP	227
MONSTER COIN	Copper		
TEAM	Not Quite Human		
DEATHMOVE	N/A		
TEAM BONUSES	Team Max HP +15		
LOCATION	Unnamed Isle		
CONDITION	After defeating Monster Arena Rank F		

Comments: Terror Talons a.k.a. Seasaw is a powerful attacker with a pretty good defence stat. It has the Whack spell, which can be dangerous when you try to scout it. Unfortunately, it isn't as effective during the higher rank fights of the Monster Arena.

SIPPY

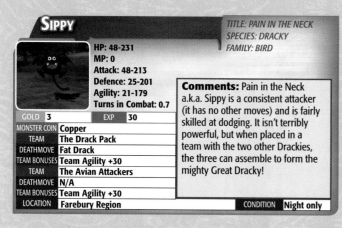

TITLE: PAIN IN THE NECK
SPECIES: DRACKY
FAMILY: BIRD

HP: 48-231
MP: 0
Attack: 48-213
Defence: 25-201
Agility: 21-179
Turns in Combat: 0.7

GOLD	3	EXP	30
MONSTER COIN	Copper		
TEAM	The Drack Pack		
DEATHMOVE	Fat Drack		
TEAM BONUSES	Team Agility +30		
TEAM	The Avian Attackers		
DEATHMOVE	N/A		
TEAM BONUSES	Team Agility +30		
LOCATION	Farebury Region	CONDITION	Night only

Comments: Pain in the Neck a.k.a. Sippy is a consistent attacker (it has no other moves) and is fairly skilled at dodging. It isn't terribly powerful, but when placed in a team with the two other Drackies, the three can assemble to form the mighty Great Dracky!

SLURPY

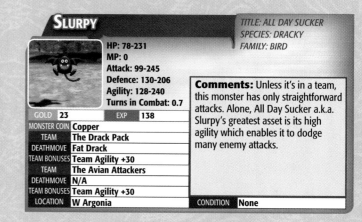

TITLE: ALL DAY SUCKER
SPECIES: DRACKY
FAMILY: BIRD

HP: 78-231
MP: 0
Attack: 99-245
Defence: 130-206
Agility: 128-240
Turns in Combat: 0.7

GOLD	23	EXP	138
MONSTER COIN	Copper		
TEAM	The Drack Pack		
DEATHMOVE	Fat Drack		
TEAM BONUSES	Team Agility +30		
TEAM	The Avian Attackers		
DEATHMOVE	N/A		
TEAM BONUSES	Team Agility +30		
LOCATION	W Argonia	CONDITION	None

Comments: Unless it's in a team, this monster has only straightforward attacks. Alone, All Day Sucker a.k.a. Slurpy's greatest asset is its high agility which enables it to dodge many enemy attacks.

SKELEDOID

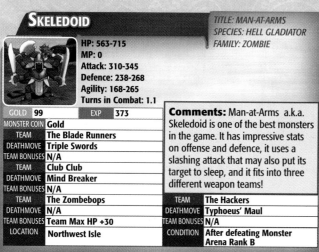

TITLE: MAN-AT-ARMS
SPECIES: HELL GLADIATOR
FAMILY: ZOMBIE

HP: 563-715
MP: 0
Attack: 310-345
Defence: 238-268
Agility: 168-265
Turns in Combat: 1.1

GOLD	99	EXP	373
MONSTER COIN	Gold		
TEAM	The Blade Runners		
DEATHMOVE	Triple Swords		
TEAM BONUSES	N/A		
TEAM	Club Club		
DEATHMOVE	Mind Breaker		
TEAM BONUSES	N/A		
TEAM	The Zombebops	TEAM	The Hackers
DEATHMOVE	N/A	DEATHMOVE	Typhoeus' Maul
TEAM BONUSES	Team Max HP +30	TEAM BONUSES	N/A
LOCATION	Northwest Isle	CONDITION	After defeating Monster Arena Rank B

Comments: Man-at-Arms a.k.a. Skeledoid is one of the best monsters in the game. It has impressive stats on offense and defence, it uses a slashing attack that may also put its target to sleep, and it fits into three different weapon teams!

SMILES

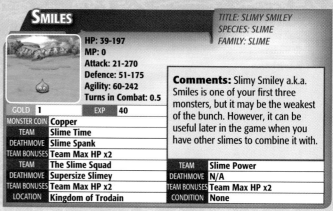

TITLE: SLIMY SMILEY
SPECIES: SLIME
FAMILY: SLIME

HP: 39-197
MP: 0
Attack: 21-270
Defence: 51-175
Agility: 60-242
Turns in Combat: 0.5

GOLD	1	EXP	40
MONSTER COIN	Copper		
TEAM	Slime Time		
DEATHMOVE	Slime Spank		
TEAM BONUSES	Team Max HP x2		
TEAM	The Slime Squad	TEAM	Slime Power
DEATHMOVE	Supersize Slimey	DEATHMOVE	N/A
TEAM BONUSES	Team Max HP x2	TEAM BONUSES	Team Max HP x2
LOCATION	Kingdom of Trodain	CONDITION	None

Comments: Slimy Smiley a.k.a. Smiles is one of your first three monsters, but it may be the weakest of the bunch. However, it can be useful later in the game when you have other slimes to combine it with.

SLIME SHADY

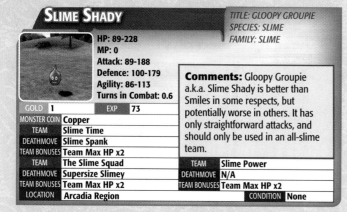

TITLE: GLOOPY GROUPIE
SPECIES: SLIME
FAMILY: SLIME

HP: 89-228
MP: 0
Attack: 89-188
Defence: 100-179
Agility: 86-113
Turns in Combat: 0.6

GOLD	1	EXP	73
MONSTER COIN	Copper		
TEAM	Slime Time		
DEATHMOVE	Slime Spank		
TEAM BONUSES	Team Max HP x2		
TEAM	The Slime Squad	TEAM	Slime Power
DEATHMOVE	Supersize Slimey	DEATHMOVE	N/A
TEAM BONUSES	Team Max HP x2	TEAM BONUSES	Team Max HP x2
LOCATION	Arcadia Region	CONDITION	None

Comments: Gloopy Groupie a.k.a. Slime Shady is better than Smiles in some respects, but potentially worse in others. It has only straightforward attacks, and should only be used in an all-slime team.

SNAP CASE

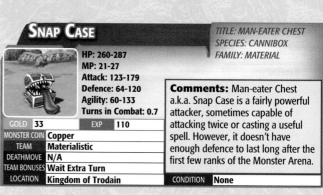

TITLE: MAN-EATER CHEST
SPECIES: CANNIBOX
FAMILY: MATERIAL

HP: 260-287
MP: 21-27
Attack: 123-179
Defence: 64-120
Agility: 60-133
Turns in Combat: 0.7

GOLD	33	EXP	110
MONSTER COIN	Copper		
TEAM	Materialistic		
DEATHMOVE	N/A		
TEAM BONUSES	Wait Extra Turn		
LOCATION	Kingdom of Trodain	CONDITION	None

Comments: Man-eater Chest a.k.a. Snap Case is a fairly powerful attacker, sometimes capable of attacking twice or casting a useful spell. However, it doesn't have enough defence to last long after the first few ranks of the Monster Arena.

SLIMEHOPPER

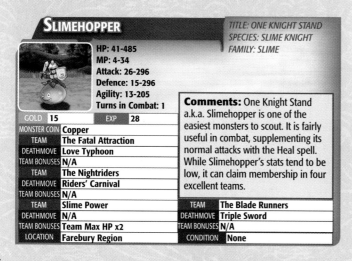

TITLE: ONE KNIGHT STAND
SPECIES: SLIME KNIGHT
FAMILY: SLIME

HP: 41-485
MP: 4-34
Attack: 26-296
Defence: 15-296
Agility: 13-205
Turns in Combat: 1

GOLD	15	EXP	28
MONSTER COIN	Copper		
TEAM	The Fatal Attraction		
DEATHMOVE	Love Typhoon		
TEAM BONUSES	N/A		
TEAM	The Nightriders		
DEATHMOVE	Riders' Carnival		
TEAM BONUSES	N/A		
TEAM	Slime Power	TEAM	The Blade Runners
DEATHMOVE	N/A	DEATHMOVE	Triple Sword
TEAM BONUSES	Team Max HP x2	TEAM BONUSES	N/A
LOCATION	Farebury Region	CONDITION	None

Comments: One Knight Stand a.k.a. Slimehopper is one of the easiest monsters to scout. It is fairly useful in combat, supplementing its normal attacks with the Heal spell. While Slimehopper's stats tend to be low, it can claim membership in four excellent teams.

SPIKE

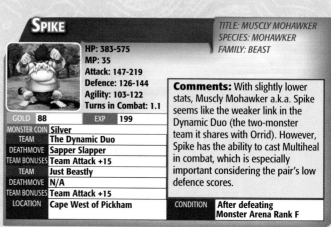

TITLE: MUSCLY MOHAWKER
SPECIES: MOHAWKER
FAMILY: BEAST

HP: 383-575
MP: 35
Attack: 147-219
Defence: 126-144
Agility: 103-122
Turns in Combat: 1.1

GOLD	88	EXP	199
MONSTER COIN	Silver		
TEAM	The Dynamic Duo		
DEATHMOVE	Sapper Slapper		
TEAM BONUSES	Team Attack +15		
TEAM	Just Beastly		
DEATHMOVE	N/A		
TEAM BONUSES	Team Attack +15		
LOCATION	Cape West of Pickham	CONDITION	After defeating Monster Arena Rank F

Comments: With slightly lower stats, Muscly Mohawker a.k.a. Spike seems like the weaker link in the Dynamic Duo (the two-monster team it shares with Orrid). However, Spike has the ability to cast Multiheal in combat, which is especially important considering the pair's low defence scores.

SQUIGGLES

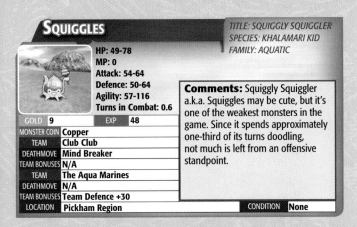

TITLE: SQUIGGLY SQUIGGLER
SPECIES: KHALAMARI KID
FAMILY: AQUATIC

HP: 49-78
MP: 0
Attack: 54-64
Defence: 50-64
Agility: 57-116
Turns in Combat: 0.6

GOLD	9	EXP	48
MONSTER COIN	Copper		
TEAM	Club Club		
DEATHMOVE	Mind Breaker		
TEAM BONUSES	N/A		
TEAM	The Aqua Marines		
DEATHMOVE	N/A		
TEAM BONUSES	Team Defence +30		
LOCATION	Pickham Region	CONDITION	None

Comments: Squiggly Squiggler a.k.a. Squiggles may be cute, but it's one of the weakest monsters in the game. Since it spends approximately one-third of its turns doodling, not much is left from an offensive standpoint.

STEROPES

TITLE: GIGANTES GANGSTER
SPECIES: GIGANTES
FAMILY: DEMON

HP: 888-959
MP: 0
Attack: 278-329
Defence: 149-200
Agility: 108-173
Turns in Combat: 0.8

GOLD	103	EXP	398
MONSTER COIN	Silver		
TEAM	Two Eyes		
DEATHMOVE	Sapper Slappers		
TEAM BONUSES	Wait Extra Turn		
TEAM	Club Club	TEAM	Far From Heaven
DEATHMOVE	Mind Breaker	DEATHMOVE	N/A
TEAM BONUSES	N/A	TEAM BONUSES	Wait Extra Turn
LOCATION	Unnamed Isle	CONDITION	After defeating Monster Arena Rank B

Comments: Gigantes Gangster a.k.a. Steropes is even more powerful than Brontes, but you can't recruit it until you defeat Monster Arena Rank B. After that, add it to your team (preferably alongside Brontes) and you'll be in good shape for the final ranks!

STONEMAN

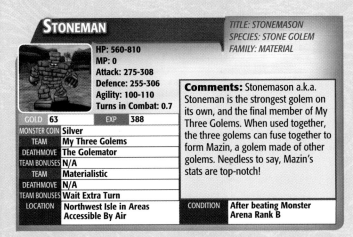

TITLE: STONEMASON
SPECIES: STONE GOLEM
FAMILY: MATERIAL

HP: 560-810
MP: 0
Attack: 275-308
Defence: 255-306
Agility: 100-110
Turns in Combat: 0.7

GOLD	63	EXP	388
MONSTER COIN	Silver		
TEAM	My Three Golems		
DEATHMOVE	The Golemator		
TEAM BONUSES	N/A		
TEAM	Materialistic		
DEATHMOVE	N/A		
TEAM BONUSES	Wait Extra Turn		
LOCATION	Northwest Isle in Areas Accessible By Air	CONDITION	After beating Monster Arena Rank B

Comments: Stonemason a.k.a. Stoneman is the strongest golem on its own, and the final member of My Three Golems. When used together, the three golems can fuse together to form Mazin, a golem made of other golems. Needless to say, Mazin's stats are top-notch!

SUGI

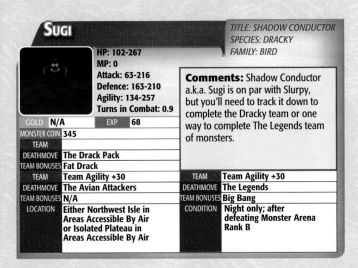

TITLE: SHADOW CONDUCTOR
SPECIES: DRACKY
FAMILY: BIRD

HP: 102-267
MP: 0
Attack: 63-216
Defence: 163-210
Agility: 134-257
Turns in Combat: 0.9

GOLD	N/A	EXP	68
MONSTER COIN	345		
TEAM			
DEATHMOVE	The Drack Pack		
TEAM BONUSES	Fat Drack		
TEAM	Team Agility +30	TEAM	Team Agility +30
DEATHMOVE	The Avian Attackers	DEATHMOVE	The Legends
TEAM BONUSES	N/A	TEAM BONUSES	Big Bang
LOCATION	Either Northwest Isle in Areas Accessible By Air or Isolated Plateau in Areas Accessible By Air	CONDITION	Night only; after defeating Monster Arena Rank B

Comments: Shadow Conductor a.k.a. Sugi is on par with Slurpy, but you'll need to track it down to complete the Dracky team or one way to complete The Legends team of monsters.

TALOS

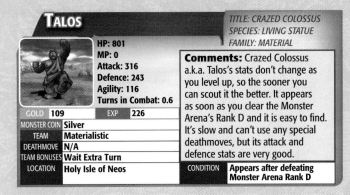

TITLE: CRAZED COLOSSUS
SPECIES: LIVING STATUE
FAMILY: MATERIAL

HP: 801
MP: 0
Attack: 316
Defence: 243
Agility: 116
Turns in Combat: 0.6

GOLD	109	EXP	226
MONSTER COIN	Silver		
TEAM	Materialistic		
DEATHMOVE	N/A		
TEAM BONUSES	Wait Extra Turn		
LOCATION	Holy Isle of Neos		
CONDITION	Appears after defeating Monster Arena Rank D		

Comments: Crazed Colossus a.k.a. Talos's stats don't change as you level up, so the sooner you can scout it the better. It appears as soon as you clear the Monster Arena's Rank D and it is easy to find. It's slow and can't use any special deathmoves, but its attack and defence stats are very good.

TORCHMAN

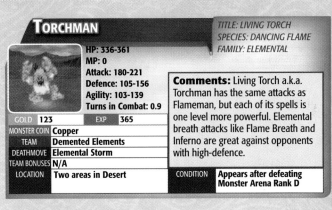

TITLE: LIVING TORCH
SPECIES: DANCING FLAME
FAMILY: ELEMENTAL

HP: 336-361
MP: 0
Attack: 180-221
Defence: 105-156
Agility: 103-139
Turns in Combat: 0.9

GOLD	123	EXP	365
MONSTER COIN	Copper		
TEAM	Demented Elements		
DEATHMOVE	Elemental Storm		
TEAM BONUSES	N/A		
LOCATION	Two areas in Desert		
CONDITION	Appears after defeating Monster Arena Rank D		

Comments: Living Torch a.k.a. Torchman has the same attacks as Flameman, but each of its spells is one level more powerful. Elemental breath attacks like Flame Breath and Inferno are great against opponents with high-defence.

TORI

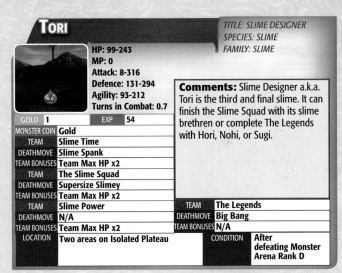

TITLE: SLIME DESIGNER
SPECIES: SLIME
FAMILY: SLIME

HP: 99-243
MP: 0
Attack: 8-316
Defence: 131-294
Agility: 93-212
Turns in Combat: 0.7

GOLD	1	EXP	54
MONSTER COIN	Gold		
TEAM	Slime Time		
DEATHMOVE	Slime Spank		
TEAM BONUSES	Team Max HP x2		
TEAM	The Slime Squad		
DEATHMOVE	Supersize Slimey		
TEAM BONUSES	Team Max HP x2		
TEAM	Slime Power	TEAM	The Legends
DEATHMOVE	N/A	DEATHMOVE	Big Bang
TEAM BONUSES	Team Max HP x2	TEAM BONUSES	N/A
LOCATION	Two areas on Isolated Plateau	CONDITION	After defeating Monster Arena Rank D

Comments: Slime Designer a.k.a. Tori is the third and final slime. It can finish the Slime Squad with its slime brethren or complete The Legends with Hori, Nohi, or Sugi.

TRICK BAG

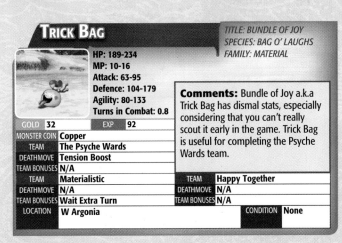

TITLE: BUNDLE OF JOY
SPECIES: BAG O' LAUGHS
FAMILY: MATERIAL

HP: 189-234
MP: 10-16
Attack: 63-95
Defence: 104-179
Agility: 80-133
Turns in Combat: 0.8

GOLD	32	EXP	92
MONSTER COIN	Copper		
TEAM	The Psyche Wards		
DEATHMOVE	Tension Boost		
TEAM BONUSES	N/A		
TEAM	Materialistic	TEAM	Happy Together
DEATHMOVE	N/A	DEATHMOVE	N/A
TEAM BONUSES	Wait Extra Turn	TEAM BONUSES	N/A
LOCATION	W Argonia	CONDITION	None

Comments: Bundle of Joy a.k.a. Trick Bag has dismal stats, especially considering that you can't really scout it early in the game. Trick Bag is useful for completing the Psyche Wards team.

TWIGGY

TITLE: ROOT OF EVIL
SPECIES: TREEFACE
FAMILY: PLANT

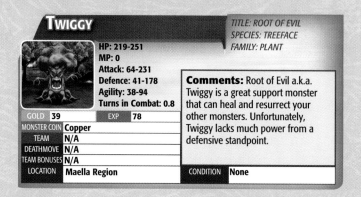

HP: 219-251
MP: 0
Attack: 64-231
Defence: 41-178
Agility: 38-94
Turns in Combat: 0.8

GOLD	39	EXP	78

MONSTER COIN	Copper
TEAM	N/A
DEATHMOVE	N/A
TEAM BONUSES	N/A
LOCATION	Maella Region

Comments: Root of Evil a.k.a. Twiggy is a great support monster that can heal and resurrect your other monsters. Unfortunately, Twiggy lacks much power from a defensive standpoint.

CONDITION	None

BISHOP

LOCATION	Two areas in Maella Region
CONDITION	Appears after defeating the game

HEV

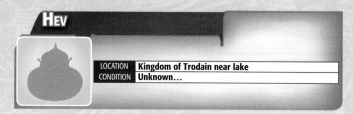

LOCATION	Kingdom of Trodain near lake
CONDITION	Unknown…

FRILLSAUR

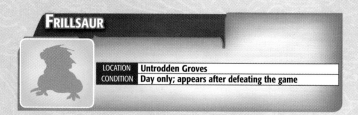

LOCATION	Untrodden Groves
CONDITION	Day only; appears after defeating the game

MORNSTAR

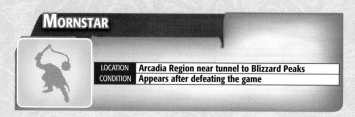

LOCATION	Arcadia Region near tunnel to Blizzard Peaks
CONDITION	Appears after defeating the game

GRYPHUS

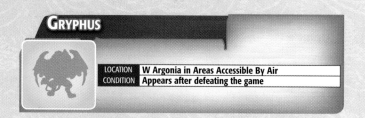

LOCATION	W Argonia in Areas Accessible By Air
CONDITION	Appears after defeating the game

SPOT

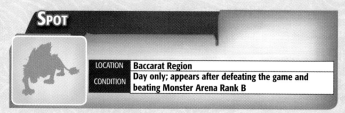

LOCATION	Baccarat Region
CONDITION	Day only; appears after defeating the game and beating Monster Arena Rank B

MORRIE'S MONSTER ARENA

UNLOCKING THE MONSTER ARENA

When you first meet Morrie atop the keep near Pickham, he asks you to track down three particular monsters, fight them, and send them back to him. Unlike normal monsters, these guys are visible on the field and are among the first of over 70 "infamous monsters" you'll encounter.

The party acquires 3 memos.

After you defeat all three, Morrie hands over a key that allows you to enter the Monster Arena at any time. Here you can send a handpicked team of monsters into combat with parties assembled by other monster scouts. Your starting team consists of the three monsters you defeated for Morrie. It's also possible to recruit additional infamous monsters, provided you can earn their respect by defeating them in combat.

Dumbking
King of Dumbira
notso macho
(Humanoid Family)
[HP]620
[MP]: 24
Attack216
Defence193
Agility125

Yes
No

King of Dumbira looks at the party with respect. Do you wish to add King of Dumbira to your Monster Arena reserves?

Victories in the arena will earn you both items and special abilities, courtesy of Morrie. The most significant is the **Call Team** ability, which Morrie teaches you after you conquer Rank E. This skill enables you to call your Monster Team to replace your normal party in battle for a certain number of turns!

Here comes Wyld Stallynz!

HOW BATTLES WORK

You can enter a battle by talking to the man in red behind one of the counters in the Monster Arena. The tournament is divided into eight ranks and you must conquer them in order, starting with the lowest (Rank G). There is a small fee to pay to enter each rank, but the potential prizes for winning are worth the price of entry. You can challenge a previously defeated rank for free, but you won't win any prizes.

* : Welcome to the Monster Arena registration counter.

Each rank consists of three rounds. Your enemies' monsters may appear to be ordinary monsters, but they have enhanced stats, making them formidable opponents. Also, your foes always begin at full health, while your team does not recover lost HP or MP between rounds.

A night fox draws near!
A night emperor draws near!
A night sneaker draws near!

During battles, your monsters fight on their own. You can't give them specific commands, so the strategic element lies in scouting the best monsters and identifying the correct mixture of attributes to fashion an all conquering team from your ever-expanding roster.

SCOUTING MONSTERS

As noted previously, you assemble your team from infamous monsters, which are the more powerful versions of normal monsters that you face in random monster encounters. Once Morrie makes you an official monster scout, any infamous monster you defeat will ask to join your team after you defeat it. The monsters you begin with are among the weakest in the game, so try to replace them quickly.

Initially, there is space for only three monsters, so recruiting a new monster means releasing an old one (it returns to its original location). As you ascend the Monster Arena ranks, Morrie will reward you with additional storage space in your reserves and even a second team! You can only enter one team of three monsters in each fight, but you can swap between teams and your bench before you register.

A few tips for catching monsters:

 When you see an infamous monster, try to attack it from behind. This may enable you to strike first.

Some monsters only appear at night, while others only appear during the day. If an area seems suspiciously empty, try waiting until the next time change to see if a monster appears.

 Certain monsters appear only after you've conquered certain ranks in the Monster Arena. Ranks F, D, and B are the significant milestones.

Most infamous monsters appear in only one location, but some may have up to five possible appearance points! They are only in one spot at any given time, so these monsters can be tricky to track down.

 A few super-secret infamous monsters do not appear until after the game is completed, or other criteria are fulfilled later in the game.

How Infamous Monsters Grow

Infamous monsters distinguish themselves from their normal monster counterparts in many ways. They have names and higher stats and while they don't level up, they gain strength as your normal party gains strength. Note that not every monster stat is affected, and the amount by which they're affected can vary drastically. Some grow significantly as your party does (like Hackzilla), while others are as good as they'll ever be on the day you recruit them (like Talos). Note that infamous monsters grow whether they're in the wild or on your team; recruiting them early doesn't make a difference in their ultimate stats.

Talos

Crazed Colossus

[HP]:	801
[MP]:	0
Attack:	316
Defence:	243
Agility:	116

Hero Level 20

Hackzilla

Axoraptor

[HP]:	854
[MP]:	0
Attack:	320
Defence:	226
Agility:	136

Hero Level 45

Deathmoves and Special Teams

When you combine monsters of the same type, or ones that have something significant in common (they all wield the same weapon, for example), the team may gain a nickname, deathmoves, stat bonuses, or other secret traits. Your team will occasionally use a deathmove in combat automatically.

Despite their name, deathmoves aren't always offensive in nature. For example, Elemental Storm (used by a party of three Elementals) casts Bounce and Insulate on the party. If you use Call Team to summon a monster team that uses a stat-boosting or healing deathmove like this one, the effects will often carry over to your human party as well!

You can certainly get through the Monster Arena with three tough monsters that have nothing in common with each other, but it is often easier with a themed party that has a powerful team ability.

Monster Arena Prizes

Rank G
Strength ring (accessory); attack: 5; equipped by Hero, Yangus, Jessica, Angelo

Rank F
Bunny suit (armour); defence: 38; equipped by Jessica

Rank E
Ring of clarity (accessory); defence: 10, immunity to confusion; equipped by Hero, Yangus, Jessica, Angelo

Rank D
Mighty armlet (accessory); attack: 15; equipped by Hero, Yangus, Jessica, Angelo

Rank C
Saint's ashes (item); used in alchemy

Rank B
Bardiche of binding (scythe); attack: 83, does extra damage to demons, may silence target; equipped by Yangus

Rank A
Hero spear (spear); attack: 100, recovers user's HP; equipped by Hero

Rank S
Dragon robe (armour); defence: 103, reduces fire- and ice-type damage; equipped by Jessica, Angelo

Monster Arena Rounds

RANK G

Entrance Fee: 100 gold
Prizes: Strength ring, +3 Reserves monster slots

GRIMEY—THE SLIMEYS

She-slime (x2)
HP: 45
MP: 0
Attack: 45
Defence: 40
Agility: 50

Slime knight
HP: 63
MP: 10
Attack: 65
Defence: 44
Agility: 72

GRACEY—TEAM FACE OFF

Frogface (x2)
HP: 49
MP: 10
Attack: 52
Defence: 23
Agility: 52

Treeface
HP: 80
MP: 0
Attack: 66
Defence: 53
Agility: 44

GRUELLY—THE BULLY BROTHERS

HAMMERHOOD
HP: 50
MP: 0
Attack: 49
Defence: 45
Agility: 18

GORERILLA
HP: 82
MP: 0
Attack: 70
Defence: 62
Agility: 39

BULLFINCH
HP: 77
MP: 0
Attack: 53
Defence: 45
Agility: 50

RANK F

Entrance Fee: 200 gold
Prizes: Bunny suit, unlock Compete against own team option

FISHER—THE FISHER KINGS

KHALAMARI KID (x2)
HP: 66
MP: 0
Attack: 70
Defence: 68
Agility: 57

KING KELP
HP: 103
MP: 20
Attack: 82
Defence: 72
Agility: 59

FELBLE—HELL'S BELLS

DINGALING (x2)
HP: 72
MP: 4
Attack: 63
Defence: 60
Agility: 71

JARGON
HP: 120
MP: 0
Attack: 100
Defence: 71
Agility: 56

FINNEGAN—THE RED BARONS

DANCING DEVIL
HP: 70
MP: 0
Attack: 46
Defence: 45
Agility: 63

WAILIN' WEED
HP: 83
MP: 0
Attack: 77
Defence: 71
Agility: 61

REDTAIL HIPSTER
HP: 103
MP: 0
Attack: 106
Defence: 95
Agility: 70

RANK F STRATEGY

Watch out for redtail hipster's tail shake, which hits for about 50 HP to all party members. If your party is weak, this attack can eliminate multiple team members in a single turn.

RANK E

Entrance Fee: 300 gold
Prizes: Ring of clarity, Call Team ability (for Hero)

ERICSON—THE PRISON PUSSYCATS

JAILCAT (x2)
HP: 65
MP: 12
Attack: 86
Defence: 66
Agility: 80

TERROR TABBY
HP: 99
MP: 20
Attack: 120
Defence: 80
Agility: 80

ELIDOR—THE FIEND FAMILY

HIPSTER
HP: 146
MP: 32
Attack: 132
Defence: 80
Agility: 80

MINIDEMON
HP: 83
MP: 60
Attack: 58
Defence: 63
Agility: 70

WITCH
HP: 130
MP: 48
Attack: 110
Defence: 79
Agility: 80

EVIANA—THE DIRTY DANCERS

MAGIC MARIONETTE
HP: 180
MP: 0
Attack: 132
Defence: 92
Agility: 64

TAP DEVIL
HP: 125
MP: 0
Attack: 91
Defence: 89
Agility: 60

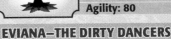

VOLPONE
HP: 183
MP: 48
Attack: 145
Defence: 100
Agility: 80

RANK E STRATEGY

The tap devil uses Underpants Dance to stun your characters for a turn, leaving them unable to fight back. If this causes a problem, find a monster that is immune to temporary stun attacks. This quality is typically found among machines and zombies.

Monster Arena

RANK D

Entrance Fee: 400 gold
Prizes: Mighty armlet, +3 Reserves monster slots

DAREN—TEAM NIGHTMARE

NIGHT FOX
HP: 161
MP: 6
Attack: 98
Defence: 73
Agility: 90

NIGHT EMPEROR
HP: 182
MP: 0
Attack: 128
Defence: 116
Agility: 60

NIGHT SNEAKER
HP: 123
MP: 12
Attack: 110
Defence: 77
Agility: 80

DARCY—THE DEADHEADS

SKELETON
HP: 145
MP: 30
Attack: 131
Defence: 33
Agility: 80

WALKING CORPSE
HP: 200
MP: 0
Attack: 130
Defence: 13
Agility: 80

MUMMY
HP: 143
MP: 0
Attack: 118
Defence: 60
Agility: 80

DEOGOL—THE PSYCHE-OS

BROWNIE (x2)
HP: 100
MP: 0
Attack: 123
Defence: 76
Agility: 75

HOOD
HP: 200
MP: 0
Attack: 166
Defence: 72
Agility: 75

RANK D STRATEGY

The brownies have a special ability that can boost their tension by two levels, making most of their attacks one-hit kills. Brownies are weak, so a deathmove may eliminate them before they cause any damage.

RANK C

Entrance Fee: 500 gold
Prizes: Saint's ashes, no prize from Morrie

CORAL—THE BEACH BABES

SEE URCHIN (x2)
HP: 161
MP: 20
Attack: 83
Defence: 45
Agility: 90

SIREN
HP: 180
MP: 50
Attack: 27
Defence: 100
Agility: 73

CRAZY INVENTOR—BAD SCIENCE

MECHA-MYNAH
HP: 178
MP: 45
Attack: 100
Defence: 135
Agility: 82

HUNTER MECH
HP: 256
MP: 0
Attack: 175
Defence: 108
Agility: 80

CLOCKWORK CUCKOO
HP: 240
MP: 0
Attack: 150
Defence: 99
Agility: 90

COUNTESS CHRISTIE—BATTLE ROYALS

FENCING FOX
HP: 320
MP: 8
Attack: 126
Defence: 92
Agility: 80

BONE BARON
HP: 316
MP: 0
Attack: 190
Defence: 116
Agility: 88

PHANTOM FENCER
HP: 400
MP: 0
Attack: 173
Defence: 95
Agility: 80

RANK C STRATEGY

Tough foes like the hunter mech and bone baron use powerful attacks on a consistent basis, and the metal monsters in the second round are immune to nearly every trick outside of direct physical damage. Construct a resilient team of your own, and use monsters that rely on direct attacks, not status conditions.

RANK B

Entrance Fee: 700 gold
Prizes: Bardiche of binding, second Monster team

BALDHERE—THE DRAG QUEENS

DRAGURN
HP: 481
MP: 0
Attack: 216
Defence: 128
Agility: 92

TYRANTOSAURUS
HP: 530
MP: 0
Attack: 221
Defence: 134
Agility: 108

SNAPDRAGON
HP: 550
MP: 60
Attack: 204
Defence: 118
Agility: 102

BOGART—THE TOUGH NUTS

STONE GUARDIAN
HP: 401
MP: 0
Attack: 209
Defence: 190
Agility: 92

BOSS TROLL
HP: 800
MP: 0
Attack: 238
Defence: 32
Agility: 82

GOLEM
HP: 560
MP: 0
Attack: 227
Defence: 126
Agility: 80

BOTHAN—THE ROCK 'N' ROLLERS

ROCKBOMB
HP: 180
MP: 40
Attack: 68
Defence: 111
Agility: 86

STONE GOLEM
HP: 612
MP: 0
Attack: 245
Defence: 156
Agility: 93

LIVING STATUE
HP: 462
MP: 0
Attack: 218
Defence: 154
Agility: 80

RANK B STRATEGY

The enemies in this rank hit hard and have lots of HP. The key to victory is having a team with very high defence since after the first round, all of the enemy monsters will use physical attacks exclusively. HP is important too, but even a monster with 1000 HP won't last long if its defence is low.

RANK A

Entrance Fee: 1000 gold
Prizes: Hero spear, unlock Rank S

ALOISE—THE BIG BOYS

FROU-FROU
HP: 540
MP: 0
Attack: 226
Defence: 157
Agility: 111

CYCLOPS
HP: 650
MP: 0
Attack: 261
Defence: 112
Agility: 94

TROLL
HP: 508
MP: 0
Attack: 254
Defence: 18
Agility: 51

'ATTABOY TOM—THE WILD CATS

JUMPING JACKAL (x2)
HP: 525
MP: 0
Attack: 230
Defence: 148
Agility: 135

GREAT SABRECAT
HP: 670
MP: 0
Attack: 271
Defence: 155
Agility: 150

AMAAN—FEAR FACTOR

ZOMBIE GLADIATOR
HP: 868
MP: 16
Attack: 256
Defence: 164
Agility: 126

TREEVIL
HP: 419
MP: 0
Attack: 145
Defence: 84
Agility: 72

BOMBOULDER
HP: 245
MP: Infinite
Attack: 80
Defence: 111
Agility: 80

RANK A STRATEGY

The final group of recruitable monsters becomes available after clearing Rank B. Take some time to recruit the final members of many powerful themed teams, like the killing machines and golems. This is a very tough rank, and it will be difficult to clear this rank without the use of some powerful deathmoves.

Monster Arena

RANK S

Entrance Fee: 1000 gold
Prizes: ???

Morrie

FIGHT ME! Become the strongest monster team owner in all the world! Our passionate encounter will take place here, in my MONSTROUS PIT!

You must clear all of the previous ranks to make Rank S appear. This rank contains the toughest battles yet, and victory may not be possible until you recruit some of the best monsters in the game. Also, boost their stats by attaining a high level for your characters.

SPECIAL MONSTER TEAMS

While you can build a team out of any three team monsters you like, you can earn stat bonuses and unlock deathmoves if the team is comprised of monsters that share a species, a weapon, a family, or some other trait. When this occurs, a special name is assigned to your team (as listed in this chapter) and you receive some bonuses shown. All deathmoves are automatically used in combat at your team's discretion. If your team of three monsters has a special two-monster sub-group in it, the deathmove for the two-monster sub-group may also be used. Some effects extend to party members, but only when the Hero summons your team in combat with the Call Team ability.

A THIRD TEAM MEMBER

Note that some special monster teams require only two monsters. However, the third member of the team must be of the same family to unlock starred bonuses!

WEAPON TEAMS

THE ANGRY ARCHERS

DESCRIPTION	Monsters that wield bows.
DEATHMOVE	Harrowing Arrow: Arrows of light hit all enemies for 116-124 points of damage.
TEAM BONUSES	Team Max HP +15

POSSIBLE TEAM MEMBERS:
Shortshooter a.k.a. Fletch (Bodkin archer)
Sharpshooter a.k.a. Archer (Bodkin bowyer)
Poisonous Sniper a.k.a. Sagittari (Bodkin fletcher)

THE BLADE RUNNERS

DESCRIPTION	Monsters that wield swords.
DEATHMOVE	Triple Swords: Team members focus attacks on a single foe, and cause 50% more damage than normal attacks.
TEAM BONUSES	N/A

POSSIBLE TEAM MEMBERS:
Old Soldier a.k.a. Bones (Skeleton)
Fantom of Chopera a.k.a. Capers (Phantom fencer)
Attack Bot Mk II a.k.a. Cybot (Killing machine)
King of Dumbira a.k.a. Dumbking (Notso macho)
Raging Rooster a.k.a. Foul Fowl (Fowlfighter)
Bone Racer a.k.a. Jockey (Skullrider)
Hollow Knight a.k.a. Lonely Joe (Restless armour)
Killer Director a.k.a. Nohi (Killing machine)
Robooster Mk I a.k.a. Roborg (Killing machine)
Man-at-Arms a.k.a. Skeledoid (Hell gladiator)
One Knight Stand a.k.a. Slimehopper (Slime knight)

CLUB CLUB

DESCRIPTION	Monsters that wield clubs.
DEATHMOVE	Mind Breaker: Team members focus attacks on a single foe, and cause the target to lose its turn.
TEAM BONUSES	N/A

POSSIBLE TEAM MEMBERS:
Big Blue Bully a.k.a. Arges (Cyclops)
Gigantes Guardsman a.k.a. Brontes (Gigantes)
Abominable Ape a.k.a. Klub Kong (Gorerilla)
Troll Patroller a.k.a. Pa Troll (Boss troll)
Man-at-Arms a.k.a. Skeledoid (Hell gladiator)
Squiggly Squiggler a.k.a. Squiggles (Khalamari kid)
Gigantes Gangster a.k.a. Steropes (Gigantes)

THE HACKERS

DESCRIPTION	Monsters that wield axes.
DEATHMOVE	Typhoeus' Maul: Team members focus attacks on a single foe, and inflict 50% more damage than normal attacks (double damage versus beasts).
TEAM BONUSES	N/A

POSSIBLE TEAM MEMBERS:
Bushwhacker a.k.a. Bush-W. (Berserker)
Axoraptor a.k.a. Hackzilla (Hacksaurus)
Hooded Hacker a.k.a. Hoodwink (Hoodlum)
Man-at-Arms a.k.a. Skeledoid (Hell gladiator)

THE JAVELINAS

DESCRIPTION	Monsters that wield javelins.
DEATHMOVE	Jolly Jousters: Team members attack eight times, hitting enemies at random. Each hit does half the damage of a normal attack.
TEAM BONUSES	N/A

POSSIBLE TEAM MEMBERS:
Occult Rider a.k.a. Deadnoble (Bone baron)
Octavius Maximus a.k.a. Octurion (Octavian sentry)
Wild Spearman a.k.a. Orcus (Orc king)

THEMED TEAMS

THE DRACK PACK

DESCRIPTION	All three drackies.
DEATHMOVE	Fat Drack: All team members merge into the Gracky, the Great Dracky!
TEAM BONUSES	Team Agility +30

POSSIBLE TEAM MEMBERS:
Pain in the Neck a.k.a. Sippy (Dracky)
All Day Sucker a.k.a. Slurpy (Dracky)
Shadow Conductor a.k.a. Sugi (Dracky)

THE DYNAMIC DUO

DESCRIPTION	Orrid and Spike.
DEATHMOVE	Sapper Slapper: Both monsters focus attacks on a single foe and also lower its defence.
TEAM BONUSES	Team Attack +15* (When third member is of the beast family.)

POSSIBLE TEAM MEMBERS:
Ochre Ogre a.k.a. Orrid (Buffalogre)
Muscly Mohawker a.k.a. Spike (Mohawker)

THE FATAL ATTRACTION

DESCRIPTION	Faunus, Hazel and Slimehopper.
DEATHMOVE	Love Typhoon: A pink whirlwind hits a group of foes for 76-84 points of damage.
TEAM BONUSES	N/A

POSSIBLE TEAM MEMBERS:
Fertiliser a.k.a. Faunus (Silenus)
Femme Fatale a.k.a. Hazel (Witch)
One Knight Stand a.k.a. Slimehopper (Slime knight)

HAPPY TOGETHER

DESCRIPTION	Two monsters happy to be together. ☺
DEATHMOVE	N/A
TEAM BONUSES	N/A

POSSIBLE TEAM MEMBERS:
Jewel Juggler a.k.a. Jewelbag (Goodybag)
Bundle of Joy a.k.a. Trick Bag (Bag o' laughs)

THE LEGENDS

DESCRIPTION	Monsters named after DQ Staff.
DEATHMOVE	Big Bang: A massive explosion hits all foes for 175-225 points of damage.
TEAM BONUSES	N/A

POSSIBLE TEAM MEMBERS:
Slime Creator a.k.a. Hori (King slime)   Slime Designer a.k.a. Tori (Slime)
Killer Director a.k.a. Nohi (Killing machine)
Shadow Conductor a.k.a. Sugi (Dracky)

MY THREE GOLEMS

DESCRIPTION	All three golems.
DEATHMOVE	The Golemator: All team members merge into the monstrous Mazin!
TEAM BONUSES	N/A

POSSIBLE TEAM MEMBERS:
Bricklayer a.k.a. Brickman (Golem)
Goldbricker a.k.a. Goldman (Gold golem)
Stonemason a.k.a. Stoneman (Stone golem)

THE NIGHTRIDERS

DESCRIPTION	Mounted monsters.
DEATHMOVE	Riders' Carnival: Team members focus attacks on a single foe, and cause double the usual amount of damage.
TEAM BONUSES	N/A

POSSIBLE TEAM MEMBERS:
Occult Rider a.k.a. Deadnoble (Bone baron)
Bone Racer a.k.a. Jockey (Skullrider)
One Knight Stand a.k.a. Slimehopper (Slime knight)

THE PSYCHE WARDS

DESCRIPTION	Monsters that build tension.
DEATHMOVE	Tension Boost: Raises the tension of each team member and party member by two levels.
TEAM BONUSES	N/A

POSSIBLE TEAM MEMBERS:
Al Gee a.k.a. Big Al (King kelp)   Bundle of Joy a.k.a. Trick Bag (Bag o' laughs)
Femme Fatale a.k.a. Hazel (Witch)
Jewel Juggler a.k.a. Jewelbag (Goodybag)

TEAM GOODNIGHT

DESCRIPTION	Certain nocturnal monsters.
DEATHMOVE	Dirge: Reduces the defence of all team members and all enemies to 0.
TEAM BONUSES	N/A

POSSIBLE TEAM MEMBERS:
Fantom of Chopera a.k.a. Capers (Phantom fencer)
Hooded Hacker a.k.a. Hoodwink (Hoodlum)
Nightstalker a.k.a. Nightwing (Night emperor)

THE TREASURE HUNTERS

DESCRIPTION	Wealthy monsters.
DEATHMOVE	Good as Gold: Both monsters focus attacks on a single foe. You gain gold equal to half the damage dealt. You *cannot* use this move in the Monster Arena.
TEAM BONUSES	Fight Extra Turn*(When third member is of the material family.)

POSSIBLE TEAM MEMBERS:
Goldbricker a.k.a. Goldman (Gold golem)
Jewel Juggler a.k.a. Jewelbag (Goodybag)

TRIPLE TROUBLE

DESCRIPTION	All three killing machines.
DEATHMOVE	Stream Killer Attack: Team members focus attacks on a single foe, and cause triple the damage of normal attacks.
TEAM BONUSES	N/A

POSSIBLE TEAM MEMBERS:

Attack Bot Mk II a.k.a. Cybot (Killing machine)

Killer Director a.k.a. Nohi (Killing machine)

Roboster Mk I a.k.a. Roborg (Killing machine)

VALENTINE'S DAY

DESCRIPTION	Monsters that use puppets.
DEATHMOVE	N/A
TEAM BONUSES	Team Agility +15, Team Max HP +15* (becomes "Not Quite Human" with another Humanoid member, thus gaining the Team Max HP +15, and also retains the Team Agility +15)

POSSIBLE TEAM MEMBERS:

Puppet Pugilist a.k.a. Dolldrums (Puppet master)

Punchin' Judy a.k.a. Moppet (Puppeteer)

TWO EYES

DESCRIPTION	The two gigantes.
DEATHMOVE	Sapper Slapper: Both monsters focus attacks on a single foe and also lower its defence.
TEAM BONUSES	Fight Extra Turn* (When third member is of the demon family.)

POSSIBLE TEAM MEMBERS:

Gigantes Guardsman a.k.a. Brontes (Gigantes)

Gigantes Gangster a.k.a. Steropes (Gigantes)

SLIME TEAMS

THE KING AND US

DESCRIPTION	Healer, Curer and Hev.
DEATHMOVE	Maximaster: Returns all fallen team members to life and heals all team members to max HP, then boosts defence of all team members and lowers defence of all enemies.
TEAM BONUSES	Team Max HP x2

POSSIBLE TEAM MEMBERS:

Angel of Curing a.k.a. Curer (Cureslime)   Heavy Metal a.k.a. Hev (Metal king slime)

Family Doctor a.k.a. Healer (Healslime)

MEGA METAL MANIACS

DESCRIPTION	Hev and Metabble.
DEATHMOVE	Magic Burst: Hev and Metabble expend all remaining MP to deal 480-520 damage to all enemies.
TEAM BONUSES	Team Max HP x2*(When third member is of the slime family.)

POSSIBLE TEAM MEMBERS:

Heavy Metal a.k.a. Hev (Metal king slime)

Metal Babble a.k.a. Metabble (Liquid metal slime)

THE METAL MOB

DESCRIPTION	All metal slimes.
DEATHMOVE	Multi Masher: Your team expends all remaining MP to attack 3 to 10 times at random. Each attack causes 110-130 points of damage. (Possible Magic Burst from any combination of two in the group.)
TEAM BONUSES	Team Max HP x2

POSSIBLE TEAM MEMBERS:

Heavy Metal a.k.a. Hev (Metal king slime)   Quick Silver a.k.a. Metaly (Metal slime)

Metal Babble a.k.a. Metabble (Liquid metal slime)

FULL METAL POWER

DESCRIPTION	Hev and Metaly.
DEATHMOVE	Magic Burst: Hev and Metaly expend all remaining MP to deal 330-370 points of damage to all enemies.
TEAM BONUSES	Team Max HP x2* (When third member is of the slime family.)

POSSIBLE TEAM MEMBERS:

Heavy Metal a.k.a. Hev (Metal king slime)

Quick Silver a.k.a. Metaly (Metal slime)

SLIME THERAPY

DESCRIPTION	Any two of the following three slimes.
DEATHMOVE	Multiheal: Restores 100-120 HP to all team members and party members.
TEAM BONUSES	Team Max HP x2* (When third member is of the Slime family.)

POSSIBLE TEAM MEMBERS:

Angel of Curing a.k.a. Curer (Cureslime)   Quick Silver a.k.a. Metaly (Metal slime)

Family Doctor a.k.a. Healer (Healslime)

SLIME TIME

DESCRIPTION	Metaly and two normal slimes.
DEATHMOVE	Slime Spank: All monsters focus attacks on a single foe, and cause 50% more damage than normal attacks.
TEAM BONUSES	Team Max HP x2

POSSIBLE TEAM MEMBERS:

Quick Silver a.k.a. Metaly (Metal slime)   Slime Designer a.k.a. Tori (Slime)

Gloopy Groupie a.k.a. Slime Shady (slime)

Slimy Smiley a.k.a. Smiles (Slime)

Metal Power

DESCRIPTION	Metabble and Metaly.
DEATHMOVE	Magic Burst: Metabble and Metaly expend all remaining MP to deal 180-220 points of damage to all enemies.
TEAM BONUSES	Team Max HP x2* (When third member is of the Slime family.)

POSSIBLE TEAM MEMBERS:
Metal Babble a.k.a. Metabble (Liquid metal slime)
Quick Silver a.k.a. Metaly (Metal slime)

The Slime Squad

DESCRIPTION	All normal slimes.
DEATHMOVE	Supersize Slimey: All team members merge into Ultrus, the Ultra Slime!
TEAM BONUSES	Team Max HP x2

POSSIBLE TEAM MEMBERS:
Gloopy Groupie a.k.a. Slime Shady (Slime)
Slimy Smiley a.k.a. Smiles (Slime)
Slime Designer a.k.a. Tori (Slime)

Trauma Centre

DESCRIPTION	Metaly, Curer and Healer.
DEATHMOVE	Omniheal: Restores all team members to max HP and restores some HP to party members.
TEAM BONUSES	Team Max HP x2

POSSIBLE TEAM MEMBERS:
Angel of Curing a.k.a. Curer (Cureslime)
Family Doctor a.k.a. Healer (Healslime)
Quick Silver a.k.a. Metaly (Metal slime)

Wizards o' Z

DESCRIPTION	Metabble, Curer and Healer.
DEATHMOVE	Zingslinger: Returns all fallen team members to life and heals all team members to max HP.
TEAM BONUSES	Team Max HP x2

POSSIBLE TEAM MEMBERS:
Angel of Curing a.k.a. Curer (Cureslime)
Family Doctor a.k.a. Healer (Healslime)
Metal Babble a.k.a. Metabble (Liquid metal slime)

Family Teams

The Aqua Marines

DESCRIPTION	All members are aquatic type.
DEATHMOVE	N/A
TEAM BONUSES	Team Defence +30

POSSIBLE TEAM MEMBERS:
Al Gee a.k.a. Big Al (King kelp)
Colossal Clione a.k.a. Clio (See angel)
Octavius Maximus a.k.a. Octurion (Octavian sentry)
Little Nipper a.k.a. Robster (Yabby)
Squiggly Squiggler a.k.a. Squiggles (Khalamari kid)

The Avian Attackers

DESCRIPTION	All team members are bird type.
DEATHMOVE	Deathmove: N/A
TEAM BONUSES	Team Agility +30

POSSIBLE TEAM MEMBERS:
Raging Rooster a.k.a. Foul Fowl (Fowlfighter)
Gryphon General a.k.a. Gryphus (War gryphon)
Pain in the Neck a.k.a. Sippy (Dracky)
All Day Sucker a.k.a. Slurpy (Dracky)
Shadow Conductor a.k.a. Sugi (Dracky)

Clank and Spank

DESCRIPTION	All team members are machine type.
DEATHMOVE	Metal Panic: The team members focus their attacks on a single foe, and cause 50% more damage than normal attacks.
TEAM BONUSES	N/A

POSSIBLE TEAM MEMBERS:
Attack Bot Mk II a.k.a. Cybot (Killing machine)
Automaton Aviator a.k.a. Mechabubo (Mecha-mynah)
Killer Director a.k.a. Nohi (Killing machine)
Roboster Mk I a.k.a. Roborg (Killing machine)

Materialistic

DESCRIPTION	All team members are material type.
DEATHMOVE	N/A
TEAM BONUSES	Fight Extra Turn

POSSIBLE TEAM MEMBERS:
Bricklayer a.k.a. Brickman (Golem)
Goldbricker a.k.a. Goldman (Gold golem)
Jewel Juggler a.k.a. Jewelbag (Goodybag)
Hollow Knight a.k.a. Lonely Joe (Restless armour)
Man-eater Chest a.k.a. Snap Case (Cannibox)
Stonemason a.k.a. Stoneman (Stone golem)
Crazed Colossus a.k.a. Talos (Living statue)
Bundle of Joy a.k.a. Trick Bag (Bag o' laughs)

DEMENTED ELEMENTS

DESCRIPTION	All team members are elemental type.
DEATHMOVE	Elemental Storm: Boosts all team members' and party members' resistance to fire- and ice-type attacks, and creates a barrier that bounces spells back at their caster.
TEAM BONUSES	N/A

POSSIBLE TEAM MEMBERS:

Cold Fire a.k.a. Blizag Jr. (Frostburn)

Living Flame a.k.a. Flameman (Dancing flame)

Big Blizzard a.k.a. Jack Frost (Frostburn)

Living Torch a.k.a. Torchman (Dancing flame)

THE DRAG RACERS

DESCRIPTION	All team members are dragon type.
DEATHMOVE	N/A
TEAM BONUSES	Team Attack +30

POSSIBLE TEAM MEMBERS:

Jumbo Dilophosaur a.k.a. Frillsaur (Frou-frou)

Axoraptor a.k.a. Hackzilla (Hacksaurus)

Potty Dragon a.k.a. Potbelly (Jargon)

FAR FROM HEAVEN

DESCRIPTION	All team members are demon type.
DEATHMOVE	N/A
TEAM BONUSES	Fight Extra Turn

POSSIBLE TEAM MEMBERS:

Arch-archdemon a.k.a. Archfiend (Archdemon)

Big Blue Bully a.k.a. Arges (Cyclops)

Gigantes Guardsman a.k.a. Brontes (Gigantes)

Femme Fatale a.k.a. Hazel (Witch)

Bone Racer a.k.a. Jockey (Skullrider)

Nightstalker a.k.a. Nightwing (Night emperor)

Troll Patroller a.k.a. Pa Troll (Boss troll)

Pelvic Thruster a.k.a. Salsa (Redtail hipster)

Gigantes Gangster a.k.a. Steropes (Gigantes)

JUST BEASTLY

DESCRIPTION	All team members are beast type.
DEATHMOVE	N/A
TEAM BONUSES	Team Attack +15

POSSIBLE TEAM MEMBERS:

Loopy Lupus a.k.a. Bladewolf (Jumping jackal)

Buffalo Bill a.k.a. Cowboy (Bullfinch)

Mole Major a.k.a. Doug (Mad mole)

Death Tabby a.k.a. Fat Cat (Jailcat)

Abominable Ape a.k.a. Klub Kong (Gorerilla)

Wild Spearman a.k.a. Orcus (Orc king)

Ochre Ogre a.k.a. Orrid (Buffalogre)

Muscly Mohawker a.k.a. Spike (Mohawker)

Greater Sabrecat a.k.a. Spot (Great sabrecat)

NOT QUITE HUMAN

DESCRIPTION	All team members are humanoid type.
DEATHMOVE	Deathmove: N/A
TEAM BONUSES	Team Max HP +15

POSSIBLE TEAM MEMBERS:

Sharpshooter a.k.a. Archer (Bodkin bowyer)

Bushwhacker a.k.a. Bush-W. (Berserker)

Puppet Pugilist a.k.a. Dolldrums (Puppet master)

King of Dumbira a.k.a. Dumbking (Notso macho)

Fertiliser a.k.a. Faunus (Silenus)

Shortshooter a.k.a. Fletch (Bodkin archer)

Hooded Hacker a.k.a. Hoodwink (Hoodlum)

Mullet Mallet a.k.a. McHammer (Brownie)

Punchin' Judy a.k.a. Moppet (Puppeteer)

Poisonous Sniper a.k.a. Sagittari (Bodkin fletcher)

Terror Talons a.k.a. Seasaw (Riptide)

SLIME POWER!

DESCRIPTION	All team members are slime type.
DEATHMOVE	Deathmove: N/A
TEAM BONUSES	Team Max HP x2

POSSIBLE TEAM MEMBERS:

Angel of Curing a.k.a. Curer (Cureslime)

Family Doctor a.k.a. Healer (Healslime)

Heavy Metal a.k.a. Hev (Metal king slime)

Slime Creator a.k.a. Hori (King slime)

Metal Babble a.k.a. Metabble (Liquid metal slime)

Quick Silver a.k.a. Metaly (Metal slime)

Gloopy Groupie a.k.a. Slime Shady (Slime)

One Knight Stand a.k.a. Slimehopper (Slime knight)

Slimy Smiley a.k.a. Smiles (Slime)

Slime Designer a.k.a. Tori (Slime)

THE ZOMBEBOPS

DESCRIPTION	All team members are zombie type.
DEATHMOVE	Deathmove: N/A
TEAM BONUSES	Team Max HP +30

POSSIBLE TEAM MEMBERS:

Wight Highpriest a.k.a. Bishop (Wight priest)

Old Soldier a.k.a. Bones (Skeleton)

Fantom of Chopera a.k.a. Capers (Phantom fencer)

Occult Rider a.k.a. Deadnoble (Bone baron)

Old-School Drooler a.k.a. Hork (Walking corpse)

Headless Flailsman a.k.a. Mornstar (Dullahan)

Man-at-Arms a.k.a. Skeledoid (Hell gladiator)

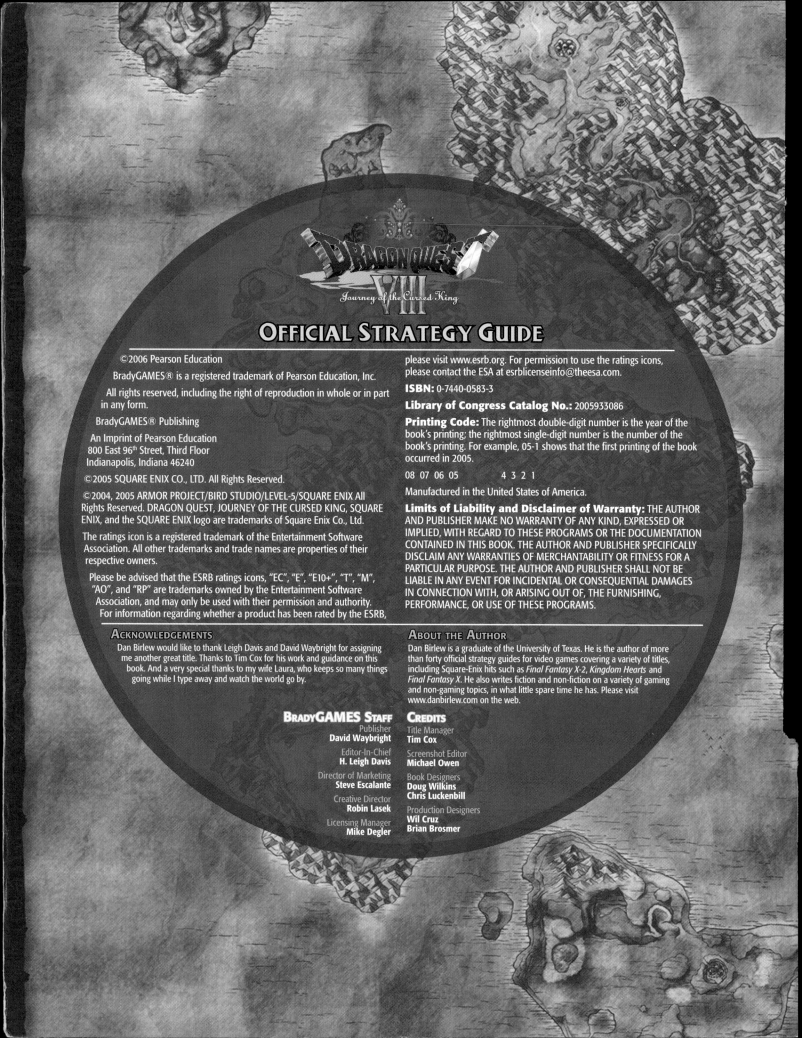

DRAGON QUEST VIII
Journey of the Cursed King

OFFICIAL STRATEGY GUIDE

ISBN: 0-7440-0583-3

Library of Congress Catalog No.: 2005933086

Printing Code: The rightmost double-digit number is the year of the book's printing; the rightmost single-digit number is the number of the book's printing. For example, 05-1 shows that the first printing of the book occurred in 2005.

08 07 06 05   4   3   2   1

Manufactured in the United States of America.

ACKNOWLEDGEMENTS

Dan Birlew would like to thank Leigh Davis and David Waybright for assigning me another great title. Thanks to Tim Cox for his work and guidance on this book. And a very special thanks to my wife Laura, who keeps so many things going while I type away and watch the world go by.

ABOUT THE AUTHOR

Dan Birlew is a graduate of the University of Texas. He is the author of more than forty official strategy guides for video games covering a variety of titles, including Square-Enix hits such as *Final Fantasy X-2*, *Kingdom Hearts* and *Final Fantasy X*. He also writes fiction and non-fiction on a variety of gaming and non-gaming topics, in what little spare time he has. Please visit www.danbirlew.com on the web.

BRADYGAMES STAFF

Publisher
David Waybright

Editor-In-Chief
H. Leigh Davis

Director of Marketing
Steve Escalante

Creative Director
Robin Lasek

Licensing Manager
Mike Degler

CREDITS

Title Manager
Tim Cox

Screenshot Editor
Michael Owen

Book Designers
Doug Wilkins
Chris Luckenbill

Production Designers
Wil Cruz
Brian Brosmer